WILLIAM NICKERSON

How I Turned
$1,000 into Three Million
in Real Estate—
in My Spare Time

NEWLY REVISED EDITION*

* *Originally:* HOW I TURNED $1,000 INTO A
MILLION IN REAL ESTATE—IN MY SPARE TIME

SIMON AND SCHUSTER · NEW YORK

To my wife, Lucille

CONTENTS

PREFACE TO SECOND EDITION

In the ten years since my book was first published, scarcely a week passes but someone asks, "Is it still possible to follow your formula to make a million? Or has there been a major change?"

Opportunities for the average person today are better than ever before. My basic investment formula has not changed. Nor is it likely to, for it has become accepted by experienced realtors the world over as the established Real Estate Bible.

Although my fundamental precepts for making a fortune will always hold true under free enterprise, I have developed numerous operating innovations from continuing analysis of the practices of successful investors throughout the country. Many refinements are incorporated in this new edition, with up-to-date references, valuations and forms where appropriate, after gleaning through the original book with a fine-tooth comb.

I have visited every major city in the United States since my book was written. In every community there are usually a few who say, "You succeeded yesterday in California. But can you do it today? And can you do it here?"

In the same cities there are always some who tell me of their current experiences in surpassing my formula. Usually two or three in every recent lecture audience say they have already passed the million mark in less than ten years of investing. My own estate, in fact, has now reached the three-million-dollar mark, tripling the amount I attained when *How I Turned $1,000 into a Million*—the first edition of this book—was published. Similar opportunities await throughout the United States for every enterprising investor who seeks a realty fortune.

My step-by-step formula in Chapter 2 shows how to make a million over a 20-year span, starting with $2,500. This time schedule has proven conservative for most who have the faith and initiative to follow my guidance. Thousands have started investing with small nest eggs since reading my books, have emulated the accelerated guidelines cited in Chapter 30, and have already become millionaires.

Is it still possible to become a millionaire in this country? At this writing in 1968 the United States has 90,000 individual millionaires, and their numbers are growing at the rate of about 30 every working day, or 8,000 a year.

This annual increase is close to the total number of millionaires when I started investing 30 years ago!

WILLIAM NICKERSON

FOREWORD

When I was twenty-five my wife, Lucille, and I started saving with my first steady earnings from the telephone company. In three years we saved the $1,000 down payment on a home. Two years later we traded our home for a pair of flats. After working twelve more years for the company, and operating rental property as a sideline, we had pyramided our estate to a half-million dollars.

This exceeded the lifetime savings of the presidents of many telephone companies and of most other businesses. There seemed little object for me to work longer on a salary. I retired at forty-two to concentrate on managing my property, with considerable time out for gardening our sunny acre in the San Ramon Valley, swimming in our back-yard pool, hunting, fishing, and traveling.

Many friends have asked the secrets of my success. I have given freely of information which would have helped me a great deal when I started to invest, information I would like my son and daughter and my friends to have, to assure their maximum success. Some have followed my suggestions and speeded their advance on the realty road to a fortune. To cover major questions on buying and operating real estate at a profit, I started writing this book. Though they verified my financial statement with Dun & Bradstreet, editors declared:

"Your success depended on starting during the depression."

"You couldn't make similar progress in these times, or ever again."

"Your experience is unique. Nobody else could duplicate it."

This challenged me to study other careers, and current real-estate markets. I found many multimillionaires whose present-day real-estate operations far overshadowed mine, and I have analyzed the secrets of their successes. Although I had not intended to increase my holdings, I found so many bargain opportunities in current markets that in two years I doubled my net estate to over a million.

My progress has been spasmodic and interrupted by trial and error.

11

By review of the factors that led to success for me and for others, I have discovered not only guideposts to follow, but detours to avoid. I have set down a guide to real wealth that promises you surer riches than any other investment, showing how, with average ability, average savings, and average luck, you can become a millionaire.

WILLIAM NICKERSON

Alamo, California

PART ONE

HOW YOU CAN
MAKE A MILLION DOLLARS

1. GROW RICH ON BORROWED MONEY

Most forms of investment pay only the paltry leavings after others deduct their expenses and fair compensation for using your money. You lend your savings to banks and insurance companies, and they capitalize on your money for their profit.

Investment in business and income property puts you on the real money-making side of the capital fence and pays you for courage and imagination. You profit not only from your own savings but also from the savings of the timid, the uninformed, and the satiated who already possess all the money they want.

Every venture presents an element of risk, but with rent-producing income property you take negligible risks and your chances for success are 1,600 times better, for example, than your chances if you start in business. With each, however, you follow the freeway that leads to wealth by harnessing the secret force of capitalism—which is the pyramiding power of borrowed money. Regardless how wisely you invest, you can't go far on your own money. Your greatest expansion is assured by making maximum use of the other fellow's money.

The road to riches is paved with borrowed money. Big-time real-estate operators buy properties worth millions without putting in a penny of their own. Multimillion-dollar deals are made by borrowing the utmost from mortgages and the balance on personal and collateral notes.

FROM ZERO TO MILLIONS BY 100 PER CENT BORROWING

Nearly all big business operates on money either loaned or invested by other than the managers. Henry Kaiser parlayed a modest road-contracting business into a multibillion industrial empire by 100 per cent borrowing of government and bank money.

The world's most outstanding pyramider probably was Henry Ford. His billionaire enterprise mushroomed faster than any other in history and eventually outstripped all except Rockefeller's. How much did Ford invest personally to found his gigantic business? Not one cent! One hundred per cent of his original capital was borrowed from others.

YOUR INITIAL FINANCING CAN BE CLOSE TO 100 PER CENT

You cannot expect to start right out emulating tycoons like Ford in the ability to pyramid through 100 per cent borrowing. But as a property investor you can approach this financing and make the maximum use of borrowed money. On an average purchase you would put in considerably less than the lender. When starting to buy income property you can normally borrow on a sound basis at least 75 per cent of the purchase price, which means that the lender invests three times as much as you. With this nominal financing your property will earn a rental return from four times the investment of your personal savings.

BUYING A HOME IS THE USUAL FIRST REALTY STEP

Buying a home by utilizing the savings of others constitutes your usual first step, as it did mine, on the real-estate road to a million. If you own your home you are already a capitalist in the sense of owning capital, along with over 60 per cent of U.S. families, according to Federal Reserve Board figures. Chances are you borrowed in order to live in your own home, like the four out of five home buyers who borrow in preference to dissipating housing payments on rent receipts. Or you might be among the 43 per cent of GI borrowers, computed by the Veterans Administration, who matched the tycoons in no-down-payment, 100 per cent financing.

It is not uncommon to buy income property with nothing down, or 5 to 10 per cent down, approaching GI financing. I have bought about $1 million worth of property with nothing down and have rejected several millions of dollars' worth of property offered on the same terms. I know of a $12,000 duplex house recently bought for nothing down, a 100 per cent mortgage. A friend bought a $100,000 20-unit apartment house with nothing down but a promissory note for $7,000. Another friend bought a 30-unit building worth $150,000 by trading in, as a token down payment, a vacant lot worth $3,000.

Of the 80 per cent of home buyers who risk mortgages, how many would ever enjoy home ownership if they waited to pay cash? More would progress from home to income property ownership if they only understood how much more they could accomplish with further use of the pyramiding power of borrowed capital. My intent in this book is to spell out in detail how you can utilize this latent power, open to all, to make a million or more.

OPPORTUNITY IS ALWAYS KNOCKING

In every year, in good times or bad, investment opportunities are always knocking, in spite of the pessimists who perennially lament, "There is no opportunity today."

My wife, Lucille, and I came from low-income families, poor in worldly possessions. Like most of our contemporaries starting to earn a living during the depression, we were obsessed with a goal of security. Our idea when we bought our first rental property was that it would be a good objective to have a clear, independent income of $100 monthly by the time I retired from the telephone company with a modest pension at sixty-five. We had no conception of the pyramiding potentialities within our grasp, until we had dawdled for many precious years. Yet we made over a million in our spare time without particularly striving for this amount, while still in our forties.

The soul-searing poverty of the depression induced for many a blinding cult of security, which of course offers a better alternative than poverty. Without losing sight of security, why not seek opportunities which can also produce comfort and luxury? America owes its founding and its great strength to leaders whose courage sought opportunity above security. The chances for success today offer less risk by far than those taken by our pioneer settlers and pioneer founders of government and industry.

Like the editors to whom I first submitted the initial chapters of this book, some of my friends now rationalize, "Nobody could start today with nothing as you did and build a fortune. There just isn't the opportunity in these times."

I remember they made the same forecasts in the courage-sapping depths of the depression. My wife and I were both working our way through Fresno State College. When we decided to marry and work together, one of our friends summed up the depressing consensus of many, "The most you can look forward to is Social Security, and if you're lucky a small company pension."

Our economics instructor advised our class, "You might as well realize that the time for opportunity is past. The best you can hope for is to keep a steady job and stay off welfare. Nobody will ever again be able to build an estate big enough to produce an independent income."

There will always be those who see only darkness today and question the possibility of a bright tomorrow. If you wait until the "time is ripe," your later years will be embittered by it-might-have-beens. Instead of a future clouded by regrets, why not enjoy along with me accomplishments that with each advancing year will make your heart sing, "Now is the best time of life"?

IT IS NEVER TOO LATE TO START

Many of our cautious friends, and our Econ teacher, too, lament today, "Wish I were in your shoes and had started saving and investing when you did. Is it too late to start now?"

It is never too late to start, although fortune favors early starters. Each day of delay loads the dice against maximum success. But I know of many successful owners who bought their first income property after retirement at sixty-five. You can always start later in life, possibly with a modified financial goal.

In contrast, some of my younger friends have asked, "Is it too early to get started?" In the Apartment Owners Association to which I belong, some members still in their twenties are already well launched on a successful income-property program. Many couples between twenty-five and thirty own 2-unit and 4-unit houses. One couple at twenty-eight owns a 30-unit building bought by conventional saving and financing. Another member retired from wage earning at thirty-five with a quarter-million estate.

Among the active members many over seventy stay younger because of their property interests. A widow of eighty-four looks and acts twenty years younger discussing her apartments. They not only pay her a comfortable retirement income but help to preserve her youthful spirit. There is no question that property ownership has added years to the lives of many older members.

President Eisenhower, when he approached sixty-five, recommended to Congress that more outside earnings be permitted Social Security pensioners. He said, "I am convinced that the great majority of our able-bodied older citizens are happier and better off when they continue on some productive work." Congress approved.

A Lloyd's of London ten-year survey indicates a greatly increased life span for those—like Grandma Moses, painting at ninety-five—who keep an active interest in worth-while production. Of a group of men who retired at sixty, the average rocking-chair addict dropped dead at sixty-three, probably of boredom and penury. Most of those with productive interests were enjoying life well past seventy.

UNSUPPLEMENTED PENSIONS PROVIDE LITTLE COMFORT

Social Security and other pensions promise a sufficient backlog to keep you out of the poorhouse. Unless supplemented by investment income they will normally clothe you only in the hair shirt of poverty, inviting death, like the Lloyd's rocking-chairers, within three years of retirement. Even a comfortable, fixed retirement income may dwindle through gradually rising prices and shunt you to the shanty town of "Just Getting By." A 1947 annuity providing $300 monthly, for example, was worth only $236 monthly in 1957 purchasing power. And a 1939 dollar plummeted 60¢ to a purchasing value of only 40¢ by 1968, indicating a continuing trend of erosion.

For comfort in sunset years the buying power of your retirement income should be not less than half your working income. For enjoyable and carefree leisure years you must earn additional income from investments whose value will grow with inflation. To build an estate large enough to assure financial independence, you must have the courage to pledge your embryo savings in order to utilize borrowed money, made available by the savings of others.

EXPECTING WEALTH FROM SAVINGS
IS AN IMPOSSIBLE DREAM

To start investing you normally have to save a nest egg, but expecting wealth from savings compares with expecting chickens to hatch from eggs deposited in cold storage. According to the Bureau of Labor Statistics, the purchasing power of savings put in the bank twenty years ago, for example, would have dropped over 50 per cent, offsetting any interest earned.

The omnipotent tax collector bars the road to riches if undertaken solely with savings, regardless how large the salary. According to a survey by Dun & Bradstreet, most corporation presidents with annual salaries exceeding $100,000 find it impossible to accumulate an estate sufficient for a comfortable retirement, and their chief worry is sufficient savings for family security. What chance is there for those earning less?

The Census Bureau reports a million persons a year passing sixty-five, adding to the more than nineteen million studied in 1968. Among those over sixty-five who have followed a savings program, only one in four had a combined income exceeding $1,000 a year from savings, pensions, and Social Security.

SAVINGS ARE A GOOD MEDIUM
FOR ACCUMULATING A NEST EGG

According to Federal Reserve surveys, three out of ten families spend more each year than they earn, and they can never make ends meet. Among the seven out of ten savers are the conservatives who cannot bear to release deposited dollars to produce more, and who make a fetish of paying cash and never owing a cent. The never-in-debt savers are usually better off than the spendthrifts who are always in debt beyond their capacity to pay. But the spendthrifts may be enjoying themselves more, at least now if not tomorrow, and often at the expense of the savers. Savers can actually be the losers by hoarding their earnings to the extent that they not only find it impossible to develop real wealth but can enjoy fewer of the pleasures of life.

The savings account provides a liquid and safe medium for accumulating a nest egg, and for building a reserve for specific purposes. The money can be withdrawn virtually any time it is needed, and it will always be there, particularly now that each institution covered by Federal Deposit Insurance insures savings up to $15,000. But, as indicated above, the relatively low returns scarcely offset inflation. After using the savings account to build a nest egg, more lucrative fields should be sought for long-term investments.

BANKERS ALWAYS FAVOR CAUTIOUS SAVING FOR YOU

In depression years I took out my accumulated savings to buy my first income property. Sincerely perturbed about my welfare, my banker forecast, "If you buy rental property during the depression you'll probably lose everything. Of course what you do with your money is up to you, but I would advise keeping it in savings. If you put it in those flats you won't be able to collect enough rent to pay the mortgage."

If I had followed this admonition I would still be treadmilling for the telephone company. Instead of retiring financially independent at forty-two, I would be looking forward to a pensioner's modest existence at sixty-five.

Although I have discounted such extreme caution, bankers have given me a lot of good advice. I have found that they like to point out all the possibilities of failure, not because they expect compliance to the letter, but to help you consider exigencies which you might otherwise overlook. Your bank officer, too, will give the most conservative counsel he can think of, because you may reproach him if his advice goes wrong.

With the low purchase prices of the depression, I found it easy to collect sufficient rents to pay all costs, including the mortgage payments. Bargains were available from owners who had let their properties run down and therefore had to sacrifice at lower prices than otherwise. Any new buyer with wages as a backlog, and with no black marks on his credit record, could secure ready financing, although this might have been impossible for a previous owner if he had been operating at a loss.

My steady telephone-company salary, though nothing to brag about, was a major factor in securing adequate financing. When you start out to invest, steady employment greatly enhances your opportunities for borrowing.

IN WARTIME

When I borrowed to buy more property in wartime my banker said, "Better not buy any more income property during war. You'll go broke trying to operate with taxes and other expenses going up, and income held down by rent control."

Again my banker's advice went unheeded because my experience had already shown that rent controls removed competition. Even though taxes and other fixed expenses increased, I was able to lower over-all operating expenses because it was no longer necessary to provide services, decorate and modernize as under a free economy. And I was able to further increase net income through legitimate devices for nominal rent raises.

IN GOOD TIMES OR BAD

With the general economy booming I have heard bankers advise, "Better not buy while times are good. You might lose out because prices are bound to go down."

Pessimists incessantly warn of collapse, but present indications are that we may very well enjoy an ever expanding economy. Increasing utilization of our Atomic Age's automation is expected to produce a continually rising standard of living and individual worth. We are bound to have periodic recessions and advances, but the inevitability of a severe depression like that of 1929 is as open to question as the inevitability of another world war. As the check of nuclear weapons should forestall another world conflict, so also the many present checks against deflation will forestall another widespread depression.

As the eminent analyst W. M. Kiplinger forecasts in *Boom and Inflation Ahead,* "There will be minor slumps, but no deep depression." Page 22 shows Kiplinger's forecasts regarding population growth.

With boom times ahead, your investment decisions today should be governed by the effects of inflation and high taxes. Tax experts agree, as will be illustrated in later chapters, that even with the phenomenal opportunities offered, the greatest tax shelter exists in real estate. And income geared to rental property will ride with inflation, adjusting upward as price levels rise with our expanding economy.

MANY REAL-ESTATE FORTUNES
ARE BEING BUILT TODAY

Investors with courage are building worth-while estates today in many fields. Among my personal friends are many leaders in real estate and business who have become financially independent, as I have, entirely through financing and their own efforts. Among well-known multimillionaires in country-wide real estate are Texans Clint Murchison and Sid Richardson, who attained huge fortunes; New York developers Louis J. Glickman and James H. Scheuer; Roger Stevens of Detroit, who bought and sold the Empire State Building; Ben Swig of San Francisco, hotel and shopping-center developer; and Conrad Hilton of Chicago, who added the Statler hotels to his Hilton hotels, to create the world's largest hotel chain.

Much in the news in 1968 were the spectacular realty exploits of billionaire Howard Hughes, busily converting into Nevada hotel casinos and other real estate a major portion of the $546.5 million in cash realized from the 1966 sale of his TWA stock.

Multimillionaires like those above plan spectacular investment and redevelopment projects. Coming to the forefront in investment attention is the rehabilitation and redevelopment of deteriorated areas, creating desirable housing and other income properties. Try as they may, induced by high profits, the tycoons scarcely make a dent in the vast areas begging for development. This leaves plenty of elbow room for investment and improvement action by every small investor who is willing to set his sights on a program that will make a million or more.

MILLIONAIRES, LIKE BANKS,
ARE MADE OF BORROWED MONEY

Show me a millionaire, and I will show you, almost invariably, a heavy borrower. In this they emulate banks and insurance companies. When banks take your savings they are borrowing from you. Insurance companies, which most strongly advocate security, owe four dollars in obligations for every one dollar in assets. Since these profit-making practices are considered sound by government regulatory bodies, a similar practice should be considered both sound and profitable for you.

Banks and insurance companies grow rich only by attracting indi-

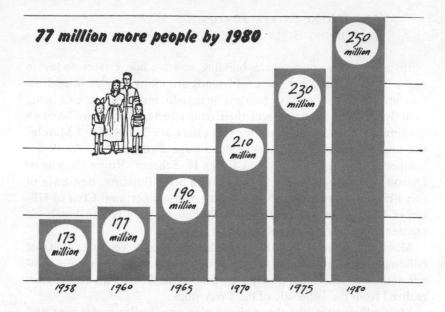

77 million more people by 1980

173 million — 1958
177 million — 1960
190 million — 1965
210 million — 1970
230 million — 1975
250 million — 1980

Reproduced from W. M. Kiplinger's Boom and Inflation Ahead *(New York, Simon and Schuster, 1958), p. 7.*

vidual savings and then reinvesting them. Fortunately they have no patents on this harvesting process any more than the tycoons have a patent on money-making property investment. Once you become aware of these basic economic facts you are free to copy them.

BANKS AND INSURANCE COMPANIES DEPEND ALSO ON INVESTORS

It is only through the siphoning of savings by these institutions that enterprising investors are able to secure funds at nominal rates. Since they deal in billions, banks and insurance companies charge only a small percentage, averaging in the 2 to 3 per cent range, for operating costs and profits.

As much as these money wholesalers need savers to provide their funds, they also depend on investors to borrow the funds. You and I, who can use the money for highly profitable enterprise, should be grateful for this funneling system, which makes investment funds available at comparatively low cost for our pyramiding to a fortune.

IF YOU POSSESS AN AVERAGE NEST EGG, YOU CAN SPEED YOUR WAY TO A FORTUNE

According to the National Consumer Finance Association, the total 1957 net worth of American families approximated a trillion dollars. A 1968 study by the Securities and Exchange Commission estimates a total net worth of 3.2 trillion dollars. This averages over $40,000 per family, including present millionaires. Federal Reserve Board figures for 1957 show the net worth of the typical median family as approximately $2,500 where the head of the household was between twenty-five and thirty-four; $5,000 between thirty-five and forty-four; $10,000 between forty-five and fifty-four. This indicates that the average family, not just the favored few, already possesses sufficient funds to found a respectable estate.

Starting with average funds can speed the way to financial success. The hardest task on the road to a million dollars is saving a nest egg. If you possess as much as $2,500 and the courage to grasp the sound opportunities offered by income property, you will find in the next chapter how in twenty years of reinvestment you can become a millionaire.

Some of my friends lament, "If you give all your secrets away, you will spoil our chances to make a million as you have."

My answer is this: Our population and income growth and time's deterioration of present buildings create plenty of room for all who are interested.

Income-property opportunities are unlimited, continuously expanding like the universe.

2.   STEP BY STEP
TO A MILLION DOLLARS

To produce financial independence your investment commitments should require only a modicum of personal attention, and the estate must be large enough for you to leave the capital intact and live in comfort from the income.

You might consider a net estate of $100,000, producing a 6 per cent net income of $6,000 a year, a sufficient goal to achieve a fair degree of financial independence. Or you might peg your minimum goal at a quarter million, producing a net close to $15,000 a year. The larger your holdings, naturally, the more supervision they will demand. But as compensation you can delegate routine tasks and decisions to employees, as I do, and handle personally only major policies.

Let's say you aspire to be a millionaire. How can you get your million, invested to pay approximately a $60,000 annual net? Let us examine my formula showing your probable expectations from an accumulative investment in rental-income property.

Let's suppose you have saved a moderately average nest egg of $50 monthly for four years. Including compounded interest this would exceed $2,500, the median savings for a U.S. family with a breadwinner between twenty-five and thirty-four. You could start with $1,000, as my wife and I did during the depression. As mentioned, I know of many recent purchases of houses and duplex apartments with down payments of $1,000 or less. But for a sound start on current markets I figure the average investor should have about $2,500. Let us take this $2,500 and see how, with average luck, you can pyramid it to over a million in twenty years. We will invest in income property by steps.

My Step-by-Step Formula to a Million Dollars

ZERO DAY

Step 1. You take the $2,500 nest egg from your savings account. Then you borrow three times as much, $7,500, making a total of $10,000. With the $10,000 you buy a rental house in need of renovation. This means you borrow 75 per cent of the total purchase price.

Most metropolitan newspapers advertise daily property opportunities asking as low as 10 per cent down. The present owner or other lender will loan nine times the buyer's investment. As mentioned in Chapter 1, experienced buyers like myself often secure 100 per cent financing. Rather than unusual opportunities, however, for our examples we will operate on average possibilities which you can readily expect to match or exceed while getting started. Typical purchases will later be detailed with approximately 75 per cent financing, which you can easily obtain as an average investor. Since taking advantage of financing is at the very heart of our plan, three full chapters, 22, 23 and 24, will later be devoted to the many aspects of borrowing which will enhance your progress.

Step 2. In addition to your $10,000 purchase price, you put in $600 more from savings each year for the next two years. This makes an accumulated investment of $11,200. With the $1,200 savings, plus any net income from the property, you arrange to paint and renovate. This increases the income value and therefore the sale value of the property so it can be sold at a profit.

TWO YEARS

Step 3. You sell the improved house for $14,000, a gross profit on your total investment of money and supervisory time of $2,800, 25 per cent for two years. This represents an over-all gross of 12½ per cent a year, a nominal profit from selective buying and renovation. You repay the $7,500 borrowed. The 6 to 7½ per cent average interest has already been paid in monthly installments from the property income. You pay 5 per cent average sales costs, $700, leaving a net profit of $2,100. You now own $5,800 at the end of two years.

In most cases, as will be shown in later chapters, you would also net the additional amount by which the loan had been amortized, paid for from rental income. To be conservative in this reckoning, we will omit these usual earnings in order to provide an extra reserve for unforeseen expenses. Even so, since you profit not only from your own funds but also from the money borrowed, your net profit of $2,100 represents a return of approximately 67.74 per cent in two years, or 33.87 per cent a year, on your $3,700 personal investment. This figures earnings on your $50 monthly savings as accumulated.

The capital value of your income property can be mushroomed with sustained success at this 33.87 per cent average rate as long as you desire to expand. Watch how the continuation of this formula will pyramid your estate.

Step 4. You take the $5,800 and again borrow three times as much, $17,400, making a total of $23,200. With this you buy a 4-unit rental-income building, 4 apartments or flats, in need of renovation.

Step 5. You put in $600 each year for the next two years, using the $1,200, plus the net property income, to pay for painting and refurbishing.

FOUR YEARS

Step 6. You sell the improved 4-unit building, with an accumulated $24,400 investment, for $30,500, again a 25 per cent gross profit. You repay the $17,400 borrowed and pay $1,525 sales costs. This leaves a net profit of $4,575 for your investment and efforts and gives you a total of $11,575 in four years.

Step 7. You invest your $11,575, together with $34,725 you borrow, a total of $46,300, in an 8-unit income-property building. You put in $600 a year for the next two years, plus your net property income. Again you arrange to have your property painted and renovated.

SIX YEARS

Step 8. You sell the improved 8-unit building, with an accumulated $47,500 investment, for $59,375 and repay the $34,725 loan. You pay $2,969 sales costs, leaving you in six years with $21,681.

Step 9. You repeat this formula every two years. With each new purchase you borrow approximately three times your own investment. Each time you buy a building, or buildings as your estate increases, in need of refurbishing. You then paint and renovate, sell for a 25 per cent, two-year gross profit, repay the loans, and pay 5 per cent average sales costs.

Compounding most forms of investment, and particularly a growing business, subjects you to a major tax bite. Your pyramiding of income property will scarcely be affected by income taxes if managed prudently, as will be explained in later chapters.

EIGHT TO TWENTY YEARS

Step 10. At the end of twenty years you would possess a net estate of $1,187,195.

In 8 years you would have $39,363.
In 10 years $70,548.
In 12 years $124,884.
In 14 years $219,972.
In 16 years $386,376.
In 18 years $677,583.
In 20 years $1,187,195.

You can conservatively expect to earn an average net return of 6 per cent, giving you an annual income of $71,232. Even as a neophyte income-property owner you should earn 6 per cent on your total investment of four times your personal equity. Realty syndicates are able to take out a sizable bite for salaries and other heavy expenses and still virtually guarantee a 6 per cent net return to individual investors who devote no time or thought to their projects. While mortgaged the property income should build your equity and net worth by repaying your loan, plus returning an operating in-pocket net of over 6 per cent on your personal investment or net estate. You would have a conservative in-pocket net return of 6 per cent on your entire investment after paying off the mortgage.

MORTGAGES ARE NOW EASIER TO PAY OFF

Changes in regular mortgage practices have eliminated the major cause of depression foreclosures. Owners who lost their properties in 1929 and the early '30s were chiefly those who had short-term mortgages with high interest. Mortgages included interest in the 8 to 10 per cent range, high monthly payments, and a balloon payment. The principal in most cases had to be repaid or refinanced within three to five years.

Many owners could have survived by renewing their mortgages, but it was often impossible to refinance. The mortgage holders foreclosed, in many cases because they were required to by the existing laws. In the case of banks, money had to be raised to meet panic withdrawals, in the absence of present-day deposit insurance.

With current income-property loans written in the 7 per cent range, and averaging twenty years to repay the principal, the nominal monthly payments automatically pay off the mortgages from income.

A Look at Probable Expectations

Do the results shown in this chapter seem fantastic? The indicated operating figures are on the conservative side, because most experienced big-time owners expect a minimum operating net of 20 per cent on their personal investment, after making mortgage payments. The operating net is the net return from rentals while running the property prior to turnover for a capital gain.

The turnover profits outlined in my "Step-by-Step Formula to a Million Dollars" are also highly probable when you follow these four cardinal principles:

1. Borrow the maximum that can safely be repaid.
2. Buy only property that needs improvement.
3. Make selective improvements that increase value.
4. Keep selling at a profit and reinvesting.

How you can best accomplish each of these cardinal principles will be described in detail as we progress in later chapters toward your accumulation of a million dollars. Later case histories will prove our outline somewhat conservative, as it is in comparison with my own experience. I started my pyramiding with only $1,000 instead of the $2,500 cited in Step 1, reinvested on a spasmodic rather than a constant basis, and still surpassed a million within seventeen years. My net estate has tripled to over three million in the last ten years even though my realty investments have remained a part-time endeavor.

THE FORMULA INDICATES AN AVERAGE
YOU CAN ACTUALLY EXPECT TO PRODUCE

You would not of course take identical steps, making major move. exactly two years apart in the formula of investing, improving, selling, and reinvesting. Some sales would be made one or one and a half years after purchase, some would be made two and a half or three years after. As your estate grows to many properties you would maintain an overlapping program of continuous buying and selling.

In some turnovers your gains would exceed the indicated 25 per cent average. I have found 50 to 100 per cent capital profits are not unusual with experience. In other deals your gain might be less where the transaction does not meet expectations. And there is always the possibility of a loss, or a profitless turnover with neither gain nor loss. But if you persevere in reinvesting capital, the example indicates an average you can actually expect to produce. Even though not fully realizing your goal at each step, you can expect success at most steps.

To show how the formula works in practice, instances of typical purchases selected from current real-estate markets will be cited in Part Two and later chapters. Then improvements which result in capital gain will be specified, and resales will be consummated at current market levels.

Most forms of investment accumulate by simple arithmetic. Sustained investment and turnover in business and income property, especially the latter, which can harness to the utmost the latent power of borrowed money, pyramid geometrically. Geometric progression will always overtake arithmetic progression, even when the latter has a big head start.

ANYONE HAS A GOOD CHANCE
TO FULFILL THE GOALS SHOWN

Anyone with the confidence to aim at the goals shown has a good chance of fulfillment. Though maximum success demands consistent effort, the realty road to riches requires neither superhuman endeavor nor superintelligence. The chief attributes of successful realty investors are imagination, enterprise and persistence. Imagination means the vision to see the inherent potentialities of property investment. Enterprise means the willingness to venture both capital and effort in pursuit of a worth-while goal. Persistence means the ability to adhere to a program till the goal is achieved or surpassed.

MY FORMULA CAN BE FOLLOWED ON A PART-TIME BASIS

The amount of time and effort required is surprisingly small compared to the resulting compensation. As with my own experience, my formula can be followed on a part-time basis by the average employee. If your time is governed by unusually heavy existing commitments, you can choose a more leisurely pace if desired and plan your steps three or four years apart. If starting late with low assets, you can plan an investment goal that can be fulfilled in fewer years. If you possess substantial savings or other resources, such as a sizable equity in your home, you can get a head start by making an initial investment at the highest step which present assets permit.

Regardless of your present residence, you can take the interstate highway at any crossroad and successfully complete a cross-country motor trip merely by following the guideposts.

And regardless of your present financial status, you can take the realty freeway to riches at any state and follow the guideposts cited until you reach the destination of financial independence that meets your goal.

3. YOUR PHENOMENAL CHANCES FOR SUCCESS

Of course other roads besides real estate may lead to riches, but with most of them the odds are heavy that you will be led astray. These roads may depend chiefly on Lady Luck, like uranium hunting or buying speculative oil stocks. Or they may offer more chances of failure than success, like starting a new business. Normally the greater your possible return the greater your risk. But this is not true of real-estate investment.

YOUR CHANCES FOR REALTY SUCCESS
ARE BETTER THAN 400 TO 1

Income property investment, which offers the greatest average potential return, also offers you better than four hundred chances for success to one risk of failure.

According to typical nation-wide computations by the Federal Reserve Board and the Home Loan Bank Board, in 1953 less than one nonfarm home mortgage in five hundred was foreclosed. These figures included neither high-risk farm and commercial foreclosures nor low-risk apartment income-property mortgages.

A comprehensive study by the Institute of Life Insurance shows that real estate held under foreclosure by all U.S. life insurance companies at the end of 1951 totaled $61,000,000, only .316 per cent of their $19,314,000,000 in outstanding mortgages. Thus for each dollar mortgaged by insurance companies on all farm, commercial, home and apartment properties, foreclosures averaged slightly under one in three hundred. Grouping the Federal computation of only one foreclosure in 500 loans with the life-insurance-loan dollar figures of one in three hundred gives an average estimate of one failure in four hundred.

The foregoing figures include mortgaged homes which provide no self-sustaining income and are more apt to be defaulted in case of death, job loss or relocation of the breadwinner. They also include farm and commercial properties which are more dependent on the personal capabilities of their owners. When you possess apartment rental property that pays for itself, your odds will be considerably enhanced over the average odds for all properties. You can therefore safely gauge your chances for success with our recommended income property as better than 400 to 1.

YOUR CHANCES ARE BETTER THAN 1,600 TO 1
COMPARED TO GOING INTO BUSINESS

According to a study by the Department of Commerce, four out of five new businesses fail to survive eight years. Fifty per cent go out of business within two years. Each year of successful business operation increases the chances for ultimate survival, but the odds are thus four to one that a new business will go broke.

Contrast these 4-to-1 odds against you in business with the 400-to-1 property investment odds in your favor. This indicates that the chances for success in income property exceed by 1,600 to 1 the chances in business.

Why such a marked difference? Perhaps one reason is that while few invest in real estate without some study, many buyers blithely exchange their life savings for a business, feeling they are bound to succeed in a field where they have worked, or in a field which they think they will enjoy. Operating a business, as determined by the Bureau of Internal Revenue, is basically a form of self-employment, with investment secondary. A business depends almost entirely on individual idiosyncrasies and health. A bank will therefore seldom lend to a business neophyte and will hold his loan application in the pending file until he proves successful.

The Internal Revenue Service recognizes rental-income property, on the other hand, as basically a form of investment rather than a business. Income property is not so apt to fail because of personal whims, since it represents chiefly an investment in real estate which requires only nominal, part-time supervision. Business loans are governed chiefly by operating experience, while real-estate loans are governed chiefly by the value of the property. Experience is usually mandatory in obtaining a business loan. Although desirable, it is no more required on an income property loan than it is on a home loan. A lending institution will lend on the appraised value of income property, even though the owner is completely inexperienced. Witness all the completely inexperienced widows and retired pensioners who have made profitable income property purchases with the aid of heavy institutional financing.

A Further Comparison with Going into Business

Our income property formula shows how you can expect an average return of 33.87 per cent on your personal investment as long as you follow a sustained program of purchase, improvement, sale, and reinvestment. Perhaps it would be well to compare this average potential rate of expansion with business returns, the only other major field that offers a comparable pyramiding potential. As with income property, we will start with a nest egg of $2,500, and see how it grows in twenty years.

BUYING A BUSINESS OFFERS A 20.25 PER CENT RETURN

The Department of Commerce study cited above showed the odds are four to one that a new business will go broke. Starting anew with average luck, you would therefore wind up with nothing. But you might combine unique ability and experience with hard work and attain a one-to-four ratio of good luck. Studies shown below indicate that the average successful business earns a return of 20¼ per cent.

Business success usually requires self-employment for more hours than you would consent to work for someone else for on a salary. And when ready to retire, you will normally find the business cannot be carried on successfully without your active, full-time participation. Nor could it be continued by survivors, as attested in partnership contracts, which in most cases exclude survivors from carrying on.

In business partnerships when a partner dies the surviving widow is usually forced to sell at book value, which may be far less than the market value. With an individually owned business, widows normally are also forced to abandon or sell at a loss. With income property, on the other hand, a widow normally finds little difficulty in continuing to operate her husband's investment.

The average business, according to a representative 1948 study by the Department of Commerce, requires an investment of $9,500. Of this, one third (or $3,167) represents borrowed money, and two thirds (or $6,333) is composed of personal savings. This means that with $2,500 already saved at $50 monthly, you would have to save for six more years to obtain the average capital invested in a business.

The Department of Commerce study also shows that surviving businesses in 1947 averaged gross sales 6.2 times the dollars invested, making total average sales of $58,900 on a $9,500 investment. Dun & Bradstreet's *Standard Ratios for Retailing* indicates an average net return, after paying management salaries, of two and a half cents for each dollar of sales. Applying the 2½ per cent ratio to $58,900 in sales would produce an investment return of $1,472.50. Subtracting 6 per cent interest, $190.02, on the $3,167 borrowed would leave a net annual return before taxes of $1,282.48. Since you profit on your own and on the borrowed money, these combined studies show you would earn a return of 20¼ per cent on your personal investment.

Suppose you followed the principle of most successful pyramiders and plowed the investment return back into the business. Assuming that you would approximate average gross sales and net return, what income could you expect in fourteen years of success, twenty years from your start with $2,500? You would accumulate a personal net worth of $69,658. Using the previously cited financing and production factors, this would produce a 20¼ per cent annual return of $14,106.

These summaries do not take into account the crippling effect of income taxes, which stunt an otherwise thriving business more than any other form of investment. They show, however, the average business-profit potential once the risks are surmounted. They also show the growth potential in pyramiding profits with the aid of borrowed money, and they help to explain amazing expansions like those of Rockefeller, Ford, and Kaiser. Mushrooming expansion is inherent in any sustained business success, the same as with income property investment.

REAL-ESTATE INVESTMENT HAS A COUNTRY-WIDE FUTURE

Now that we have briefly scrutinized business possibilities, it might be well to take a broad look at future real-estate investment. What is the over-all picture for rental-income property? Are opportunities limited to a small area? Or are future opportunities country-wide?

Rental-income-property demand is expected to rise continually with mushrooming metropolitan populations throughout the United States. The annual total housing has consistently increased about a million units a year since removal of World War II brakes. Even the business recessions of 1949, 1953–54, and 1957–58 failed to stop housing's sustained growth. These recessions affected rental property less than any other industry, in most cities having no measurable adverse influence on vacancy ratios. In fact, when FHA financing on individual homes was curtailed, lenders poured an even higher percentage of funds into apartments.

Albert M. Cole, Administrator of the U.S. Housing and Home Finance Agency, in his November 8, 1955, Miami Beach speech to the U.S. Savings and Loan League, estimated that dwelling units would continue to be built at the rate of 1,200,000 per year or a little higher.

Robert L. Rand of the Federal Home Loan Bank Board states that there will be more than 10 million new American households between 1968 and 1975, creating a huge demand for apartments.

W. M. Kiplinger, in his *Boom and Inflation Ahead,* previously cited, predicts, under the heading of "Housing Boom—The Biggest Ever," an average of one and a half million housing units per year in the 1960s, two million in the 1970s, and two and a half million in the 1980s.

What are the prospects for the more lucrative field of improving existing dwellings? Vice-President Richard M. Nixon, in his October 19, 1955, speech to the Investment Bankers Association in New York, forecast, "In the next ten years America will need the replacement of five million housing units, and the reconditioning of fifteen million more at a cost of twenty-four billion dollars."

In 1968 Secretary Robert C. Weaver of the U.S. Department of Housing and Urban Development stated that existing housing in the next 10 years should be rehabilitated at 100 times the rate of the previous 10 years.

One reason that a rising population has such a marked effect on housing is that each newlywed family calls for close to three times as much capital outlay for a dwelling unit, whether bought or rented, as for all other expenditures combined. Various estimates place the total average 1955 requirement of a new marriage as approaching $15,000, including housing, furniture, clothing, transportation, and incidentals. Of this, housing approximates $11,000 and all other expenditures $4,000.

It is an accepted realty axiom that land values rise wherever the population increases. The value of each individual improved property will rise accordingly, as long as buildings are soundly maintained and not permitted to deteriorate.

Early American real-estate giants like Astor, Goelet, and Rhinelander in New York, Field in Chicago, and Longworth in Cincinnati all owed the fantastic growth of their fortunes to rapidly expanding economies in which cow pastures were converted to commercial properties in a comparatively few years. This type of purchase founded another sound axiom for land buyers: "Buy farms by the acre in the path of city growth and hold till the land can be sold as city lots."

Since practically the entire country is expected to experience population increases, real estate is now considered a sound investment throughout most of the United States. Investors, like Texans Murchison and Richardson, previously mentioned, have bought property in all parts of the country. Roger Stevens, for another example, moved his major operations from Detroit to New York to buy the world's most valuable single piece of real estate, the Empire State Building, for $51,000,000. After selling for a profit of several millions he jumped out to San Francisco to pick up, with Seattle associates, a group of properties valued at $17,500,000 being liquidated by a syndicate. On this latter deal, incidentally, Stevens outbid San Francisco's Ben Swig and myself, who were negotiating a joint offer.

Other things being equal, the best opportunities await in the cities of the greatest population increases, either numerically or percentagewise. But there is opportunity wherever the population goes upward rather than downward.

As an example of continuing expansion trends, interesting forecasts of population growth between 1958 and 1970 are shown on the following regional map taken from W. M. Kiplinger's *Boom and Inflation Ahead*, previously cited.

A table of U.S. Census Bureau forecasts of population growth from 1967 to 1985 also follows, indicating increases in every state except West Virginia.

HOUSING IS A PRIME NECESSITY

When you invest in housing you buy a prime necessity of existence. The Department of Commerce estimates the 1968 housing value at approximately seven hundred billion dollars. This surpasses by far the next highest of any industry and exceeds the six-hundred-billion-dollar total for all 1,200 corporations listed on the New York Stock Exchange. The food and clothing industries, which involve the other two prime necessities of life, trail far behind.

To keep up with inherent demand, your chief concern will be to prevent your holdings from becoming outdated, by staying abreast of current trends on price, convenience and appearance. Salability may fluctuate with inflation and recession. But your real estate will always retain an intrinsic value which economic forces cannot destroy.

SECURITY OBSESSIONS PREVENT RICH POSSESSIONS

Riches are impossible for those who are hopelessly obsessed with security. I have mentioned cases of several present-day successes, including my own comparatively modest achievement in becoming a millionaire. In spite of this, a sincere friend, who is an outstanding executive in the life insurance field, advises, "According to all the

Population increase: Regional growth by 1970

Reproduction of Regional Map from Page 30 of W. M. Kiplinger's
Boom and Inflation Ahead, *published by Simon and Schuster, 1958. The*
accompanying table shows later figures for individual states within each
region.

research information my company sends me, it is now absolutely impossible to build a substantial estate. The only means even to provide security is through life insurance."

My friend has arrived at an above-average state of security, but he is still searching for financial independence. Since protection is the chief purpose of life insurance, investment to such an insurance man is secondary. Your insurance representative, like your banker, will be guided by his exclusive training. He is obsessed with security considerations and is indoctrinated to make funds as insured of safety as possible.

Insurance provides the maximum estate for your survivors in case you die young, but the preponderant odds destine your living to a ripe old age. The average American at age twenty-five, according to the Federal Office of Vital Statistics, can expect to live past seventy. Increasing age adds to your total life expectancy. Why not chart your main course to get the most out of your prospective years? It is wise to plan for probable eventualities. It is tragic to toil and save chiefly for death, when all the time you seek an abundant life.

Business and professional men, whose chief asset is their personal production, may load heavily with insurance when they fail to make self-sustaining investments. If you want to follow a consistent investment plan that leads to wealth, you should consider life insurance chiefly for protection to tide survivors over emergencies. In case of

POPULATION GROWTH 1967 to 1985
U.S. Census Bureau Forecasts

*Fastest Growing, Exceeding 22% U.S. Average

	GROWTH			GROWTH	
	Numbers	*%*		*Numbers*	*%*
Alabama	585,000	17	Montana	100,000	14
*Alaska	77,000	28	Nebraska	100,000	7
*Arizona	945,000	58	*Nevada	225,000	51
Arkansas	245,000	12	*New Hampshire	185,000	27
*California	9,835,000	51	*New Jersey	2,050,000	29
*Colorado	630,000	32	*New Mexico	425,000	42
*Connecticut	845,000	29	New York	3,080,000	17
*Delaware	170,000	33	North Carolina	775,000	15
*Dist. of Col.	240,000	30	North Dakota	30,000	5
*Florida	3,655,000	61	Ohio	1,905,000	18
Georgia	890,000	20	Oklahoma	190,000	8
Hawaii	80,000	11	Oregon	380,000	19
Idaho	115,000	16	Pennsylvania	665,000	6
Illinois	1,775,000	16	Rhode Island	70,000	7
Indiana	770,000	15	South Carolina	340,000	13
Iowa	60,000	2	South Dakota	20,000	3
Kansas	140,000	6	Tennessee	600,000	16
Kentucky	210,000	7	*Texas	2,515,000	23
*Louisiana	865,000	24	*Utah	335,000	33
Maine	75,000	8	Vermont	50,000	12
*Maryland	1,190,000	32	*Virginia	1,085,000	24
Massachusetts	740,000	14	Washington	515,000	17
Michigan	1,145,000	13	West Virginia	−135,000	−8
Minnesota	600,000	17	Wisconsin	675,000	16
Mississippi	270,000	12	*Wyoming	75,000	24
Missouri	435,000	10			

U.S. TOTAL   42,842,000
AVERAGE   22%

Note substantial numerical growth in populous states like New York, Ohio, Illinois and Michigan, each gaining more than a million, even though below the 22% national average in percentage growth.

heavy mortgages, mortgage insurance provides an additional safeguard, paying off loans in case of death of the breadwinner. Insurance as an investment pays only for the one out of five who is unable to save by any other method.

BANKS AND INSURANCE COMPANIES
INVEST MOST OF YOUR MONEY IN REAL ESTATE

As mentioned in Chapter 1, banks and insurance companies prosper only through utilizing your savings. Suppose you put all your money into a savings account and life insurance. After deducting necessary expenses, where do they place your funds? They invest a major portion in real estate, chiefly in the form of mortgage loans. According to the Institute of Life Insurance, "Real estate mortgages have been a major area for investment of life insurance funds down through the years."

An estimate prepared by the American Bankers Association shows approximately a 50 per cent cumulative total invested in mortgage loans by all banks and insurance companies from time deposits, private repurchasable capital and policy reserves. Federal Reserve Board figures reveal that by 1968 their total mortgages approximated two hundred billion dollars, considerably surpassing their other major investments in securities and commercial loans.

The foregoing figures indicate that real-estate mortgages represent the major investment preference of both banks and insurance companies, proving that their officers select real estate as their soundest paying investment. They are willing to invest in property, through loans, considerably more than you and I when we borrow.

YOU CAN MATCH THE BANK'S MARGIN OF SAFETY

Banks and insurance companies own billions in real estate. As mentioned above, most of their property investments are made by means of real estate mortgages. This gives them the margin of safety which is the difference between the market value and the loan.

You can also operate with as large a safety margin by specializing. As the lending agencies concentrate on mortgages, you can concentrate on properties that will respond at nominal cost to improvements which will greatly enhance value. This is the field that makes most real-estate fortunes.

After such improvements you can frequently secure, as I have, a new loan for an amount equal to or greater than your total outlay for the original purchase plus improvements. This gives you a safety margin between total cost and market value as great as the usual margin between loan and market value. Although the general economy may fluctuate, this cushion makes your investment as safe as the bank's or the insurance company's.

YOUR SUCCESS IS ENHANCED
WHEN YOU CONTROL YOUR INVESTMENT

Your success with income property is enhanced because you can retain control of it. In contrast, those who attempt to pyramid with stocks relinquish control of their investment funds, except for choosing when to buy or sell. Hired management chooses expansion, improvement, and retrenchment steps to be taken. Operating decisions concerning the firms in which they invest are entirely out of the stockowner's hands.

Many, of course, have made money in stocks. Some have heeded analysts who have made comparatively consistent winning strikes. Many also have lost. A study by the Cowles Foundation for Research in Economics at Yale has shown that if you followed all the suggestions of a particular stock analyst for five years you would have broken about even from the standpoint of capital. Even expert analysts are prone to enumerate their successful selections and forget their flops.

By comparison, you can retain personal control at all stages in the selection, operation and improvement of your income property. The scientific and most successful farmer chooses for his greatest benefit the seeding and cultivation practices which will produce maximum harvests. So at all times you can select and consummate the property improvements which inherently will produce for you the most bountiful profits.

The sustained growth of metropolitan areas throughout the United States promises continually increasing demands for rental housing.

This offers you an ever expanding choice of real-estate investment opportunities which will make you a millionaire.

PART TWO

BUYING YOUR FIRST PROPERTY

4. SHOPPING FOR
A $10,000 INCOME PROPERTY

As population growth results in economic expansion, any growing city warrants consideration for rental-housing investment. Your success will be most assured if the speculative gamble of increased location value, as in buying a vacant lot, is subordinated to the primary objective of an earned gain from making profitable improvements. Although economic expansion was the chief growth factor for early real-estate fortunes, this factor falls to third in importance for today's financiers, with maximum financing first and property improvement second.

Besides physical improvement of property, you can also increase value as you gain experience by improving operations, an objective which I will cover in later chapters. Succeeding chapters will also detail information on appraisal, purchase, and operation of larger properties. This and the next two chapters will deal chiefly with choosing and buying a small run-down property in the $10,000 range.

COMMERCIAL PROPERTY IS RISKY
FOR THE NEW INVESTOR

With large holdings to cushion against loss of income from an individual property, various properties might prove safe investments, as long as their shortcomings are accounted for. Apartment houses require a minimum of employees in ratio to gross income. Hotels and office buildings, which may otherwise offer a good return, normally require a high ratio of employees. Being more subject to labor stoppages and a growing tendency of labor costs to devour profits, they can successfully be operated only by experienced managers. They are considered by the Internal Revenue Service as a business operation, not primarily an investment like an apartment house.

Large commercial units, like retail stores and industrial buildings, offer a good return with minimum supervision when leased to established businesses. But on the termination of a lease they may suffer long vacancies with no income even to pay the mortgage. A successful business may give up a lease because of a need for larger space, and a failing business is apt to abandon a lease. Commercial properties are therefore far more risky than apartments for the new investor. They are a sound investment only for the owner with many holdings, who has other income to offset the loss from a possible vacancy.

Commercial property might offer considerable opportunity for capital gain from enhanced location value, being more subject to development trends, but for the same reason it entails a greater risk of loss in value.

RENTAL DWELLINGS ARE YOUR SAFEST REALTY INVESTMENT

By following the lead of the seven million owners in the private-housing industry and concentrating your investments as I do in rental dwellings, you can heed the financial admonition against putting all your eggs in one basket. Each dwelling unit constitutes a separate income producer to which you can give individual attention. By alert management you can hold vacancies in soundly bought apartments and flats to a negligible factor, even less than national averages between 2 and 5 per cent found by the Department of Commerce in various surveys between 1954 and 1968.

In order to produce the capital gain required to expedite expansion, property should offer maximum possibilities to increase value. The property should be of basically sound design and construction, so that you can make improvements that will bring the building up to date at less total cost than new construction. To compete successfully it is obvious that the cost of an older building plus the cost of renovation must total less than the cost of a comparable new building. You can make marked transformations at minimum cost by such improvements as painting, landscaping, replacing antiquated fixtures, and modernizing surface architectural features. Details of money-making improvements will be covered in Chapters 7 and 8.

The property when bought should pay a fair return, at least sufficient for mortgage payments and expenses, and should promise sustained and possibly increased rents. As previously mentioned, big-property buyers usually demand a return of at least 20 per cent on their personal investment, in addition to paying all expenses including mortgage payments. Even as a small-property buyer you should expect the income to pay off expenses and the mortgage and to net a return of not less than 6 per cent on your personal investment. After the mortgage is paid off, the property should return a minimum of 6 per cent on the total invested by you and the lender.

Each mortgage-principal payment, although borne by the property, increases your net estate to the extent that it reduces the outstanding loan balance. In addition, if working toward maximum expansion, you should plow back all possible property earnings to speed improvement. Thus you can resell with the least delay and reinvest the profits in larger property. Such turnovers can pyramid your holdings rapidly. In a minimum number of years the properties should be large enough to pay all expenses including mortgage payments, and also produce a net in-pocket income sufficient to warrant your early retirement from your present occupation.

COMPETITIVE RENTALS ARE YOUR SAFEST HOUSING INVESTMENT

To minimize vacancies it is always better to aim for a rent somewhat under, rather than over, the market. Competitive rental housing should cost the tenant less than the average housing expense for the area. For example, the 1960 housing census showed that in metropolitan areas with more than 50,000 population, housing expenses averaged $85. The general level on a national basis was $60 for apartments without bedrooms, using folding beds of the wall, closet or sofa type, and ranged to $100 for apartments with bedrooms.

Owners of highest-quality rental units designed for executive incomes may be in a safe position with sound financing, good location, attractive buildings and grounds, and desirable interiors. However, high rentals are usually hardest hit with vacancies in times of severe competition, because of the small percentage of prospective tenants. In the moderately competitive rental market of 1954, for example, luxury apartments were second only to undesirable "conversions" in their high vacancy ratio. As competition increases the rentable luxury level declines.

RENTS SHOULD NOT EXCEED AVERAGE WEEKLY TAKE-HOME PAY

In an industrial area rental units will suffer excessive vacancies if rents exceed the average worker's weekly take-home pay, a principle violated by some investors to their sorrow. As another example, the Department of Labor estimates the average factory worker on a national basis in 1968 earned $118 a week. This average included the South, where the median wage is considerably lower than that of the rest of the nation. In an area where the wage scale approximates this average a monthly rent of $125 would result in frequent turnover and vacancies. In the same area a rent of $110 would encourage a full house, as long as the housing units compete for convenience and appearance with other available units. With this in mind, the safest property you can buy will meet competition and pay a fair return on your investment at rentals under the weekly wage of the average potential renter.

For faster progress it is important, particularly in the first steps, to invest in the biggest self-supporting property that available funds can buy. Although financing fluctuates, you can normally borrow about three times your investment and still keep mortgage payments low enough for the property to pay for itself. Assuming you have saved $2,500, you could buy property costing about $10,000, as in Step 1 in Chapter 2. With $5,000 to invest you could look for property in the $20,000 range, and with $10,000 for a $40,000 property. Larger purchases will be examined later, but for the present we will scrutinize the market for you as a prospective buyer who now has $2,500 to invest.

HOW WILL YOU FIND YOUR $10,000 INCOME PROPERTY?

The two chief leads on property for sale are:

1. Newspaper advertising
2. Real-estate brokers

Most property buyers consult newspaper classified or display ads. To become acquainted with various brokers, check the classified section for pertinent ads in your price range, then contact the realtor who has the listing. You condition the broker to serve you more wholeheartedly if you concentrate his attention by answering his ad, rather than approaching him initially with nothing specific to discuss. Answering an ad makes you a "hot prospect," whereas a "cold turkey" approach might draw a more indifferent response, classing you with the curious, dead-end shoppers who are merely killing time.

After discussing the property advertised tell the broker what kind of buy you are interested in. Do not begrudge the sales fee, which will be paid by the seller. The broker will earn his commission by handling many details of the transaction, and by negotiating a better deal and securing better financing than you might. It is surprising how often a good broker can secure additional funds to consummate a deal, when it may first appear that the sale will collapse for lack of financing.

SOMETIMES THE BEST BUY WILL
BE FOUND THROUGH AN AD

A sample survey shows that one third of the completed real-estate transactions were initiated by newspaper ads. Often an ad will lead to a realtor who keeps his best buys up his sleeve so other brokers cannot learn about them. Local customs vary. In some areas listings are tied up predominantly by individual brokers on an "exclusive" basis, so the property cannot be sold without paying a commission to the broker who has the listing. In others most listings may be "open," so that any selling broker would earn the commission. In most areas both types of listings will be made, and the broker who has a listing and the one who sells the property will co-operate by sharing the commission. But advertising exposes a "hot listing" to an unscrupulous broker who may steal the sale. Besides, if the property appears to be an especially good buy, the broker who has obtained the listing feels there is a good chance to make the entire commission instead of sharing it with another broker. Ads are used not only to sell a listed property, but also to get prospects for other property, thus serving for the mutual benefit of other sellers and prospects. A realtor whose ad interests you will usually have several similar listings, sometimes better buys than the property advertised.

At each stage of progress, in order to select the particular property to meet our specifications, we will choose from up-to-date listings and shop current real-estate markets. All but new property can usually be bought for between 10 and 25 per cent less than the asking price. Also sound purchases are often made with more than 75 per cent financing. So we should check the ads in which the property is listed between $10,000 and $15,000, where it appears the down payment may not exceed $2,500. Looking over four columns of ads under "Rental Dwellings for Sale" in a leading city newspaper, the *Metropolitan,* we find within our requirements ten ads which merit further checking.

EARNEST SHOPPING BEATS DRY RUNS

There is not too much advantage in dry runs, just looking at property from the outside, except to consider improvement possibilities. This would give you no idea of community and district price ranges, which will be an important part of your education. It is fine to appraise various districts to see which suits you. You might as well use the same time to best advantage by shopping in earnest.

In 1955 I served as chairman of the Manse Committee of the First Congregational Church of Oakland, California. We were charged with finding a home for our minister, Dr. Clarence Reidenbach, in the general neighborhood of the church. We could have spent many fruitless meetings discussing price ranges and could have drawn no valid conclusions. We let our wants be known to various realtors. The minister's wife selected from their listings seven suitable homes, enough to take up a full Saturday of shopping. Before we started, none of us had any conception of price levels for the type of home wanted. By the end of this one day's shopping every member of our committee of five had formulated a solid idea of market prices and values for the quality of home sought.

Though perhaps hesitant to plunge, you should find it just as easy to draw sound conclusions once you get started. After a dozen or so contacts you will begin to know values in the price range you have set. Before making your first purchase you will normally want to look over many listings in various districts. Thus you can observe whether a particular district is on the down- or upgrade. Although you may look for several weeks or months before selecting a suitable buy, be alert from the start. A choice bargain might appear when you answer your first ad, as the biggest trout in the pool may strike when you first cast a lure to test the distance.

WHY NOT BUY WITH LESS DOWN?

The ads show that some properties can be bought for as little as 10 per cent down, one $10,000 property for $1,000 down. Why not buy after saving only $1,000, as I did, and get a faster start? You should start as soon as possible, with financing as heavy as possible, always with the safety proviso that the mortgage payments can be handled from the property income after expenses are paid. Sometimes the best buy will demand less, sometimes more, than the minimum down. In citing examples I prefer to choose the conservative, which you can more readily equal or excel.

You will want to mark all the ads within your requirements, rating them by degree of interest, and then contact the advertiser for each ad. We will list the more interesting of the ten ads and look for desirable and undesirable features as we check over the respective properties. The following ads are quoted verbatim except for minor changes, such as names, addresses and telephone numbers.

OLD, BEAT UP AND ROUGH, AND NO FOUNDATION

> A—2 units, $9950; old, beat up and rough but in good district, above Broadway at High Avenue. Tremendous possibilities. Phone 224–3910.

This might be just what we are looking for. Brutal advertising is used to attract attention. The property might not be quite as bad as described, so we phone the listed number and obtain the address. When we drive up to the property, however, we meet with a shock. In the forepart of the lot is a 2-story wooden building, with 4 rooms on the ground floor and 2 bedrooms on the upper floor. The front gable is high-peaked and trimmed with ornate carving fifty years out of date and difficult to camouflage without high expenditure. Several windows are broken, drawing attention to large cracks in the upper corners of the casings, clues which cast doubt on the structural soundness. Screens are hanging loose, except for one which has fallen to the ground.

A weedy, gravel drive leads to a small jerry-built cottage in back of the lot. Papers are scattered over the yard, which is bare of trees, shrubs or grass. Obviously nobody has lived on the property for several months, a bad sign. If rental units are not occupied and drawing income when for sale, there usually is something radically wrong which makes the property unrentable. The quoted rents may be too high, or the property may have slipped under the slum line and become unfit to live in.

CONSTRUCTION KNOWLEDGE IS UNNECESSARY

It is not necessary for the income property buyer to have a detailed knowledge of construction. Along with most property investors, you can be content with surface examinations and can base final remodeling conclusions on the advice of architects and contractors. Experienced owners usually have foundations inspected by an expert before consummating a purchase. I always have a qualified contractor give me a cost estimate if there is any question regarding the approximate cost to remedy apparent deficiencies. Until you gain experience you can obtain expert advice regarding even routine improvements on which you later will be able to make fairly accurate "horseback" estimates. Most contractors will give an approximate estimate without charge where they stand a good chance of securing work.

There is no object in calling an expert until you have selected a property you are ready to buy and are prepared to give a contract if purchase and improvement costs can be worked out satisfactorily. Additional points to safeguard your purchase will be covered as we proceed with shopping, now and in later chapters. Meanwhile you can reject obviously poor buys, like this property and the next, with their major, glaring faults.

REHABILITATION COSTS HERE WOULD BE PROHIBITIVE

In examining any structure, all visible flaws should be regarded as possible indications of poor construction or advanced deterioration which may be costly to remedy. Even a beautiful-appearing building may be miraculously held together by a thin shell of plaster, with most of the foundation and underpinning eaten away by dry rot and termites.

On the other hand, a vacant building invites vandalism. A basically desirable property may appear hopelessly dismal only because of minor problems like broken windows. Before rejecting a property which on surface examination looks broken-down, it is well to make a thorough inspection, as long as the property may otherwise be of interest. We will check this first advertised property further before making up our minds.

The small cottage at the back of the lot is composed of three rooms, which have been converted from two connecting garages. One garage has been divided into a living room and kitchen, the other into a bedroom and bath. The floors are the gray concrete of the old garage floor, partially covered with the cheapest, battered linoleum print. Thrust through a pane in the only front window is a black, 6-inch vent pipe, connected to a bulky circulating gas heater located just inside the window.

This obviously inept conversion is typical of units too unappetizing to draw tenants even with cheap rents. In back of the cottage a 4-inch vent from a kitchen gas stove protrudes from a small window. We glance under the cottage's back porch, and then under the sagging back porch of the main building to the main foundation. There is no concrete or brick under the sills, the only foundation consisting of rotted wooden mudsills. This explains why the doorways and windows look off-square, and why the doors sag, although sagging doors may sometimes signify only easily repaired, loose hinges.

Without inspecting the main interior it is obvious that the cost of rehabilitation would be prohibitive. Before remodeling it would be necessary to level and square the building by jacking it up and installing an adequate foundation. This alone, if contracted, would cost about $5,000, depending on the problems that develop and how badly the structure is damaged.

RECONSTRUCTING A "JUNKER" MAY COST MORE THAN A NEW BUILDING

The converted cottage would no doubt be condemned upon city inspection. Often it would be cheaper to build anew than to reconstruct and modernize such a structure. Some shortsighted work horses buy such cheap buildings, called "junkers," so dilapidated that they can make a profit on rehabilitation only with prodigious personal labor.

Against my advice a retired carpenter of seventy bought for $6,000 a wreck of a 5-room house about to collapse from dry rot and termites. He knew what he was getting into, but he considered it a challenge to show his ingenuity and youthful stamina. He put in a new foundation and completely rebuilt the superstructure, taking a year's hard labor to complete his renovation project. His material expenses came to $3,500, and he incurred no labor costs. He triumphantly sold for $12,500, to take a $3,000 monetary profit. He said that all the time he was working on the house he was drawing Social Security, whereas if he had been working for wages these payments would have stopped.

If he had hired the work, he would have broken about even, or taken a thousand-or-so loss. He seemed to enjoy his expenditure of time and energy. But he could have made considerably more money by working on a less deteriorated property, such as we will choose. There are too many good buys in basically sound buildings to waste much time on junkers.

MAKE NOTES AND SKETCHES

As you appraise various properties, it will be helpful to make notes and sketches of the existing situation and possible improvements. Some shoppers take snapshots of interesting properties as an additional memory refresher. This is fairly inexpensive if you use small negatives, as on 35 mm. film. Your notes should also cover existing rentals, as a continuing survey of the rental market keeps you up to date on the actual rentals for different types of units.

Even while you are getting started your notes can include rough estimates of improvement costs. As you gain experience your original estimates will usually prove close to actual costs quoted by a reliable contractor.

Now let's move to the next ad.

ANOTHER AWKWARD CONVERSION, AND POOR DRAINAGE

FLATS, $10,950 full price, only $1,000
down; level location. Parkway Terrace
district. Phone 728–2913.

A small 5-room cottage, with a neat, white exterior and a trim front yard, has been converted into two 3-room apartments. The owner lives in one, in which a folding bed is pulled out in the living room. The bedroom is crammed with a double bed, a couch, two dressers and two chests of drawers, emphasizing the lack of closets. The kitchen has been built on a 6-by-8-foot back porch landing. The dishes rattle in the cupboards as we walk gingerly over the springy floor, calling attention to inadequate floor joists.

The owner's brother lives in the 3-room adjoining apartment. A toilet and a washbasin have been installed in what was originally one of his closets, and a Sears Roebuck sheet-metal stall shower in the remaining built-in closet, an awkward arrangement to give each apartment separate bath facilities. The brother's only clothes-storage space is a portable pressed-wood closet, leaning drunkenly from the corner of his bedroom, too flimsy to stand upright under top-heavy clothing.

POOR DRAINAGE

We descend a number of steps into the back yard. Although the ad reads "level," the back of the lot is about ten feet lower than the front. This is a moderate slope which would not normally be questioned except for the inaccuracy of the ad. A quick look at the basement shows high enough headroom in back, but the readily usable space is insufficient for conversion to an additional apartment. The higher ground at the front of the basement has been shored by two 2-by-12-inch planks supported by 2-by-2-inch posts. This is evidence that the earth has shifted, probably because of excessive drainage.

The ground behind the planks is mucky although it has not rained for several days. The surrounding concrete foundation is spotted white with a moist fuzz. Both signs of dampness are proof of poor drainage or a broken sewer pipe. The sewer pipe runs into the ground at the rear of the building and is apparently intact. We look outside at the front of the building and note that the downspouts from the gutters empty onto an oval slab of concrete about eighteen inches in diameter. This stops soil erosion, but it fails to prevent the water from draining into the basement. Two major items of repair are needed to correct the drainage problem:

1. Installing an adequate drainage line to carry the water away from the house.
2. Replacing rotted foundation sills, joists, and studding.

This is our second example of poor foundations, which result from poor original construction or from neglect. Before moving further, you might glance at the sketch on page 53, showing the terminology for a typical framing section, including the foundation. Although it is not required information, it might be of interest to iden-

tify such items as sills, girders, and joists when they are mentioned.
As a matter of information, one of the yardsticks of your foundation inspection will be that foundation walls should be a minimum of eight inches thick at the top. Poured concrete foundations are best, although concrete blocks may be acceptable if properly set. As an anchor against shifting, foundation walls should lie on footings twice the width of the foundation.

The two inadequate foundations which have been cited help to emphasize the importance in all such building purchases of your having the foundation inspected by an expert, just in case there is major damage. He will inspect all framing members for termite and dry-rot damage, and for sagging and bad cracks. The latter two items indicate inadequate underpinning, which might require major replacement. Cracks may be caused by the inadequacy of cuts for pipes or by failure to reinforce them.

VISIBLE DAMAGE MAY BE REPAIRED AT NOMINAL COST

Contrary to popular belief, most termite and dry-rot damage can be repaired at nominal cost, only a fractional portion of the resulting enhancement in value. Most visibly deteriorated buildings may be damaged only to a slight extent; for instance, only a single sill may be rotted. Minor inadequacies might be handled for $50 to $100. But a major foundation replacement, as required in the first-inspected, High Avenue property, can be prohibitive, running to $5,000 or $10,000. Or a high-cost drainage line may be needed besides, as indicated in the second property.

Most buyers reject a property in dismay at the least sign of rotted beams, visualizing framing completely eaten away by termites. This phobia helps to create bargains for the knowing buyer who is willing to correct minor damage. There are forty-five types of termites in the United States, and they can be a serious menace. As forests and orchards are depleted, termites move from this natural food to buildings. Their total damage is estimated to cost the nation about $250,-000,000 a year. But termites are not nearly as destructive to individual properties as most people imagine. Far more structural damage is caused by dry rot from decaying fungi, cultured by dampness from poor ventilation or drainage as in this Parkway Terrace property.

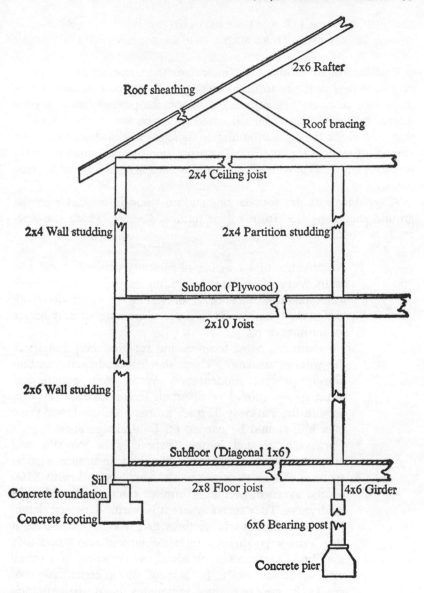

TERMINOLOGY FOR TYPICAL FRAMING SECTION

Note: Although framing varies with different types of construction, this diagram will help identify framing members. Details of plates, bridging, etc., are omitted.

FOUNDATION INSPECTION
IS CHEAP INSURANCE

If either rot or termites are indicated, the suspect beams can be probed with a penknife to discover the extent of the damage. If it is major, the place may be rejected; if minor, the property may be considered further. In any case, a licensed expert on termites and foundations will check the actual foundation damages or drawbacks and give you an estimate of repair costs. The inspection fee on a small property is usually about $10, which is cheap insurance against a possible error in selection.

A building with dry foundations and no wood in contact with the ground should be free from rot or termite damage, which can normally be controlled by:

1. A minimum of six inches of masonry between wood and earth. Very often careless grading or depositing of earth when planting shrubbery, or sliding of earth downhill, brings earth and wood in contact, creating an easy access for termites or rot.
2. No moisture. Most termites and rot-producing fungi will die without moisture. There should be adequate ventilation to prevent condensation. Water from gutters and drain spouts should be diverted. Excess rain or seepage, as with the Parkway Terrace property on the lower slope of a hill, should be carried off by drainage lines.
3. Chemically treated lumber, especially in the sills and other underpinning. This is the best insurance against termites. The cost, for example, would be as low as $100 on the average dwelling. Termites can't stand cold, light or dryness. They thrive where it is warm, dark and damp. If other conditions favor them and wood is untreated, if they cannot go directly from the ground into wood they may build earthen tunnels about the thickness of a pencil up foundation walls. In case of block construction or cracks in concrete they sometimes build their tunnels inside the foundation. But if you can see completely around the inside and outside of a concrete foundation, and there are neither earthen tunnels nor cracks in the concrete, then there should be no termites.

As in our appraisal of the first property, we have seen too many faults in this Parkway Terrace offering to warrant further consideration. It is time to move to the next ad.

A THIRD AWKWARD CONVERSION, A CHEAP PAINT JOB, AND A LEAKY ROOF

A—Open Sunday, 1 to 5:30, 5314 MacKenzie Avenue; one 3 and one 5-room apartment; level lot, approximately 60x180, zoned for business. $14,950; terms. Manny Kelvink. Phone 536–7209.

There are three vacant stores within a half block of this listed property. The small neighborhood shopping district has lost out to a two-block-distant supermarket with ample parking space. Business zoning, therefore, is no inducement. But we are primarily interested in the value for apartment rentals, so we proceed with our appraisal.

Here we find a 2-story wooden building sloppily sprayed with a cheap coat of white over an old gray paint that shows through in streaks and splotches. This ineffective one-coat paint job, lacking proper preparation and using poor paint, is a typical attempt to cover blemishes cheaply and calls more attention to a need for paint than if the building had been left in its original state. A buyer is usually better off with worn paint that can be soundly painted over than with cheap new paint, which may present more problems to cover, as some paints are incompatible. The cost of repainting should always be included, of course, in improvement estimates. A property should not be rejected purely because of a poor paint job, as this usually can be corrected at nominal cost compared with the possibility of producing a spectacular increase in value.

Paint on a wooden building will normally stay in fair condition for about five years. On concrete or stucco buildings the life expectancy is nearer ten years. In appraising older paint, notice whether it has aged naturally by powdering or chalking or whether there is telltale blistering and peeling or flaking. The latter, along with vertical streaking, is evidence of condensation between the walls, which causes rapid paint deterioration. We will bear the cost of complete repainting in mind as we proceed with our further appraisal.

SOME CONVERSIONS ARE INSANE

From the building design we can see that originally there was a single-family 6-room house which has been converted into two flats. The lower 5-room flat is now vacant but, according to the salesman, Mr. Kelvink, "has been renting for $90 a month." On the upper floor a vacant 3-room apartment has been converted from a former bedroom. It has a kitchen where the back porch used to be. "The owner is asking $75 a month rent. Both apartments are being left vacant in case the new owner wants to move into one of them." This sounds like an alibi to cover up the indication that the crude vacancies cannot be rented even at these low prices without costly remodeling. Both are awkward conversions, sharing the front entrance and one bath.

Physical conversions of property fall, like spiritual conversions, into two categories:

1. Natural, transforming into a new, complete entity
2. Unnatural, falling into an awkward distortion of the original

Natural conversions of property are made when the space converted may be used as a standard dwelling unit and looks as though it might have been included in the original building design. Examples which may attract tenants are attics and aboveground basements, full-sized for square footage and height. Unnatural conversions are made by using too limited or unsuitable space or by skimpy, awkward subdivisions of standard units. Typical are the garage-cottage in the first ad and the two apartments in this and the second ad. These ugly-duckling types of harum-scarum conversions repel tenants and suffer the highest vacancy factors. They should be shunned by the prudent investor even more than luxury apartments.

Some conversions appear so incongruous that the owner's sanity might be questioned. Many were made to circumvent rent controls. Whereas the 6-room house was probably "frozen" at an unusually low rent, converting to two apartments permitted two new and higher rents. Although shortsighted, this may have seemed a good economic move during rigid controls when space was at an unusual premium and the apartments could then be rented. Now the two apartments will be more difficult to rent than the one standard 6-room house they replaced.

Many conversions are sound. The buyer should be wary of those whose cost has been increased in an attempt to increase income and the actual income not only fails to repay the additional capital outlay but is now less certain than before. This conversion is too uneconomical to warrant further consideration of the property.

Where you see a drawback like this, which merits summary rejection, there is no need to waste further time appraising other items, such as foundations and roofs. In this instance we will take a look at the roof while we are here, for additional items in your education.

A LOOK AT THE LEAKY ROOF

Dark stains and peeling paint on the porch ceiling indicate a leaking roof which should be investigated if the property were still under consideration. There is a rusting downspout on the outside wall of the back porch. By climbing on the outside landing rail and standing tiptoe we can look into the gutter and onto the roof above. The elbow joining the gutter with the downspout is jammed with bits of crumbling shingle, showing that the roof is wasting away. The shingles remaining on the roof are curled and broken, proving that their useful life has about ended. The roof is too far gone for patching, and a replacement will probably be needed before the advance of winter.

Replacement with similar cedar or redwood shingles, to tie in with the existing gable-style architecture (see next page for five common roof styles), would cost about $1,000, giving a new roof that could be expected to last from twenty to thirty years. Fire-resistant, asphalt-composition shingles would cost around $750 and could give good service for ten to twenty years. Now installed on 80 per cent of all pitched roofs, this would be our choice if we were to replace this roof. The cheapest replacement would be asphalt-composition roll roofing, which could be installed for about $500. Besides being unsightly, roll roofing is highly susceptible to cracking and usually forms bubbles and ridges after one season. It would give an average life expectancy of only five years.

Unsightly metal roofing such as galvanized iron, used on barns and older residences particularly in the South, is subject to rusting and could not be considered. Lifetime aluminum shingles and sheet roofing are coming into more extensive usage, replacing copper for ultra-expensive private dwellings; but for rental property the cost of this, as of slate or tile, would normally prove prohibitive.

Tar-and-gravel roofing, built up with several alternating layers of felt and hot tar, and covered with gravel or mineral surfacing im-

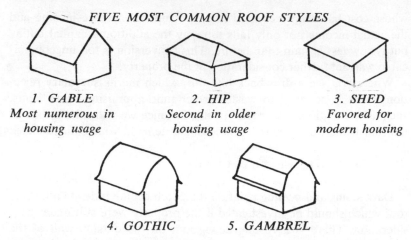

FIVE MOST COMMON ROOF STYLES

1. GABLE
Most numerous in
housing usage

2. HIP
Second in older
housing usage

3. SHED
Favored for
modern housing

4. GOTHIC   5. GAMBREL

Previously favored only for barns (large hay capacity), Gothic- and gambrel-roofed barns have been converted to housing, especially in New England. Now used in new construction.

bedded in hot tar, could not be installed on a steep-pitched roof such as this. However, this would be a conventional installation on a slightly pitched or flat shed-type roof, where the pitch usually runs less than four inches per foot. An existing roof of this type, favored in modern architecture, can be adequately inspected only from on top. From ground level it usually is impossible to spot imperfections which would be apparent on a steep sloping roof. Points to look for include cracks in the felt and spots barren of mineral surfacing. Neither mineral nor gravel has much effect on whether a roof leaks or not. Their chief purpose is to preserve the life of the felt by preventing the evaporation of tar from the full force of sun and wind.

While appraising a roof, look for worn-out corroded flashing in the valleys, and at vents, chimneys and parapet walls. Also inspect the gutters and downspouts to see if, like the rusted ones here, they need replacement.

Many unimaginative buyers reject all buildings, regardless of size, which need new roofs. Since we are looking for basically sound property in need of improvement, we would leave this, like most individual appraisal factors, open to question. If other factors appeared favorable, we would not cross a property off our list, even if, as here, a complete roof replacement was required. The approximate replacement cost of $750 would not be prohibitive if little else than painting, for example, were necessary. The point at which total improvement costs outweigh potential profits will be discussed more fully in the next chapter.

It should be mentioned that the importance of a single item such as a new roof decreases with the number of units involved. On an individual home the cost per dwelling unit would be the total cost, or $750. On this 2-unit house it would be $375 per unit. On a 24-unit building, such as we will buy later in the book, the identical cost would be about $31 per unit, which would be relatively inconsequential.

A NEWER PROPERTY OFFERS LITTLE CHANCE TO INCREASE VALUE

Since we have seen three disappointing older duplexes, for our fourth ad we select a newer single-family house:

> AT 247 BALMY TERRACE
> Open Sunday, modern stucco house,
> two blocks Broadway, $11,400 FHA
> commitment, see, make offer. Ames.
> Phone 283–6535
> LEE BROS. REALTY
> 9517 Main St.

Arranged in four identical pairs, eight cottages occupy all but one corner lot of a full block, facing the same street. Each pair of houses is composed of two L-shaped, one-story buildings, with the bases at the back of the lot and a common driveway running between them. The floor plans of the buildings are identical, except for the symmetrical reversing of design in each pair. A red-brick veneer covers the concrete foundations up to two feet above ground. Above that is white stucco for three feet. The remainder of the outside walls up to the eaves is covered with clapboard, also painted white. In each building the front entrance is at the top of the L, fronting on the street, and the rear entrance is at the end of the base of the L, facing the driveway.

NO GARAGES OR ADEQUATE LAUNDRY FACILITIES

There are no garages. The driveway common to each pair of houses leads to a concrete parking area across the back of the lot, sufficient for four cars. Galvanized wire is strung in four lines high enough for cars to clear, so that the parking area may be used for clothes-drying during the day. There are no indoor laundry facilities, not even a service porch with laundry trays, which is common to this type of housing.

A well-kept lawn fills the space between the main sidewalk and the buildings, down the entire block of cottages. A hawthorn tree is planted in front of each cottage in the parking strip, an Italian cypress accents the outside corner of each building, and compact shrubs underline the front windows. The shrubs have intertwined and should be thinned, their growth indicating they were probably planted five to ten years previously.

We ask the salesman why only one of the eight cottages is for sale, instead of the entire group. The salesman explains that they were built by a developer who sold each to a separate owner. There is an FHA commitment for $7,500. The owner will take a second mortgage from a responsible party who lacks funds for a full down payment. The cottage for sale is vacant. The salesman says, "You can easily get one hundred and twenty dollars, as that is what these houses all rented for when they were built three years ago. The owner has moved to a single-family home with more room and left the place vacant, so you will be able to move in if you buy it." "What does the cottage next door rent for?" "That one happens to rent for ninety dollars because the tenant is probably a relative or something like that."

SKIMPY SPACE AND CHEAP CONSTRUCTION

Inspection of the vacant unit shows a 3-room cottage with smaller-than-average rooms, the type found more often in premium-spaced downtown apartments than in a residential-district house. Heat is provided only in the living room by a combination wall-floor furnace of a type seldom installed in recent years. There is no thermostat for heat control, an item marking cheap construction. There is one small bedroom, with a tiny closet. The cramped bathroom has a stall shower, but no tub. Many lending agencies will not loan on housing without a tub.

There is no dining room. A compact breakfast nook adjoins the kitchen, which is the only room not below average in size. There is a deep sink suitable for clothes-washing, installed to make up for the previously noted lack of laundry trays. The linoleum in front of the sink shows four holes that seem to have been gouged out by a washing machine. The whole interior needs painting. The brown grease stains above the gas stove emphasize inadequate ventilation and look like an accumulation of at least five years. There are cracks one-quarter- to one-half-inch wide between the ends of the oak planks in the living-room floor. The shortened boards indicate that green, unseasoned lumber was used. The bathroom, breakfast-nook and kitchen floors are covered with inlaid linoleum in fair condition except for the worn area in front of the kitchen sink.

We ask, "Did you say this was built three years ago?"

"Yes, that's right."

WE VERIFY THE AGE INDICATED BY SHRUBBERY, CONSTRUCTION, AND CONDITION

We dismiss the salesman by telling him we will consider his listing while looking over other properties. After he has departed, we return to the cottage with the "For Sale" sign. While on the premises we might as well get as true a picture as possible, though this does not appear to be the kind of buy that offers much chance for profitable improvement. To verify the age, we follow an old real-estate practice. We go to the back of the building and look in the meter box. Alongside the electric meter several white cards are tacked, one marked "Electrical Inspection," one for plumbing, and several for other inspections made at the time of installation. The dates on the inspection cards indicate that the building is ten years old.

IT ALWAYS PAYS TO VERIFY RENTALS

To check the rentals we try to interview a tenant in each cottage, saying that we are considering buying the place that is vacant and want to find out what the similar units actually rent for. There is no response from one. All six tenants queried in the remaining cottages willingly answer questions. In two cottages the rent is $95. In one it is $85. In the other three, the rent is $90. One of the tenants paying $95 volunteers that she has lived here since the cottages were erected. All rented for $95 when new, but they were raised to $125 three years ago when a freeway construction gang took over most of the rentals in the area. When they moved on the rents had to be lowered. Most of the new tenants moved to larger quarters or bought their own homes.

"For the one hundred and five dollars I was paying here I was going to rent a two-bedroom flat where an old-maid teacher had moved out when her rent was raised. But when I told my landlord about moving he cut my rent to ninety-five dollars, so I decided to save the ten dollars and stay. But these places are awfully crowded for a family with children. With my oldest sleeping on a sofa, and my second outgrowing her crib, I can't stand it much longer, doing without two bedrooms."

If these were 2-bedroom dwelling units as in most rental houses, they would rent readily in this area for $125. But, unfurnished and excluding utilities, their space is inadequate to warrant over $95. The cramped design causes the number-one tenant gripe and offers no possibilities for converting additional rental space. There is little opportunity for capital enhancement.

. . This listing serves as a warning that rental value cannot be judged on original or previous rentals but must be appraised on existing and potential rentals. With rent control, for example, new construction often rented above the going market, whereas most older property was frozen below the market. Concentration on older property will present better opportunities to find under-the-market buys because of lower rents.

A Good Income, but Already Developed

Here is an interesting 2-unit ad, showing for our fifth inspection a good present income for the probable purchase price:

> OPEN every afternoon; three-bedroom house, plus apartment facing rear street; two garages; income $155 month; loan $12,500 payable $115 month; make offer above loan. 4210 Majestic Street.

In a neat-appearing house with five small rooms, renting for $85 monthly, the original dining room is now being used as a bedroom. At the rear of the lot, over two adequate-sized garages, a small 3-room apartment has been built. It has modern fixtures in kitchen and bath, is furnished in economical but attractive style, and rents for $70. The rent will apparently hold because the location is close to regular industrial employment. From Mr. Bokay, the realtor, we gather that the property can probably be bought for $1,000 over the loan. The owner has died, and the heirs want to sell and divide the proceeds.

Rents are low. In this generally poor neighborhood they would have to remain low in order to prevent vacancies. Even so, this would be a fair income producer for a buyer looking solely for income. It offers, even with reasonable maintenance allowances, a fair 10 per cent net. It is not unusual, however, to find properties of this type, in a deteriorating district such as this, paying 15 to 20 per cent net after allowing for fixed expenses and maintenance.

The property does not meet our requirements because the practicable improvements have already been developed. There is little opportunity for meeting our goal to increase capital value.

Your average shopping experience will find fewer such obvious rejects as the foregoing. They have been selected to emphasize shortcomings to be wary of.

If you have any doubts, always have a qualified expert inspect possible deficiencies and estimate the cost of proposed improvements before you consummate a purchase.

5. CHOOSING YOUR FIRST PROPERTY

We tell the realtor, Mr. Bokay, that we are especially interested in property that might compare with this already-developed Majestic Street offering, before the remodeling was done to build up the rental income. We prefer something in a better district, not so run down. We want a building that has not already been remodeled but could stand adding a unit or renovating the present units, something of basically sound design that may be badly in need of painting and may need other work.

"Got dozens of listings right up your alley. Let's see, now, we better go back to my office and I'll pick out some humdingers for you."

WHAT DO TENANTS WANT?

We have already looked over and rejected five property examples. Before proceeding further, let's summarize what we are looking for by checking certain specific requirements which satisfy tenants. A study of buyer desires by the Housing and Home Finance Agency reveals that a good location tops the wants of almost every buyer. Large rooms were second and ample closets third. A confirming survey by the same agency of the specific complaints of 1,000 home buyers also reveals considerations which would cause tenants to complain:

1. Rooms too small, 50 per cent
2. Inadequate storage and closet space, 45 per cent
3. Unsatisfactory laundry arrangements, 33⅓ per cent
4. Inconvenient layout of rooms, 25 per cent
5. Not enough space for furniture in bedrooms, 23 per cent
6. Inadequate working or eating space in kitchen, 19 per cent

We can conclude, therefore:

1. Desirable property should be situated in a location considered good by the average potential tenant.
2. It should have a basically sound design in which most tenants' requirements are already contained or may readily be realized by improvements.

A PROPERTY THAT MEETS OUR REQUIREMENTS

The agent thumbs through his files and selects five cards with details in front and a snapshot pasted on the back. He shows us pictures of two duplexes and three single-family houses. For various reasons we tentatively reject all but one of the buildings. We get into Mr. Bokay's car to look over the chosen property, listed for $11,500, a 5-room house over a full basement.

The realtor says, "I have other good deals if this one doesn't suit you, but I think this is just what you should buy. It's a sound house on A Avenue that needs fixing up. And you can easily make it into a legitimate duplex."

A REVIEW OF FAVORABLE POINTS

Although we set our sights on a duplex when we started shopping, our cursory appraisal shows we have found a house which will probably meet our requirements. As with my own initial purchase, a single-family house is the first property bought by most realty investors. In 1968, houses constituted 42 per cent of all rental dwellings. We therefore decide to make a fairly extensive review of favorable points.

Price and Financing Favorable. Mr. Bokay volunteers that the house is about twenty years old. He thinks he can pull the price down to $10,000, and the owner will sell with as little as $2,000 down.

Zoning O.K. The district is zoned for multiple dwellings, as he points out on a zoning map. "There would be no zoning problem if somebody wanted to make money by building a flat in place of the basement."

General District Good. The general area is regarded as good. There are several duplexes, also apartment houses and older, single-family residences. No industries have invaded the area, and present zoning prevents their encroachment.

Immediate Neighborhood Good. The house is situated on A Avenue, previously a streetcar artery, which has been converted into a residential boulevard. The trolley tracks have been taken up in the last few years. A curbed planting strip has been installed in the middle and filled with variegated low shrubbery.

This has evidently encouraged adjoining owners to spruce up their front yards, as many new shrubs and lawns are in evidence. Most of the yards and buildings in the area appear well maintained, a good sign that there is no general area deterioration. Another good sign is a new 4-unit apartment house under construction four lots up the street.

WHAT MAKES A GOOD NEIGHBORHOOD?

Since a good neighborhood is the number-one desire of tenants we might well examine further distinctions that mark a neighborhood good. This is a generally good neighborhood because it is on the up-grade and there are no substandard buildings in the area. The lack of paint on the building we are inspecting makes it the most uncared-for in the block. Further neglect, or many more similar eyesores, would pull the whole neighborhood down.

The U.S. Housing and Home Finance Agency considers an area for designation as a special urban renewal project, eligible for consideration under the rehabilitation and conservation phases of the Federal Housing Act, if 20 per cent of the housing has deteriorated to substandard. This would mean that if one out of five dwelling units in the neighborhood looked dilapidated, the whole area could be considered a slum instead of a good district.

If the area is generally as good as this, there is an added incentive to renovate a particular building. Once rehabilitated its value will be enhanced by the general values of the neighborhood. On the other hand, it would be uneconomical to beautify a single dwelling in an all-slum district, because the value of the renewed dwelling would still be held down by the neighborhood. The exception would be where the whole area is being rejuvenated, as under a general renewal program, such as is being encouraged in many cities by the Housing and Home Finance Agency and by ACTION, the American Council to Improve Our Neighborhoods. Various real-estate groups, and the U.S. Chamber of Commerce, too, are vitally interested in renewal.

DETERIORATION CREATES OPPORTUNITIES FOR IMPROVERS

In past years Americans have devoted so much energy to expanding new production that much wasteful deterioration has occurred from neglecting to conserve the already-built. In 1954 the government took special note of the need for improving housing when President Eisenhower stated in his housing message that the nation's primary housing problem is to insure the conservation and rehabilitation of existing housing wealth. Eisenhower asked Congress for comparable financial assistance for older as for new construction, and the FHA improvement-loan maximum was then increased to $10,000. By late 1955 the FHA further encouraged improvement loans by tightening loans for new housing, but continuing liberal loan policies for replacement, reconstruction, repair, alteration or improvement.

According to a 1954 study by the Housing and Home Finance Agency, 79 per cent of all housing was built before 1945, 41 per cent prior to 1920. The agency estimates that 20 million dwelling units need some rehabilitation and about one fifth of all housing should be rated inadequate. In prewar rentals the percentage of dilapidation is even higher. Rental housing has deteriorated at an accelerated rate because normal incentives for improvement were killed by rent controls.

Older Housing Can Be Rejuvenated
by Improvements

Neighborhoods do not decay merely because of age. In European countries and some older sections of America there are many desirable communities with well-maintained and improved housing hundreds of years old. To remain adequate, housing has to keep up with the times by adding improvements such as plumbing and other fixtures that are recognized as necessary for comfort and convenience. As simple an improvement as installing a shower head over a bathtub can make a dissatisfied tenant happy. In addition, appearance must be maintained both inside and out so that there is a general look of functional beauty, which creates satisfaction, rather than ugliness, which arouses disgust.

Signs of an Undesirable Neighborhood

There are many signs to mark a neighborhood as undesirable, a slum or deteriorating into a slum.

1. The aforementioned deterioration of individual buildings.
2. Overcrowding of buildings, jamming them with far more tenants than they were planned for and thus creating noise and confusion, delinquency, health and fire hazards.
3. Overcrowding of land with buildings, blocking out sunshine and air and leaving no room for gardens and trees.
4. Unplanned or poorly planned land usage, with housing built next to tanneries, churches situated next to bars, and schools surrounded by noisy trucks or locomotives.
5. Heavy passenger or truck traffic funneling through a district. Auto speedways down residential streets drive away desirable tenants who would help maintain good housing.
6. Lack of public facilities and services. Absence or inadequacy of schools, playgrounds, parks, neighborhood organizations.
7. Lack of convenient transportation facilities.
8. Lack of adequate shopping facilities.

ADDITIONAL POINTS FOR APPRAISAL

Fortunately none of these detractions that mark an undesirable neighborhood are apparent here. Now that we have examined salient points by which to check a neighborhood, let us return to our further appraisal of the A Avenue house at hand.

Transportation Convenient. A city bus line runs down the street and the closest bus stop is only a half block away. A major crosstown bus stop is two blocks distant, where A Avenue intersects another boulevard.

Schools Satisfactory. The nearest grammar school is four blocks, and the junior and senior high schools about six blocks, distant.

Shopping O.K. For nearby convenience there are a small drugstore and a grocery within two blocks. It is about ten blocks to a supermarket shopping center.

Lot Terrain and Size Are Fair. The 40-by-100-foot lot slopes moderately, with the back rising about ten feet higher than the front. We verify the lot lines with the salesman by locating tiny crosses notched in the cement curb to mark the boundaries. The front lawn is full of weeds and the shrubbery on the boundary lines and in front of the building needs trimming, but these items can be corrected without much expense.

Garage Is Fair. There is a two-car garage in fair condition facing an alley in the rear. It has a concrete slab floor and newly installed overhead doors.

Front Porch Is Convenient. A sloping cement walk minimizes steps by climbing halfway up the lot to the side of the building, where there is a stairway and a porch leading to the front door. The porch is enclosed with 2-by-4-inch railing, chewed at the ends from frequent renailing. The tongue-and-groove porch floor sags toward the upper side, calling for a close check when we look at the foundation. The porch is sheltered by a pitched roof—a desirable protection, as another pet gripe of tenants is about having to fumble for a key in the rain.

Outdated Fixtures Are Cheap to Replace. The gangling electrical fixture in the dining room, suspended to just above head level, plus the badly chipped, small white hexagonal tiles on the kitchen drainboard, date the original construction in the 1920s. A large circulating heater is installed in the living room. The bathtub is of modern appearance, flush with the floor, but the porcelain faucet handles are cracked.

Large Rooms and Closets Meet Tenants' Number-Two and -Three Desires. All the rooms are fairly large, and there are roomy closets in the bedrooms. The kitchen cabinets are fairly adequate.

Floors Are Fair Except for Kitchen. The kitchen floor is covered with worn linoleum in need of replacement. The bathroom floor is of ceramic tile in fair condition. There are oak floors in the living room, dining room, and bedrooms, all of sound construction but in need of refinishing.

Needs Paint, Which Will Help Drive a Good Bargain. The house is badly in need of paint inside and out. Both the inside plaster walls and the outside stucco are in good condition otherwise.

Age, Too, Will Help Drive a Bargain. The telltale inspection slips in the meter box show the structure was built in 1926.

Roof, Gutters and Downspouts Fair. The pitched gable roof is covered with green asphalt-composition shingles in fair condition. The galvanized gutters and downspouts are sound. The downspouts are located at the four corners and pour onto concave concrete slabs which slope away from the sides of the building.

Service Porch and Laundry Facilities Satisfactory. Inside at the rear is a service porch with two concrete laundry trays. The porch leads to an outside landing. The floor is of 1-by-4-inch tongue-and-groove, the same as the front porch. An outside stairway runs from the landing to a wide concrete step on the ground. The landing and stairway are protected by 2-by-4-inch railings, all in sound condition. From the landing a pulley-type galvanized-wire clothesline runs to a pole at the rear corner of the lot.

Main Foundation Good. The outside foundation on the vulnerable upper side, where earth might pile up, shows a foot above ground level, double the safe minimum. The top of the concrete foundation runs six inches or more above ground all around. The concrete is dry on the inside walls, and shows no signs of dampness.

Basement Good. The full basement has a good cement floor about two feet above ground level in front, and one foot below ground level at the back. In case the basement should be converted into a flat there is ample height for the eight feet of headroom normally required, as the bottom of the floor joists is ten feet high.

Main Underpinning Sound. The girders supporting the floor joists are 2 by 8 inches. To double-check for termites or rot, we attempt to thrust our pocketknife into the girders and the foundation sills, and find them sound as new. The underpinning is all of sound construction, with 2-by-6-inch floor joists spaced 16 inches apart, with cross bridging every 8 feet, and with subflooring installed over the joists on the diagonal.

A Sagging Porch Foundation Helps Drive a Better Bargain. On the upper side of the front porch, which is enclosed with frame and stucco from the floor to the ground, dirt has piled a foot above the porch foundation. A pocketknife probed into the porch foundation sill and wall studs finds them soft and spongy with rot. No wonder the porch sags.

Porches are usually built on entirely separate foundations. Although this front porch is joined to the main building, its inadequate underpinning normally would have no bearing on the main foundation. But a sagging porch will pull down the over-all value far out of proportion to the cost of repair, by casting suspicion on the soundness of the main structure. A porch that can be repaired for $200 may reduce the sale price by as much as $2,000. Some improvement-minded buyers specialize in seeking homes with "For Sale" signs where the front porch is about to cave in. If the house is otherwise sound except for the need of paint, they can buy at a heavy discount, repair and paint cheaply, and possess a sure-fire profit maker.

Present Low Rent Can Be Raised. The house, including some dilapidated furniture, is now renting for $90 a month. The tenant pays for all utilities. The tenant says she has been living here for eight years and has always paid the same rent.

Even in its present condition the house could be rented for $120 to $130, since it has the two bedrooms required by families with additional adults or one or two children.

Summary of Favorable Factors. The house is in a good rental district, meeting tenants' number-one demand, with desirable immediate and general neighborhood. Other tenant desires are satisfactorily met. The basic design is sound. Rooms and storage facilities are ample. Kitchen and laundry are satisfactory. The building is built square, with no gingerbread trimming nor impractical offsets. The needed painting and incidental rehabilitation are the types of improvement we welcome, which produce maximum increase in value at minimum cost. Here is a place that meets our requirements if we can buy at the right price.

YARDSTICKS OF VALUES

A lending institution usually averages several types of appraisal valuation, such as gross income, net income and replacement values, to arrive at a composite evaluation. To buy on an advantageous and sound basis, you should use various types of valuation as a guide, but you should always figure that your total appraisal shall not exceed the income value. If the replacement cost is higher than the income value, which should always be the case with older property, you should not raise or average your appraisal but hold to the income value. If replacement costs are less than income value, which frequently occurs with new construction, you would lower your valuation to the replacement costs, rather than strike an average.

Capital Value. On single-family homes and on duplexes in fair condition a common yardstick for establishing a fair market price is to multiply the gross monthly income by 100. This means the monthly gross is 1 per cent and the annual gross 12 per cent of the existing income, or capital value. With a gross rental of $90, we multiply by 100 and arrive at a base income valuation of $9,000.

In this type of rental tenants usually pay for utilities and minor repairs. Thus the owner's fixed expenses consist of taxes and insurance, which normally can be paid by two months' rent, leaving the owner with a 10 per cent net before loan payments. In this case two months' rent equals $180, slightly exceeding the total of $152.50 for taxes and $20.50 for $8,000 fire insurance.

In addition to deducting 5 to 10 per cent, for repairs, from the base income value, lenders usually also deduct 5 to 10 per cent for an average vacancy factor. This is usually assessed on an arbitrary basis regardless of the rent schedule. However, the rent is considerably under the market in this case, so we can give full credit to the present rentals and estimate a sound income valuation as the full base of $9,000.

It should be mentioned that with larger properties there are innumerable expense variations which should be accounted for before arriving at the fixed net income, and the formula of 100 times the monthly gross would not apply. With more units than a duplex the usual yardstick is ten times the annual net income. Several detailed examples will be cited in later chapters.

Replacement Value. For an appraisal of replacement costs,

we measure the building with a tape and find it 30 feet wide by 48 feet deep. This makes 1,440 square feet. Comparable new construction would cost about $12 per square foot, or $17,280. Normally 10 to 50 per cent would be discounted for depreciation on all but new buildings, covering the age, the state of upkeep, and features such as lack of paint and old-fashioned electrical and plumbing fixtures that need replacement. Here the fixtures are only partially inadequate. Poor neighborhood and poor design would also be considered, but in this instance we have good neighborhood and good design.

To stay on the conservative side, we will compute a 40 per cent depreciation in this case, allowing $7.20 per square foot, or a fully depreciated value of $10,368. The 20-by-22-foot garage and full basement total 1,880 square feet, on which we will figure half regular building costs, or $6 per square foot for new construction. Depreciating 40 per cent to $3.60 per square foot would make their depreciated value $6,768, giving a total depreciated buildings' value of $17,136. We add no credit for the furniture, most of which has outlived its usefulness, but add a nominal value of $3,500 for the lot, which does not depreciate. Our total replacement value thus would come to $20,636, including the lot and a 40 per cent depreciation on the buildings.

In addition to square footage, lenders make a "horseback" room appraisal for a quick check of usability. They figure a certain maximum allowance per room, based on the quality of construction, age, and state of maintenance, the same as on the square-footage appraisal. In addition to the 5 rooms in the house, the basement and double garage might each be counted as a room, making 7 rooms. In this case a $1,500 room valuation might be applied, totaling $10,500. The lot value of $3,500 would again be added, to make an over-all room and lot appraisal of $14,000.

Buy on Lowest, not Average Appraisal. To recapitulate, you should never pay more than the income value or the replacement value, whichever is less. If you hold to the principle of buying older property on the basis of existing income, you will always buy for less than the cost of replacement. You can maintain an enviable competitive position with low initial cost—

1. You can rent below the market for comparable new housing.
2. You can compete successfully with new housing for appearance and convenience by selective renovating.

3. You can compete successfully with older housing which fails to match your renovation.

PROBABLE INCREASED VALUES FOR A PROFITABLE RESALE

Of course we would not reveal to the agent any ideas on improving the operation of the property, as this could increase our purchase price. But, in addition to our other appraisals, we would review in our minds factors which would increase the net income and therefore the resale value.

Increasing the Gross Income. Comparing rentals in the vicinity, we decide that the house should readily rent for $150 after decoration and renovation. This would result in a resale value of $15,000.

Reducing Costs by Removing Furniture. The house would look more presentable unfurnished than with the much-used furniture. After a rent raise the present tenant probably will move, and then the salable furniture should be sold to a secondhand dealer and the balance junked. Two-bedroom houses in this area rent almost as well unfurnished as furnished and in the long run may draw a more stable tenant who does not like to move his furniture. The national trend with rental units having bedrooms is toward cutting expenses by providing a minimum of furniture. Providing new furniture seldom pays for the expenditure involved except when you can buy at wholesale prices. With the discounted prices available through most Apartment Owner Associations, new furniture can give you a competitive advantage in many areas.

Cost of Renovation. Our rough estimate, which an inexperienced investor would verify with a contractor before buying, indicates that the house could be put in attractive condition for a maximum of $2,000 if all the work is contracted. This could be reduced to about $1,400 if the more unskilled half of the labor is done by the owner. Details of renovation work and costs will be covered in Chapters 7 and 8.

What Profit Can We Expect? With all the foregoing factors in mind, we can estimate a good purchase price as $9,000. If we can buy for $9,000 and renovate for not over $2,000, our over-all costs would be $11,000.

Since we could probably sell for $15,000, our anticipated gross profit before sales costs would be $2,000. This 36 per cent capital gain means our outlay for improvements would triple in value, which constitutes a nominal expectation. This possible turnover profit exceeds our 25 per cent formula in Chapter 2 and indicates we are aiming for a readily attainable goal on the realty road to a million.

WILL THE INCOME PAY EXPENSES
PLUS LOAN PAYMENTS?

Now that our appraisal has prepared us to make an offer, we should figure whether the income will pay expenses plus loan payments. Anticipating a purchase price of $9,000 and a loan of $7,000, the loan payments should be not over $70 monthly, or $840 per year. We previously arrived at a net return of approximately $900 after paying taxes and insurance, but before loan payments. This net was based on ten months' income from the present monthly rent of $90. Only $60 per year would be left after making loan payments. If rents could not be raised in the near future, the margin would be too close for sound operations, as there would be an insufficient reserve for repairs and other possible emergencies.

Prior to committing additional funds for renovation, however, the rent can be raised conservatively to $120 a month, or $30 a month additional, giving us $360 annually to add to our $60 reserve. The total of $420 after loan payments would provide an ample in-pocket operating net on our expected 21 per cent down payment of $2,000.

Compare offerings of several brokers before buying. Look over numerous listings before settling on the best buy. When you find a suitable property, make sure that negotiations on price and financing prove advantageous.

6. HOW TO BUY PROPERTY

Buyers and sellers who dislike bargaining may establish a firm figure and state, "That's my price. Take it or leave it."

When they do this in real-estate transactions they are usually left with no deal or a poorer deal than they could realize by tactful negotiation. After a certain amount of dickering the average seller, especially if his place has been on the market for several months, will accept an offer 25 per cent under his original asking price, although he would refuse so low an initial offer. A competent realtor often convinces the seller to set a price near market value; so the broker's listing may already be considerably lower than the seller's initial asking price. Subtracting 25 per cent from the asking price is of course no final gauge of value, since the knowing seller prices high to begin with. But we can use the resulting figure as a guide after checking other value factors. Discounting the listed price of $11,500 by 25 per cent gives us $8,625 as an approximate target.

Before making an offer it is well to fix in mind the lowest price the seller might accept, then also set the top price you will pay, so that you are not apt to be swayed by subsequent sales pressure. In this case, discounting our target figure by about 5 per cent to $8,200 would represent a bargain. Increasing the $8,625 about 5 per cent to $9,000, the figure we arrived at when making our appraisal, would give us a good buy. To the target price about 10 per cent might be added, making $9,500 our top price. If the offer is too low the seller might shy off completely and refuse to negotiate without a higher starting offer. If the offer is too high, negotiations will be difficult to complete within the boundaries set. The first offer should probably be about 10 per cent less than the $8,625 we aim for, rounded to $7,750.

How to Negotiate a Bargain

Make mental and written notes of defects, but don't point them all out to the realtor as you go over a property. The agent can be better conditioned to negotiating a low price if the worst defects are enumerated as a prelude to giving an offer. You can be sure the salesman will repeat your knocks and add his own to pull the seller down. We tell Mr. Bokay the building is closer to forty years old than to the twenty he mentioned, since the inspection cards show it was built in 1926. We were looking for a place that needed fixing, but this is rougher than we had anticipated. The foundation looks bad, the way the porch is sagging. The place is badly in need of paint. To make it look decent some of the electrical and plumbing fixtures and all the furniture should be replaced. Instead of being worth the $10,000 the realtor mentioned, the actual gross rents of $90 a month show that from an income standpoint the place is worth only a base valuation of $9,000. And that figure should be discounted considerably to take care of the painting and other much needed expenditures.

Mr. Bokay expostulates, "Although I mentioned $10,000, that is pretty close to rock bottom. The owner is asking $11,500. The house is now renting for $90, it is true, but should rent for more even in its present condition. It might rent for as high as $200 if you fix it up. Besides, there is the full basement which could be converted into a new flat, and the two rentals could turn the building into a gold mine."

We say that if we were selling we would expect to sell on the basis of the actual income, and that when we consider buying we apply the same yardstick. Any additional income that could be obtained would be eaten up by the cost of painting and remodeling, so all we can go on is what the building is actually taking in now. If the place can't be bought on that basis we might as well forget it and look at something else.

Mr. Bokay tries to pin us down on how much we would pay. We say the place is probably worth a top price of $7,000, taking into account all the money that has to be spent on it. The agent repeats that he doesn't think he can get the owner below $10,000, but he finally agrees to write up our offer for $7,750.

What the Purchase Contract Should Cover

Now we are ready to examine the details involved in making the original offer. Here is where it is possible for the investor to come to grief if he fails to check the essential terms closely. Real-estate laws differ in various states. In most, an offer binds the tentative buyer to a specific contract which might be costly if he fails to protect himself on every possibility. Generally the offer is binding as soon as the seller accepts. In most cases it can be retracted at any time prior to acceptance. Some brokers, however, insert a binding clause, such as "irrevocable for ten days." If the offer is sound, the buyer in most cases will become involved in further negotiation before the contract is completed. But if the offer is unfavorable to the buyer he is apt to be tied to an undesirable contract by having it immediately accepted by the seller.

Realtors for the most part are basically honest and conform to the fine code of ethics of the National Association of Real Estate Boards. But agents make their living by closing sales, and, like salesmen in general, they are prone to exaggerate. It is up to the buyer to protect himself from a bad deal. Before signing any paper relating to real estate it is advisable to check carefully every point that should protect you. Until you gain experience it would probably be well to have the broker draw up a tentative offer, then to hold the papers for a day or so for re-examination before signing. Many buyers feel it good insurance to consult an attorney prior to signing any papers. A title guarantee company can be depended upon to clarify any ambiguities surrounding a clear title. If a loan is being obtained from a bank, an insurance company or another experienced lender, they will check into title matters, in addition to appraising the value of the property.

Sometimes the broker will attempt to rush your signature by saying that another party is just on the verge of making an offer for the property, and that any delay will cause you to lose a hot buy. All such hoary sales dodges should be ignored. Once you make up your mind it is best to take action, for it is better to act and make mistakes than not to act at all. Usually there is plenty of time for examining items about which there is any doubt. After all, if someone else should buy the property, something comparable can eventually be found if you continue to shop the market.

Most brokers fill out, often with a minimum of consultation with the buyer, a standard printed form called a Deposit Receipt, a Real Estate Agreement, or similar title. Such forms are usually acceptable if you are careful to insert the conditions which will protect you and also are careful to check for gimmicks every word of the print, regardless how fine.

Now let's review the items which should be included in the offer: The date, description of the property, total amount of the offer, total down payment, the deposit, all financial arrangements, and all conditions of the sale should be clearly indicated.

DEPOSIT AND DESCRIPTION OF PROPERTY

The deposit is customarily 5 to 10 per cent of the purchase price.

The property should be described as completely as possible, including the legal description of the boundaries, the address, the approximate size of the lot, and all items in addition to the real estate to be included in the sale. Sometimes the salesman says the lot includes certain property, for instance a portion of land to the rear or side of the building, and after a contract is signed the buyer finds that the lot is much smaller than he had been led to expect. In real-estate sales the buyer and the seller are generally bound only by what they execute in writing, so the buyer would suffer if not protected by his written offer.

Any failure of the seller to perform a condition written in the offer gives the buyer the right to cancel the contract and have his deposit refunded. If furniture and other items such as drapes and curtains are not included in the written contract, the buyer often finds to his disillusionment that the seller will remove them before giving up possession of the property. Here is a sample wording covering the deposit and the description of the property.

> *November 5, 1963*
> *Received from Joseph Enterprise and Mary Enterprise the sum of FIVE HUNDRED AND NO/100 DOLLARS ($500.00) as a deposit on account of the purchase of that certain real property in the City of Metropole, County of Metropole, State of Columbia, described as: Commonly known as 4210 A Avenue, consisting of a house and garage on a lot approximately 40 by 100 feet, Assessor's Block 51, Lot 34 as described in Volume 17, folio 9; together with all furniture and furnishings, and personal property of any kind contained therein which is owned by the present owner, where the use of such personal property is included in the rental paid by tenants in said real property.*

PURCHASE PRICE AND DOWN PAYMENT

The difference between the purchase price and obtainable loans usually governs down payments. If other financing is inadequate the seller will normally take a subordinate loan, such as a second mortgage, in order to complete the sale. The owner may establish the down payment in the first place when his property is listed with the broker, as in this case, where the owner asked $2,000 down. The down payment is subject to negotiation, the same as the purchase price and other conditions. Your maximum down payment would be your total savings, in this example $2,500, if escrow charges can be worked out so that no additional cash will be required. A reserve should be held if possible, unless an unusually advantageous bargain can be made by committing all available funds.

If the owner had asked $3,000 or more down we might offer $2,000. Since he asks only $2,000, we might expect to meet this request before completing negotiations, as this would still leave a reserve of $500. But we may as well offer $1,500. In case it is accepted we would hold a larger reserve of $1,000 for emergencies or for financing improvements. To cover the down payment:

> Total purchase price is SEVEN THOUSAND SEVEN HUNDRED FIFTY AND NO/100 DOL- LARS ($7,750.00), and the balance is to be paid into escrow within 30 days from date hereof, as follows: Buyer to pay additional down payment of ONE THOU- SAND AND NO/100 DOLLARS ($1,000.00), making total down payment of FIFTEEN HUNDRED AND NO/100 DOLLARS ($1,500.00).

Never Leave Financing to Chance

Some brokers or sellers will tell the buyer, "We can easily get the loan you want, so no need to make unnecessary complications by putting it in the contract."

It is extremely important that all terms of proposed financing be written in the contract, and that it be specifically stated that the sale is subject to obtaining such financing. Otherwise, if the buyer fails to secure the necessary financing he would forfeit his deposit, which would be shared by broker and seller. The broker will work much harder to obtain financing if his commission depends on it. If a loan for the required amount cannot be obtained from other sources, the buyer would not have to make concessions or plead with the seller to take a second mortgage. The seller, in order to consummate the sale, would be forced to take a second mortgage to make up the balance of the loan. In any event, if specified in the contract, the buyer can let the broker and the seller worry about financing.

The loan should be paid off on a monthly or quarterly basis, with no large "balloon" payment due at the end of a fixed period, like five years, as was formerly common. Some buyers have been told it would be easy to negotiate new loans when their short-term mortgages fell due, and then they have lost their properties or have been coerced into paying stiff brokerage fees for loan extensions. It cannot be overemphasized that there are no guarantees outside the written contract. As mentioned previously, practically all real-estate loans are now arranged to liquidate by monthly or quarterly payments. Payments as low as possible should be stipulated in order to reserve maximum funds for improvements. The usual payment on private financing of older property is about 1 per cent per month including interest. This would be $62.50 monthly on a $6,250 loan. But we can offer a reasonable lesser amount, like $50. An "or more" clause should always be inserted if possible, enabling you to pay off the loan without penalty if you wish to obtain new financing for improvements or to facilitate resale. Most insurance-company loans, for example, can be paid off with a small penalty during the first two or three years and can be paid off without penalty thereafter.

You should attempt to obtain the lowest interest possible. Property financing costs will average between 6 and 8 per cent interest, depending on the lender, the age and desirability of the property and the ratio of the loan to the appraised value. The average buyer can obtain a sound first mortgage at 7 per cent. Interest of 7 to 8 per cent is usually charged on a second mortgage taken back by a seller, and on first mortgages where the loan exceeds 80 per cent of the appraised value or where the property is substandard. Second-mortgage money from an outside source usually costs 7 to 10 per cent. Here is a paragraph to cover financing:

> *Balance of SIX THOUSAND TWO HUNDRED FIFTY AND NO/100 DOLLARS ($6,250.00) to be covered by mortgage or deed of trust payable at FIFTY AND NO/100 DOLLARS ($50.00) per month, or more, including interest not to exceed 6 per cent. Sale is subject to Broker or Seller obtaining aforesaid mortgage.*

TERMITE-AND-FOUNDATION AND OTHER INSPECTIONS

As previously covered, foundation inspection should always be included in the contract, regardless of outward appearances. Unless protected by an "escape clause," the buyer usually must accept the property "as is," even though it might be crumbling from rot or termites. An exception might be made where the buyer can prove in court that the seller failed to divulge damage of which he was aware. If his contract so provides, the buyer can reject any such deteriorated property unless it is repaired. For example:

> *Sale is subject to inspection, by a licensed inspector or contractor, of the foundation for termites, rot or other damage, any such damage to be repaired at cost of Seller, otherwise Buyer may cancel contract.*

YOU MAY STIPULATE AS MANY INSPECTIONS AS YOU WISH

At this point it would be well to cover various checks which a new property buyer may insert to protect himself against a possible error in judgment. You may stipulate as many inspections as you wish. With this in mind you can feel free to make an offer, with no further safeguards. It is better to see whether your proposed offer will be accepted by the seller before you arrange additional checks. They might prove time-wasting if no deal can be consummated.

SPECIFIC APPROVAL MAY BE REQUIRED

My wife's two younger brothers, Lemuel and Laton Willis, decided to follow our lead in real-estate investment. Both asked me to help them shop for good buys. I advised them, as I tell all interested friends, that the only way they could learn values was to shop the market and make choices entirely on their own, following a few yardsticks which I gave them. After they found properties that looked good, they could make an offer without fear of mistake. All they had to do was insert in the offer:

> *Subject to inspection and approval of property and contract by William Nickerson.*

The deal could then be canceled or revised if I did not approve.

Within a few weeks after starting to shop, each of my brothers-in-law found a desirable property and made an offer. In each case the property and the contract were acceptable, so my inspection was not needed.

Lemuel made the first purchase, buying a 3-unit apartment house. He borrowed on his home to make the down payment. He decided to continue living in his home and rented all three apartments. After development the three apartments were traded for a 12-unit building. Laton bought a 4-unit apartment house, using for his down payment funds he had been saving to buy a home. He moved into one of his rental units. The seller took back a second mortgage to complete financing. Laton made his first subsequent pyramiding step by trading his developed 4-unit building for a 14-unit property.

Both of the initial purchases of my brothers-in-law have worked out as good investments. Several of my friends, including three ministers, have followed similar patterns in making sound initial property purchases. In all cases their choices and contracts were acceptable without change. This shows that with a few yardsticks to follow, the odds favor your making a desirable choice.

Many Appraisal Sources Can Safeguard You

Of course, many more appraisal factors are included in this book for your guidance than I could possibly convey in a short oral check list to friends. You can specify a similar safeguarding clause where you have a trustworthy acquaintance who is an experienced investor, realtor, appraiser, or building contractor. Although few could take the time to do your realty shopping for you, many would normally be glad to check your selection and contract.

Lacking a personal contact, you can call on a professional appraiser, listed in the phone book under "Appraisers" or "Real Estate Appraisers." A typical fee schedule shows a charge of only $25 to appraise a $10,000 residential property. In the contract you could stipulate:

> *Subject to inspection by a Licensed Appraiser, such inspection to meet approval of buyer.*

As previously mentioned, where improvements are contemplated, until you gain experience you should always obtain a cost estimate from a licensed contractor. In this case the following clause should be inserted:

> *Subject to improvement cost estimate from Licensed General Contractor, with terms satisfactory to buyer.*

Normally at least three bids would be obtained before proceeding with any extensive work. One estimate would be sufficient before consummation of the purchase, however, as this would tell you the maximum cost for which your projected improvements could be undertaken. At the same time that you discuss improvements with the contractor, you can get his estimate of the general condition of the building and its reproduction cost.

SOME INSURANCE BROKERS MAKE
REPRODUCTION APPRAISALS

Insurance brokers who specialize in handling income and business properties often have experienced appraisers on their staffs. These appraisers are qualified to determine reproduction costs and normal depreciation factors in order to establish insurable values. You can find such insurance brokers through your telephone book, your local Real Estate Board, or your local Apartment Owners' Association. Insurance appraisals are given without charge where the broker anticipates a bona fide purchase which will result in your insurance order.

CONVENTIONAL LENDERS MAY BE
THE BEST APPRAISERS OF ALL

In this purchase of the A Avenue house the seller is taking back the first mortgage. Where a conventional loan is to be obtained, this may often prove the best appraisal of all. A bank or an insurance company will look the property over objectively before making a loan. Many times, in a tight lending market, they will make an appraisal of actual market value, then deduct a discount factor in order to spread their loan funds. Usually they will divulge their actual appraisal figures if you ask.

Even though the seller is willing to take back a mortgage, some buyers would stipulate that they be permitted to seek a conventional loan first. An attempt could thus be made to better the seller's proposed financing with more satisfactory terms, perhaps a longer payoff period, less interest, and smaller monthly payments. This at the same time would provide for a free professional lender's appraisal. Usually if the loan applied for is not granted there is no charge. If the loan sought is granted, whether accepted or not, a nominal appraisal fee would be charged.

If there is a neighborhood bank or branch, the manager will sometimes be familiar with the property you consider buying. At least he will know of general conditions and values in the neighborhood. Although naturally on the conservative side, bankers are in a position to offer much sound appraisal, giving you good and bad points to consider before making your final decision. I have found bank managers always willing to give freely of advice. Most bankers like to give advice, as there is always the chance that this may lead to your opening an account.

PROVIDE FOR TITLE INSURANCE

A guaranteed title, issued by an established title insurance company, should be obtained where available. Practices differ in various states. In some it is customary for the seller to give a warranty of title, which of course is only as good as the financial condition of the seller. In others a quitclaim deed may be executed, giving the buyer the rights of the seller, whatever they may be. This provides no guarantee that the seller actually possesses a clear title, nor that he has not placed an undisclosed mortgage on the property.

Guaranteed-title policies are almost universal in the West and are becoming more common in Eastern states. Whatever the prevailing practice, all title clouds can be cleared for the buyer's protection if he demands a guarantee from a title insurance company. The title company will search the records to ascertain that the seller has a clear right to sell, and then will issue a policy guaranteeing to reimburse the owner if the title later proves faulty.

A title insurance policy specifically insures against any loss resulting from an error or omission in examining the title. It also insures against losses because of "clouds," possible defects against a clear title, which would not be revealed by the most thorough title examination, such as:

1. Acts of incompetents such as the insane or feebleminded
2. Acts of minors
3. Community interest of spouse not exposed by records
4. Documents void by reason of lack of legal delivery
5. False court affidavits, as in the settling of an estate
6. False impersonation
7. Forged documents

While you expect none of these experiences, any might be catastrophic. More than one property has been sold under each of these title clouds, and later the buyer after costly litigation has found his purported title revoked.

VOID BY LACK OF LEGAL DELIVERY

I know of a case illustrating point 4 above in which a housekeeper took possession of a home upon the death of her employer because he had shown her a deed giving her the property. The deed had never been given to the housekeeper and remained in the deceased's safe-deposit box. The court ruled that legal delivery of title had not been made and ordered the property turned over to distant heirs.

IMPERSONATION AND FORGED DOCUMENTS

In a case covered by both points 6 and 7, a son, whom we will call John Smith, Jr., innocently impersonated his father and signed a deed for him, leaving off the "Jr." The father was bedridden and unable to get to a notary. Rather than pay for a notary to come to him, the father told the son to go to the title company, where his signature would be notarized, and sign the father's name for him. This seemed perfectly logical, since the son actually had the same name, except for the "Jr." The property later increased a great deal in value. After the death of the father, twelve years later, two daughters secured a court order to return the property to the estate of the deceased, since the father had never signed the deed.

ERROR OR OMISSION IN TITLE EXAMINATION

Undisclosed liens may later develop which the buyer has to pay if he is not covered by title insurance and is unable to collect damages from the seller.

In one 24-unit purchase, $8,000 in income-tax liens was recorded against the property but was not discovered at the time of title examination. In a 48-unit purchase the title-company search missed $6,500 in defaulted property taxes. The title companies paid both of these liens, clearing title for the buyers. The title company later collected from the seller of the 48 units, but the 24-unit income-tax defaulter had departed for South America.

Title insurance protecting against such eventualities costs a small percentage of the purchase price. Typical base rates are:

PURCHASE PRICE	POLICY FEE
$ 5,000.00	$ 57.00
7,500.00	72.00
8,750.00 (Our final purchase price)	79.50
10,000.00	87.00
15,000.00	112.00
20,000.00	137.00
30,000.00	177.00
50,000.00	237.00
100,000.00	387.00

Make sure the policy equals the full purchase amount. Base rates for title insurance include all regular escrow services except for the preparation and recording of documents, on which there would be a few dollars' additional charge.

In some sections the buyer customarily pays title costs, in some the seller, and in others the costs are shared. All costs are subject to negotiation, so it is just as well to stipulate in the original offer that the seller will pay, as in the following:

> *It is hereby agreed that the evidence of title shall be a Guaranteed Policy of Title Insurance in the amount of the purchase price, issued by a responsible Title Company, to be furnished and paid for by the Seller, and to show title to the said property free of all encumbrances, except as herein provided. In the event the title to said property shall not show as provided, and Seller shall not have perfected same within 30 days from date hereof, the Buyer shall have the option of demanding the return of the aforesaid deposit, and shall be released from all obligations hereunder.*

PROVISION AGAINST DAMAGE

Sometimes a property can be damaged by fire, windstorm or other action before the buyer takes possession. This contingency should be insured against in the contract. For example:

If the improvements or aforementioned personal property on said property are destroyed or materially damaged between the date hereof and consummation or settlement of this purchase, this contract shall at Buyer's election immediately become null and void, and the aforesaid deposit shall be refunded to Buyer on demand.

PRORATION OF TAXES, INTEREST, INSURANCE AND RENTS

Taxes, interest, insurance and rents are customarily prorated, effective either on the date of turning over or recording the deed and closeing the escrow in the title company, or the date of turning over possession of the property, whichever occurs first. Unless stipulated to the contrary, possession becomes the legal right of the buyer and should be given up by the seller upon closing of the escrow.

Whenever the seller or his representative resides on the property possession should be specifically mentioned in the contract, with a phrase such as, "Possession to be given immediately on closing of escrow," or "Possession to be given 30 days following close of escrow." In the latter case it is well to stipulate a rental clause, such as "Seller to pay $100 monthly rental from closing of escrow." Otherwise, even though the seller has no further rights in the property, he may hold possession for several months until he finds it convenient to move. The rental instead of being fixed would have to be negotiated, and the seller could not be legally dispossessed except after a court order. In this example the seller lives elsewhere, and possession should present no problem.

It is fair to both buyer and seller to prorate any income and continuing expenses, such as taxes, interest on any loan taken over, and insurance if retained. The buyer is usually better off, however, to cancel existing insurance and order new policies through his own broker. In most cases the existing policies will prove inadequate on examination by a qualified broker, and it is best to have one competent broker responsible for all your insurance. The last-mentioned items may be covered as follows:

Taxes, interest on the aforementioned loan, and rents of said property shall be prorated from date of closing transaction. Existing insurance policies are to be canceled, and Buyer will deposit new insurance policies in escrow.

STIPULATE A LIMITED TIME FOR ACCEPTANCE

Time is a weapon you want on your side, and one to avoid having turned against you. If your offer is low the broker may ask for considerable time, like sixty days, to obtain acceptance. This allows him to file your offer in abeyance while using you as a lever to prod another prospective buyer into a higher bid. The seller, too, may hold your offer as insurance while he waits for other brokers to produce additional prospects with higher offers. Thus it is essential to circumvent delay and to speed the seller's response by dating the offer and stipulating a limited time for acceptance. Except in unusual circumstances, such as an owner living overseas, or an estate requiring court approval, seven to fifteen days should normally be adequate. Like Hank Greenberg's offer for the San Francisco Seals, some offers allow only one day. Time can be covered as follows:

> *Time is the essence of this contract, and the Agent is granted 10 days to obtain the acceptance of the Seller, and if this offer is not accepted within said 10 days, the deposit will be refunded to the Buyer.*

THE VALLEY OF DOUBT IS OFTEN TRAVERSED

You sign the offer and await developments. On major transactions, like contracting for property or marriage, the parties often traverse the Valley of Doubt on the way to the Peak of Conviction. In the sacred contract of marriage this normal reaction is guarded against by a public announcement of betrothal and the giving of an engagement ring. In real estate hasty repudiation is counteracted by paying a deposit. After agreeing to a transaction, many a new buyer becomes panic-stricken with doubt and rushes to the broker demanding the return of his deposit. The experienced realtor knows this is a natural reaction and reassures the buyer by recapitulating favorable sales points. The experienced buyer anticipates his passage through doubt, in which the unfavorable aspects may loom in mind, and will reconsider the favorable conditions that counterbalance the issues in question. Some are thus able to eliminate doubt in short order. Others find they cannot reach the Peak of Conviction until the consummation of the contract, when possession is taken.

You Proceed to Negotiate

Two evenings after taking your offer Mr. Bokay, the broker, rings your doorbell and tells you, "I've been working like a dog to pull the seller down, but he won't take a penny less than $9,750. At that price, you would be getting a steal that you can make plenty of money on. Don't you think the smart thing for you is to meet that figure so we can get this deal closed before somebody else snaps it up?"

You tell the broker you appreciate his efforts, but if that is the best he can do he might as well forget the deal and refund your deposit. However, you might consider raising your sights a little. The broker asks how much. You say $8,250. The broker argues, but you stand firm, and he agrees to submit your increased offer.

Early the next evening Mr. Bokay advises that he didn't think it was possible, but he has got the seller to come down to $9,250, and that is his rock-bottom price from which he will not budge. "You had better snap it up quick before the seller changes his mind. There is another party in the picture now who is mighty interested in the property. If you don't agree to the $9,250 right away, this other buyer will probably snatch the sale right out from under you, especially if he finds out how cheap the owner has consented to let it go."

You say you will come up to $8,500, and that is your final offer. At this point the seller may balk, and you could raise your offer to $8,750 or $9,000. Or the seller might suggest a compromise. Final negotiations will depend on how long the property has been for sale, how desperate the seller feels, and how worried he may be that you will withdraw unless he accepts. Agreements sometimes may be concluded with scarcely any negotiation, and a desperate seller may accept a low bid immediately rather than chance losing a sale. Sometimes bargaining may be protracted on each item of the contract. Many an independent-minded seller has carried on complex negotiations for over a year before completion, especially where extensive financing, trade, lease or other contingent arrangements are involved. It is important at each stage to give no indication you have in mind any figure higher than your offer.

Two hours after his previous contact Mr. Bokay phones and says he is calling from the residence of the seller, who has agreed to take $9,000. Will you accept? You offer a compromise of $8,750 and ask the broker not to bother you further, but to return your deposit if this offer is not accepted. Mr. Bokay says he will call back after further discussion with the seller.

The seller agrees to $8,750, providing you will pay $2,000 down, $70 a month and 7 per cent interest on the resulting $6,750 loan, which he may carry himself. If a seller agrees to a figure previously refused, he may propose more stipulations as much to save face as to enhance the contract. This is the first time a counteroffer has been made on anything but the purchase price. The other items may not be very important to the seller, or he may have held them in abeyance pending settlement of the purchase price. You offer $62.50 at 5½ per cent, holding to a $1,500 down payment. You finally settle on $1,750 down, leaving a $7,000 loan, with monthly payments of $65, including 6 per cent interest. Under these terms the loan will be paid off in thirteen years.

The usual broker's commission, for which the seller is responsible, is 6 per cent on small improved property and 10 per cent on vacant land. Commissions are less, percentagewise, on a sliding scale in larger transactions. They can be adjusted in most cases where extensive properties are involved and should average under 5 per cent.

The buyer would have no commission to pay unless he had contracted for the broker's special services, such as incurring specified appraisal, financing, or travel expenses. Sometimes an unscrupulous broker will collect a commission from both buyer and seller if the buyer appears inexperienced. I have known of naïve buyers after completion of a routine sale asking the broker how much the bill would be for his services. In such cases, most brokers reply that the seller pays the commission, but some give a quotation, figuring if baby holds out candy they will grab before somebody else does. One astute broker, instead of quoting a fixed amount, which would be more apt to get him in trouble with his real-estate board, responds, "Whatever you think it is worth to you." If the buyer asks what is customary, he answers, "The usual commission on that kind of a deal is five per cent."

COMPLETION OF THE TRANSACTION

Two weeks after you and the seller have signed the concluding sales agreement, Mr. Bokay phones and invites you to come to the title company to make final arrangements. He asks that you bring a check for the $1,250 remainder of the down payment. You take the money

from savings and obtain a cashier's check, which is turned over to the
title company to be held in escrow until the transfer of the deed. The
title company's escrow officer presents an imposing array of legal documents which he has prepared. Requiring your signature are four documents, the first two to be notarized by the title company notary:

1. The mortgage, which pledges the real property, consisting
   of the lot and buildings, against the loan (in many states
   a deed-of-trust form is used in place of a mortgage).
2. The chattel mortgage, pledging the inventoried furniture
   against the loan.
3. The note promising to pay the loan, stating the amount,
   interest, monthly payment, and due date.
4. Your "buyer's instructions" to the title company, confirming what you are to receive and what you are to give
   in making the bargain.

In addition to the foregoing, there are five other major papers:

1. The notarized deed, signed by the seller, transferring the
   title from seller to you.
2. The "preliminary report," covering the title-guarantee
   tentative policy, with a map and a complete legal description of the property, and detailing the various restrictions
   which the property is subject to.
3. The receipted tax bill previously paid by the seller.
4. A statement from the seller, covering the rent amount and
   due date.
5. A "cover note" from your insurance broker, stating that
   the property will be protected by your new insurance
   from the date of closing the transaction, and that copies
   of the policy will arrive later.

Title Companies Handle Complex Paper Work

Title companies are so experienced with the mysteries of real-estate
documents that they can handle the most complicated problems with
economic efficiency. In most cases all paper work can be entrusted to
them with complete confidence. But the most competent title officers
are human and sometimes make mistakes, either through momentary
negligence or through misunderstanding of the desired arrangements.

Some brokers prefer to draw up all documents, which would then be checked by the title company. In some areas the title companies customarily draw up the papers; in others they are nearly always executed by attorneys. Where the loan is made by a regular lending institution they will often prepare all papers involving the mortgage. In any case the buyer should check all documents closely. If desired it is always permissible, regardless of custom, to secure the advice of an attorney, although this should not be necessary except in unusual circumstances, like buying from an estate.

Inspection shows the main foundation in sound condition, but the front porch foundation is affected by dry rot, which undermines the supporting structure and damages the floor. The repair cost is estimated by a reputable contractor at $180. Instead of waiting to consummate the sale after the repairs are completed, the seller agrees to credit your account, and the $180 is to be held in escrow until you complete the stipulated repairs.

You Receive $64.84 to Close the Deal

The week following your visit to the title company, on December 4, the escrow officer is ready to close the transaction. Since you did not prorate fire insurance, you have sixty days to pay the $20.50 bill for $8,000 insurance which you will receive from your broker. The seller pays the $79.50 for $8,750 title insurance. He has previously paid the first installment, one half of the real-estate taxes of $152.80, so his account is credited and yours charged for $11.46. This covers the remainder of half the fiscal tax year, ending December 31. The prorating of $90 in rent, collected December 1 by the seller, more than pays the escrow charges against you and leaves you with a credit balance of $64.84. For a complete statement from the title company, see the following page.

On income-property purchases the closing date often can be jockeyed to fit the rent schedule so that the buyer will receive funds from the escrow settlement, rather than having to put up additional funds. The title company records the deed in your name in the County Recorder's office December 4, one month after your original offer was made. This means you are now the legal owner of the A Avenue house.

Tactful negotiation usually earns better deals. You may stipulate as many inspections and approvals as you wish. Never take financing for granted. To be binding all terms of a real-estate purchase must be in writing.

. . . .

METROPOLE LAND TITLE INSURANCE COMPANY
ESCROW STATEMENT
Escrow No. 37446   Metropole, Columbia, Dec. 4, 1963
ACCOUNT OF Joseph and Mary Enterprise

. . . .

DEPOSITS AND CREDITS

Deposit	$ 500.00
Balance down payment	1,250.00
Loan—Deed of Trust to Seller	7,000.00
Prorate rent $90 Pd. Dec. 1	81.00
Credit for foundation repairs	180.00
TOTAL	9,011.00

. . . .

DISBURSEMENTS AND CHARGES

Purchase price	$8,750.00
Prorate taxes, first installment pd.	11.46
Recording deed	1.50
Recording deed of trust	3.20
TOTAL	8,766.16

. . . .

SETTLEMENT
Held for foundation repairs $180.00
    Check herewith   64.84   Balance due . . . .

. . . .

GRAND TOTALS   9,011.00   9,011.00

. . . .

KEEP THIS STATEMENT FOR FUTURE REFERENCE

. . . .

PART THREE

HOW TO IMPROVE
YOUR PROPERTY FOR PROFIT

7. IMPROVING OPERATIONS
AND THE EXTERIOR

Having completed negotiations and taken possession, we are
ready for our next step, the improvement of our newly bought property. An accepted axiom among realtors is "You can't increase the
value of your property just because your name is Jack Robinson."
Although continuing population growth and inflation generally increase values, you cannot depend upon them over any specific period
of time.

You have to make a worthwhile change to assure making property
worth more. As most real-estate fortunes are built on improvements,
the latter are essential to assure your major success in property investment. All buildings are subject to depreciation, and seldom will they
hold a constant value. If you do not improve a building and thereby
enhance its value, it is liable to become obsolescent and diminish in
value. An obsolescent building reduces income by causing rents to be
low and vacancies high. An improved building raises income by drawing high rents and holding vacancies low.

Government studies, as previously mentioned, show that national
vacancies have approximated between 2 and 5 per cent from 1954 to
1968. Even these nominal figures can be reduced to 1 per cent or less
by the competitive owner who makes continued selective improvement. Vacancies are especially heavy in non-competitive apartments,
both old and new:

1. Many over-financed and over-priced new projects with
   rent schedules above area levels experienced high vacan-

cies, continuing from 1954 through 1968. Some maintained a bankrupting 50 per cent vacancy factor after six months' operation, and a number stayed as high as 20 per cent vacant considerably longer.

2. Older properties allowed to run down, with no modernization or rehabilitation to offset obsolescence and deterioration, suffered continued alarming vacancies, some averaging 30 per cent.

IMPROVEMENTS INCREASE BOTH INCOME AND RESALE PROFITS

The owner who "bleeds" a building by spending all the income finds under competition that he is forced to revise his rents lower and lower to combat increasing vacancies, until he finally reaches a point where expenses cannot be met. A survey by the Division of Research of the National Association of Real Estate Boards shows that rents continue increasing for well-maintained rental units, while deteriorated properties suffer rent decreases. It is the shortsighted owners of such slipping properties who may join the fewer than one in four hundred who fail. Their negative operations, by reducing the income value, may force a loss when they sell, creating a bargain for an alert buyer who is willing to make improvements. Besides the satisfaction of building up rather than tearing down, the improver realizes a far more dependable income and can earn a substantial gain when he sells.

IMPROVING MANAGEMENT OPERATIONS

There are two major ways of improving property: by physical change, or face lifting, and by improvement of management operations. Physical improvement covers painting, modernizing design and fixtures, and landscaping, and it breaks down into two natural divisions, the interior and the exterior. The purpose of management operations is to improve the net income, which also leads to two natural divisions:

1. Increasing gross income by increasing rental value and eliminating vacancies.
2. Decreasing operating expenses.

Other management aspects will be covered in greater detail later, after we examine larger properties. For the present we will outline essentials pertinent to the A Avenue house.

RAISE PRESENT RENTS IMMEDIATELY IF WARRANTED

The first consideration should be the present rent schedule. The house now rents for $90, but our inspection indicated that by comparison with others it should rent for $120 to $130 a month. An investor who planned to move into the house could give the tenant a dispossess notice and be better able to show the property when he is ready to sell.

We will assume that, like many rental owners, you prefer to remain in your present residence and plan not to move into the house bought for investment. In this event, when should you raise the rent? Tenants whose rents are below market levels expect increases from a new owner. Their chief concern is how much, and some tenants may move in anticipation of higher rents than the new owner plans. Thus rents should be raised as soon as practicable.

If the premises are unusually dilapidated, or if major reconstruction is required, the owner might dispossess the tenants before proceeding with renovation. With improvements as contemplated here, the work can be done while tenants continue to pay rent. Tenants are willing to put up with resulting inconveniences even at increased rents in exchange for enjoying better living conditions.

Details on collecting rents, and the wording and presentation of legal notices such as rent raises, will be cited in Chapters 15 and 16. The tenant would commonly be given a notice on the next rent date, in this case January 1, to take effect on the following due date, or February 1. The amount should be governed not only by prevailing basic rents in the area, but also by the number of occupants. Where you might raise a couple to $120, for example, a larger family should pay more. In this case there are four occupants: a couple with two daughters in high school.

On being given a raise notice to $130, the tenants say they have been expecting an increase. They have been living there for eight years at the same rent. But they will just not pay $130 and will have to find another place. However, by their February 1 rent date they pay the $130 rent, for they now realize that comparable space in a similar neighborhood would cost as much. The mother says, "Guess we'll be staying after all. We haven't found anything we like as well for floor space, and my children hate to move out of this neighborhood. But our place needs painting—it hasn't been touched since we moved in. Are you going to paint our place now that we're paying more?"

We advise the tenant that we plan a gradual program of improvements, including painting inside and out, which we will take care of as soon as it can be managed.

"We don't mind paying the extra rent," says the mother, "as long as you're going to do some painting and fixing up."

Improving Housing Is Big Business

Stimulated by FHA Title I and other improvement loans, the repair and improvement of housing has become a twenty-billion-dollar business. The Housing and Home Finance Agency finds that nearly seven out of ten home buyers immediately undertake repairs and improvements. Look how this activity has mushroomed. Department of Commerce figures show that five billion dollars was spent in 1953 for rehabilitation and repair of owner-occupied homes. Later studies find that about 70 per cent of all homeowners, some 18,000,000, spent an estimated seven billion dollars on repairs and improvements in 1954. Expenditures for 1955 were estimated at nine billion dollars, and by 1967 homeowners passed the twelve billion level. FHA estimates for 1968 indicate a total of twenty billion a year spent on both owner-occupied and rental properties, approaching the expenditure for new housing.

We are a nation of prodigious builders, who to a great extent build and turn to new projects and let our buildings go to pot. Like the engineer who develops a run-down gold mine, you can reap a phenomenal harvest by developing these deteriorated properties. Contrary to the uncertain profits from mining, however, profits from property development are almost certain, and ultimate profits can be as spectacular as from the richest mine. A comparatively few dollars spent to revivify a money-losing property can often transform it into a fabulous money-maker.

INCREASE VALUE AT MINIMUM EXPENSE

Making money on improvements will be influenced by methods of financing and by sound, selective buying. But for the present we will concentrate on the choice and application of materials and equipment which can increase value at minimum expense. To beat competition your best yardstick is to make your property, as far as practical within expense limitations, what you yourself would want if you were operating on the budget of the average prospective tenant. How would it please you if you were looking for a place to live in? In addition to convenience, a dwelling should present a pleasing appearance, so that tenants may feel proud rather than apologetic when visited by friends.

You should keep in mind that overimprovement may be more unprofitable than underimprovement by pricing the unit out of the rental market. It pays generally to stay within a neighborhood level. It does not pay to compete with luxury housing. Some items, such as a dishwasher, an individual automatic launderette, or luxurious furnishings, might be worth while in luxury rentals. They would be installed in a home as a matter of personal choice. But from an investment standpoint, in the average rental unit they might cost more than they would repay. Over-all costs should be kept low enough so that new construction cannot compete in price, since lower rental is the chief competitive advantage of older housing. To keep rents low enough to beat competition, you must determine which improvements are most productive within an allowable budget.

Prime examples of value-producing improvements with minor installation problems are modern kitchen cabinets, stoves, and refrigerators. Profit-making examples involving justifiable labor costs are painting, replacing obsolete or worn-out electrical, plumbing or heating fixtures, and landscaping.

A sizable project, such as rehabilitating and modernizing an entire building, sometimes looms as insurmountable to a new investor. It does not prove so difficult to accomplish if the intended changes are all listed and then scheduled in segments. Emergency repairs should be listed first, and those which will immediately increase income next. Any other jobs can be handled in stages. If we plan to change a basement or an attic to an apartment or to add rooms for rent, that might be the first job to complete after repair work if sufficient funds are available, because it will result in an additional rental. If improvement of an existing apartment will increase rents, we should probably tackle that.

If we contract the work, emulating most experienced owners, it would save money to complete all similar jobs at the same time. For example all electrical work could be handled in one contract, all plumbing in one contract, and all painting in one contract. If the owner plans to move into one of his apartments and do most of the work himself, it normally would not affect cost and it would be more convenient to complete the rental units one at a time, finishing first the apartment he is living in, and then successive units.

DO-IT-YOURSELF vs. CONTRACTING

Interests and skills of investors naturally vary. Some are as eager to spend both time and energy to meet their goal as a teen-ager with his date, and they perform work that others would contract. There are certainly no inflexible "all or nothing" rules. The value of personal labor increases the chances of selling for a profit and provides an additional margin of safety against a drop in the market or a mistake in property selection. The chief advantages of your own labor are thus greater profit on the individual transaction and greater safety margin.

The average owner can take care of all but the most difficult tasks. Probably 75 per cent of homeowners, if we measure purchases in paint stores, do all their painting. Only the most highly skilled trades, like repairing a TV set, require an expert craftsman. The effort of making home improvements helps to assure initial success when applied to income-producing residences. Often a stable tenant will provide labor for improvements if the owner buys the material, especially if encouraged by a promise not to raise the rent for a period, for example, of at least a year.

According to one authoritative estimate, half the total of improvements are accomplished by do-it-yourself projects. The cost of materials for owner labor, however, according to the National Home Improvement Council, is only one-third the total, equaling half the expenditure to contractors.

Sometimes you can best take advantage of bargains in older property which needs improvement if you join the expanding do-it-yourself ranks. With low initial funds in the early steps of investment, you can often progress faster, and gain additional experience to guide sound future planning, by handling personally as much as practicable of the improvement labor.

PERMITS AND LICENSES

While we are considering the subject of do-it-yourself, mention should be made of permits and licenses which are the responsibility of the contractor when you place contracts. Permit and license restrictions should be investigated in the particular locale before undertaking personally many types of improvement or repair work. Painting and landscaping, for example, are types of improvement that can be done with impunity by an owner, and so are plumbing and electrical repair jobs like fixing or changing leaky faucets or portable appliances. But permits are required in most areas for do-it-yourself projects, as well as for work performed by licensed contractors or craftsmen, for most plumbing installations like putting in a tub, a heater or a stove, and for electrical wiring and equipment permanently attached to a building. Construction alterations or additions, like adding a room, would require a permit. Permits should be obtained where required, in order to avoid possible penalties, including the expense of removing work already installed.

Costs of permits vary, but they average about 1 per cent of the market value of the work, a $1,000 construction job costing a $10 fee. Fees for permits to install a gas stove or a heater usually run from $1 to $5. License and permit laws are intended for the protection of the public, the cost of permits usually offsetting the cost of inspection to insure that work is correctly performed. With a heater or a tub, for instance, the work would be checked to see that water, gas, and vent connections are of adequate dimensions and material and that they are properly installed. Whether performed by an owner or a licensed contractor, most projects would be acceptable if a permit is obtained and the work passes inspection. If a project is unacceptable, most building inspectors will point out the changes necessary to pass inspection.

OWNER SHOULD BUDGET RENTAL VALUE OF OCCUPIED UNIT

Whether you move into your rental property or not, you should plan to retain savings and rent in your personal budget on the same basis as before. Many investors falter at this point because they omit savings, and sometimes rent, from their budgets and raise their personal expenses accordingly. If the owner moves in, the fair rent for the owner-occupied unit, in this case $130, should be paid from the wage earner's personal budget into the building account, to be applied the same as a tenant's rent against fixed expenses such as loan payments, and against repairs and improvements. This would be similiar to the arrangement necessary when buying a home.

CONTRACTING SAVES TIME AND SPEEDS RESALE

Most investors contract some labor, and many contract all work, limiting their personal efforts to supervision. The chief advantage of hiring the work is faster turnover. While it may take two or three years for an owner to rehabilitate and modernize, if the same work is contracted the property can be readied for resale in a few months. This time factor increases in importance with the size of the property under consideration. As an investor progresses he should periodically review his methods of operation to see if they require revision. Many conscientious workers become stymied at an early stage because they stay in a rut and fail to change from their originally praiseworthy habit of personally handling all labor. By the time you own larger apartments your time will always be more productive in supervision and management than in personal labor.

Many widows and single women, and professional men like doctors and lawyers, make money on rental property without contributing any personal labor. So that you can emulate them if you choose, all labor will be contracted in our examples.

Most experienced investors would contract all the projected work at once, including converting the basement if desired, and arrange financing accordingly. Contractors would specify the changes to be made, and you would be involved very little with improvement details. Since we will assume this to be your first investment in improving rental property, it might be well to develop experience by refurbishing the present house on a detailed, step-by-step basis, and mainly from current income to start. This should help you to make a decision on the basement conversion and on the improvement possibilities of later property purchases.

IMPROVING THE EXTERIOR

The first undertaking might be the interior improvement of the flats, but we have a mandatory repair to be made on the front porch. And since the yard and exterior of the building look run-down, their immediate improvement, especially in front, will make it easier to hold tenants at the increased rents. The sooner any planting is completed, the more presentable the yard will look when we sell. And the sooner the exterior is painted, the less deterioration it will suffer.

Improvements will be expedited if you set a reasonable completion goal. If you are aiming to finish the work in two years, you might break planning into workable segments. In the first six months you might schedule emergency repairs, gardening, painting and other improvements to the exterior. In the next twelve months you could renovate the interior. In the fourth six-month period you could convert the basement to a second rental, if you so decide, and complete any other items still needing attention.

MAKE AN IMPROVEMENT OUT OF A REPAIR JOB

Our only emergency repair is the sagging front porch, which might cause an accident if left in its present state. The concrete foundation of the porch is adequate, and on the outer side all of the supporting structure is sound. The previously reported dry rot, caused by the one-foot accumulation of earth and debris, is all in the upper sill, siding and supports. The partial rot has collapsed the porch slightly, damaging the rail and floor. The foundation contractor has agreed to repair the damage for $180, including his $7.50 inspection charge, which he would be paid if someone else does the work. Should we have him make the repairs? Or should we improve the structure instead of merely repairing it?

Often a complete modernization can be made for little more than the cost of repairs, and additional capital outlay can cut future repairs. It is good practice to compare a feature to be repaired with the more pleasing designs of similar structures in up-to-date buildings. The existing porch siding is stuccoed like the main building. The steps, of 2-by-8 planks, are at the side; 2-by-4 rails run up the outside of the steps and around the edge of the tongue-and-groove porch floor. By checking new front-porch installations and choosing a composite of the more desirable features, we find that our most attractive arrangement would consist of red-brick steps and floor, and wrought-iron rails.

The steps show up plainly from the front. They run down the side of the building from the porch toward the street. Installing the red-brick steps and the wrought-iron rails would considerably enhance the front appearance, besides improving the apparent and real soundness of the structure. We ask the contractor for a bid to include the desired features in addition to repairing the porch. He figures the whole job for $300, $120 more than the repairs. At this point we must decide whether the proposed change will materially increase the sale value of the property in proportion to the cost, or whether it will add too much to our tentative improvement budget.

Our objective is to transform the house into a modernized building that will present to a prospective buyer, both at first glance—which is often decisive—and upon thorough inspection, the appeal of a desirable, newly built structure. A front porch or steps can add or detract as much as any other item of architecture. The brick steps and wrought-iron railings will change the first appraisal from discredit to credit. Our tentative improvement budget figured a $2,000 maximum. We could easily finance any sound modernization from several sources, for instance from an FHA improvement loan. But a check of expected income for our time allotment of two years shows that the projected improvements can be made without additional financing, unless we undertake the basement remodeling.

RESOURCES ARE SUFFICIENT WITHOUT BORROWING

We would total our expected improvement resources by adding our present funds to expected net income. The latter would be obtained by taking the gross income and deducting fixed expenses:

RENTAL INCOME LESS EXPENDITURES
FOR 24 MONTHS

GROSS RENT FOR 24 MONTHS

First month	$ 90.00	
23 months at $130 monthly	2,990.00	
TOTAL RENTAL INCOME		$3,080.00

EXPENSES AND LOAN PAYMENTS FOR 2 YEARS

Taxes at $152.80 per year	$ 305.60	
Insurance at $20.50 per year	41.00	
23 loan payments starting Jan. 15		
at $65 monthly	1,495.00	
TOTAL FIXED EXPENDITURES		1,841.60
NET IN-POCKET RENTAL INCOME		$1,238.40

Since we are planning continuous improvement, all repairs from a budget standpoint will be considered as contributing to the improvement of the property. In addition to rental income, our resources for two years would include $1,200 budgeted savings at $50 a month.

Our present bank balance is $814.84. This is arrived at by deducting our $1,750 down payment from our original $2,500, then adding our escrow credit check of $64.84.

To compute all our expected investment resources, we add:

Present bank balance	$ 814.84
Budgeted personal savings	1,200.00
Expected net rents	1,238.40
Escrow credit for porch	180.00
TOTAL	$3,433.24

This gives a respectable margin over our $2,000 expected maximum requirements in case of emergencies or expanded improvements. Since improvement financing looks satisfactory, we should recapitulate capitalization. Our net purchase price was $8,750 less the $180 the seller advanced for fixing the porch, and less the $64.84 obtained in escrow, making an actual cost of $8,505.16. Adding $2,000 to this would make a total net cost when ready to sell of $10,505.16. If we can produce for that price a modernized building with a rental value of $150 a month, we should have little difficulty meeting our current objective of selling for a 36 per cent gross profit. We have a comfortable margin to achieve our 25 per cent previously scheduled goal for each turnover.

Since $180 would have to be spent for repairs, the additional $120 would be about 6 per cent of the total improvement allotment, not enough to disrupt the budget. Although we plan to contract all necessary work, a few owners would tackle the entire job of carpentry and stucco repair, and the brick and wrought-iron installation, and could save over half by their own labor. Amateur bricklaying may suffice on terraces and barbecue pits, but few amateurs can properly finish an eye-catching installation like a front porch.

We tell the contractor that before letting the contract we would normally get a competitive bid. Would he discount his estimate if we give him the job immediately? He discounts the 10 per cent normal padding, usually added to cover "unforeseen contingencies," and agrees to do the work for $270. We settle on this proposal.

LANDSCAPING CAN MAKE A MAJOR TRANSFORMATION

After disposing of emergency repairs, as soon as weather permits we should plant the garden so that it can start filling out. We can buy young, inexpensive trees and shrubs if they are planted as soon as possible, and they will look presentable by the time we are ready to sell. In this case it is midwinter, and—since we are in a warm climate —the sooner the garden is planted the more it will benefit from winter rains and spring growth, to be well established before the dry summer.

Realtors have found that transforming an eyesore yard by good landscaping can increase the resale value of a home as high as 50 per cent. The over-all increase in value would be smaller in ratio with a larger number of dwelling units on a lot, but even with the largest income properties value may be increased by 10 per cent. Landscaping adds more than the value of the work, because it counteracts the loss from its lack. A buyer or appraiser normally arrives at an appraisal figure, then deducts for poor landscaping. Good landscaping not only offsets this deduction but earns an added appraisal valuation. On our house we can expect landscaping to increase value between 10 and 25 per cent, and it is surprising how comparatively little money will be required to make a major transformation. One landscaping project that cost me $350 using young, inexpensive shrubs and trees, was appraised by an insurance company for loan purposes five years later at a value of $12,000.

Effective landscaping should be planned for a pleasing, over-all picture when the planting reaches maturity, blending the building, the foundation planting, and the framing on the borders. Owners who wish to plan the gardening but are inexperienced can get good ideas from examining new and pleasing landscaping. For a nominal fee a landscape gardener will design your garden and give you a bid for necessary plants and labor. When you buy your plants from them, most nurseries are glad to give advice on what will grow to look the best in your area. They will also recommend a competent gardener.

Before making our final decision, we look over new landscaping where similar problems exist. We then contact a large, nearby nursery for advice and comparative costs. With a nurseryman we stand across the street and survey our property objectively. He recommends a desirable landscaping arrangement, which we decide to follow.

WE DECIDE WHAT TO RETAIN, WHAT TO DISCARD, AND WHAT TO PLANT NEW

By an inventory of the presently deteriorated yard we decide what planting to retain by judicious pruning, what to discard, and what to plant new. Directly in front of the building at each corner stands a moth-eaten Italian cypress, and over between the front porch and the hedge is another. They exhibit more brown deadwood than greenery, and the yard would look better if they were removed. The one next to the porch distorts like a sore thumb the porch addition to the otherwise rectangular building. The two cypresses in front make the building look narrower and accentuate the height of the house above a full basement.

If placed to the side of the corners instead of the front they would improve the appearance by making the building look wider and lower. It would be advisable to remove all three yellow-green Italian cypresses and replace the two in front with other accent shrubs. For the two accent shrubs at the corners we choose blue Lawson's cypresses, pyramidal in shape and a distinctive blue-green in color. For balance we will plant a smaller cypress on the porch side. This plant can be kept trimmed as it matures, while the cypress on the opposite side will stay taller by growing unrestrained.

On a low, one-story building, front-foundation planting should be uneven in order not to decrease the height. But to de-accent further the height of our upper-slope, two-story house, we want a uniform grouping across the entire front of the building. For this foundation planting we select five Rosedale pyracanthas, or fire thorns. They can be trimmed once a year to four or five feet, will have shiny green leaves the year round, and will be blanketed with white flowers in the spring and with bright red berries in the fall. To blend the porch with the building, rather than sore-thumbing it as the outstanding cypress does, we want a shrub in the corner behind the porch. We choose a eugenia, a shiny evergreen with small flat leaves. It will grow erect and fairly compact to a level below the porch roof, and it can be restrained by once-a-year trimming.

On the front-porch side of the building a hedge of golden privet runs the full length of the lot, from the street curb to the alley. On the opposite side of the lot the hedge runs from the street to the front corner of the building. The privet has grown thin and scraggly to a height of ten feet from lack of trimming, but fortunately it has not yet deteriorated past reclamation. We can cut it to two or three feet and it will thicken into a desirable hedge. The privet planted on the lot lines in the front parking strip makes the lot look narrow and should be removed so that the hedge will start just beyond the sidewalk. Many of the homes and apartment houses on this street have recently planted hawthorn trees in the parking strip. The nurseryman says hawthorns have been designated by the city as A Avenue's official tree. To widen the lot's appearance and de-emphasize the slope we decide to conform by planting two Lavalle Rose hawthorns, one at each end of the parking strip on the boundary lines.

At the nursery we buy for $3 each in 5-gallon cans the two hawthorns and the eugenia, all 8 feet high. Two blue Lawson's cypresses in 5-gallon cans cost $3.50 each. We select one 5 feet and the other 7 feet high. If we plant the five fast-growing pyracanthas now, we can save by buying them 2 feet high in 1-gallon cans for $1 each.

The parking strip and the front yard have been planted in lawn, which has been mowed and tended irregularly and shows more bare spots and weeds than grass. In the center of the yard is a planting circle of dried-up calla lilies, about five feet across, surrounded by white-painted brick set on edge in a saw-toothed effect. This old-fashioned planting arrangement is an eyesore that should be removed and replaced with the same ground cover as in the rest of the front yard. Planting areas on lawn borders are generally acceptable, but interior plants ruin the appearance of a smooth lawn. The lot looks narrower because the lawn runs all the way from the building to the street curb. It would be preferable to have a planting in the parking strip different from the ground cover between the building and the sidewalk. The parking strip is level, but much of the slope of the lot rises between the sidewalk and the building, making it difficult to maintain a lawn under the best of care. On comparable sloping yards in the area, the best-appearing are covered by dense, low-lying shrubs like horizontal junipers, or by creeping plants like ivy.

THE NURSERY ALSO HANDLES GARDENING

Since it will cost considerably less than shrubs, we choose ivy, buying sufficient small plants in flats for $15. In order to retain a little lawn, we plan to renovate the grass in the parking strip. Sufficient lawn seed costs $1.50. This brings our plant cost to the modest total of $37.50. We ask the nurseryman if he can recommend a good, reasonable gardener to dig out discarded plants, trim the retained shrubs, and plant the new. He replies that his nursery also handles gardening, and he gives an estimate of $90 for the projected labor, making a contract total of $127.50, including the plants.

We tell the nurseryman we appreciate all his advice, and we may still buy the plants from him, but we should get at least one competitive bid before giving a contract. Is there a possibility of reducing his price? He says they would do better later, but not at this time because of the Christmas rush. We settle on doing the work in the slack time between Christmas and New Year's for $110.

By the end of two months both the porch and the garden transformations are completed at a total expenditure of $380. The yard had been so run-down that the tenants had lost interest in looking after it. Now that it is in desirable condition they agree to keep it in good shape, taking care of mowing the small lawn and watering and trimming. In the basement the previous owner had left an old lawn mower and a few necessary garden tools, including spade, hoe and rake, longhandled pruner, hand pruning shears, hedge clippers and pruning saw.

PAINTING THE EXTERIOR

In this part of the country, a good time for painting the exterior is the early spring, when the rains are over and before the shrubbery grows very high. Then the surfaces to be painted can be expected to stay thoroughly dry. After rain, outdoor painting should always be postponed for at least a week of sunny weather. The outdoor temperature during the day can be expected to stay about 50 degrees, the minimum for satisfactory results.

Anyone with no experience can, if he wishes, do a first-class paint job with a little care and can save about two-thirds of the average contractor's charge, as such labor usually costs at least twice as much as material. Since we plan to contract the work, we will get several bids to compare costs and specifications. Owners need no prior experience, because reputable contractors will give detailed specifications on each improvement job. One can be checked against the others. Each contractor will add to our education on price levels and on how the job should be done. In order to have our exterior color scheme look modern and attractive we check several new similar installations for up-to-date ideas, then discuss possibilities with three different contractors.

The original paint was white, now become quite dingy, with the window frames painted dark green and the sash pink. In this area the checkerboard effect of contrasting colors on frames and sashes has become passé. Contrast is obtained by painting the doors in striking colors and painting different sections in contrasting colors, but within the section painting all surface and trim the same. Paint application can be used to improve architectural appearance. Here the chief architectural drawback is the exaggerated height in relation to width, accentuated by placement on an upper slope. Our landscaping rearrangement has helped to relieve this effect. A further contribution to flattening the appearance can be made by painting in horizontal bands.

We decide to paint the entire base of the building dark gray, which will cover in one solid band from the ground up to the first-floor level above the basement. The rest of the surface up to the roof we will paint a light pink, which creates a pleasing contrast with the gray. For individuality we will paint the front door a glossy rose.

A WIDE RANGE OF BIDS

One large and reliable paint contractor, selected from a display ad in the telephone book, gives a bid of $975 to paint both main and garage buildings. He specifies a good two-coat job, providing thorough preparation, "well scraped, brushed, calked and sealed," and two coats of a good-quality paint.

A second contractor, recommended by a friend, gives a bid of $550 for the same-quality paint and same specifications. The reason for the startling price differential is that the first contractor has a heavy overhead, working with foremen and an office staff. Adding profit and contingency percentages to his base cost further pyramids the over-all bid. The second bidder does all the work himself in conjunction with a partner.

The foregoing exemplifies that the most economical contractor works on the job himself, has little overhead, and is satisfied with a minimum profit above wages, an ideal combination if the job is small enough for him to handle.

A Fly-by-Night Advertiser

The third contractor we contact through a newspaper ad which states:

BEST PAINTERS
We Defy Competition
For Lowest Prices in Town
Phone 223-8091

Although we ask for a two-coat job, this advertiser states, "I specialize in one-coat work. My special process is just as good as the average two-coat application." He bids $495 for one coat. We ask for an address where he has worked, and he says there is no use giving any addresses, because there are none anywhere close to this neighborhood. He specifies no preparatory work in his contract and when questioned says, "No need to put all that in the contract. I always do a good job regardless."

The brand of paint is also omitted, and when prodded the painter agrees to include this item. He writes in the name of a cheap off-brand, which he says is "just as good as the highest-priced you can get."

Some advertising boasts of good one-coat exterior paint, but a professionally finished appearance usually demands two coats of good-quality paint throughout. It always pays to specify good paint, even though expecting an early resale. Besides much longer durability, the small per-square-foot cost differential at $2 or $3 per gallon is more than offset by easier application and improved appearance. Cheap paint may look "just as good" in an ad, but it shows up on exposure. Many a misguided speculator has applied cheap paint for a "quick slick-up" and found a second application necessary before resale because of glaring checks, runs and spots such as those revealed on the MacKenzie Avenue property in Chapter 4. Some cheap products will wash through to the original paint after only one heavy rain.

Besides good paint and a two-coat job, preparing the surface distinguishes the work of a conscientious professional. A tyro or fly-by-night contractor often slaps paint with abandon over holes, cracks and loose surfaces without the slightest preparation, hoping the film of new color will hold the surface together and camouflage the defects. If the old exterior paint is checked or unusually heavy with too many coats, it may be necessary to burn off the excess. If a worn surface is basically sound, it can be put in good condition by scraping and wire-brushing the most weathered portions, such as window sills. Loose sills and window framing and other insecure boards should be nailed fast. Any cracks should be filled with calking compound, and any loose or crumbly putty on the windows should be cleaned out with a scraper and replaced. Paint should cover the putty, both old and new, plus a hairline over the glass in order to completely seal the putty and prevent excessive drying and cracking.

Most satisfactory results will be obtained if the undercoat is painted a similar color to that chosen for the finish. An interval of at least one week, but not more than two weeks, should be allowed before second-coating, so that the first coat will be thoroughly but not excessively dried.

WE CHOOSE THE LOWEST SOUND CONTRACT

The third contractor's specifications fail to meet our requirements. The first and second bids, although differing considerably in price, appear comparable otherwise. We advise the $550 contractor that we like his specifications and the job he did on our friend's house, but that we have a bid lower than his. Will he cut his bid if we agree to give him the job? The painter says he needs the work and will accept $500. Could we pay half when he finishes the first coat, and the balance as soon as he completes the job? To this we agree.

The painter and his partner complete the preparation and the first coat in one week. They then take a week out to go on another job. During the third week they complete the exterior painting. This concludes our improvement of the exterior, and we are ready to turn our attention to improving the interior.

Our buildings and grounds from the outside present an entirely different appearance from the house bought six months previously. The exterior appearance now compares with nondiscounted new construction.

This transformation, entirely contracted, has cost a total of $880, including the exterior painting and revitalizing the porch and the garden. Nearly half of all improvement funds nationally are spent on exteriors. Our project has cost close to the same percentage of our total budget.

The $40 additional monthly rental increases the base sales valuation by $4,000, more than $4 for each $1 expended.

8.   MONEY-MAKING INTERIORS

New paint and wallpaper will make the greatest improvement in the interior of our house. A new investor, particularly if he lives in the place to be modernized, finds it difficult to restrain himself from tackling first the paint job that will most radically change the appearance. All work should be co-ordinated, however, and painting left toward the last. Otherwise the paint will be botched by carpentry, electrical and plumbing changes. Plumbing and electrical work cannot be made until carpentry remodeling is roughed in. Finished carpentry would follow the plumbing and electrical work. As in building a new house, almost all changes should precede painting. In this case no major carpenter projects requiring preliminary roughing in are planned.

Our scheduled six months' exterior work has been completed as planned. In our preliminary planning we also set a goal of completing all interior work in twelve months. Now we might tentatively schedule bimonthly completion goals as follows:

Months	1 and 2	Plumbing and heating
	3 and 4	Electrical
	5 and 6	Carpentry
	7 and 8	Tile and linoleum
	9 and 10	Painting and decorating
	11 and 12	Furniture and furnishings

PLUMBING AND HEATING MODERNIZATION

Plumbing often presents the biggest interior modernization bills. It is well to have a reliable inventory of plumbing problems. Through the Apartment Owners Association we secure a competent and reasonable plumber who reviews with us the complete plumbing requirements. Special attention should be given to obsolete installations like old-fashioned bathtubs on legs, lack of modern facilities such as showers, and worn-out fixtures such as cracked sinks.

The modern-type bathtub, flush with the floor, is in good condition, and so is the washbasin. The individual hot- and cold-water faucets with porcelain handles should be modernized by changing to mixing faucets with chrome handles. The large porcelain shower head above the bathtub looks like a drooping sunflower and has no spray adjustment. It should be changed to a compact, modern chrome fixture with built-in adjustments for fine, coarse or needle spray. The porcelain mixing faucet with shower diverter over the bathtub is cracked. It should be replaced with chrome to match the other changes.

The kitchen sink is in good condition, but the chrome on part of the mixing faucet has worn off. It should be replaced with a new chrome faucet. The plumber says all these plumbing fixtures, including good-quality fittings, can be installed for $45, including labor and material. They will make a marked difference in the next buyer's appraisal of the bathroom and kitchen.

HEATING SHOULD BE CONSIDERED ALONG WITH PLUMBING

Heating facilities should be considered along with plumbing. Many firms specialize in heating installations. Most plumbers also handle the average heating problems. There is a satisfactory small built-in electric heater in the bathroom. In the living room, looking quite archaic by modern standards, is a bulky gas circulating heater. The name plate shows a 25,000 BTU capacity, insufficient for chilly mornings. There is no thermostat. Adequate heat would maintain 70 degrees in the coldest weather. In this climate the floor space would require 45,000 BTU, according to a chart which the plumber has obtained from a heating-equipment firm. An additional heater of 20,000 BTU could be installed, but changing to a more modern adequate single replacement would greatly improve the appearance.

We could install a central heating system or a wall furnace. Either would be adequate. Central heating would present a tough installation problem and would cost about $750 installed. A wall furnace of 45,000 BTU capacity would cost only $185 including thermostat. The nearly flush appearance on the wall does not interfere with furniture or rugs. The furnace we select is a 45,000 BTU, dual-wall type, with thermostat. One grill of the heater will face into the living room, and the other will open into the central hallway to heat the remaining rooms.

A plumber's charge could run between $50 and $200 additional for the labor and material, depending on the work required on the gas line and flue. Enlarging the heating capacity would sometimes necessitate larger gas and flue lines. In this case the existing half-inch gas line and 4-inch flue are adequate. The new heater can be installed adjacent to the old one, simplifying the change-over. Our plumber agrees to a reduced price of $175 for installing the heater, making it $220 for plumbing and heating changes. He says this is a discounted price, which he would give only to members of the Apartment Owners Association. Two additional bids would often be in order, but this bid seems low, so we tell the plumber to go ahead with the work.

He cuts out a section of wall and mounts the heating element within the regular 14-inch space between the 2-by-4 studs. The gas line, flue, and thermostat are connected. Then the grill on each side, projecting only two inches from the wall, is attached to the heating element, forming a plate which conceals the rough edges where the wall has been cut. The replacement of the ugly old heater not only enlarges the heating capacity but enlarges and enhances the appearance of the living room.

ELECTRICAL MODERNIZATION

In the third month of interior modernization we are ready to check the electrical fixtures. Push-button switches and outdated types of hanging fixtures mark a dwelling as ancient, and they should be replaced. The switches are already the toggle type. But the living-room switch works only half the time. The one in the bathroom does not work at all, so the lights have to be turned on and off at the fixture.

When a light fails it pays to check first whether the bulb is burnt out and then inspect receptacle and switches for a loose connection. None of these faults is evident. We have an electrician recommended by the Apartment Owners Association replace both suspect switches. The two new switches operate their light circuits satisfactorily.

Many older living rooms have obsolete overhead fixtures. Ceiling fixtures are generally out of date except where appropriate in kitchen, bathroom and dining room. The easiest way to cover them where undesirable is to remove the fixture entirely, cut the wires close, tape the ends and push them above the ceiling. If the receptacle projects, it can be removed and the hole plastered over. If the receptacle is flush, it can be sealed over with tape, then papered or painted. There is no ceiling fixture in the living room, and the switch at the door controls the lamps plugged into the wall outlets. A long wall should have more than one outlet. There are sufficient double outlets in each wall.

The close-to-the-ceiling fixtures in both bedrooms are satisfactory and in this instance do not warrant replacement or removal. If desired they could be replaced with modern, completely flush fixtures, or they could be removed entirely. Fortunately the bathroom has satisfactory lighting, with an electric outlet for a shaver adjacent to the medicine cabinet, a wiring must. In the dining room hangs a dangling monstrosity, and from the kitchen ceiling an exposed bulb projects with no shielding globe. We have the electrician install a ceiling-hugging, flush-mounted fixture in the dining room, and a three-bulb fluorescent fixture in the kitchen. Since all fixtures replace existing ones in the same locations, the installation cost is nominal. The total cost, including switches, electrical fixtures, and labor, comes to $42.

CARPENTRY IMPROVEMENTS

In planning our carpentry improvements, starting the fifth month, we want especially to check shelves, cupboards, closets, walls, floors, and general plan and trim. Are there any outdated features like ornate picture moldings or fireplace mantels which should be modified or removed before painting and decorating? Luckily we have no such changes to make. The closets and shelf space appear ample except in the kitchen. A previously mentioned government survey revealed that 45 per cent of housewives complained of inadequate storage space. We should give this item special attention. What is adequate?

Builders consider 60 square feet the minimum kitchen cupboard shelf space, plus a minimum of 20 square feet of kitchen drawer space. The kitchen has 28 square feet of drawer space, 8 more than the minimum. There is also a broom closet with shelf space overhead. The cupboard shelf space totals 54 square feet, only 6 short of the 60-foot minimum. All the cupboards are above the sink-and-drainboard area. The kitchen wall is bare above the refrigerator, where an additional cabinet would be desirable. In this space we have a carpenter install a factory-assembled, unfinished, Douglas-fir wall cabinet, 30 inches high, 30 inches wide, and one foot deep. The cabinet costs $45 installed. When painted it will match the other cabinets in the kitchen. The new cabinet has three shelves which add 7½ square feet of cupboard shelves, making a new total of 61½ square feet. This just exceeds the minimum. This shelf deficiency was comparatively easy to solve. In many older kitchens shelving must be doubled in order to become adequate.

In the bathroom the shower has washed off the paint and eaten into the plaster behind the tub. Holes surround the edges of the tub where some of the plaster has completely disappeared. The wall could be patched and repainted, but replacing the plaster around the tub with colorful tile would modernize the room. Ceramic tile would be most desirable, but also the most expensive. The cheapest ceramic-tile installation would cost $150, twice as much as economical plastic or metal tile. The latter comes in various sizes, 4¼-inch and 8½-inch squares being the most common. Marbled tileboard, however, in standard 4-by-4-foot and 4-by-6-foot panels costs the least and can be installed by any carpenter. The bathtub is 5 feet long by 31 inches wide, and the three-sided area would require two 4-by-6-foot panels to cover to an average height of 4 feet. The carpenter agrees to install the tileboard for $38, including labor and accessories, using chrome molding. This is a good example of a compromise modernization at least cost, and it brings our total carpentry expenditure to $83.

TILE AND LINOLEUM

By the seventh month of interior work we are ready for tile and linoleum renewal. The tile floor in the bathroom is in good condition. In the kitchen the small hexagonal tiles on the drainboard are badly chipped and pitted around the edges. The drainboard surface could be replaced with new ceramic tile, with stainless steel, with a plastic, like Formica, or with any number of substitutes. Formica is most common with new construction. Stainless steel may be featured in luxury housing. After checking into durability and cost and comparing with more pleasing new installations, we conclude that the best replacement would be modern ceramic tile, both for the drainboard and for the splashboard. We obtain estimates from two contractors. The lowest bid is $95, and we let the contract for ivory-colored tile.

In the kitchen large sections of the pattern have worn off the linoleum in front of the sink, the stove, and the door to the service porch. We might replace the worn linoleum with modern inlaid linoleum of a colorful marbleized or geometric design, or of the tile type that is normally laid in 9-inch squares. Two linoleum houses bid. The lower quotation, including material, taking up the old linoleum, and laying a geometric inlaid-linoleum tile, is $75. We accept the latter. When the old linoleum is removed the underlying tongue-and-groove pine flooring is found in fair condition. This makes it unnecessary to install plywood or other smooth undercovering, which would otherwise have been required at an extra cost.

PAINTING AND DECORATING THE INTERIOR

In the ninth month since we started on the interior, we are ready for painting. We contact the same painter who handled the outside and discuss over-all specifications preparatory to getting his bid. To make our house look like a choice, newly decorated dwelling, we want a first-class preparation job, as on the exterior. All walls having an accumulation of dirt and grease should be washed. This particularly applies to kitchens and sections where dirt accumulates, for instance over a heater. Heavy varnish on woodwork should normally be removed with the help of varnish remover. Any loose paint should be wire-brushed and sanded and, if this does not produce a satisfactory surface, scraped or treated with paint remover. All loose wallpaper should be pulled off and scraped down. Where there are several layers of wallpaper all of it should be removed, whether the surface is to be painted or repapered. If the wallpaper is stuck too tight for scraping, it should be loosened with a chemical or by an electric steam wallpaper remover.

Happily there is no varnished woodwork, and no paint so loose or checked that it cannot be handled with wire-brushing and a light sanding. The wallpaper in the dining room and bedrooms is faded, but it adheres to the wall except for occasional tears around the edges and a few nail holes. All holes and cracks in the woodwork are to be filled with self-sizing paste wood filler. In the plaster ceilings and walls, including those papered, large cracks or holes are to be filled with patching plaster, and smaller ones with spackling paste or compound.

In discussions with the painter we decide whether to paper or to paint a high-gloss or semigloss enamel or a flat paint compounded with oil or latex. We should consider the surface to be covered, the over-all effect to be obtained and the wear and exposure to which the paint or paper will be subjected. Wallpaper is sometimes suitable in living rooms and can give an especially colorful effect in dining rooms, breakfast nooks, or bedrooms. Striking decoration can be obtained by papering only one wall where appropriate. We decide to paper the breakfast nook at one end of the kitchen.

In kitchens and bathrooms it is wise to specify enamel which will withstand moisture and can be washed. We decide on a semigloss enamel for a finish coat in the kitchen and bathroom. For durability in the living room we specify a good oil-base flat paint. In the dining room and bedrooms a latex-base flat wall paint will cover over the wallpaper, since it was butted, with no overlapping edges. If it had been overlapped, it would require removal or texturing-over in order to present a smooth surface.

TWO COATS ARE NEEDED FOR A GOOD INSIDE PAINT JOB

Advertising to the contrary, a good inside paint job takes two coats in most cases, the same as outside. The exception is where the present surface is in fair condition and the new paint is similar or darker in color. Painting an undercoat also permits selecting any new colors desired, regardless of previous colors. In the bedrooms and dining room the painter will undercoat over the wallpaper with the same latex-base paint as the finish coat. The living room, kitchen, and bathroom will require special undercoats. The same type of paint will be applied on the ceilings as on the walls, but with contrasting or matching colors. Where the walls are to be papered in the breakfast nook, we specify the same semigloss on the ceiling as on the kitchen ceiling. An undercoat will be applied in every case, and all closets and cabinets will be painted inside, as they will detract in the view of a prospective tenant or buyer if left unpainted.

If the hardwood floors were in bad shape they could be covered with wall-to-wall carpets. Since they are in fair-to-good condition, it will cost considerably less to renovate them. The hardwood floors in the dining room and bedrooms are in good shape. But in the living room there is considerable scratching and scuffing in the traffic lanes, and dark, heavy coats of varnish on the outer edges. On the living-room floor paint-and-varnish remover should be used to soften the heavy varnish, which should then be peeled off with a scraper. Next, the floor should be washed with a cleaner and a bleaching agent, and the holes and cracks filled with a paste wood filler. The floors of the bedrooms and dining room will look like new with touching up, so they should be scrubbed with a cleaner. The filler in the living room should be sanded smooth, and also the scuffs, scratches and worn spots in all hardwood-floored rooms.

The living room, where all varnish is to be removed, should have one full coat of sealer and then a coat of varnish. In the other rooms, where the varnish appears satisfactory except for the spots which are to be sanded lightly, an oil stain should be applied to the worn spots to match the rest of the varnish. Then a coat of varnish should be painted over the spots. After this has dried for twenty-four hours, the spots should be lightly steel-wooled and a finish coat of varnish should be applied over the entire floor. The scuffed tongue-and-groove pine floor of the service porch should be covered with two coats of porch-and-deck enamel. The foregoing floor renewal can be handled by a floor or paint contractor.

WE REQUIRE A FIRM CONTRACT

After reviewing all the specifications, the painter suggests, "You know I do good work at a reasonable price. Let me work on a time and material basis instead of a fixed contract. I will charge just for the material and my labor. I won't have to add the usual extras to make sure I don't lose out, so you will save money by not having a contract."

The suggestion sounds plausible, and it is no doubt made in good faith. But it is amazing how the most conscientious contractor usually changes in attitude, material savings and labor speed when working on "time and material." All who are familiar with the operation of wartime "cost plus" contracts can testify to this. Material, for example paint and wallpaper, would be billed at the full retail list price, unless specified otherwise, on a "time and material" job. It would be discounted more nearly at wholesale on a close-figured contract. Labor on contract is closely supervised to prevent wasted time. More extra trips for forgotten tools and material seem to develop when you are paying for the time. We tell the painter we know he means well. But to be certain of how much expense we are getting into, and whether we will have enough money to pay for the work, we must have a firm contract. We suggest going easy on the "padding" and sharpening his pencil, as we are getting at least two other bids. After considerable figuring, the painter arrives at a "rock bottom" contract of $375. We get other bids of $525 and $750, showing again how contractors' bids can vary. After giving the contract to the first painter, we are ready to discuss color schemes.

COLOR CAN TRANSFORM THE APPEARANCE OF A ROOM

Many misfit rooms can be made more pleasing by an apt choice of color arrangement. For example, high ceilings appear lower when they are painted darker than the walls, and when horizontal bands are painted on the walls. Horizontal bands also broaden a narrow room. Low ceilings appear higher if painted lighter than the walls, and if vertical bands are painted on the walls. Any room that looks depressing because of drab colors can look cheery and inviting with bright colors. The trend in decorating is away from lackluster whites, and toward creams, bright yellows, pinks, green and light blues. With rental housing, colors cannot be overexuberant—with deep purples, reds and blues, for example—for fear of clashing with tenants' furnishings and color phobias. However, interesting color schemes with bright harmonious colors invite tenants.

From the painter's voluminous color charts we select for the living-room and dining-room ceilings the same tint of aquamarine, and for their walls a contrasting light rose. The kitchen and breakfast nook are now both a dingy white. White used to be the rage for kitchens but has been supplanted by bright colors here as in other rooms. For the kitchen and breakfast-nook ceilings and also for the adjoining service-porch ceiling we choose a light-cream paint. The breakfast wall we have papered with a colorful pattern. We have the kitchen wall painted a light green. For the service porch, which was medium brown, we choose a dusty-pink paint. We choose a light aquamarine for one bedroom ceiling, with light pink walls. For the other ceiling we choose a creamy yellow, with light-green walls. To brighten the bathroom we have the ceiling painted cream and the walls rose-pink.

When the decoration is completed, we can see how our choice of colors works out in practice. Paint on a color chart always looks different, sometimes not as good and sometimes better, when applied. In this case the results are good, and the tenants are happy with the chosen transformation.

By the end of March 1965, the eleventh month on the interior, the house is completely decorated. Our total modernization cost to date is $1,770, and all that remains is furniture and furnishings.

TIME TO RECHECK THE RENT SCHEDULE

Any changes in furniture would normally be held up until the present tenants move after we raise the rent to the level warranted by all our improvements. The tenants had put up with the inconvenience of modernization in anticipation of enjoying the results, but they expect our expenditures to be offset by further raises. At this point it would be wise to recheck rentals for similar accommodations in the area. The rental market could have moved up or down in the seventeen months since we bought. We answer two ads in the $150 bracket at which we expect to rent and find that both are less desirable than our place. In fact they compare more with our house before decoration. We check one ad for $155, one for $160, and another for $167.50, and we find all three comparable to our modernized interior and exterior in their present condition. All are unfurnished (as ours will be if the tenants move), further evidence that this is the practice for this type of unit.

Armed with this information, we decide to raise the rent for the present tenants to $150. If they move we will review the furniture needs and then advertise the vacated flat for $160 instead of the $150 top we had originally planned. The increased figure will still compare favorably with the present market, and the rent can always be reduced if response is too slow.

We notify the tenants on May 1 that their rent will be $150 starting June 1. This time they say they can't afford more rent and will have to move before the end of the month. We ask if this is a definite notice, and the husband says yes.

FURNITURE AND FURNISHINGS

If we did not plan a major furniture change, we would at once advertise the expected vacancy. A new tenant could be ready to move in when the present tenant moves out, thus preventing a loss in rent. But we plan to remove most of the furniture, as the new paint and wallpaper accentuate the dilapidated condition of most of the furniture and furnishings.

As previously mentioned, it is not advisable to reclaim furniture from a tenant. But the national trend is toward renting unfurnished those units which have bedrooms, especially two or more. As furniture deteriorates it should be renovated, replaced, or removed. The latter is obviously most economical as long as unfurnished units in the area rent for little less than furnished. If we adopt the policy of renting unfurnished and the present tenants ask for furniture repairs or changes, they should be advised that they will have to pay for such repairs or they can elect to buy replacements at their own expense.

The tenant moves out the morning of May 29, the Saturday before the end of the month, leaving us free to make any desired furniture changes. The only furniture to consider retaining might be such essential equipment as the stove and the refrigerator. In many multi-room rentals these two are owned by the tenants. However, in this area they are often included with unfurnished rentals. We will plan to provide a stove and a refrigerator, and we will remove all other furniture.

It is surprising how a single object of furniture, like an obsolete stove or refrigerator, can detract from an otherwise desirable apartment and negate much modernization work and expense. Any furniture to be retained should be checked for appearance and condition. The refrigerator is acceptable, being an 8-cubic-foot Frigidaire about five years old. The gas range is the outdated upright type that stands on spindly black legs, like a giant spider, with the oven mounted to the side and higher than the surface burners. The oven thermostat does not work. There is no storage space underneath. The finish is a cream-colored enamel trimmed in black.

We decide to buy a modern, table-model kitchen range, with a good oven thermostat and with the oven and storage drawers under the regular cooking surface, so that the entire assembly is mounted flush with the floor. A small, 20-inch-wide, apartment-type "rangette" cheapens a family-size kitchen, so we want a standard 36-inch range with hotter burners and a good-sized oven. Where a 20-inch rangette would cost $100, a suitable 36-inch range can be bought for $140. We can trade in the present stove for $25, making a net cost of $115 for the new, copper-colored range.

In checking furnishings we look over carpets, rugs, screens, shades, drapes, and curtains. In this type of dwelling unit we use rugs over hardwood floors instead of carpets. If we rent unfurnished, the tenant would provide rugs, along with curtains. Screens and shades are normally provided by the owner. The screens, including the frames, are in fair condition, as they were tightened and painted by the painter while working on the exterior. The shades are satisfactory except for two in the living room and one in the master bedroom. The shade in the master bedroom can be repaired by taking the cloth off the roller, trimming both ends, then reversing the cloth and attaching the previous bottom to the roller. In the living room, however, the shades are too deteriorated for repair, so we arrange to replace all three. For $7.50 we get three new plastic shades of fair quality affixed to our old rollers, which are still in good condition.

In this area drapes are provided sometimes by the owner, sometimes by the tenant. The drapes and curtains in the living room, which faces the street, are fairly new and quite desirable, so we decide to leave them. They will be attractive to a prospective tenant or buyer and would have little value if removed. We remove the rest of the curtains and drapes, as all of them are faded and worn.

We offer the furniture to a secondhand dealer. He says that not much of it is really worth hauling out, but he bids $95 for the salable items, including rugs and dining-room and bedroom sets. We accept this offer, with the proviso that the dealer will remove all unsalable items, like the forlorn sofa, and leave the house clean and ready for renting. The dealer agrees, gives us $95 in cash, and immediately starts loading his truck.

The $95 windfall reduces our $122.50 outlay for furniture and furnishings to a net of $27.50. If we had replaced with modest new furniture our cost would have run about $750. It could be about as difficult to rent in this area for $170 thus furnished as for $160 unfurnished. This is another good example of an economical choice which increases net by reducing expenditures.

RENTING OUR VACATED HOUSE

To rent our vacated house, we place a cardboard "Vacancy" sign in the front window where it can be seen from the street. On the front door we tack a card with our telephone number. In the leading newspaper, the *Metropolitan,* we advertise under "Unfurnished Houses for Rent":

> A Avenue. Redecorated 5 rooms, garage. Adults. $160. Phone 233–4127.

The best advertising draws bona fide prospects and eliminates those who would neither be interested nor qualify. It is therefore advantageous to specify, besides desirable features, the area location, the amount of rent, whether furnished, and whether restricted to adults. Since advertising is an important factor for successful operations, considerably more information on this subject will be offered in Chapter 12, after we own more rental units.

Renting to tenants with children would have been all right when the house was in the condition in which it was purchased. Now that it is completely decorated, and since it should be kept looking its best until the property is sold, we would be foolhardy to rent to any but adults. We place the ad for one month, starting Sunday. This insures the lowest rate, and it can be canceled as soon as the house is rented. If the vacancy is not rented at $160 within two or three weeks, the price could be reduced to $155 or $150. An owner testing the market might reduce the rent early if planning on especially stable tenants for long-term investment. But our sale price will be determined by the actual rent in effect at the time of sale, so we should consider waiting possibly a month or so before decreasing the rent.

By 1 P.M. Sunday our telephone has rung fourteen times in response to the ad. We have been scheduling appointments starting at 2 P.M. to show the vacancy. By 3 P.M. we have rented to desirable tenants—a middle-aged couple, both working, and the wife's sister, recently widowed, who has moved from Idaho. They have been staying in a 3-room furnished apartment with one bedroom, and the sister had to sleep on the living-room sofa. Our redecorated house is just what they have been looking for. They wanted two bedrooms, and they were attracted by "redecorated" and "adults" in the ad, as they prefer a nice place undamaged by children. The sister has stored her furniture, and it will fit nicely.

We arrange for the new tenants' rent to start the same day, May 30, gaining two days' rent, since the vacating tenant paid to the first. This more than offsets the cost of the ad, which we cancel the next day, thus being charged for only two days.

On June 1, 1965, eighteen months after our purchase, our gross rent has thus increased to $160 a month. Because of these changed circumstances, it is well to review our over-all planning in the light of our recent experience and the new conditions, before we proceed further. Our $30 additional monthly rental increases the base sale valuation by another $3,000.

CONVERTING THE BASEMENT
WOULD NOT RESULT IN A WORTH-WHILE GAIN

Originally we had considered converting the basement into a flat in our fourth six-month improvement period. Now we are ready to check the soundness of this possibility. After consulting with two general contractors, who draw tentative plans, we get a bid of $12,240 from one and $12,960 from the other for labor and material complete. The latter estimates exactly $9 per square foot, and the former figures a slight discount on this amount.

Many investors would add the new flat because of the bargain cost, 75 per cent of the $12-per-square-foot cost of comparable new construction. After thorough study, we decide against the change. Figuring a $150 dependable monthly rental, the added flat would increase the base sale value $15,000. Discounting a 6 per cent added sale cost, $900, would bring the sale value uncomfortably close to the improvement cost.

For a worth-while profit plus a safety margin, every dollar in conversion cost should earn at least $2 in projected capital gain. Converting the basement for $7,500 would be a paying undertaking. But selling for close to a $13,000 cost would mean money and effort spent for nothing and would build the property to a total cost where greater sales resistance would be met. Here is a point where many a misguided investor makes a wrong decision. What profit is there in spending $1 which increases the value only $1?

The money would be well spent if the basement could be soundly converted for around $15,000 to two apartments rentable at $150 each, resulting in a $30,000 additional capital value. But the basement and lot layouts make only one rental unit practicable.

An owner who would do the work himself at a cost of approximately $7,500 would gain a productive, increased income and would have a sound investment for resale. However, the possibility of doing the work yourself does not appear attractive when balanced against the probable requirement of a year's added time. Our plan of accelerated pyramiding requires turnover as rapid as possible. This addition would project the total turnover time on a do-it-yourself basis to two and a half years. By its elimination we are ready for resale within one and a half years and can expect to be making progress on a 4- to 8-unit building in the year it would take to rebuild the basement.

As with most new building construction, complete remodeling, such as turning a rough basement into an apartment, may pay an adequate income return. It might not pay too well from the viewpoint of increasing capital value for resale, unless the investor is prepared to do the work involved, or unless a high ratio of rental units can be obtained from the available floor space. The investor interested in capital expansion will gain most by restricting his initial efforts, as we have done, to rehabilitation and modernization of basically sound existing dwelling units.

INCOME HAS PAID FOR TOTAL OUTLAY

Eliminating the basement conversion has cut elapsed time from twenty-four to eighteen months, thereby reducing available funds by six months' savings and net rentals. Increased rent and judicious contracts have enabled us to keep on a pay-as-you-go basis, however, making it unnecessary to borrow additional funds to pay for improvements. Total repairs to date have cost only $28.60 for plumbing, since other minor repairs have been handled without additional charge by various workmen on the premises. Adding the $28.60 to our $1,797.50 improvement cost gives a total outlay for maintenance and remodeling of $1,826.10, arrived at chronologically as follows:

CAPITAL OUTLAY

CATEGORY	COST
Front porch modernization and repair	$ 270.00
Garden transformation	110.00
Painting exterior	500.00
Plumbing and heating modernization	220.00
Electrical modernization	42.00

Carpentry additions	83.00
Tile and linoleum rejuvenation	170.00
Painting and decorating interior	375.00
Furniture and furnishings	27.50
SUBTOTAL	$1,797.50
Plumbing repairs	28.60
TOTAL FOR REJUVENATION AND REPAIRS	$1,826.10

In our eighteen months of operation, our income has built up as follows:

INCOME STATEMENT

Bank balance December 4, 1963, at close of purchase	$ 814.84
Received from escrow after porch repair	180.00
Personal savings for 18 months at $50 monthly	900.00
Net rental income	965.05
TOTAL RESOURCES	$2,859.89
Minus Capital Outlay	−1,826.10
BALANCE ON HAND, JUNE 1, 1965	$1,033.79

Here is the capitulation to arrive at our $965.05 net rental income:

NET INCOME CAPITULATION
GROSS RENTS

1 month at $90, 1/1/64	$ 90.00
16 months at $130, 2/1/64 to 5/1/65	2,080.00
1 month at $160, 6/1/65	160.00
GROSS RENT TOTAL	$2,330.00

EXPENDITURES

Taxes and insurance, $173.30 per year, $259.95 1½ years (Includes half-year tax reserve, not paid)	
17 loan payments at $65 monthly	1,105.00
TOTAL FIXED EXPENDITURES	1,364.95

NET SPENDABLE INCOME AFTER FIXED EXPENSES AND LOAN PAYMENTS $ 965.05

We have paid for all improvements from current resources, and we still have a reserve of $1,033.79. Our total capital outlay to date is $10,331.26, adding the net purchase cost of $8,505.16 to the improvement and repair cost of $1,826.10.

Personally handling the practicable work would have cost about one third less, saving approximately $600. But for the average worker this would also cost another year's time, making two and a half years instead of one and a half.

We can stay within our turnover objective of two years, even though it takes another six months to sell our property and buy a larger one. This should prove ample time to meet our turnover profit objective of 25 per cent to carry us along on the realty road to a million dollars.

We have contracted all improvements for an expenditure of $1,826.10. Our modernized house is now ready for resale within one and a half years of the purchase date.

The rent has jumped from $90 to $160, a net raise of $70 monthly. This increases the capital valuation by $7,000. Now that improvements are completed, every $1 expended has earned a value of close to $4.

PART FOUR

BUYING YOUR SECOND PROPERTY

9. SHOPPING FOR
A $40,000 INCOME PROPERTY

Now that our house is completely modernized and compares favorably with desirable new construction, we are ready to put it on the market. We have built a sizable personal equity in our property, chiefly through capital improvement. Also, the seventeen loan payments have paid the interest and have reduced the loan principal by $530.91, further increasing our equity by this bonus amount. We are in the position of forty million homeowners, who possess a nucleus that can be expanded toward a fortune.

Many real-estate investors at this point would rest on their laurels. Others bent on building an estate would sell for cash, waiting until they knew how much could be realized before looking for a larger place to buy. This step would result in extra income taxes on the capital gain, and it could result in several months of idleness for investment funds which should be working continuously. Therefore the present property should not be sold until a larger property is found. But the larger property cannot be bought until the present property is sold. How to solve this dilemma?

TRADE FOR A LARGER PROPERTY

Find a larger property first, then offer to trade your equity for the equity in the larger property. Such an offer, if handled properly, will be accepted more often than refused, particularly if both properties are in the same city. A high percentage of ads, examples of which will be cited, express a willingness to trade. I have found that a trade can be worked out with most owners, even though they may shy from an original trade offer.

Both Up-Trader and Down-Trader May Benefit

Many owners of larger properties may liquidate part of their holdings from time to time by trading down and also taking back mortgages. This is a logical step for older owners desirous of partial liquidation. Usually the smaller property is easier to dispose of, and the mortgages which are taken pay a better return than most investments.

I know of a couple in their mid-seventies who decided to sell one of their mortgage-free properties, a 30-unit apartment house valued at $150,000. They took in trade for the down payment a $25,000 equity in a $40,000 home which had a $15,000 mortgage. For the $125,000 balance of the apartment-house sale price they carried a fifteen-year first mortgage at 6 per cent. They later sold the home for the traded value by taking back a second mortgage.

The homeowner who traded up for the apartment house was a retired utility executive of sixty-five who preferred an investment like apartments, which could maintain his productive interests. The large home had become a white elephant for him and his wife, since all of their children were married. Its loan payments, high taxes and other expenses ate a big hole in his pension without producing income and reduced his spendable income to a niggardly amount. After improving the apartment house and increasing rents, he found that his spendable income was higher than when he worked on a salary.

Five Advantages of Trading Up

Trading is a device to buy and sell in one transaction. It offers a fivefold advantage:

1. *You can make a bigger profit.* The profit on property traded for a larger property can be substantially greater than the profit from a cash sale.
2. *You can buy a bigger property.* A larger property can be secured by trading than by selling for cash and buying for cash. (A "cash sale" in real estate means "no trade," but it usually involves financing.)

3. *You save income taxes.* You pay no income taxes on property traded up at a profit. This advantage may accrue partially to the owner trading down.
4. *You can obtain increased financing.* Loans are governed by both appraisal valuation and sale price, and they are limited by whichever is lower. A low cash buy lowers financing proportionately. By trading you can stipulate a maximum market value on property to be financed, thereby increasing your loan potential.
5. *You can keep your funds working.* No investment time is lost between sale and purchase.

When you trade your equity for the equity in a larger property, you assume a larger loan to make up the difference in value. New investors sometimes feel timorous about owning a large property with a large loan. With the same financing ratio, it is safer in actual practice to handle the loan on a large property than on a small one, because greater gross income provides more leeway for transferring accounts to meet emergencies. The bigger the number of units, the smaller the vacancy ratio created by a single vacancy. For example, a tenant vacating an apartment in a duplex house creates a temporary 50 per cent vacancy ratio. One unit vacant for one month in a year creates a 4.2 per cent annual vacancy factor. In a 40-unit building one vacancy creates a 2.5 per cent temporary vacancy ratio. If one month's rent is lost in a year, the resulting annual vacancy factor is only about .02 per cent.

Regardless of how desirable a property may appear, however, as previously stated, loan arrangements should always be made so that the payments can be handled from the income and the property will be self-liquidating.

How to Determine Your Equity

For maximum expansion you should determine first your marketable equity and then the largest potential property the equity will buy. Multiplying the existing rental value of $160 monthly by 100 gives a sale valuation of $16,000, close to a figure that will hold, with the present attractive buildings and grounds. The possibility of converting the basement into a flat is an added inducement for the next buyer. We could establish $16,000 as a fair value and arrive at an asking price by adding about 20 per cent. This would make $19,200, which could be raised to $19,500. If our negotiations result in selling outright, we could set a rock-bottom minimum of $15,000. Unless at least this amount is received we can afford to await a suitable offer while drawing the present income.

To determine our salable equity we deduct the outstanding loan balance from the fair sale value of $16,000. The $65 monthly loan payments, including 6 per cent interest, have been made from the property income. By June 15, 1965, at the end of eighteen monthly payments, the balance on the principal has decreased from $7,000 to $6,436.44. This gives an equity of $9,563.56, or approximately $10,000. We multiply this equity by 4 and find we can buy a property in the $40,000 range.

This means we should look at property listed between $35,000 and $60,000. An owner who had performed most of the work on the same time schedule would look for property in a similar bracket, as his equity would be increased by $600, to $10,163.56.

Any homeowner who has been making payments and improvements would build an equity between his sale value and loan balance and could board our financial ship at this point. He could plan to trade for income property valued at about four times his equity. I know of many instances, besides the example cited earlier in this chapter, of trading the equity in a home as the down payment on substantial income properties.

Another recent trade on a smaller scale involved a couple in their twenties who traded a $3,000 equity in a 6-room GI home for a 4-unit apartment house valued at $20,000, incurring a $17,000 mortgage. The liquidators in this case were two brokers who had taken the building free and clear as commission on a $300,000 sale of an office building.

HOW TO COMPUTE POTENTIAL PROFITS

While only the foolhardy spend unhatched chickens, it pays to count your chickens before they hatch, contrary to the old saw. Otherwise how can you gauge your possibilities for further progress? At each stage it is again well to review accomplishments. Before proceeding further we might examine the potential profit that can be realized from our eighteen months' efforts. On a probable sale price of

$16,000, we have figured our equity, or net estate, at $9,563.56. What would the profit amount to?

Deducting our total cost of $10,331 for purchase and improvements would make a gross sale profit of $5,669, or 54.87 per cent. A sale commission of $800, averaging 5 per cent of the sale price, would normally be paid, leaving a net sale profit of $4,869. To this we add the $564 loan reduction, arriving at an over-all net profit of $5,433.

To compute the potential earnings on our personal investment, we first add:

Original investment, $1,750 down less $64.84
    from escrow $1,685.16
Accumulated $50 monthly savings for 18 months   900.00
Bank reconciliation
    Balance at time of purchase $814.84
    June 15, 1965 balance   968.79
    Total net deposits over withdrawals   −153.95

TOTAL EXPENDITURE
OF PERSONAL FUNDS $2,431.21

If we sell for $16,000 within two years after the original purchase, what would our profit percentage be? On our personal investment of $2,431 the net return of $5,433 would total 223.4 per cent, or 111.7 per cent a year.

The improvements on the A Avenue house are typical of what you can expect to handle profitably, and they are cited at 1965 costs with ample time allowances for completion. In this specific example the profits are more than triple the 33.87 per cent a year on personal investment shown in Step 3 of the "Step-by-Step Formula to a Million Dollars" in Chapter 2. Other specific examples will also considerably exceed the moderate pace of Chapter 2, indicating the comparative conservatism of our guide to a million when matched with actual case histories.

By combining judicious initial investment, maximally sound financing, and profitably selective improvements, it is not exceptional to double net worth in two years, as I have, along with many other realty investors. With experienced guidance to help chart your operations, you can consider Chapter 2's over-all capital gain of 25 per cent every two years—which will make you a millionaire in twenty years—as a reasonable minimum expectation.

THE SALESMAN WHO NEGOTIATED YOUR PURCHASE
WILL SELDOM MAKE A PROFITABLE RESALE

When ready to sell, many investors blindly place their fortunes in the hands of the salesman who negotiated their original purchase, giving him an exclusive sale listing. If the salesman appraises your improved property at full market value, there is no harm in giving him an open listing. But be wary of tying up your property. In many cases an unimaginative salesman will be so dominated by the price he knows you paid that he will not be able to condition himself to make a profitable resale. Often he will not even credit your property with actual expenditures for improvements. He might discourage you from setting a maximum resale price, whereas a new salesman, even in the same broker's office, would appraise afresh at fullest market value. Mr. Bokay might well be contacted regarding subsequent deals, but there is little likelihood that he can be of any assistance on the property which he sold us.

Some investors interested in trading make a practice of listing their properties on an open basis with several realtors, describing what they have to trade and what kind of property they desire. This sometimes leads to a trade. In most cases the greatest opportunities will be found by shopping as though you were a cash buyer for properties in the correct price range. When a desirable buy is found you can then propose a trade, offering your property as the down payment.

INCOME PROPERTY OPPORTUNITIES
ARE INEXHAUSTIBLE

After they learn of the opportunities offered by income property investments, many of my friends say, "With such a money-making gold mine, how soon will the lode run out?"

I reassure them that income property represents an inexhaustible treasure trove in which there are more opportunities than treasure seekers. For every eager investor wanting to buy or trade up there are many liquidators wanting to sell or trade down. Basically desirable property may be sold at discounted prices on favorable terms for business or personal reasons. Among the sellers I have encountered who have offered bargains or unusually good terms are:

1. Unimaginative owners who allow their properties to deteriorate
2. Stubborn owners whose net incomes drop because they refuse to change
3. Shortsighted milkers who feed no income back into improvements
4. Multiple heirs who let a property go to pot, because no one is responsible
5. Heirs in a hurry to divide estate proceeds
6. Spendthrifts who sell cheap to pay for personal indulgences
7. Improvidents forced to sell to pay personal debts
8. Absentee owners who do not keep abreast of actual rental or sale values
9. Would-be investors in other fields, such as a business
10. Part-time owners whose employment has been relocated
11. Older owners who wish to liquidate and take back mortgages

AGAIN WE WILL SHOP FROM CURRENT NEWSPAPER ADS

To seek further opportunities at prevailing prices, we will select our $40,000 purchase from current newspaper ads. With income property, as with private homes, the larger the property the smaller the number of prospective buyers. Also, the number of advertised listings of larger properties will normally be less when you are ready to buy. However, in looking over a single recent issue of the *Metropolitan,* we find that in two columns of ads under "Rental Dwellings" there are fourteen listings which might be handled by our finances. Nine merit our further consideration, and five we summarily reject.

Perhaps we should first cover the drawbacks of the listings which would normally be rejected without wasting time for detailed investigation. As in Chapter 4, the ads will be quoted as written except for minor changes, such as names, addresses, and telephone numbers. In Chapters 4 and 5 we explored physical appraisals. In this and the next chapter we will concentrate more on special economic factors which spotlight a poor or good buy.

NOT ENOUGH UNITS FOR POTENTIAL PYRAMIDING

Here is an ad offering an exchange:

> JAMES near Terrace; new duplex;
> $35,000; consider exchange. Real-
> wealth. 4617 Broadway. Phone 226–
> 3784.

The words "consider exchange" might arouse your interest because of an apparently easy opportunity to trade. But we anticipate little difficulty arranging an exchange and are interested only in a good buy. Other factors being favorable, we want as many rental units as possible. In order to increase capital value, our basic objective is to increase rental value. If we buy for $35,000 and spend $5,000 for improvements, for example, a 25 per cent minimum gross profit goal would mean an added capital value of $10,000. This would require increasing the net income after improvement by $1,000 a year, or $83.33 monthly. The more units you have to work with, the easier to accomplish this. It would be much easier to increase the rental value on four apartments $20.84 each, for example, than to raise the rent on two apartments $41.68 each.

If you anticipated only a 25 per cent gross profit, as exemplified in Chapter 2, and possessed an equity in the $6,000 range, you might be satisfied with doubling your holdings from a house to a duplex. With a $10,000 equity you would normally seek a minimum of four apartments, unless you found an especially attractive buy in a 2- or 3-unit building. From the duplex we jump to a 20-unit ad, also suggesting a trade.

TOO BIG TO HANDLE

> INCOME over 12% net; modern 20-
> unit apartment building near Mercy
> Hospital; will consider trade. Phone
> 221–2568 or 225–2063.

"Modern" can mean any age from two to twenty years, or an older renovated building, just as anything under two years is "new" or "nearly new." A phone call reveals that this is a building in fair condition in the $120,000 range. The owner would take a trade of a minimum equity of $20,000 in a smaller apartment building, or would take a smaller equity, with cash to make up the $20,000. The requirement for double our equity places this property out of our sights. From twenty units we drop to twelve.

"UNRESTRICTED" MEANS SLUM PROPERTY

Here is the beginning of another rejected ad:

> An unrestricted 12-plus rooms, furnished; near Evergreen and 7th St.

"Unrestricted" in realty advertising means no racial restrictions, and it also may connote slum property that should probably be condemned. Racial restrictions are gradually softening as property owners become reconciled to having members of any race as next-door neighbors. Many Negro families, for example, have bought homes in desirable neighborhoods and are winning acceptance from fairminded neighbors.

WHAT ABOUT RENTAL INTEGRATION?

Full integration is bound to come eventually. The question is, when? There are many organized efforts by religious and other groups to overrule prejudice by reason in an attempt to alleviate segregation in housing as well as in church membership and other phases of social life. As an example, the Evanston Assembly of the World Council of Churches declared unanimously, "Segregation in all its forms is contrary to the gospel, and is incompatible with the Christian doctrine of man and with the nature of the Church of Christ."

The United Church of Christ, of which I am a member, has a standing Committee for Social Action, which is continually promoting "racial integration in the churches and in housing." So are the Commission on Law and Social Action of the American Jewish Congress, and the Department of Social Welfare of the National Council of the Churches of Christ in the U.S.A.

Others among the many organized groups which have taken strong stands in favor of housing integration are:

American Veterans Committee
Americans for Democratic Action
Catholic Interracial Council
Congress of Racial Equality
Council of Spanish-American Organizations
Episcopal Diocese of New York
National Association for the Advancement of Colored People
National Committee Against Discrimination in Housing
International Ladies Garment Workers Union
United Automobile Workers
Urban League of Greater New York
Women's City Club of New York

The foregoing, along with scores of other organizations, have endorsed state and Federal bills to prohibit discrimination in housing rentals and sales. Their efforts have culminated in the 1968 Supreme Court decision that housing discrimination is unconstitutional.

HOW ARE RENTAL UNITS AFFECTED?

Integration has progressed smoothly in some housing developments, spread as far apart as Honolulu and New York City. Metropolitan Life's 8,700-family Stuyvesant Town housing development in New York City has taken in several score Negro families without apparent repercussions. Including Metropolitan's project, over a billion dollars has been spent in New York State alone to build housing subject to antisegregation laws. This would indicate that forced integration does not discourage builders. Rental integration has been tried in many cities besides New York and Honolulu, including public housing on a country-wide basis and specifically in Chicago, Philadelphia, San Diego, San Francisco, Seattle and St. Louis.

Despite praiseworthy efforts such as those cited above, in many areas human nature will tend to keep desirable housing on a restricted basis for some time. Tenants in general find it easy to move if they are dissatisfied. In many areas they move out when a member of a minority race moves in. Rental owners as a group would be more receptive to integration if they did not fear such tenant reaction and the possibility of a resulting income loss. Where housing is scarcer than in most areas—as in New York, where rent controls are still in effect—prejudiced tenants will not leave so quickly, and integration is easier to accomplish.

NET INCOME MAY INCREASE AFTER INTEGRATION

In many examples I have studied, where an open-minded apartment-house owner has attempted integration, the following pattern has been general:

1. A member of a minority race is permitted to rent an apartment.
2. Some prejudiced tenants move out immediately.
3. Within a few months most of the other tenants move out.
4. The owner suffers a period of heavy vacancies and reduces rents.
5. Eventually the building is filled with minority race members.
6. Rents are then restored to previous levels, or in many cases increased.
7. Services may be curtailed, thereby increasing the net income.
8. Where services are maintained, income usually increases.

Integration progresses slowly. Although minorities have improved their housing, little desegregation has taken place in many such instances. From an investment standpoint, the results are a temporary income loss which eventually stabilizes and often develops into an increased net.

BUY ONLY BASICALLY SOUND PROPERTY

Getting back to the Evergreen ad, you stand a better chance of prospering if you hold to the previously quoted rule of owning and improving property that you would choose to live in if you were on the budget of the prospective tenant.

Slum property often pays the greatest return for the money invested, but may offer little opportunity for capital enhancement, since capital values are more apt to decrease than increase. Making improvements or building anew where an entire area is undergoing rehabilitation, as in many cities, should be profitable. But building an isolated desirable property in a slum is like building a mansion next to a garbage dump. The mansion does not increase the value of the dump, but the dump drastically slashes the intrinsic value of the mansion.

This ad points to a typical example of a slum dwelling basically unsound when built and now deteriorated past reclamation except at prohibitive cost. The instance of unsound construction prevails even with some newer buildings, as with jerry-built, "temporary" government housing, which was intended to last only till the end of the war. Most slums would be demolished if building codes were rigidly adhered to, a contingency that will probably be enforced eventually. From the viewpoint of good conscience and of good economics, you would be wise to restrict your purchases to basically sound property suffering only surface deterioration.

The "Return on Equity" Gimmick

Another rejected ad dangles a special bait for the uninitiated:

> A brand-new 6-unit apartment house;
> always full; 18% return on $15,000
> equity; near Parkway district. Phone
> 357–4021; or 229–0452.

Here is an apparently new building with the chief gimmick an "18 per cent return on $15,000 equity." In buying single homes and duplexes, often owner-occupied, our basic valuation was the gross monthly income multiplied by 100. On desirable income property of four units or more the generally accepted yardstick is the fixed annual net income multiplied by 10. This would mean that the annual net income would be 10 per cent of the sale price. This annual net is arrived at, as a regular practice, by deducting fixed expenses from the gross income and does not account for repair costs, vacancies, and depreciable capital expenditures. These additional factors will usually leave an actual net of about 6 per cent for the average property. All these figures are based by conscientious dealers on the total cost of the property, rather than on the down payment, which would be the original equity.

An 18 per cent return on a $15,000 equity would be $2,700. The property in question would be valued at ten times this net figure, or $27,000. For a quick check we phone the first listed number and ask the full price of the property. The answer is $60,000. On this price the fixed net should be $6,000, showing that the property from an income standpoint is overpriced more than double. Any ad that blows up the return from the equity should be ignored, because such advertising is almost invariably designed to catch the unwary by covering up the fact that the net income is low in relation to the total purchase price.

BUY PROPERTY ON THE BASIS OF THE ACTUAL NET INCOME

The net income may be far below normal because the building cost considerably more to erect than the actual income would warrant. Although replacement costs are an additional check on whether a listing represents a good value, the cost of replacement never guarantees income. Types of property for which rents seldom pay construction costs are luxury housing built in low-income districts, middle-class housing built in the slums, and any housing built next to tanneries, dumps, and isolated or other shunned locations.

Property should be bought on the basis of actual net income and only if it cannot be replaced for less than the valuation determined by the income. It should never be bought on the basis that it has cost a certain amount to build and therefore will carry a certain income. There are many white elephants of both old and new construction that cannot pay expenses. Many apartments were built during and after World War II with inflated FHA mortgages which exceeded building costs. Because of excessive costs, rents, to pay even a modest investment return, have been set at more than potential tenants would pay. The vacancy rates in these projects have gone as high as 50 per cent and the incomes have been insufficient even to pay off the mortgages.

These uneconomical practices are far from normal examples of private enterprise. They are typical of business and investment under government supervision, and distorted by wartime pressures:

AN OVERPRICED NEW PROPERTY

> 6 New Units—Brockhaven. $10,000 Down—Price $64,000. Payments $410 —Income $610. Annual income $7320. Tenants pay all utilities; 6 carports and storage spaces; fully occupied; best rental area in county; near dozens of industrial plants; close to schools, shopping and transportation.

Owner leaving area. You'll seldom
find a better return on investment.
Call 633–2714, or 859–8122.

This property appears to be within our price and financing range. It
might prove sound from an income standpoint and seems worth investigating. Our previous appraisal of the Balmy Terrace cottage in Chapter 4 showed there was less chance of increasing capital value on
newer property. What are the prospects with this new property? As a
check, we phone the first-listed number. The owner's wife answers
and gives the address, and we journey to the outlying Brockhaven
district for a personal inspection.

We ring the bell of apartment 1, marked "Manager," and are
greeted by the owner's wife. After a few leading questions she tells us
that the building is just six months old and was built by her husband,
who is a general contractor. When they sell they plan to move to a
different section, closer to town, where the husband is building another apartment house. Apparently here is a contractor who builds for
speculation. We can be fairly sure that he has built at minimum cost,
using the cheapest construction where it will not be too apparent. We
can expect this to be camouflaged by a few showy items like the
wrought-iron sign over the front door:

The Brockhaven

We ask if the $610 advertised income is net or gross and are told it
is gross income. There are two 2-room apartments renting for $85
and four 3-room apartments renting for $110. All are unfurnished
except for stoves, making the rents about as high as possible in this
outlying suburban area. The annual net after deducting taxes, insurance, water and scavenger service, paid by the owner, comes to about
$5,400. This means 8.4 per cent net on their price. "Dirt cheap," says
the wife, for such a nice, new property.

The income figures include the full rental value of $110 for the
owner's apartment. Since the owner also serves as manager, allowance
for a manager's services are omitted, although this item is normally
included in property of this size. With 6 units a tenant-manager should
receive between 20 and 30 per cent rent concession.

As a further check we ask what the total floor space is and are told
about 3,200 square feet. Allowing $6,000 for the lot, $8,000 for the
6 carports, paving and landscaping, and $12 per square foot for
apartment construction, we figure that the property could be repro-

duced new for $52,400, including contractor's fees. The income is fair for the cost of construction, but low for the listed price. If we are interested in this type of property, we might as well build it ourselves. Building new apartments or other rental property might well be considered after gaining experience. But for the new investor the ramifications of new construction are far riskier than improving older property. An experienced owner I know confines his purchases, for example, to properties at least three years old, where rents are proved but improvements can be made in operations and updating.

A HOTEL IS A BUSINESS MORE THAN AN INVESTMENT

We next choose our hottest potential ad, a listing of 20 units which we might be able to buy with our equity of approximately $10,000, after negotiation.

> ASKING $12,000 down! Grossing $2,000 monthly! Twenty rentals! Call 232–4201.

The salesman gives us an address in a good rental district. He says, "The total asking price is $92,500. The owners are giving up a hot deal only because they are moving out of the state and can no longer supervise the property. They have set a firm figure and the purchase price is not subject to negotiation; but the down payment may be, depending on the buyer's experience and responsibility. You can look the deal over and take it as offered, or leave it. You can make enough net profit to get your down payment back in less than two years, and from there on in you would be riding the gravy train. The place is such a gold mine it would pay $600 a month net over and above all expenses, including the payment on the mortgage."

It seems too good to be true, to be able to buy this income and 20 rental units in a desirable district with only a $12,000 down payment requested. As soon as we drive up in front of the property we are immediately disillusioned. Instead of an apartment house, it turns out to be, according to the sign in front:

MARGIE-JOE HOTEL, DINING ROOM
HOME COOKED MEALS

Any but an experienced restaurant or hotel operator should reject such a setup regardless of how attractive the figures appear. The rate of failures among new restaurant owners is considerably higher than the four-out-of-five average previously cited for all businesses.

The 20 rentals are all hotel rooms, not apartments. In order to arrive at the proposition he had outlined, the salesman had figured that all rooms would be full at hotel rates the year round, that the dining room would operate on the basis of full board for the twenty occupants, and that the owners would handle personally without salary not only the rentals but the cooking and serving of meals.

We mentioned that at fair rentals, in a good district, and with capable management an apartment house can be operated at close to 100 per cent capacity the year round. This is far from true of even the best-operated hotels and restaurants, which are susceptible to seasonal, work-day, and weekend business fluctuations. The hotel should have been advertised with other hotels under "Business Opportunities," rather than under "Rental Dwellings." Hotel operations are basically a form of business employment, not a form of investment. On income tax returns apartment income under normal operations is listed under INCOME FROM RENTS. Hotel income is listed under PROFIT (OR LOSS) FROM BUSINESS. The tax collector thus anticipates the possibility of loss.

No Chance for Capital Gain

Discouraged with this 20-unit listing, we reverse our field and tackle next a 5-unit ad where the owner offers to trade:

> A—Bequette Realty Co.
> Start right with us. Investigate the following property offered for your approval.
> 6-year-old stucco 5-plex, 4 large 4s and one 5-room; near Midway and Elysian Ave. May take home as part payment. Call Jim Dollman. Phone 345–3940; evenings 273–8147.

Investigation shows a fair income for the sale price, and workable financing. But the building and grounds are already in good condition and offer little opportunity for capital enhancement. We move to a 4-unit listing.

"4 FULL 5S" PROVE TO BE EMPTY AND DISPLACED

A—James K. Powers Co. Broadway
at Iona. Phone 329–0467.
FLORADALE DISTRICT
One of Metropole's finest apartment
houses, 4 full 5s in perfect condition;
11% return, excellent financing.
We have several other fine listings
in Metropole. Shown by appointment
only. Phone 329–0467; evenings 448–
2742.

The realtor gives us the address, with the admonition that the interior is not to be inspected without an appointment. At our request he gives us a statement, shown on the next page, listing the rents and expenses. There is good reason for the fine print at the bottom of the statement, intended to nullify the broker's responsibility for omissions of expenses, or discrepancies of income. Omitted in this case are customary manager's expense, and water and scavenger service, usually paid by the owner in this area even if the tenants pay other utilities. We will want to check these expenses and also how the actual rents compare with the listed schedule. Possibly the price and down payment can be pulled down considerably after verifying these items.

This is the number of units we expect to buy, and the $9,375 annual net is good for the possible purchase price. But the rentals seem excessive. We would have no further interest except for the statement that the 5-room units are full, which indicates the rents are at fair market levels.

On our arrival at the property, a newly painted 2-story stucco building, it is a few minutes after 1 P.M. A painter in white uniform is just approaching the front door. We intercept him and ask if this is the apartment house advertised for sale by the Powers Company. The painter says it is and he is just completing a bit of touching up. Did we want to see the building?

There are no curtains or drapes at the windows, which eye us with an empty look. We ask the painter if anyone is living there. He says no, he is just finishing a complete painting job, inside and out, and nobody has moved in yet. However, he would be glad to show us around if we are interested.

JAMES K. POWERS CO., REALTORS
Metropole, Columbia

BROADWAY AT IONA
Phone 329–0467

We Sell the Earth—Complete Real Estate and Insurance
Service

FLORADALE APARTMENTS

GROSS INCOME, ANNUAL		$10,800.00
Monthly income $900.00		
Four 5-room apartments at $225 per month		
ANNUAL EXPENSES		1,424.71
Taxes	$1,236.33	
Insurance	188.38	
TOTAL	$1,424.71	
NET ANNUAL INCOME		$9,375.29

PRICE: $85,000.00

FINANCING: Will take $15,000.00 down
or equivalent equity in smaller property.
Balance $500.00 per month, 7% interest.

SHOWN BY APPOINTMENT ONLY

The information above has been obtained from sources we deem to be reliable, and while we do not guarantee it, we believe it to be correct. The acceptance of this statement obligates the person accepting it to conduct all negotiations regarding this property through James K. Powers Co., Realtors. We assume no liability for representations as to values or for errors or omissions in this statement.

"FULL 5S" HAS A DOUBLE MEANING

We mention that the ad stated "4 full 5s" and ask how it happens that all units are empty.

"The owner won't rent a thing," says the painter. "Wants to keep it looking new for the next owner. But they are full fives. They have a dining room, besides two bedrooms, and a living room, and a kitchen. You don't count the bath as a room, of course. These junior fives that some people call fives don't have a dining room—just a breakfast nook. That's why these are legitimate full fives."

The lot is completely devoid of landscaping, with roughened terrain having the no-man's-land look of a vacant lot on which a new building is being constructed. Yet the building shows unmistakable signs that

this cannot be new construction. There are old-fashioned floor furnaces in each apartment, 6-inch baseboards, picture moldings on the
walls a foot below the ceilings, which are ten feet high, glass doors
between the living rooms and dining rooms. All are contrary to new-
construction practices, and they reveal age as surely as wrinkles on a
woman's hands and throat. We needle the painter for additional information.

We tell the painter his paint job looks very good and then ask why
there is no garden of any kind as would be expected on a lot with a
building this old. The painter says the owner is planning to landscape
the lot later if the building doesn't sell without it. There isn't any
garden because this was a vacant lot until a few months ago. The
building was moved from its former location in the path of a new
expressway.

We remark on the improbability of moving such a large building,
and the painter says they had to split it down the middle in order to
get it through the streets. The building used to have an all-wooden
exterior and has been completely stuccoed to cover up the dissection
and cracks caused by moving.

"You've certainly done a good job slicking everything up," we
compliment the painter. "You seem to know all about the owner's
plans. Do you know him very well?"

"I ought to. I am the owner."

"Well, you have developed a nice building here. But why don't you
start collecting rents instead of leaving everything vacant?"

REALTY STATEMENTS MAY NOWHERE
APPROACH REALITY

"Why, I'm making so much money on some of my other projects, I
don't need to fuss with collecting rents. Just have to pay it back out in
income taxes. So I'm taking no chances on a bunch of careless tenants
messing up my new paint. Besides, if you buy the place, you would be
better off to pick your own tenants."

"Don't you think two hundred and twenty-five dollars is too high to
rent?"

"Not a bit. Had lots of people stop in here perfectly willing to pay
that much and more, even while I was still working on the place. But I
wouldn't give in to them. No sir! Going to leave the whole business
vacant till I sell to the next owner."

Obviously the foregoing barefaced statements nowhere approach reality. They merely serve to warn that it is poor business to accept any information at face value. It is always wise to heed the Roman law of *caveat emptor*, "Let the buyer beware." Yankee traders translate this into "Look at the horse's teeth before you buy."

Here is a prime example of how reality may differ from realty statements or advertising. The apartments are about the same dimensions as our A Avenue house. They are not as modern and would not rent for over $150 per month. One hundred forty dollars would be closer to their realistic market level. Anyone would be foolhardy indeed to accept at face value the stated rent schedule on a completely vacant building. There is not a single actual rent to check against except on a neighborhood basis. Probably the only potential purchaser will be someone who thinks he is getting a generous allowance for his traded building, failing to realize that he is giving his property away and paying an exorbitant boot.

While some of the offerings you find will be obviously poor buys, not worth investigating, your average shopping should turn up several acceptable properties.

10. CHOOSING YOUR SECOND PROPERTY

Since the vacant 4-unit Floradale Apartments have proved disappointing, we raise our sights an additional unit. This time we select an ad covering a 5-unit property:

THIS IS IT

> NEAR Mercy Hospital; modern five
> units; income approximately $5,000;
> $42,500. Small payment. Trade. Mr.
> Murga, 2947 Broadway; Phone 743–
> 5232.

This offering might be right up our alley. We phone the broker and ask what he means by a small payment. He tells us the owner is a widow anxious to sell. For the down payment she will take as little as

$5,000 cash or a sound trade up to $10,000 in value. We agree to meet in front of the property, which is on B Boulevard, a residential street in a good rental district in East Metropole.

A gold-lettered plate-glass sign hanging from the front-porch ceiling of a 2-story building reads:

> ## BELVEDERE APTS.

There are three structures on a 50-by-150-foot level lot. Behind the main building is a one-story cottage, and in its rear on an alley is a one-story garage. The structures are about twenty years old, according to the broker, Mr. Murga. The two-story building in front is of white clapboard and consists of four 5-room flats, all furnished. The two front steps and the porch deck are built of terrazzo-surfaced concrete, badly cracked, with an irregular pattern of polished marble chips. The front porch and the balcony above it on the second floor are protected on the sides by clapboard running 30 inches high. The balcony has a 2-foot picket railing in front.

On each side of the front steps is a 3-foot-high, 18-inch-square stone pillar, capped with a 2-foot-square concrete slab 4 inches thick. The pillars are slightly off balance. Large cracks between the steps and the porch, and between the back of the porch and the building, indicate that the foundation under the porch and the steps has settled.

The pitched roof is hipped in front and has a small gable. Its composition shingles seem fairly new. The eaves overhang about two feet and present a barnlike appearance, with no ceiling to cover the exposed rafters.

The lawn in front needs cutting. Shrubbery grows rank on the sides and in front of the building, but the yard on the whole appears well planned. It would be suitable without change except for a good trimming.

The four-car garage on the rear alley is clapboard-sided, with three car spaces in one enclosure and a fourth car space separately enclosed, and with a tool- and workroom adjoining. The owner lives in the green shingled cottage between the garage and the main building. All three buildings are badly in need of exterior paint. The salesman says the owner's husband recently died from a heart attack. The price includes the furniture in the four flats, but not that in the cottage.

The climbing roses in front of the cottage have rambled so far out of bounds that the shoots over the front door have to be pushed aside to gain entrance. Mr. Murga introduces us to the owner, Mrs. Ballcryn, a stout, comely woman of forty. The absence of make-up accentuates the dark circles under her eyes. The cottage has been recently redecorated inside, except for the kitchen. The kitchen is of average size and presents a modern appearance, with ample cabinets, tile drainboards, and new inlaid linoleum on the floor. The bathroom has a modern flush-mounted tub, with a chrome shower overhead. There are a fairly large bedroom and living room, and the latter has a folding wall bed. The dining room is compact, with two built-in china closets. The whole interior is in good condition, except for the kitchen's needing a painting.

As soon as we finish inspecting the cottage, Mr. Murga starts out the door. He frowns impatiently when we ask Mrs. Ballcryn why she is selling. Salesmen often try to discourage much discussion between principals, so we ignore him and give our attention to Mrs. Ballcryn.

"I would like to keep the property, because it's easy to look after and pays good. But it's too depressing to stay here where I just keep being reminded of my husband. He passed away in the night in that bed with me beside him, and I couldn't sleep there since. Have to use the wall bed. I plan to go back to teaching school in Metropole, but I want to move to a different location and forget about this place.

"My husband was a farm-equipment salesman. We planned to stay in the cottage and live off the income from the four flats after he retired. My husband intended to fix the whole place up, inside and out. But it seemed that being on the road and fishing and hunting used up most of his spare time; so he took the last couple of years to make the cottage decent enough to live in. It was very run-down when we bought it five years ago. It took him three years, working occasional weekends, to completely remodel one of the flats, and that and the cottage were all he got around to. The other three flats were renting for $90 a month, but we rented the remodeled one for $125 as soon as it was fixed up."

WE SUGGEST THE POSSIBILITY OF A TRADE

We say we will have to inspect the remodeled flat and also the others, and we ask Mrs. Ballcryn if she would consider taking in trade a nice house in top condition. She asks how many rooms it has. We say five. She says she would like to look at our property and then she could tell whether she would be interested in trading. She wants a house with two nice bedrooms, as she plans to have a teacher friend live with her to keep from being lonesome. We assure her there are two good-sized bedrooms, both newly decorated, so she and her friend would both be pleased.

Mr. Murga asks how much we want for our property. We say $19,500, and that it is spick-and-span, just like new. Mrs. Ballcryn says that if we want to make a trade we should just let her know, and she could go right over and look at our place. We say we will first have to think over the possibilities, after making a more complete inspection of Mrs. Ballcryn's property. We can then get in touch with her or Mr. Murga. Mrs. Ballcryn says that if we have any further questions at any time she will be glad to answer them.

THREE FLATS NEED MODERNIZING

The lower flat renting for $90, Number 1, badly needs paper and paint. The condition is comparable to that of our A Avenue house before it was rehabilitated, but the flat appears to be a fcw years older in style. The kitchen is most in need of decoration, with faded wallpaper hanging loose from the walls and the ceiling. The kitchen is compact, with a small breakfast nook at the end. The refrigerator and kitchen range are fairly new. Off the kitchen is a service porch with a double laundry tub. The service porch opens on a sheltered backstairs landing.

At the other end of the kitchen is a doorway into the dining room. In the center of the dining room is a large oval table of oak, darkened by many coats of stained varnish and surrounded by six sturdy oak chairs. A large closet projects three feet out and occupies most of the inside wall of the dining room, opposite the windows. At one end of the closet is space for hanging clothes. Most of the closet is occupied by a bulky double bed, with heavy cast-iron framing and folding legs. The wall behind the closet is finished with the same oak paneling as the dining room. Apparently the boxed-in folding bed was built as an afterthought to the original design.

We ask if all the flats are arranged the same, including the wall-bed arrangement. Mr. Murga answers yes, in all but the remodeled one next door, from which the folding bed had been removed. Each flat already has two bedrooms and there is little need for a folding bed.

In the dining room, between the kitchen door and another doorway, is a built-in buffet which projects eighteen inches and runs from floor to ceiling. Between the buffet and the other door is a large circulating gas heater. The other door leads into a small hallway, which opens into the master bedroom and the bathroom. The bathtub is the old-fashioned type, standing on cast-iron legs, with exposed galvanized pipe running to the overhead shower. The furniture in the master bedroom is in fair condition. In a smaller second bedroom at the rear there is a couch that can be opened into a double bed.

At the end of the dining room, opposite the buffet, are two 4-foot sliding doors, forming an 8-foot-wide doorway, which leads into the living room. Gangly light fixtures hang from the living-room and dining-room ceilings. The living-room sofa is lumpy and the upholstery is worn through at the arms. All floors are hardwood in fair condition, except for the kitchen and bathroom, both of which are covered with worn linoleum.

In the two remaining flats renting for $90, on the second floor, conditions compare with the $90 flat on the first floor. None has as dilapidated a sofa, however, nor are there showers over the other tubs. In the lower flats the original stoves and refrigerators have been replaced with new ones in recent years. The kitchen in Number 3 on the second floor has a small rangette, instead of a range, and an archaic GE refrigerator with the coils exposed on top. Number 4 on the second floor has a spider-legged, black-surfaced range which looks more ancient than the one we replaced at A Avenue.

One Flat Is a Ready-Made Model for Modernization

In the $125 flat, Number 2 on the first floor, we have a ready-made model of what can be accomplished with the identical floor plans in the other three flats. The modernized flat has been attractively furnished and decorated throughout. The sliding doors and the partition between the living and dining rooms have been removed. So have the cumbersome wall bed and its closet and the built-in floor-to-ceiling buffet in the dining room. This surgery has created an appearance of greatly increased spaciousness.

The circulating heater has been exchanged for a large wall furnace. There are a new range and a new refrigerator in the kitchen. New inlaid linoleum has been installed in the kitchen, and a new ceramic-tile drainboard and splashboard for the sink.

A new, completely square peach-colored bathtub has been installed, surrounded by ceramic tile on three sides to a height of five feet. An all-tile stall shower has been built alongside. Ceramic tile has been laid also on the bathroom floor. Opposite the tub and shower, the washbasin has been enclosed in a built-in cabinet, which extends three feet to the side to provide a make-up bar. A square mirror fills the wall above the make-up area, and a full-length mirror covers the door leading to the master bedroom.

An automatic washer has been installed on the service porch. The overhanging lights have been completely removed from the living room, and the outlet concealed by plastering over, then stippling and painting the entire ceiling. All other electric fixtures have been replaced, in the kitchen and bathroom with fluorescent lighting.

Although we would modify the changes made, the present $125 rent and the appearance of the renovated flat show the potentialities in remodeling the other three flats. Here the owner worked out a basically sound improvement, then bogged down. If he had changed from his slow Do-It-Yourself Freight to the Contract Express, all four flats would have been remodeled long before this at a good profit.

A Review of Financing and Income

Outside, we ask how it is planned to work out the additional financing if the owner is willing to take as little as $5,000 cash. Mr. Murga says that either the present $21,500 insurance-company loan can be taken over or a new first mortgage of $25,000, with the same 6 per cent interest, can be obtained. In any case Mrs. Ballcryn is willing to take a second mortgage to make up the difference. She is asking only 6 per cent interest, which is very reasonable for a second loan. Mrs. Ballcryn is not in need of any cash, as her husband left her a few thousand dollars' insurance.

We ask how the "income approximately $5,000" in the ad was arrived at. Since the 3 $90 flats plus the one for $125 come to $395 monthly, or $4,740 a year, this apparently is a gross instead of a net figure, is it not? The salesman says no, the $5,000 represents net income, because the rental value of the cottage is figured at $75 and the fixed expenses come to only $68 a month. The tenants pay all utilities except water, scavenger service, and hall lights.

He says that if we take the $68 expenses from the $75 cottage rent we get an additional $7 a month net income, making a total of $4,824 as the actual annual net. "And that doesn't account for the fact that the three flats now renting for ninety dollars could easily be rented for one hundred and twenty-five apiece without touching them." Mr. Murga gives us a written statement of income and expenses.

BELVEDERE APARTMENTS
Statement of Income and Expenses

GROSS INCOME, 1 Cottage and 4 Flats, all furnished:

3 flats, Nos. 1, 3, 4, @ $90	$270.00	
1 flat, No. 2	125.00	
Cottage	75.00	
Total Monthly Rent	$470.00	
	× 12	
Total Annual Rent	$5,640.00	$5,640.00

ANNUAL EXPENSES, Actual, for previous 12 months:

Fire insurance	$ 94.74	
Taxes	535.16	
Water and Scavenger Service	163.20	
Hall lights	28.00	
Total Annual Expenses	$821.10	821.10
NET ANNUAL INCOME		$4,818.90

"The flat now renting for one hundred and twenty-five ought to get one hundred and fifty. This proves a one-hundred-and-twenty-five-dollar value as is for the others," states Mr. Murga. "There certainly isn't more than twenty-five dollars' difference in rental value between the fixed-up flat and the others."

WE KEEP CONTROL OF OUR PROPERTY

We tell Mr. Murga we will think the whole deal over and might later be willing to make an offer for a trade. Mr. Murga asks the amount of the outstanding loan on our house, and we tell him $6,436.

"You said you were asking nineteen thousand five hundred. Then you figure you have about a thirteen-thousand-dollar equity, eh?"

"That's pretty close."

"Well, let me take a look at your property now, and we'll see whether we can work out a deal."

The broker attempts to pin us down and get a commitment to list our property for sale or trade with him exclusively for six months. This might prevent our working out the best arrangement, because we would be denied the right to free-lance in search of better buys if we failed to arrive at a satisfactory bargain. If we were interested in an outright sale rather than in trading, we might give a broker an exclusive listing to compensate for his advertising our property and giving it special attention. A broker often will ask for an "exclusive" for three to six months, and sometimes for a year. However, it is usually unwise for an owner to agree to more than ninety days, for the listing can always be renewed if the broker's efforts are considered satisfactory. On the other hand, if the property is tied up for more than three months, a broker often has a tendency to put the listing in the back of his files and devote his attention to short-term listings, or listings soon to expire, on which his time is limited. Here again is an instance of an owner's taking care that time works in his favor.

Some brokers attempt to take property control completely out of the owner's hands into theirs, so that they can better manipulate deals to their advantage rather than the owner's. Since we wish no strings on our freedom to look for other property, we agree to no exclusive listing with Mr. Murga. We tell him that we definitely would not sell and give up our present income except to trade for larger property. We will not show our property to anyone until we work out in our mind a satisfactory offer for a trade in which our property would constitute the down payment.

However, we agree to an appointment at our residence the next evening, in case we have any further questions or are ready to write up a tentative offer. We wait in our car, jotting notes, until the broker drives off; then we go back to the meter box to search for clues regarding age.

VERIFYING THE AGE

Mr. Murga said the buildings were about twenty years old. Although they appear to be in sound condition, certain telltale items like the older-type, terrazzo-surfaced front porch and the leggy bathtubs date the age closer to thirty or forty. Salesmen are quick to point out new buildings, and they may boast like a centenarian of unusual age. But of buildings that are neither new nor antique, realtors can be as evasive about ages as middle-aged women. For a building up to five years old typical salesmen may say, "It is almost new," and for one between five and ten, "only three or four years old." Between eleven and twenty will be described as "around ten," and between twenty and fifty "about twenty years old." An age between fifty and a hundred comes "in the twenty-five year range." For a house over a hundred, apologies may change to an accolade of "a well-preserved antique."

A check of the meter box shows not an inspection card in sight, as they apparently have all been removed. Down in the lower corner of the meter box, however, behind an electric meter, we spy a triangular segment of yellow cardboard, held by one tack. With a pocketknife we pry the tack and paper loose, then edge it free from the corner. The piece of cardboard turns out to be the lower section of an inspection card. Alongside the signature of "Jno Gilhooley, Framing Inspector" is a blurred date, "August —, 1924," which means the building is forty-one years old.

THE OWNER DIVULGES FURTHER INFORMATION

Mrs. Ballcryn notices us pass her cottage, opens her door and asks if there is anything else we would like to see or know. We say we would like to learn more about the present loan arrangements. What are the present payments? Mrs. Ballcryn invites us into the cottage and gets her passbook out of a desk drawer.

"The payments are two hundred dollars a month, and here's what I still owe." She points to the last balance of $21,457.58. "This loan is from the Double Security Insurance Company."

We note that the original loan was for $25,000 and that the interest rate is 6 per cent, as Mr. Murga has indicated. Mrs. Ballcryn continues, "The Double Security Company wanted us to take out mortgage insurance. Would have cost us only one-half per cent more tacked onto our interest, six and a half instead of six per cent. My husband wanted it so that the loan would be paid up and give me enough income to get along without working in case he died. But I told him no, we might as well save the extra ten dollars a month. I wish I had let my husband decide. He was so thoughtful, only thinking of me."

After an interval Mrs. Ballcryn volunteers that in order to make a quick sale she is willing to sell the place for what it cost, including their improvements, even though they got a good buy to start with. She doesn't expect to make a penny. We ask what she paid originally.

She says it is pretty hard to tell exactly because they traded in their home, but she figures that they were out about $32,000. In addition, they spent a little over $5,000 remodeling the Number 2 flat, buying new furniture, and fixing up the cottage. Of course the quoted price of $42,500 includes Mr. Murga's commission, which he said would be about $2,000. And Mr. Murga said they would have to come down from their asking price, so they put it up a little to start with.

From our inspection of the property and our discussion with Mrs. Ballcryn, all indications point to the probability of negotiating a favorable trade which will advance us one more step on the realty road to a million.

CHECKING THE POSSIBILITIES

Now that we have selected a suitable larger property, we are ready to determine the fair market value on which to offer a trade. Values are not usually stated in a trade offer, as either there will be an even trade or boot will be given by one of the traders. Some realtors attempt to bypass entirely the establishment of an actual value on the property to be assumed. They can manipulate the mechanics of a trade so that you may think you are buying low and selling high, when you are selling cheap and buying at an exorbitant price.

I know of many trades which were favorable to both parties, and of other deals where the neophyte trader lost his shirt because he thought he was making a fortune on his own property. In the next chapter, therefore, we will explore in more detail some of the mechanics of working out a trade. At this point we will further assess the possibilities presented by the B Boulevard property.

The Yankee trader trying to get rid of a balky horse still takes a good look at the other horse to make sure it isn't spavined, smitten with the heaves, or about ready to collapse into the glue yard. It is most essential before you make a trade offer to establish in your own mind the fair market values of the property you are selling and the property you are buying. We have already figured $16,000 as the fair market value of our flats. What is the fair market value of Mrs. Ballcryn's property?

We mentioned that building costs do not necessarily determine income values. Neither are they established by purchase-plus-improvement costs, as with Mrs. Ballcryn's $37,000 figure, but on the basis of actual net income, modified by the condition of the property. What is a reasonable valuation on the present net income? How much will it cost to put the buildings in good condition?

FIGURING THE NET INCOME

To get the net-income base, we take the present listed gross income of $470, including the stated $75 rent for the cottage, and deduct the fixed expenses. Actually, however, the cottage should have approximately the same rental value as the $90 flats, being in better shape, but having one less bedroom.

The stated fixed expenses come to $68.43 monthly for fire insurance, taxes, water and scavenger service, and hall lights. To this we add an estimated cost for managing the property, including janitor and yard work. These are customary costs that should be included with fixed expenses, although they are often overlooked, as in this and other examples previously cited. We figure that a competent resident manager, who should live in the rear cottage or the $90 lower flat, could be obtained for a rental allowance of about 30 per cent, or $30. The manager's duties would include collecting rents, keeping up the halls and yard, and handling minor repairs. This rental allowance would make the total fixed expenses $98.43.

Deducting these fixed expenses from the $470 gross would leave a net monthly income of $371.57, or $4,458.84 a year. The present rents seem somewhat under the market, even in the units' present condition. Even so, and although the building is basically sound, the fact that it is badly in need of paint inside and out would warrant a 10 per cent discount from gross income to cover repairs and vacancies. These are normally inevitable with increasing competition, even with low rents, until considerable painting and decorating are completed. The discount would leave a net-income valuation of $3,895 a year. Multiplying this by 10 would give a fair market value of $38,950, close to $39,000. This is $2,000 over what the present owner paid for original cost plus improvements.

Mrs. Ballcryn's $37,000 cost, for which she is willing to sell, would represent a fair buy, as long as remodeling can be worked out profitably. Although Mrs. Ballcryn expects to receive her cost, plus the commission cost, she has also received free rent for five years, plus a net income. She will no doubt settle on a total price of $37,000, which might be taken as a tentative purchase figure.

FIGURING THE COST OF REMODELING

Our next step is to figure the probable cost of improvements which will put the buildings in condition for a profitable resale. In this case the Number 2 flat makes a ready-made model which can serve as a reliable guide, since its improvement has resulted in a $35 increase in rent. What yardstick should we use as a basis for modification?

Mrs. Ballcryn has stated that $5,000 was spent on the property, plus her husband's labor, in order to raise the rent $35 on the one flat. Since the widow has said the cottage was quite dirty and uninhabitable when the Ballcryns moved in, it might be assumed that its rental value has been increased about $15. This would make a total increase in income valuation of $50 monthly, or $600 annually. Since there would be little effect on expenses, this would increase the sale valuation ten times as much, or $6,000.

Estimating the value of Mr. Ballcryn's labor at $1,000 would increase the value of expenditures to $6,000, or a $1 expenditure for each $1 of increased valuation. The expense has resulted in a 10 per cent return, a fair increased income. But it compares with income from new construction and does not enhance resale value over actual costs. There is obviously no profit in reselling for $1 an item with an original cost of $1.

One of the greatest mistakes of investors is to put more money into a property than can be regained, figuring that the investment will be retained forever. Circumstances are always subject to change. The Ballcryns intended to keep the property for retirement income and made expenditures from which only a nominal return could be expected. Their case points up the general rule that income property should be handled with the thought that it might eventually be sold or traded.

For a profitable resale, a $6,000 increased value should be earned for not more than $3,000, holding to our yardstick of making at least $2 for every $1 spent. In reverse this means the Ballcryns' expenditure of $5,000 plus personal labor is worth only $3,000 to us, assuming we bought the building before remodeling. The foregoing analysis signifies that we must modify the Ballycryns' changes so that our cost will result in an increased value of at least $2 for every $1 spent. We will eliminate all unprofitable expenditures, arrive at resulting costs, then compare costs with potential income.

A high proportion of the $5,000 was spent on expensive new furniture. After each flat is remodeled, its rent will be raised. If the tenant moves we would plan to remove all furniture except for a stove and a refrigerator. Thus the only new furniture to consider would be a new refrigerator for one flat, and new stoves for two flats. Mrs. Ballcryn probably would exchange her stove and refrigerator in the cottage for our stove and refrigerator at the A Avenue house.

We would make comparable changes in internal appearance, as in the Number 2 flat, except for eliminating or modifying nonproductive changes. We would plan a similar change in painting and decorating and would remove the built-in beds and buffets from all three flats. Changes in electrical and plumbing fixtures would be similar, but we would omit the stall shower. A new bathtub with modern shower overhead would be satisfactory. We would use ceramic tile for the sink drainboard and splashboard only, and we would specify marbled tileboard around the bathtub and plastic linoleum on the bathroom floor.

Rather than install automatic washers, we would remove the existing one as soon as the present tenant vacates. A tenant will overload equipment more than an owner. Tenants who desire automatic or other washers for individual use expect to provide them. An automatic washer for rental purposes not only results in unwarranted initial expense but also will be a source of excessive repairs. They should be installed only on a self-liquidating, coin-operated, community-laundry basis, where the income pays for capital and repair expenses.

From our experience in the A Avenue house, and accounting for our projected modifications, we estimate that the interiors of the three flats could be put in desirable shape for about $1,000 each. The exteriors of the main building, the cottage and the garage could be revamped for $3,000, making a total of $6,000. Adding this to our tentative purchase price of $37,000 would give a total rehabilitated cost of $43,000. A 25 per cent gross profit on this cost would be $10,750, resulting in a target resale figure of $53,750, which we round to $54,000.

Can We Resell for a 25 Per Cent Profit?

Our next step is to figure whether we could sell for a minimum gross profit of 25 per cent after modernization. We have a made-to-order income yardstick, as well as a modernization model, in the Number 2 flat renting for $125 furnished. We could assume that with a similar change, and with most of the furniture removed, each of the four flats would readily rent for $120. And the cottage would rent for $120 if the kitchen and the exterior were painted and the yard trimmed. This would make a new gross income of $600 monthly.

Deducting the previously figured fixed expenses of $98.43, which should not appreciably change in spite of increased gross income, would leave a new net of $501.57 monthly, or approximately $6,019 annually. Multiplying by 10 would result in a potential income valuation of $60,190. This estimated possible increase gives us a healthy margin over our $54,000 minimum resale target.

What Is the Replacement Value?

We make a quick appraisal to check if the property is priced lower than the cost of replacement. The building is 40 by 60 feet, making 4,800 square feet for two floors. As with the A Avenue house, comparable new construction would cost about $12 a square foot, making a reproduction cost for a new building of $57,600. To offset obsolescent fixtures, general depreciation, and lack of paint, an appraiser would discount 30 to 50 per cent on this old a building. Even discounting 40 per cent—as we did when appraising A Avenue—to $7.20 a square foot would give a figure of $34,560. The cottage is 30 by 30. On the same basis as the flats, its 900 square feet at $7.20 would appraise at $6,480. The garages would cost about $3,000 to reproduce, and their depreciated value would be $1,800. This would make a 40 per cent depreciated total of $42,840 on all improvements.

The lot, of course, would not be subject to depreciation but would be appraised on the basis of sale value if unimproved. This is a better rental area than A Avenue. Many new apartments and modern offices for doctors have recently been built, or are in the process of building, in this Mercy Hospital district. An empty lot would readily sell for $7,500. This makes a total value of $50,340 for lot and depreciated buildings.

What Was the Loan Appraisal?

As another check we can take the original amount of $25,000 on the present insurance-company loan and figure what the lender had appraised. An owner might sell for 10 per cent down and accept a note for 90 per cent, so a private individual's loan is an unreliable check against appraisal value. Other lending agencies might loan up to 75 per cent, but an insurance company would not exceed 60 per cent of appraisal value on this old a property in this condition. The Ballcryns were fortunate in obtaining an insurance-company loan without a more definite commitment to improve the property. The insurance company is unlikely to have loaned over 50 per cent of their appraisal, in which case their valuation would have been $50,000. Their minimum appraisal, on the basis of a 60 per cent loan, would have been $42,000.

OUR $37,000 TENTATIVE PURCHASE PRICE IS SOUND

With our various checks confirming our income valuation of $39,000, we feel that our $37,000 tentative purchase price is a sound figure. Before setting our actual purchase target we want to review the implications of the present owner's asking and previous purchase prices.

11. HOW TO TRADE YOUR PROPERTY

Previous sale prices, if obtainable, may help to establish a present sale-price level, but they are an unreliable guide to current values. The property may have greatly depreciated through neglect, obsolescence, and neighborhood deterioration. Or it may have greatly appreciated through building, lot, and neighborhood improvements. We were fortunate to learn the Ballcryns' $32,000 original purchase price, but this could be secured on an approximate basis in most cases by tallying the revenue stamps at the County Recorder's office.

WE SET A PURCHASE TARGET OF $36,000

As in our previous purchase, we could discount the $42,500 asking price by 25 per cent to get a possible lowest zone of negotiation of $31,875, which would come close to the present owner's cost before improvements. Mrs. Ballcryn said that the price allowed for bargaining, and any seller of other than new housing expects to settle for something below his asking price. With the information obtained we would judge the asking price in this case not so inflated as often is the custom. Instead of 25 per cent, we discount 15 per cent, $6,375, and arrive at an approximate figure of $36,125. We round this to a firm purchase target of $36,000, which is $1,000 under our original tentative figure.

By adding 10 per cent, as on A Avenue, we would arrive at $39,600 as our top price. Deducting 10 per cent, $3,600, from our $36,000 target would give us $32,400 for a first offer.

Working Out the "Boot" for a Trade

We now have to translate our sale and purchase figures into terms of boot, to know where we stand in trading. There are many methods of working out the mechanics of a trade. Most common is to trade on the basis of free and clear valuations, then figure out the terms of boot and financing. Thus A Avenue, with a $16,000 target sale price, would be traded plus a boot of $20,000 for B Boulevard, with a $36,000 target purchase price. This establishes the actual boot.

The second commonly used method is to trade equities "across the board," adjusting the loans on the larger property so that no boot will be expressed. In this method we would take our $16,000 sale valuation and deduct the loan balance of $6,436.44, giving us our previously arrived-at equity of $9,563.56. This same equity would be deducted from the target purchase figure of $36,000, leaving $26,436.44 as the amount of loans to be taken over on the B Boulevard property. With a first mortgage of $25,000, Mrs. Ballcryn would be given a second mortgage of $1,436.44 to make up the difference. This method is commonly favored by owners trading down, as it minimizes the sale price of the larger property.

However, as up-traders we want to emphasize the amount of boot, so we employ a third method. The maximum boot figure can be stated in terms of trading our property, including the loan, for Mrs. Ballcryn's property free and clear, subject to obtaining a satisfactory loan. With this method we add our $6,436.44 loan to the actual boot of $20,000 to arrive at a stated boot figure of $26,436.44. We round this to a target of $26,400. As you will note, all of the three foregoing methods make the same basic transaction.

WHAT LOANS WILL BE REQUIRED?

This latter figure will also be the amount of financing required to buy the larger property without putting up additional cash. Usually loans can be arranged on traded properties so that no cash changes hands, and any money in savings can be reserved for subsequent improvements. To cover the $26,400 in boot and our tentative commission to Mr. Murga of $500 would require total loans of $26,900 on the B Boulevard property.

WILL NET INCOME PAY FOR FINANCING?

After estimating the prospective loans to be arranged, a verification should be made whether the present income on the new property will pay for the expenses plus loan payments. On the $26,900 in loans, payments not exceeding 1 per cent, or $269 monthly, could be readily arranged. Deducting this from the $371.57 monthly net after fixed expenses leaves $102.57 monthly in reserve for repairs or other emergencies. We can therefore safely figure that the income on the basis of present rents will carry all expenses, including loan payments.

TRANSLATING THE BOOT INTO TERMS FOR TRADING

Before making our offer we should take the boot target arrived at by our chosen method and then figure the maximum and the amount we should offer. To get our new top boot figure, including the $6,436.44 loan, we take the $26,400 target and add the allowable $3,600 previously calculated. This would make $30,000 as the maximum we would normally pay in boot. In a pinch we could add to this the $1,000 difference between our target sale price of $16,000 and our minimum sale price of $15,000 to establish an absolute maximum of $31,000. But when trading up the owner of the larger property expects to make the larger concession. The smaller property owner can usually negotiate a fair sale price on his property and a discounted price on the larger property.

Chances are Mrs. Ballcryn is thinking in terms of the difference between her asking price of $42,500 and our asking price of $19,500, making her probable expected difference $23,000. This would be increased to $29,436.44 by including our loan, or $29,400 in round figures.

To arrive at our first offer we deduct the previously figured $3,600 from our boot target of $26,400 to arrive at a boot of $22,800. This could be adjusted to $22,750. Now we are ready to work out with the broker the terms of our offer to trade.

MAKING THE OFFER TO TRADE

When Mr. Murga looks over our property he expresses surprise at its modern appearance and says he had not expected our building to look so new. He takes a few notes as he gives our house and garage a top-to-bottom appraisal. When he comes to the meter box he whistles when he notices the inspection tags.

"Think I'll just put these in my pocket," he says as he pries them loose. "I'll keep them on file at my office. Why, the average person wouldn't think this place was over five years old."

Usually in an exchange the owner of the smaller property acts as the buyer and makes the offer to trade. Rather than a Deposit Receipt and Sales Agreement form such as used in buying our A Avenue property, an Exchange Agreement would be used to cover the terms of a trade. No cash deposit would be made since acceptance of the offer binds the properties traded.

On a trade, as on an offer to buy, a broker often omits some of the clauses which should be included in order to protect the negotiator. It is normal practice for the broker to write the offer, but it is up to each participant to require the inclusion of terms which will guard his interests. All the terms of our exchange agreement will be listed, as in the A Avenue purchase, with comment only on the items which differ.

DESCRIPTION OF PROPERTIES

The undersigned Joseph Enterprise and Mary Enterprise of the County of Metropole, State of Columbia, hereinafter called the First Parties, hereby offer to exchange the following described property situate in the City of Metropole, County of Metropole, State of Columbia, to wit:

Commonly known as 4210 A Avenue, consisting of a house and garage on a lot approximately 40 × 100 feet, Assessor's Block 51, Lot 34 as described in Volume 17, folio 9.

For the property owned by Amalie Ballcryn of the County of Metropole, State of Columbia, hereinafter called the Second Party, situate in the City of Metropole, County of Metropole, State of Columbia, to wit:

Commonly known as 3680 B Boulevard, consisting of 4 flats and a cottage on a lot approximately 50 × 150 feet, Assessor's Block 107, Lot 15, as described in Volume 56, folio 21.

FINANCING OF A AVENUE PROPERTY

The disposition of all loans should be specified. If Mrs. Ballcryn needed cash, several thousand dollars could be realized by an increased loan on our improved A Avenue house. She has indicated her funds were sufficient from her husband's insurance. We can assume she will take over our existing loan, as this will keep her payments lower. This item might be specifically checked if in doubt; otherwise it could be changed by subsequent negotiation.

Terms and Conditions of Exchange

The First Parties agree to deliver to the Second Party the first described property, subject to the present loan balance of approximately SIX THOUSAND FOUR HUNDRED THIRTY-SIX AND 44/100 DOLLARS ($6,436.44), which loan the Second Party agrees to assume; and an additional sum of TWENTY-TWO THOUSAND SEVEN HUNDRED FIFTY AND NO/100 DOLLARS ($22,750.00).

FINANCING OF B BOULEVARD PROPERTY

The transaction could be handled by the present loan on the B Boulevard property and a second mortgage from Mrs. Ballcryn. But this would create no additional operating funds for our use. Mrs. Ballcryn would give a second mortgage to make the deal, but naturally would not advance any cash for our benefit. We expect to spend about $6,000 for modernizing, and it would be desirable to obtain as much money for this purpose as possible in the first mortgage.

Chances are the subsequent negotiations will eliminate any cash difference between the first mortgage and the boot, but the offer should be planned on the basis that it may be accepted, however remote the probability. You never know when a desperate owner may accept your first offer, fearing that it may be withdrawn instead of increased, and that it could turn out to be the best offer received. The property might decline in value, and the owner might eventually have to settle for less from another buyer.

Subject to the Second Party or Broker obtaining a loan for the First Party on the second described property in the amount of TWENTY-FIVE THOUSAND AND NO/100 DOLLARS ($25,000.00), payable at TWO HUNDRED AND NO/100 DOLLARS ($200.00) per month, or more, including 6 per cent interest.

Mrs. Ballcryn might assume that accepting the offer should result in any cash from this increased loan being credited to her account. To avoid controversy this contingency can be covered by a clause such as:

The Second Party agrees to deliver to the First Parties the second described property free and clear of encumbrances.

This would mean that the new $25,000 loan would be turned over to the title company, which would pay off the present loan. Mrs. Ballcryn would receive the difference between the $22,750 boot and her present loan of $21,457.58. The balance, $2,250, would be credited to our account.

DISPOSITION OF FURNITURE

A clause should be inserted to cover each owner's tenant-used furniture and other personal property. Mr. Murga said that all the furniture was included except the cottage furniture, which Mrs. Ballcryn planned to keep. However, we could offer to exchange all furniture as is. We could leave our furniture and take over Mrs. Ballcryn's or bargain for a compromise.

If all or any portion of both above described real properties is rented furnished, or, if any personal property of any kind is owned by the owner of said real property and used by tenants or in the management and maintenance of said property, then the seller shall convey all of such personal property to the purchasers by Bill of Sale, free of encumbrances, without additional consideration.

FOUNDATION AND OTHER INSPECTIONS

We know that our recently inspected foundation is in sound condition, but we want to check the buildings we are buying. An equitable arrangement should specify that all foundations will be inspected. As with the A Avenue purchase, any other inspections, such as by a licensed appraiser, could be included here. Many buyers would stipulate inspection by a general contractor to determine the cost of proposed improvements.

> This exchange is subject to inspection of both properties by a licensed inspector or contractor of foundations for termites, dry rot, or other damage, any such damage to be repaired at cost of respective selling party, otherwise respective buying party may cancel contract.

GUARANTEED TITLE INSURANCE

Factors involving the title could be covered in the trade offer as follows:

> It is hereby agreed that each party hereto shall supply as the evidence of title for their respective properties described herein a Guaranteed Policy of Title Insurance, in amounts to be agreed upon, issued by a responsible Title Company, to be furnished and paid for by the present owner, and to show title to the said property free of all encumbrances, except as herein provided. In the event the title to either respective property shall not show as herein provided, and the respective seller shall not have perfected same within 30 days from date hereof, then the respective buyer shall have the option of declaring this Agreement null and void, and shall be released from all obligations hereunder.

DAMAGE CONTINGENCY

Possible damage to either property should be covered:

> If the improvements or aforementioned personal property on either property are destroyed or materially damaged between the date hereof and consummation or settlement of this ex-

change, this contract shall at buyer's election immediately become null and void.

TAKING POSSESSION

Mrs. Ballcryn plans to move from the cottage to our house. Since it is rented, there will be a delay before she can give a vacate notice and dispossess the tenants. She should therefore pay the $75 rent Mr. Murga placed on the cottage. This will be more than offset by the $160 rent she will receive on the A Avenue house which she is waiting to occupy.

Possession of both properties will be given on the date of closing. If a unit of either property remains occupied by the selling owner, a rental of $75 monthly will apply from date of closing.

PRORATIONS

Prorating of income and expenses should be specified for both properties. Taxes, interest and insurance should always be mentioned. In this case there are additional expenses—the hall lights, water and scavenger service, which should also be covered. We want to order new insurance, but Mrs. Ballcryn may choose to continue ours.

Rents, taxes, interest on the aforementioned loans, and other expenses affecting such properties shall be prorated from the date this Exchange is completed and consummated. Insurance on each property is to be prorated from date of closing transaction, unless buyer elects to cancel existing insurance, in which event new insurance policies will be deposited in escrow.

TIME AND CONTROL

We should always keep control of our property and take advantage of time. Mr. Murga, wishing no time limit for acceptance, suggests the phrase, "This offer is good until canceled." He also wants to write in the contract, "This offer is irrevocable for a period of twelve months."

We tell the broker we are amazed at such an outlandish suggestion.

Mr. Murga protests he very often writes up offers this way, even though he expects to work out a deal in a few days.

We advise Mr. Murga that under no circumstances would we tie up our property as he suggests. The state law says an offer can be withdrawn any time before acceptance. How can he ethically ask for terms which are contrary to the state law?

Mr. Murga lamely says the "irrevocable offer" is put in for psychological reasons mainly, as he doubts it would stand up if taken to court. He confesses his ideas for tying up our property were recently picked up from the convention speech of a nationally known broker. This broker had made a million-dollar fortune by tying up clients' properties for long periods on an irrevocable basis, then speculating personally with multiple trades. His recommendations, although frowned on by many respected realtors as being contrary to the tenets of an "honest broker," had received national attention.

"Are you talking about the broker who jumped off the bridge the other day?"

"Yes."

Mr. Murga says he will write up the time factor as we desire:

> Time is the essence of this contract, and the Agent is granted 10 days to obtain the acceptance of the Second Party, and if this offer is not accepted by Second Party and presented to the First Party within said 10 days, the First Party shall consider this Agreement null and void.
>
> Dated this 11th day of July, 1965.

Negotiating the Commission

You sign the exchange offer and turn it over to Mr. Murga. On an offer to trade, the agent customarily gets each party to sign a separate agreement concerning the commission, since each party is disposing of property. On similarly priced improved properties, the commission in most parts of the country is 5 or 6 per cent from each party on the sale valuation of his property. A fixed commission may be sacrosanct in the argument of the realtor. On a trade, particularly, the sale amount of each property and the resulting commission are subject to negotiation. Brokers usually attempt to set the sale value on the basis of the listed price and sometimes encourage high listings in order to increase commissions.

Mr. Murga shows us a Commission Agreement form. "You're asking nineteen thousand five hundred on your property," he says. "My commission from you if I can work out this deal should be six per cent. But I'll do you a favor and make it only five per cent. Let's see, that would be nine hundred seventy-five dollars. I'll just fill the amount in here, and you can sign it."

Once we sign the agreement to pay $975 we would be obligated for that amount as long as a deal is completed. Subsequent negotiations might involve trading our property for a lesser figure, down to our $15,000 minimum. If we tell Mr. Murga we will pay a $750 commission on the basis of $15,000, he will logically place that value on our property and be mentally conditioned to negotiate accordingly, thus working out a poorer deal for us. Many traders submit to a high commission in order to keep their price high in the agent's mind.

This dilemma can be overcome by offering a lower, fixed, round figure not tied to a specific sale valuation. A figure based on approximately half the asking price may prove acceptable if the broker is working alone and does not have to split commissions with other brokers: Since the agent expects a larger commission from the seller of the larger property, he may sometimes agree to modify the commission from the smaller property. If the deal cannot be made otherwise and, as sometimes happens, the parties will not budge from figures only a few hundred dollars apart, the broker may forgo the commission on the smaller property entirely in order to retrieve a commission from the larger property.

We tell Mr. Murga, "Of course you should be paid for your efforts, but you'll be getting a fairly large commission from Mrs. Ballcryn. We'd like to make this deal, but we don't feel warranted in paying as much as you ask."

"What did you have in mind?"

"Five hundred."

Mr. Murga feels on the defensive because his ethics have been questioned. He agrees to the $500 and fills in the amount on the form, which we sign:

Commission Agreement

In consideration of the efforts of Aloys Murga, Realtor, to effect an exchange of our Property in conformity with the Exchange Agreement this day signed by us, we hereby agree to pay to him in escrow upon acceptance and consummation of said Exchange Agreement by the other Party thereto, or any modifications thereof authorized or accepted by us, the sum of FIVE HUNDRED AND NO/100 DOLLARS ($500.00) as commission for services rendered us; and consent is hereby specifically given by us for Aloys Murga, Realtor, to also act as agent for and receive compensation from the other Party to said Exchange.

MRS. BALLCRYN LIKES OUR HOUSE

At six the next evening, Mr. Murga brings Mrs. Ballcryn to inspect our property. Mr. Murga acts as guide and extols all the modern features as we proceed. We let him do the selling while we tag along to answer questions. Many an owner, particularly in selling his own home, has frightened away a prospective buyer by appearing over-eager to get into the sales act. An experienced salesman pursues a particular line of presentation in order to lead up to a tentative commitment from the prospect. An inopportune owner can ruin carefully laid groundwork by interrupting the train of thought. Many agents prefer to show property without the owner's being present at all, and this often works out for the best. Where the owner can let the salesman do most of the talking, there sometimes is an advantage in tagging along to answer questions, and also to check personally the reactions of the prospective buyer. You can better judge how high to hold your sale price if you know whether a prospect is enthusiastic or lukewarm.

We show Mrs. Ballcryn around the yard and garage before it becomes dark; then we cover our house with a thorough inspection. Mr. Murga tells the tenant Mrs. Ballcryn is a prospective buyer. Mrs. Ballcryn does not conceal her approval of the modernized interior. We next go down to the basement and Mr. Murga shows how sound the construction is. He points out that although Mrs. Ballcryn would have a good deal without the added flat, she could make a good income from building it whenever she wanted to.

Mr. Murga than takes the prospect out to his car. We discuss various details, such as the tax and insurance costs, and that the tenant pays all utilities, including water and scavenger service. The broker asks Mrs. Ballcryn if she has any further questions.

"There's only one thing that bothers me about this, besides getting a fair price," she says. "I would like to move my stove and refrigerator over here, and my living-room and dining-room furniture. I don't mind trading bedroom sets, but I want to keep my other personal furniture. I would want to move here, as it would be convenient for me. How about making a trade so that I can keep the furniture that I want from my cottage, and you can take your furniture to make up for it?"

"Of course your own personal furniture is nicer," we agree. "But if we can work out a deal, we'll be glad to exchange the furniture as you want it."

Mr. Murga says that he and Mrs. Ballcryn will discuss the matter further while he takes her home, and he will get in touch with us the following evening.

MRS. BALLCRYN PHONES US DIRECT

At ten o'clock the same evening, we are aroused by the ringing of the telephone. Mrs. Ballcryn is on the line. She says, "Mr. Murga has just left my place, and he is going to contact you tomorrow. We have talked things over, and anyone can see your offer of only $22,750 to boot is ridiculous. But you no doubt started out with such a low figure expecting to bargain.

"Mr. Murga wants me to hold out for thirty thousand. But I'm getting sick and tired of fooling around with him, so I'm calling to see if we can get down to brass tacks. You have a cute little place, all fixed up nice, and I'd like to get moved. Now I'll give you my best price, and we can get things settled. What do you think of a boot of twenty-seven thousand five hundred? Of course I'd have to get the benefit of keeping my own furniture, as you agreed, to give you a price like that."

We check our figures and mentally note that our target was $26,400. We say we appreciate Mrs. Ballcryn's calling us direct, and would like to accommodate her. But we can't see working out a deal as she suggests. We would be willing to settle on $25,000, including the exchange of furniture.

Mrs. Ballcryn says she couldn't sell as low as that, it is just out of the question. Couldn't we come up to her figure?

It is apparent that she has firmly fixed on $27,500, and that further time will have to elapse in order to make a further adjustment. Additional discussion now might cause her to make a positive statement which, in order to save face, she would not later retract. We suggest that we all sleep on the matter, and Mrs. Ballcryn can get in touch with us when she feels she can make a further change. Mrs. Ballcryn asks us to do the same and not to breathe a word of her call to Mr. Murga, but she will tell him she wants to settle for $27,500.

MR. MURGA WORKS OUT A COMPROMISE

Mr. Murga shows up at six the next evening. He tells us a cock-and-bull story, taking credit for the state of negotiation we have already arrived at with Mrs. Ballcryn. He is like the average salesman who likes to exaggerate his prime importance negotiating a deal in which he may have had little part. He says Mrs. Ballcryn refused to take a penny less than $30,000, but after much persuasion he has talked her into accepting $27,500. We discuss the matter and tell the agent we will come up to $25,000. This leaves us at the same impasse we arrived at with Mrs. Ballcryn.

Mr. Murga leaves us to go direct to Mrs. Ballcryn. He returns at 9 P.M. with the news, "Mrs. Ballcryn has agreed to compromise fifty-fifty at $26,250, providing you pay the costlier title insurance on her larger property, and she will pay the title insurance on your property. Also she must keep her furniture as she requested. I'm surprised at the importance Mrs. Ballcryn has attached to her cottage furniture, far beyond its actual worth. If it weren't for that, I know she would not have come down nearly so low."

We agree to the proposed arrangements, providing the financing is satisfactory. We ask Mr. Murga if he thinks the first mortgage can be raised, say to $27,500, since we have used most of our funds to improve our property and cannot put up any cash.

WE ASSUME THREE LOANS

He says no, he has already checked. The insurance company will not exceed their previous full loan of $25,000. They will come up to $25,000 again and keep the interest at 6 per cent, providing we carry life insurance with them sufficient to pay off their mortgage. Mr. Murga might get a larger loan from another company, but it would probably be at higher interest, 7 per cent. What would be the use, when Mrs. Ballcryn is willing to take a second mortgage for the difference?

We say we appreciate that, but if we are unable to obtain funds from an increased first mortgage, it would be necessary to postpone his $500 commission also. Mr. Murga says not to worry about that, he will be getting cash from Mrs. Ballcryn and will be glad to take a third mortgage at 6 per cent to cover his commission from us.

We make arrangements to take over the $25,000 first mortgage, with payments of $200 a month, plus $10 monthly to cover mortgage insurance. The latter will cost .5 per cent monthly on the declining balance and it insures paying off the first mortgage in case of the death of the breadwinner. In view of Mrs. Ballcryn's unfortunate experience, we feel the proportionately slight additional monthly payment a worth-while expenditure. And the cost is offset by a lower interest rate.

On the $1,250 second mortgage to Mrs. Ballcryn, making the difference between the agreed boot and the first mortgage, we arrange to pay $15 monthly, including 6 per cent interest. Mr. Murga first asks for full payment of his $500 at the end of six months. On our request, he readily agrees to $10 monthly instead. All three loans total $26,750, and payments will start approximately one month after closing the escrow.

The uninitiated may turn down an otherwise good deal because they are repelled by second, and especially third or fourth, mortgages, I know of a widow who was left a home free and clear. She refused an offer involving a second mortgage, although the latter constituted an absolute bonus compared with her later sale price. There was a loan commitment of $8,000 from a building and loan association. After she put the place on the market, the first offer she received was for $15,000, including $4,000 cash and a second mortgage for $3,000. The widow would not accept, because her husband had told her, "Never take a second mortgage." The best subsequent offer, which she accepted four months later, was for $12,000, including $4,000 cash and taking over the $8,000 first-mortgage commitment. Thus any receipts from the offered $3,000 second mortgage would have been a pure profit.

A second mortgage would be sound for a seller willing to take the property back for the value of the first mortgage. It is a common misconception that a second-mortgage holder must pay off the first mortgage in order to foreclose. In the foregoing case, if the second mortgage had been defaulted, the widow could have taken over the property by assuming and making payments on the $8,000 first mortgage, and then she could have resold. There would have been little likelihood of default when the buyer had put in $4,000 in cash. Defaults are remarkably low even with 100 per cent GI financing.

Second and third mortgages offer no cause for worry to the buyer if the total payments can be kept down and handled comfortably from the income. In our purchase the monthly payments on all three mortgages, including the first-mortgage insurance, will be $235. This is less by $34 than the $269 monthly we were prepared to pay on all loans.

WE RECEIVE $430 FOR FOUNDATION REPAIRS

The foundation inspections show our A Avenue property to be in sound condition, free of termites and rot. The main foundations of the B Boulevard flats, cottage and garage are sound, but the front steps and porch have been affected by rot and settling. This was caused, according to the inspection report, by lack of concrete footings and by accumulated dampness from lack of ventilation. Adequate air vents had been installed for the building, but not for the porch and steps. Ventilators should be installed at either side of the porch. The cracked porch foundation should be replaced and supported by adequate footings. The rot and the settling of the foundation have caused the partial crumbling of the supporting beams, which have to be removed and completely replaced. The estimated cost, $430, is credited to our escrow account, since we agree to proceed with the work in the near future.

WE ARRANGE AN ADVANTAGEOUS CLOSING DATE

All four B Boulevard rentals are collected on the first. A prorating date immediately after will credit our account with sufficient funds to pay for escrow charges, including title insurance, and prorated taxes and other costs. Rather than trust to luck, we arrange for the title company to close the escrows and record the transferred deeds effective August 5. We arrange for payments on all three loans to start September 10. Mrs. Ballcryn pays one month's rent on the cottage, since she expects to take a month to notify our tenant and move.

We Receive an Escrow Check of $537.53

Our escrow account is credited as follows:

	DEBITS	CREDITS
Prorating of $395 Belvedere rents		$331.29
One month's cottage rent from Mrs. Ballcryn		75.00
Prorating of $160 A Avenue rent	$122.59	
Credit $535.16 Belvedere taxes from July 1		52.03
Debit $152.50 A Avenue taxes from July 1	14.83	
Credit A Avenue fire insurance at $20.50 to Dec. 5		6.83
Credit contracted Belvedere porch repairs		430.00
Belvedere title insurance	207.00	
Fees and revenue stamps, A Avenue	13.20	
Check to us from title company	537.53	
TOTALS	$895.15	$895.15

Before arriving at the amount of fire insurance to be placed on the Belvedere, our insurance broker arranges an appraisal of replacement costs less depreciation. The insurance company establishes a depreciated combustible value of $48,750. This is the amount we order, plus six months' rental insurance of $3,000. The annual premium, based on annual billing of a three-year policy, comes to $84.59, about $10 less than Mrs. Ballcryn paid for $10,000 less coverage. After paying the insurance premium and reserving $430 for foundation repairs, we wind up the escrow about even.

All escrow costs have been paid, and we have $22.94 remaining from the escrow proceeds. Adding this to the accumulated bank account of $1,388.79 gives a total cash reserve of $1,411.73 as we take over the Belvedere Apartments.

The insurance appraisal is added evidence that we have made a sound buy. After our planned modernization, we should have no difficulty realizing our 25 per cent minimum profit goal.

PART FIVE

INCREASE VALUE
BY IMPROVING OPERATIONS

12. HOW TO ADVERTISE
YOUR APARTMENTS

Now that we have traded for the four flats and the cottage at B Boulevard, it is timely to review some of the phases of day-to-day operations which help to assure maximum success. As previously mentioned, a lending institution will loan on income property even though the owner has no experience, because a neophyte owner can still reap a good profit.

SOME OWNERS SHUN MANAGEMENT

I know many owners, investors as well as in-and-out speculators, who make money even though they completely shun the management of property. Some prefer to pay management fees to real-estate brokers. Many large and small investors turn all problems over to the growing ranks of property managers, usually a necessity for estates and absentee owners. An increasing percentage of realtors are management specialists, who have formed an Institute of Real Estate Management. Their fees vary, chiefly according to property size, averaging about 5 per cent of gross income. For the most part they earn their fees. But the fees take the "cream off the top" of investment income, better retained by the owner who can devote a little time to management.

SPECULATORS MAY IGNORE MANAGEMENT

A pure speculator interested only in turning over property for a quick profit may afford to ignore management. One speculator I know has stopped selling each year for the past twenty years when his total profits reached $50,000, usually within six to nine months. This unique speculator never has entered into or studied property management, confining his efforts to "buying low and selling high." He merely buys underpriced property and sells for a nominal profit. His secret is turning over property by tying up no money of his own. He has a broker's license, but he spends no time selling, except on property he has optioned.

Most of his efforts are spent seeking property that pays a 12 to 20 per cent net. He could tie up the property on a low net listing, then sell for a high markup. The owner would receive the amount stipulated as his "net" price. The broker would keep all sale receipts in excess of this net price, instead of a nominal percentage. However, this could be considered unethical if unreasonable profits resulted, and it might culminate in revocation of his license. If the owner became suspicious and refused to go through with the deal, the most the owner would probably forfeit on this type of listing would be the customary commission, in the 5 per cent range.

To take the legal position of a potential buyer, rather than that of a broker, this speculator usually ties up the property with a six-month option. He optioned to buy, for example, a property with an asking price of $100,000 which netted a minimum of $12,000, making a 12 per cent net. He put up no cash, but he gave a note for $5,000, which he said would be paid off by his commission when he sold the property. Once the owner signed the option agreement, he had to abide by it or suffer a damage suit for the buyer's loss of potential profits.

Leaving the owner to continue running the building, the speculator then found an investor who bought for $120,000 on the usual basis of 10 per cent net. The speculator pocketed a $20,000 capital gain, plus the $5,000 commission. He retrieved his $5,000 note and paid off $95,000 to the first owner. The latter received his asking price of $100,000, less the 5 per cent commission. And the speculator made $25,000 without putting up a cent! Two deals like this, and he has met his annual quota of $50,000 in profits.

A spectacular transaction of this nature was Roger Stevens' reputed buying of the Empire State Building on earnings of 12 per cent net, and selling to new owners on the basis of their earning 8 per cent net. Stevens thus realized a 50 per cent gross profit, or approximately $25,000,000. Unlike most speculators, Stevens often improves both operations and buildings in order to sell for a maximum profit.

A speculator may make spectacular profits with minimum effort. However, since he adds nothing to intrinsic property value, he stands a greater risk of suffering a loss. In one such example a speculator bought a large modern home whose value was discounted because the exterior was badly streaked with an experimental-type white stucco paint. He would not pay for the obviously needed painting, as his policy was not to spend a cent for improvement. He advertised extensively, but his white elephant sat for some time unsold.

He finally sacrificed to my wife's sister Helen and her husband, Dr. Wilson Matlock. They spent only $500 for painting the exterior an attractive dusty-pink rose. Within a month after the paint transformation they received a bona fide purchase offer $10,000 over their cost. Thus every dollar spent for painting increased the value $20.

Successful Investors Gain Management Know-How

We are concerned with the sure path of investment and improvement, where we add to the basic value of property. Physical improvements are obvious. We mentioned that one method of improving property was to improve operations.

Executive Vice President Gordon Neilson of the National Apartment Association cites a significant 1968 study of Houston, Texas, apartments. The operating costs of more successful owners ran 9 per cent less than the average and as much as 20 per cent less than the least efficient owners. Of course such savings in operations resulted in between 9 and 20 per cent higher profits.

For the long pull, improving management operations can be more important than physical improvements. Successful management details will therefore be covered in this and succeeding chapters.

How About Advice from Former Owner or Broker?

To get the most out of property and to insure maximum progress, you should take advantage of advice developed by experienced successful management. Many new owners instinctively turn for management advice to the former owner or to the realtor who sold the property. But the average agent like Mr. Murga, despite his knowledge of selling real estate, knows next to nothing about managing and maintaining income property.

Following the advice of a former owner often leads to sloppy operating methods which may have resulted in poor net revenue, which, in turn, caused the owner to sell. Most owners with a satisfactory net income could easily earn more by exercising a little forethought and imagination. It is unbelievable how often owners "play by ear" on a hit-or-miss basis, with a complete absence of method or plan.

To give an example of improving the operations of previous owners, I have never failed to increase net income on property purchased. On properties bought from unimaginative individual owners it was fairly simple to do this by improving appearance and then raising rents. One 27-unit apartment house bought from a building and loan association had been foreclosed by them during the depression on their 8 per cent, 5-year mortgage. I expected to find it difficult to improve operations, since the seller had had extensive experience in property ownership and supervision. Yet that property responded as much as any other to all three of the previously mentioned possibilities for increasing net;

1. Increased rents by improving appearance and convenience
2. Reduced vacancy-loss factor by
    a. Decoration and improvements which satisfied tenants and reduced turnover
    b. Productive advertising and salesmanship which filled vacancies without rent loss
3. Reduced costs through analysis of all expense items

I have concluded that all properties can stand a close look to improve operations, and that a capable individual owner can usually outproduce institutional management. Except for a possible month or two to analyze a building, it does not pay to follow blindly the practices of the average former owner.

WHERE TO LOOK FOR GUIDANCE

Beyond the guideposts set forth in my books, the best source for day-to-day guidance is the local Rental Owners Association, like the

Alameda County Apartment House Association of Oakland, California, to which I belong. The aid of such an organization will prove invaluable in solving routine rental problems and will result in money savings far surpassing the nominal dues. The purchase at wholesale of one stove or refrigerator, for example, through their contacts, will pay the average owner's nominal annual dues.

Usually, from their staffs you will get experienced advice on routine and on unusual problems. When legal counsel is needed, you will be directed to attorneys specializing in real-estate law. Not only do the associations handle individual problems, but their regular monthly meetings normally cover new aspects of common problems. A high proportion of local groups are affiliated with the National Apartment Association and state property-owner organizations. All foster laws favorable to free enterprise and resist legislation inimical to private ownership.

The best education in operations, particularly in the early stages of ownership, is actually managing an apartment house. In the case of our B Boulevard property you could plan to move into the cottage when Mrs. Ballcryn moves out, and you could manage and maintain the property. Whether or not you find it feasible to take over the management of your first apartments, certain fundamental knowledge and certain tools help to promote success.

Even if you start out as a do-it-yourselfer, you should eventually allocate all physical labor to others as your experience and property increase. And so it will be with management. As holdings enlarge you will delegate direct operation of property to others and confine your efforts to over-all supervision. But regardless how big your estate, you can more soundly direct your individual managers if you gain management know-how yourself.

ARRANGING FOR A RESIDENT MANAGER

Two weeks after the property transfer date of August 5, the tenant moves from A Avenue. Mrs. Ballcryn is anxious to be in her new home and immediately moves in from the B Boulevard cottage. She takes her furniture as agreed and temporarily stores ours in the basement.

In this example we will assume you are unable or prefer not to take over the on-the-premises management of the apartments, but want to secure a manager to succeed Mrs. Ballcryn. With property of this size it normally would not be mandatory to have a resident manager, as the rents could be handled by the owner from another location, or by a real-estate office, or by a nearby apartment manager or other agent. Laws and codes vary in this respect, but the typical state law requires a resident manager only if there are over sixteen living units.

However, there is a substantial advantage in having a responsible tenant on the premises to collect rent, show vacancies, keep order, and handle the janitorial, yard and garden duties. Such an arrangement usually can be made for a nominal rent allowance, which costs less than hiring each individual job. The amount of the allowance would depend on the number of units. With four units to manage, it would normally run between one fourth and one third of the usual rent, depending on duties and rental values.

Before renting the cottage to a resident manager, we must determine the changes to be made in it and its market value with the alterations completed. We can set a tentative rent and allowance which can be modified according to the amount of response and the reactions of prospects. The cottage, except for the kitchen, is already in good condition, having recently been modernized by the Ballcryns.

Juggling Furniture

We decide to rent the cottage unfurnished. As we found at A Avenue, with tenants in this area the potential rent including older furniture will be close to the same unfurnished. Many tenants are more willing to buy their furniture in areas where a high percentage of them expect later to own their homes. The conversion of furnished to unfurnished rental units has been a national trend among alert owners seeking to offset increased costs of operation. The chief exceptions are utility units which have no bedroom, and for which complete new and modern furniture is bought. The increased rent in the latter case may pay a profit on the additional capital cost when you can buy at wholesale prices.

Available furniture on hand can be used among the present tenants, and the residue can be disposed of. For example, the bedroom set in Number 1 is the least desirable, so we will give the tenant in Number 1 the desirable set from the cottage and junk the Number 1 set. A secondhand or junk dealer will normally make nominal transfers of furniture in exchange for the excess. The disposition of our stove, refrigerator, and other furniture in the A Avenue basement can be deferred until the cottage is rented. Many unfurnished units provide a stove and a refrigerator. In case we find a desirable tenant-manager wanting these items we will leave them in the cottage. But first we will attempt to rent the cottage without them. Number 4 flat has the ancient range, so we could junk it and move over the one from A Avenue. Our refrigerator at A Avenue could replace the archaic coil-top model in Number 3. If we can make the foregoing changes, the only remaining equipment requiring replacement would be the rangette in Number 3. This might later be replaced without buying a new one if we can further juggle furniture as additional flats become vacant.

REAPPRAISING RENTAL VALUE AND MANAGER ALLOWANCE

We previously figured the rental value of the cottage in its present condition at $90, and with the kitchen and exterior painted and the yard trimmed at $120. The exterior will have to be delayed for spring sunshine, but we can promise a prospective tenant that it will be painted as soon as weather permits. If we were renting to other than a resident manager we would arrange to spruce up the yard, mow the lawn, and prune the shrubbery, including the rambler roses in front of the cottage. Also we would have the kitchen painted. But we will arrange for the new manager to handle all these items, and we will provide the necessary paint and tools.

After a study of current ads for similar housing, we decide to ask $90 for the cottage, including the garage which was used by Mrs. Ballcryn. We will plan a tentative allowance of $30, or one third. With the foregoing plans in mind we are ready to advertise for a tenant-manager to live in the cottage.

A SHORT, SNAPPY AD GETS RESULTS

We will consider at greater length, in Chapters 20 and 21, the securing and supervising of managers. In this chapter we will deal chiefly with advertising for tenants. It suffices for the present that we place the following classified ad for one day in the *Metropolitan* under the heading of "Help Wanted—Couples":

> Handy, trustworthy manager, 4 apts.
> Rent allowance. Metro Box 561053

There are thirty-one replies to this ad. As our number-one choice we select the Wisters. Mr. Wister works as an auto mechanic for the nearest Ford dealer and has been looking for a place close to his work. Mrs. Wister has been working as a telephone operator but will be staying home because she expects a baby in three months. This is another reason they want to move out of their present unfurnished apartment into a ground-floor house. The couple readily agree to take care of the apartments and pay a net rental of $60. This shows that our original appraisal was realistic.

The Wisters have all the necessary furniture, including a stove and a refrigerator. A used-furniture dealer agrees to (a) move the stove and the refrigerator from A Avenue to Numbers 3 and 4, (b) move the bedroom set from the cottage to Number 1, and (c) give us $25, in return for the discarded furniture at both properties. In addition the dealer agrees to connect the gas range in the Number 4 flat.

A VACANCY OCCURS

On September 1, scarcely after the Wisters have become settled in the cottage, the tenants in Number 4, the Goldens, give notice when they pay the rent that they will be moving October 1. Mrs. Golden says they have just bought a GI-financed home in the outlying suburbs, paying nothing down. Their son is three, and another child is expected in four months, so they are anxious to move into their newly bought home.

We ask Mrs. Golden if they intend to move October 1, the date she mentioned, or would they vacate the day before when their rent terminates? She says they figured on staying till their rent was up, and wouldn't that be October 1? We point out that their rent starts the first and a full month covers from September 1 to September 30, inclusive, terminating at midnight. Additional rent would be due if they moved October 1. Mrs. Golden says in that case they will be out by September 30. A proper-type receipt, to be shown in Chapter 15, should have made this discussion unnecessary.

A National Trend

The Goldens' move exemplifies a national turnover trend, especially among families having or expecting children. Renters just don't stay put the way they used to. The National Association of Real Estate Boards estimates that eight and a half million families move each year. Of these, two thirds stay in the same county and one third move to a new county. The availability of low-cost, no-down or low-down-payment, and long-term government-financed or -underwritten homes is a major contribution to the 10 per cent vacancy factor found in some areas.

The alert operator of rental housing will not bemoan this trend but will welcome the swelling of the approaching two-thirds property-owner majority. Each new owner helps to counteract the dwindling minority who seek punitive legislation against property owners. Rental owners should have no qualms about serving the transient newlyweds who will eventually buy a home, as well as the childless couples and single persons who occupy apartments indefinitely.

Apartments in metropolitan areas offer many natural advantages over suburban living besides the saving of commuting time and costs. Many confirmed "cliff dwellers" dread the care of home and garden and prefer the convenience of a well-kept apartment where the owner shoulders the responsibilities. Drab, old-fashioned apartments drive tenants to homes in the suburbs. But cheery, modern accommodations not only hold tenants but draw back many disillusioned homeowners who have tried suburban and exurban living.

Long-Range vs. Interim Planning

In our over-all plans for the B Boulevard property we want to remodel. Now that we have an unexpected vacancy, should we remodel this one flat or merely decorate to put it in rentable condition? Either decision may be made, depending on the progress of our plans, on financing, and on the present condition of the vacant unit.

In this case the flat is in fair condition except for the bath and kitchen, which need painting. We decide to paint them for the time being, and we get a bid of $50 from our A Avenue painter. With this small expenditure we will try to rent for $110, unfurnished. We leave the refrigerator and the newly connected stove in case they are needed. The rest of the Number 4 furniture, including two 9-by-12 rugs, we sell to a secondhand dealer for $30.

THREE WAYS TO AVOID VACANCIES

Points have previously been mentioned which help the rental owner to keep his tenants longer and to rent to new tenants without vacancy lags:

1. Maintaining an attractive appearance
2. Adding the improvements tenants desire
3. Keeping rents at fair market value and within a moderate price range

With all these points in the owner's favor, he should still recognize that he is bound to experience a certain amount of tenant turnover, and that in a competitive market he must take additional steps to keep his vacancy factor to a bare minimum of 1 or 2 per cent. Property can be managed with alert attention to changing conditions so that there will be scarcely any loss from vacancies. With the month's notice received on the Number 4 flat, we can have a new tenant move in when the Goldens vacate, thus suffering no revenue loss, if the flat is in shape to rent.

THREE MORE WAYS TO KEEP A FULL HOUSE

An apartment can be rerented immediately if:

1. The outgoing tenant gives ample notice, leaving sufficient time to advertise and show the premises. The tenant is more apt to give adequate notice if properly conditioned by the terms of a lease, which will be covered in more detail in Chapter 14. The lease, of course, should provide also that the owner may then show the premises to prospective tenants until rented.
2. The vacancy is competently sold to prospective tenants. Important details of salesmanship will be covered in the following chapter.
3. The vacancy is adequately advertised. This is the most important factor of all. The best apartment bargain may

lie vacant unless prospective tenants are informed through advertising.

Six Chief Ways to Advertise

Advertising can effectively draw tenants through six chief mediums. Here they are, starting with the least economical for the average rental and working to the most fruitful:

1. Television
2. Radio
3. Real-estate brokers
4. "Vacancy" signs
5. Contacts with sources of rental prospects
6. Newspaper classified advertising

1 and 2. television and radio

These two mediums are mentioned together, as neither is worth the cost for the average owner. TV costs are prohibitive for the response. Radio has been tried extensively by multithousand-unit owners like the Metropolitan Life Insurance Company. But for average operations the cost is considerably more, and the response less, than with judicious newspaper advertising.

For the most part these mediums are used in desperation when other means fail to fill units that overprice the going market. But they are no more able than any other medium to perform miracles, such as selling above the competitive market.

3. real-estate brokers

This refers to rentals supervised by the owners and turned over to a broker to rent, not to the many rentals managed by realtors for a fixed management fee or a percentage of gross income.

While rentals were tight under price controls, a high proportion of tenants paid commissions to real-estate brokers for locating apartments. And many owners and managers circumvented rent control by turning all vacancies over to rental brokers, with agreements that owners and brokers would split the exorbitant rental fees.

Most business leases are handled through brokers, but the use of brokers has virtually been eliminated by the majority of managing apartment owners. With competitive rentals, the owner and not the tenant pays the broker's fee. The apartment owner can normally obtain faster and surer results by spending considerably less than broker's fees on newspaper advertising.

4. "VACANCY" SIGNS

Some apartment owners rely exclusively on a "Vacancy" sign in the manager's window or in front of the building. This practice often is of merit as an addition to other advertising, but it should never be depended upon exclusively, except in a tight area where no resulting rent loss occurs. The sign's field of attraction is limited to a comparatively small number who pass and notice it, while newspaper ads reach prospects in the whole area.

I know of apartment houses on major boulevards which keep almost full by using nothing besides a "Vacancy" sign. Most apartment owners will draw some of their tenants by the use of a sign. But I know of others who use no other advertising, chiefly because a sign brought them a full house during tight rent controls, and who suffer heavy vacancies as a result.

I recently found a 30-unit apartment house with ten vacancies, a prohibitive 33⅓ per cent factor that forced the owner to make up mortgage payments out of his savings. The building was fairly attractive, the individual apartments were kept in good condition, and the rents were somewhat under the market. But the location was on a quiet residential street where there was no through traffic. The owner's sole method of advertising was to hang inside the glass front door a sign, "Apartment for Rent."

This sign had kept the building full during rent control, chiefly by stimulating word-of-mouth advertising by the tenants. Now, although the apartments were a good buy pricewise, tenants would not recommend them to their friends because of a bellicose, alcoholic manager. As competition increased and higher vacancies developed, the owner failed to analyze and correct his operations. There had been not fewer than five vacancies at any time during the past year.

With so many vacancies, I suggested running two 10-word newspaper ads, one to cover three vacant 3-room apartments, and one to cover seven vacant 2-room apartments. Since the rents were competitive, the three 3s were all rented over the first weekend. The seven 2s were rented by the end of the second weekend. Incidentally, a change of managers helped to retain tenants.

Although a "Vacancy" sign used to be frowned upon as detracting from the appearance of a desirable building, it is now almost universally accepted as a legitimate medium of advertising. Probably its extensive use in business locations and plush motels has contributed to this general acceptance. To summarize, the "Vacancy" sign will usually draw some tenants. It seldom can be relied on exclusively. It will rate second for some locations, but on the average will rate third in producing results.

5. CONTACTS WITH SOURCES OF RENTAL PROSPECTS

Many apartment managers draw a good proportion, and some all, of their tenants through personal contacts with sources of rental prospects. This is a lucrative field completely ignored by some owners, and exclusively relied on by others. Its productive value for the average owner is second only to newspaper advertising.

An efficient manager will establish friendly contacts with sources within the logical rental area and advise them when a vacancy is available. Examples are:

a. Cultivate major sources of prospects—
    Large offices, such as utility or chain-store headquarters
    Personnel are often transferring
    Factories
    Transfers or new personnel
    Hospitals, whether private or service
    Doctors, nurses, orderlies, office and other help
    Service headquarters
    Air, Army, or Navy personnel
b. Cultivate neighborhood sources which often refer prospects—
    Neighborhood stores
    Service stations and garages
    Delivery men, such as the milkman and the cleaner
c. Cultivate friendly rivalry with nearby managers.
    Apartment managers in an area are in general competition for prospective tenants, but they can be of mutual help by staying on friendly terms. Neighboring

managers may refer prospects on a reciprocal basis when they have a full house, even though the rentals are similar, but most co-operation will come from managers of dissimilar units. Where the B Boulevard flats are 2-bedroom units, for example, and a neighbor has 1-bedroom apartments, managers may refer to each other tenants desiring the different-sized accommodations. The same would hold true where different prices or qualities prevail, or where one building is furnished and the other is unfurnished.

d. Cultivate friendly tenant relations.

A grumpy manager like the aforementioned alcoholic will repel prospective tenants, will cause present tenants to move, and will discourage them from recommending the building to friends. A friendly manager makes each tenant a salesman for the building; when a vacancy occurs, tenants will recommend the accommodations to any prospects they may happen to know. Often an outgoing tenant, leaving for reasons other than dissatisfaction, will make a special effort to obtain a replacement. I know one sweet-tempered manager who has earned such high loyalty that nearly all her vacancies are filled through current and vacating tenants.

Such contacts as the foregoing often take care of sporadic vacancies, but they may prove woefully inadequate when utilized to the exclusion of other advertising. One manager of a 36-unit apartment house did not lose a single day's rent in two years. Occasionally a prospect would drop in because of the "Vacancy" sign out in front, but the manager relied chiefly on tenant referrals and on her own contacts with nearby organizations with reservoirs of potential tenants. These included within a three-mile radius a naval hospital, a chain-store headquarters, and an Air Force base. She suddenly had five vacancies at once, four 2s and one 3. Two of the 2s were rented by nurses from the naval hospital, leaving three units which remained empty for two weeks, without a prospect in sight. This manager was skeptical that an ad would produce results, until my inquiry developed that occasional drop-ins from the "Vacancy" sign had volunteered that they had answered ads for other buildings in the neighborhood. They were "shopping" all nearby buildings before making up their minds.

On my advice two separate 10-word ads were inserted in the leading daily, one ad for the 2s and one for the 3. As a result the two remaining 2s were filled in one day. By the third evening the second ad had rented the 3.

6. NEWSPAPER CLASSIFIED ADVERTISING

Depending on any single medium will result in more vacancies than utilizing all mediums that can apply. When one normally productive method fails, others should be resorted to. The most dependable tenant seducer of all is a properly worded classified newspaper ad, which most prospective tenants will read.

Successful advertising must be based on the actions of prospects who will respond to the ad. With rentals, we study the course of most tenants and act accordingly. Most prospective tenants shop through the classified section, looking for certain essential information that fits their desires. They select the ads that may be pertinent, just as we did when looking for rental property to buy. Then they phone the listed numbers, seeking additional information to guide them. Should the rental unit be eliminated from further consideration? Or should it be included on a preferred list to be checked in person? Thus all pertinent information does not have to be in the ad. In fact some selling points should always be held back to stimulate further interest for the telephone caller. But the ad must contain enough information to win a telephone response.

So that we will have a tenant ready to move into the Goldens' vacated Number 4 flat, here is the ad we phone to the *Metropolitan* to be listed under "Unfurnished Flats for Rent":

> B Boulevard. Spacious 5 rooms. Garage. Adults. $110. Phone 581–4137.

This ad incorporates the essentials that potential tenants respond to, based on extensive studies of ads that get results. The necessary information to obtain response can usually be included in a 10-word, or 2-line, ad—the minimum stipulated by many metropolitan newspapers. Some charge by the word, others by the line. Two lines average 10 words.

Many owners waste money on elaborate ads which get no better results than the one listed above. Often these ads repel tenants, who think, There must be something wrong with the property or the price, or they wouldn't have to spend so much on advertising. Major dislikes of ad prospects are lengthy, flowery expressions that convey no specific details, and excessive use of abbreviations.

THE BULL'S-EYE AD

With more than one type of vacant unit, for example if we had both the flat and the cottage vacant at the same time, better results would usually be obtained by bull's-eying a separate ad for each—keying each ad to separate prospective tenants—rather than shotgunning a bigger ad to cover both units.

Shooting for more than one group of tenants in one ad is like aiming at more than one duck at a time. If you aim at a single duck you are apt to score a hit. If you aim between two, with hopes of getting both, you most likely will hit neither.

The one-third-empty building previously mentioned probably would not have been filled in ten days by a single shotgun ad. Best results were insured by a separate 10-word ad for each of its two sizes of units.

If the cottage were vacant and no manager-tenant were involved, we could advertise under "Houses, Unfurnished, for Rent":

> East Metropole. Redecorated 4 rooms.
> Garage. Adults. $110. Phone 581–
> 4137.

With the two foregoing ads as examples, we will review the essentials for ads that produce results. The chief purpose of the ad is to draw response from prospective tenants who will rent the advertised unit. An additional purpose is to weed out those who obviously will not be prospects, thus conserving the telephone line and the manager's time and attention for productive prospects. To accomplish these purposes the following information should be included:

1. At least one *attention word*
2. Location
3. Price
4. Number of rooms
5. Telephone number
6. Other essential information

1. THE ATTENTION WORD

Some advertisers call this the "kicker," or the "sex appeal," in an ad. This is the invitation that encourages response, the most important part of a successful ad. For many prospects it means the difference between passing over the ad and listing it as a possibility for telephoning. Owners have inserted ads from which they received no replies, have changed the ad to include one attention word, and then have become swamped with calls.

In the sample cottage ad, as with our ad for the A Avenue house in Chapter 8, the attention word is "redecorated," which may cause more tenants to respond than any other. This shows the importance of redecoration in the tenant's mind. "Redecorated" of course should be used only when appropriate. The ad should always honestly reflect conditions that will withstand inspection. No purpose is served by getting the prospect's attention if he will later be disappointed and fail to rent.

In this case, the Ballcryns had fairly recently decorated the entire cottage with the exception of the kitchen. If we were not renting to a manager-tenant we would have had the kitchen finished by the time a prospect appeared, leaving the convincing odor of fresh paint. The best sales appeal is earned by having the decoration completed, as many imaginations are limited to the optical image. However, many tenants will be satisfied if told the work will definitely be done within a prescribed time. Adverse reaction can be offset by telling the tenant that their choice of colors will be given consideration and thus the completed work can reflect their own personal taste.

In the sample ad for the flat the attention word is "spacious," which answers tenants' number-one desire, after a good neighborhood, for lots of room. This especially appeals to those grown claustrophobic from the cramped quarters in many newly constructed units.

Other examples of attention words, all inviting, are: *attractive, desirable, modern, new, sparkling, lovely, sunny, beautiful, view, luxurious, modernistic.* Attention words should catch the eye and warm the heart.

Change Wording When Results Wane

It pays to alter the wording of ads at frequent intervals when results wane. Some unimaginative owners run the same ad for a year or more. A large building with normal turnover calls for fairly continuous advertising. As a given mountain of prospective tenants gets mined out it is wise to change weekly the wording in the ad, including the key word, or first word.

Previously nonproductive prospects either have rented elsewhere or, if still shopping, will pass over an ad too often repeated, which they may already have checked off. But experience shows they will still respond to a differently worded ad for the same accommodation.

Sometimes the attention word may be listed first as the key word. But most prospective tenants look first for the heading of chief interest, such as "Furnished Apartments," or "Unfurnished Flats for Rent." Then they check each individual ad for the general area of their first choice.

2. LOCATION

This usually makes the location the key word in an ad. Listing a complete address may sometimes be advantageous, but generally the geographical area is all that is necessary. Before calling in person, most tenants telephone, because then they can get the exact address and travel instructions. The general location can usually be given:

> A well-known street, such as "B Boulevard"
> A familiar district, such as "Mercy Heights" or "Mercy Hospital"
> A definite area, such as "East Metropole"

Experiment will show which geographical description reaps the greatest response, and that description can be used first when advertising. If response then slackens a new reservoir of tenants can be secured by switching the geographical description.

I know of one 40-unit apartment house which was built one block from the city line, and which had twelve vacant apartments at the time it came to my attention. The owner continuously advertised the apartments as being in East Metropole, an area extending ten miles from the business center to the eastern boundary line. Prospective tenants answering the ad for "East Metropole" were disappointed to find the location so far out. Public transportation fares were on a zone basis, and the apartments were in the third fare zone from downtown Metropole.

Just one block away commenced a desirable residential subdivision incorporated as Cherry Heights. The apartment house owner, at my suggestion, switched his advertising heading to "Cherry Heights," and he filled his apartments in three weeks with prospects who wanted to live in that area. Now the owner advertises chiefly under "Cherry Heights." But when response slows periodically, he dips into the built-up reservoir of East Metropole prospects.

The name of the apartment house can be inserted from time to time. Since only a certain number of key words will be appropriate, it is not necessary to attempt dreaming up new starting words continuously. The key word can be merely rotated, after two or three weeks returning to the first-chosen word, as by that time a new group of tenants will be reading the ads.

3. PRICE

Should the amount of rent be listed or not? Some owners always indicate the rent. Others prefer a coy word such as "reasonable" or habitually omit all mention of rent. Which gets the best results?

Thousands of studies have been made by large advertisers, by newspapers, and by telephone companies interested in the ever expanding use of the telephone for shopping. I myself conducted some of these studies while with the telephone company. All agree that it pays to show the price, just as in a department store's large display ads. The price not only draws more response from legitimate prospects but weeds out time-wasting calls from the curious and from those who cannot afford the rental.

Out-of-date owners figure that if they list a big ad with many selling points, it would be better not to insert the price, because tenants may respond who would pay more than they had anticipated, after seeing the premises. This harks back to the leisurely days of cheap transportation when more shopping was done in person, more bargaining took place before a price was set, and buyers in general might not have been so budget-conscious. The owner who makes the most of his advertising will cater to up-to-date shopping methods.

A prospective tenant checks the ads with listings in a certain price range that fits the budget, just as we checked ads within certain ranges when shopping for property to buy. Tenants whose rental budget allows the $110 rent we are asking may check all pertinent ads from $95 to $125, having in mind that anything below $95 would be too undesirable and that they could go as high as $125 if nothing suitable can be found for less. In most cases where no price is listed they don't bother to call at all, figuring the price must be out of line. Why waste time on a pig in a poke when there are plenty of rentals with the amount advertised to choose from?

Some advertise "$110 per month" or similar superfluous wording. The "per month" is a waste of space and expense, as tenants know the rent is by the month unless specified otherwise.

Even though the base rental is fixed, the amount can be changed in the ad and thus draw from different groups of tenants if there are fringe accommodations which may vary the price. Most common is an available garage. The ad could first include the garage. If the unit fails to rent within a week, "garage" could be omitted from the ad and the price lessened by its market value, in this case $5. A tenant may respond to a $105 ad, then decide to pay the additional $5 to keep the garage. Otherwise it could be offered at that price to the tenant who at present has no garage, or it could be rented to someone in the neighborhood. With the continually expanding percentage of car owners, there is a shortage of garages in most rental areas, making spare garages easy to rent if fairly priced.

Other factors which may vary the rental are the inclusion of utilities, furniture, or special services. Some rentals have a flat price including utilities and an option of renting without utilities, but most owners have a fixed policy for an entire building. Some apartments give a choice of renting with or without furniture. But unless strictly controlled, this might require excessive storage and stand-by capital. Many buildings include janitor or maid service on an optional basis.

4. NUMBER OF ROOMS

Either the total number of rooms or the number of bedrooms should always be specified. This is essential information which the prospective tenant checks before selecting the ads to follow up. The specification can be switched to draw from different groups. For example, in place of the "5 rooms" used with our starting ad, the wording can be changed to "2 bedrooms" to cover the same accommodations.

5. TELEPHONE NUMBER

A charge for two words is often made for listing the telephone number, one for the exchange and one for the other numerals. The phone number is essential for maximum ad response, better than the address, as most tenants want to check by phone before calling in person.

6. OTHER ESSENTIAL INFORMATION

Much essential information is covered in metropolitan newspapers by the various classified headings. The headings "Unfurnished Home for Rent" and "Furnished Apartment for Rent" tell whether the rental unit is a home or an apartment, and whether it is furnished or unfurnished. If not covered by an appropriate heading, this information should be listed in the ad. If it is given in the heading it is a waste of advertising expense to repeat the information in the ad, as many owners do. For an otherwise unfurnished rental, specific items, like "stove, refrigerator," could be mentioned in the ad if desired.

Some larger metropolitan papers also have a geographical breakdown for various districts, such as "Central Metropole," and "North Metropole." They also often give the dividing street or streets, as "North Metropole, North of 40th St." Where these geographical areas are listed separately it is wasteful to repeat them in the ad. If there are many competing ads within the geographical area, the street could be listed, as we listed B Boulevard. Otherwise the address information could be omitted entirely where there is a geographical breakdown in the heading.

Utilities

If included in the rent, "utilities" should always be stated, preceding the amount of rent. One word is all that is necessary, as "including utilities" carries a superfluous word. If partial utilities, such as heat and water, are included they could be mentioned. If there is only a small item, such as water or scavenger service, it is normally just as well to save the information as an additional selling point when the prospect phones. Minor services seldom govern whether the prospect calls.

Children

If the accommodations are restricted to adults, this should be mentioned. Again one word, "adults," is sufficient. "Adults only" uses another superfluous word. This information will encourage calls from adults who prefer not to be in a building with children, and it will weed out profitless calls from families with children.

On the other hand, if children are permitted this may or may not be covered. Most parents will call where there are sufficient bedrooms to meet their needs, if child restrictions are not mentioned. If ad response is not satisfactory it would be desirable to test, including the one word, "children," in the ad, for the additional encouragement this will give.

Pets

Pets are permitted in most home rentals and forbidden in most furnished apartments. They may or may not be restricted according to the owner's judgment, balancing increased wear and tear against an increase in potential tenants. In most cases it is just as well not to mention this subject in the ad. There is no particular point in listing "no pet," as some owners do. If pets are not permitted, the comparatively few tenants demanding pets can be eliminated later. A pet-owner might feel antagonistic and refuse to answer a "no pet" ad, but I have had several answer such ads and make other arrangements for their pets in order to take the accommodations. Some leave them at boarding kennels. Others lend or give their pets to friends or relatives who can care for them.

Services

The inclusion of regular janitor service or maid service should be mentioned. The trend is to reduce these services as much as possible, because of rising labor costs. Luxury renters, those able to pay high premiums for personal services, tend to utilize hotel suites like those at the Waldorf-Astoria. But the average tenant chooses the least personal service for the least rent. Witness the armies of new home buyers who seek low monthly payments and expect no personal services.

Personal-service rentals cannot compete with home ownership pricewise. Rental units with no maid or janitor services can meet any but taxpayer subsidized price competition. Since these services are less customary, they should always be cited where provided.

Other Information

Other essential information to present where appropriate includes *launderette, yard, playground, pool, patio, barbecue, sauna bath, garage, air-conditioned, sun deck, view*. Words like these can be alternated to attract different groups of tenants.

The Goldens move out of the Number 4 flat the morning of September 30. When the ad for the flat is phoned into the leading Metropole daily, we are asked how long it should run. The salesgirl says it can run four days for the price of three, and a week for the price of five days. If the unit is rented before the end of a week we can cancel the ad and be charged only for the time run. We therefore place the ad for a week, a sufficient period for most individual rentals. If the flat is not rented at the end of the week, the ad can be renewed and reworded. We arrange to start the ad Saturday October 2 by which time the kitchen and bath will be painted and the cleanup completed.

We are asked to pay for the ad before it expires. On larger properties it is advisable to arrange for advertising and billing on a monthly basis. In the latter event discounts are usually offered both for volume and for payment within a specified time, such as ten days, after billing.

Now that that our ad has been placed, we should be prepared or have our manager prepared, when a prospect responds. This brings us to selling the accommodation so that the prospect will become a renter—which is a field we will cover in the next chapter.

The best apartment bargain may lie vacant unless prospective tenants are informed through advertising. The most dependable medium is a properly worded classified newspaper ad, short and to the point.

13. HOW TO SHOW
AND RENT APARTMENTS

Some owners attract tenants by advertising and then chase them away because of a cold or indifferent presentation of the premises. Many a prospective tenant is lost who could be retained with nominal salesmanship. Choice apartments may act as silent salesmen, but it takes active selling by the manager to change a prospect into a rent payer.

Most experienced owners know that a rental unit has to be sold on the premises, but many overlook selling when the prospect telephones in answer to an ad. Lackadaisical response to a telephone call can discourage the caller completely and nullify the appeal of the ad. What merit to a provocative ad if the tenant is not encouraged by telephone to visit the premises?

Selling should therefore be divided into two distinct phases:

1. Selling by telephone
2. Selling on the premises

SELLING BY TELEPHONE

Like all selling, obtaining results by telephone requires planning rather than depending on haphazard methods. Some personalities intuitively know the right thing to say at the right time, but even the best natural salesman can improve his results by planning. Witness the thousands of planned sales courses conducted in all industries.

While I was a training supervisor with the telephone company I designed courses and gave considerable instruction in both telephone and on-the-premises selling. This background has proved invaluable for the efficient selling of apartment rentals. I have tested the following suggestions through practice, and I now pass them on to my apartment managers, as you will no doubt do.

Instruction concerning the telephone contact can be more easily assimilated and applied by breaking it into natural steps:

1. Be prepared
2. Sing response
3. Find desires
4. Give sales punches
5. Say goodbye

1. Be Prepared (By Telephone)

The placing of the ad is the first preparation; then the manager should be ready when the ad response comes over the telephone. The Good Manager, like the Good Scout, will be prepared for possible eventualities.

The telephone should be located for convenient and quick answering, placed adjacent to or on a table or desk where notes can be taken and where pertinent information can be readily available. The line should be kept free for expected calls, and it should be an individual, or private, line, not subject to interruption or use by other parties.

Pencil and blank paper should be at the telephone; also any street maps, showing streetcar or bus lines, which may be needed in guiding a prospect to the premises. A copy of the ad should be on hand. It is well also, especially until you are more experienced, to have an outline by the telephone, with pertinent information about the unit and points which should be covered in the telephone contact. These can then be checked off on each contact. Thus any vital unchecked items can be included before the call is irrevocably terminated by hanging up the telephone.

It is now the Saturday morning that our ad first appears in the morning edition of the *Metropolitan*. Our flat is all spick-and-span. The kitchen has been repainted with a cream-white ceiling and light green walls.

2. Sing Response (By Telephone)

The caller on the other end of the telephone line cannot see the smile that reveals your pleasing personality. He has only the smile or the gloom in your voice to judge you sunny or a sourpuss. The caller will be attracted by a pleasing response and will be repelled by a harsh or indifferent attitude. Thus when you answer make a conscious effort until it becomes instinctive to respond with a lilt that will take the place of a smile.

Some advertisers answer their telephones with "Yes?" in a challenging tone. Or they merely say, "Hello." Both are unbusinesslike and uninviting. When expecting business calls such as the response to a rental ad, you should answer the phone by giving the name of the establishment, such as "Belvedere Apartments." Or the name of the person, "Mrs. Wister."

Both may be given if desired—"Belvedere Apartments, Mrs. Wister."

It is a matter of choice whether to add the word "speaking" or similar wording to the name, but this is not necessary. Normally with a short, abrupt name like Murga a more euphonious response is gained by "Mrs. Murga speaking." With a longer name like Enterprise, the name is sufficient in itself.

The last syllable should have a rising rather than a falling inflection. The latter discourages the caller. The former carries an invitation, like opening the door of the premises to a visitor.

The telephone rings for the first call of the day at 10:30 A.M. The Wisters have agreed that the wife will be the one who will normally answer the telephone. She responds, "Belvedere Apartments—Mrs. Wister," with an inviting lilt on the last syllable.

3. Find Desires (By Telephone)

This is a fact-finding step. The prospective tenant will ask questions to clarify points in the ad and elaborate on other conditions not mentioned. If discussion suggests an unsuitable caller the manager can also inject the minimum questions needed to eliminate the undesirable tenant. Most of the manager's checking, however, will take place at the premises. The chief object of the telephone contact is to encourage the prospective tenant to visit the premises.

ON WITH OUR FIRST CALL

A feminine voice on the other end of the line asks, "Is this the place that has an ad in the *Metropolitan?*"

"Yes, we advertised a spacious five-room flat."

"Does it have three regular bedrooms, or is that just two bedrooms?"

"It has two nice bedrooms, one fairly large. Then there's a folding wall bed in the living room."

"We have to have three bedrooms. We have a son in college, and now my mother is moving in with us. So your place wouldn't suit us."

Before the party hangs up, Mrs. Wister tries again. "Do you think you could make out with the folding bed in the living room to take the place of a third bedroom? I would be glad to have you come out and take a look at the whole place and see how it might work out. I'm sure you'll like everything if you come out to see it."

"No, my mother has to have a separate room, and so does my son so he can study. We have to have three bedrooms. Goodbye."

In this contact the desire-finding step revealed that the rental unit was unsuitable. When a prospect wants a certain number of bedrooms or has some other specific requirement, it is best to determine this as soon as possible. The tenant will usually ask about these specific items early in the contact.

When a specific desire cannot readily be met, it is a waste of time to attempt further sales appeals other than pointing out possible substitute arrangements. The review of desires eliminates the unsuitable and selects the suitable.

4. Give Sales Punches (By Telephone)

The sales punches that win the prospect cannot normally be delivered with one attack any more than the average boxer wins with one blow, but they are delivered at every opportunity. There is bound to be some sparring. Except for purely elimination questions, most replies can contain an appeal which we call the punch in the contact.

ANOTHER PROSPECT CALLS

In a few minutes the phone rings again and another woman is on the line. "Do you have a flat for rent?"

"Yes, we have a nice, spacious five-room flat."

"What's the address?"

"Three-six-eight-oh B Boulevard, and it's a nice neighborhood in the Mercy Heights district. Would you be coming by bus or car?"

"In our car."

"Do you know how to get to B Boulevard?"

"Sure. One thing I want to know before I come out. Is this a regular apartment building, or one of those screwy made-over houses you're trying to rent?"

Here is an opportune time to try a sales punch.

"It's a good-sized regular flat in a nice four-flat building. The name is the Belvedere Apartments, right over the front. That will be a good landmark to help find it."

"Is there a garden or yard where you can get some sunshine?"

Another opening.

"Oh, yes. There's a secluded yard on the south side that stays sunny all day. It has a sunny exposure and is shielded by shrubbery."

5. Say Goodbye (By Telephone)

Enough information has developed to close the contact by asking the prospect to make a personal visit. It is best on the telephone to avoid lengthy conversation, which may do more harm than good. All questions, whether favorable or adverse, should be answered by a pleasing response that attempts to satisfy the tenant. A pleasant manner will indicate a willingness to answer questions, but the sooner the prospect can be committed to visiting the premises the better.

An easy way to obtain a commitment is by the "left-handed" or "contained decision" approach. Some salesmen call this "closing on a minor point." Instead of asking, "Why don't you come out?" ask, "What time can you come?" The establishment of a time "contains" the decision to come.

In this contact Mrs. Wister says, "I'm sure you'll like everything if you see it. When would you be able to come?"

"About one o'clock. Will you be there then?"

"Yes, I'll be here all day. Could I have your name so I'll know who it is when you get here?"

"Mrs. Allen."

"Thank you. Then I'll be looking for you at one." Mrs. Wister pauses for a moment to see if Mrs. Allen has any further questions and to give the caller the opportunity of terminating the call.

Mrs. Allen agrees, "That's right. Goodbye."

Full many a prospect like this one has been sold on the idea of making a personal visit and then has been frightened away by the manager's not knowing enough to say goodbye. Do not attempt to overload with information. A prospect can be built up to a commitment, and after that point prolonged selling pours over his head like cold water. One of the vital essentials of efficient selling is to know when to say goodbye.

MORE PHONE CALLS

The phone rings four more times before the arrival, at one thirty, of the Allens, the first visitors. One more prospect agrees to look over the flat but refuses to give a name.

ONE PROSPECT WANTS NEW FURNITURE

Another prospect says that the only furniture she has is a TV set. In addition to our stove and refrigerator, would we provide the rest of the necessary furniture? All they would need is a bedroom set, a dinette set, a sofa set, rugs, lamps, and odd tables and chairs. They are just a couple with no children. Both employed. Would be good tenants. Would be permanent if this furniture could be bought for them. Don't require anything fancy, but would like everything modern and in good taste. Later on they plan to buy all their own furniture, and we could then use ours somewhere else.

Most of this furniture we previously possessed and disposed of. Should we revise our previous decision, change our plans, and buy new furniture in order to secure this apparently desirable tenant?

GIVE PLANS AN HONEST TRIAL BEFORE CHANGING

Here is where some new owners might get panicky, toss out their planning, and agree to the prospective tenant's request. Once a course has been set, the owner should attempt for at least two weeks to rent as planned before changing. In this case we have not even shown the premises to the first visitor. Very likely the "permanent renter" might be the first to move, or might change her mind and not move in at all. The most demanding tenants are apt to be impossible to satisfy.

After fruitless attempts have been made to follow original plans, a change may be considered, like buying additional furniture for a desirable tenant, further decoration or modernization, or a rent reduction. All other steps should be exhausted before reducing the rent.

The caller is advised that the place will be rented without furniture, except for the stove and the refrigerator. But they are welcome to come out and look the flat over. Perhaps they will find it just what they would like, and they could buy the necessary furniture themselves. It could all be bought on time, of course, if that would be more convenient.

The caller says no, in that case they will look elsewhere.

THE RED-INK ROAD TO RUIN

One might wonder why they replied to our ad for an unfurnished flat, instead of answering ads for furnished accommodations. This is a typical example of the perversities of human nature, and it serves as a warning that if the owner is to progress it is up to him to operate as he sees fit. He should be open to, but not unduly swayed by, suggestions.

Well-meaning friends or tenants are apt to offer an owner conflicting advice on how best to operate. A new owner is especially fair game to a would-be adviser. Often the most insistent advice comes from the rankest personal failure. Such words of wisdom are seldom of value, since sound counsel can usually be given only by another successful owner.

As the red road to hell is paved with "good intentions," the red-ink road to ruin is paved with well-intentioned advice.

DON'T BANK ON PROMISES

Most prospects who agree to visit the premises intend to keep their promise. But, with the intention of checking a certain number, they will call all ads of interest. Mrs. Allen, for example, might answer fifteen ads and select five to be visited. She might visit all five before making up her mind. She could be dissatisfied with all and start a new round of visits another day. Or she could fall in love with the first place visited, automatically eliminating the remaining four. The owner can only hope that his ad will be toward the head of the list and that his premises will not be eliminated by a prior choice.

This is one advantage of downtown rentals. A tenant may check over rentals in various locations. Wanting to be as close downtown as possible, other things appearing equal, he usually starts with the closest in and works out. Outlying rentals may be selected when they offer more in convenience and appearance. Otherwise they will be chosen more for cheaper rent or extra amenities than for location.

SELLING ON THE PREMISES

In order to do a good job of showing the flats to Mrs. Allen and other visitors, we will examine the five steps of the premises contact. They are similar in outline to the telephone steps:

1. Be prepared
2. Be inviting
3. Find desires
4. Give sales punches
5. Say "Buy" and say goodbye

1. BE PREPARED (ON THE PREMISES)

All necessary forms, such as leases and receipts, should be ready at hand. Besides having a presentable rental unit it is essential that the manager who shows the property be presentable.

Apartment Should Be Spick-and-Span

With most vacancies, rent can be collected continuously by showing the unit to a new tenant while the outgoing tenant is still in possession. This is especially true where a building is already in top rental condition. In such an event the apartment would present a lived-in appearance, and furniture in use would help to cover dust. A prospective tenant is not so apt to poke thoroughly into a current tenant's cupboards, closets, stove and refrigerator.

But we plan considerable sprucing up in order to raise rents and resale value. Most often our apartments, while undergoing an improvement program, will be vacated for a few days. This means the apartment would be vacant when shown to a new tenant. The prospect will feel free to examine the vacant apartment with an eagle eye. The rental unit should therefore be spick-and-span, welcoming a thorough inspection.

Dirt Costs Money

I know of one apartment building with twenty-four small 2-room furnished units where the rents were as low as $60 monthly, 'way below the market. Vacancies were still hard to rent because the owner, an elderly widow who managed the building herself, had a policy of renting "as is." It didn't matter how much dirt, grime, and debris were left by the outgoing tenant. The filth was left for the new tenant to clean up. Why?

The widow suffered from arthritis, which kept her from doing the cleaning, and she felt she would gain in the long run by saving the cost of having the work done. This was an extreme example of being "penny wise and pound foolish."

I advocated giving each vacancy a thorough cleaning, including mopping bathroom and kitchen, and cleaning out the stove and the refrigerator. This was done for a labor cost of $10 per apartment. Then, with no other changes except needed painting, the apartments rented readily at $90 a month, a 50 per cent increase.

At my suggestion the $10 cleaning cost was charged in advance to the incoming tenant, so removing the dirt did not cost the owner a cent. The tenants accepted the cleaning charge without protest, glad to move into a spick-and-span apartment.

Manager Should Be Neat and Trim

The manager who shows the property should appear neat and trim. Desirable tenants judge a building and the caliber of tenants who will be their neighbors by the appearance of the manager. A sloppily dressed, unkempt manager can rent only to similar tenants, whereas a neat-appearing manager will draw desirable tenants.

Some owners spend freely to attract tenants by keeping building and grounds in tiptop appearance. Then they hire a tenant-repelling witch for a manager. Perhaps it would be prudent not to mention too specific examples which might be recognized. Among hundreds of desirable apartments inspected I have found scores of managers who would fall into one of the following general categories:

1. Dirty Doras with strong, unwashed-body odors, the I-take-a-bath-once-every-spring type

2. Raggedy Anns with filthy, sometimes tattered, clothing, the I-can't-work-in-decent-clothes type
3. Tugboat Annies with belligerent attitudes, the You-scum-I-really-don't-want-you-as-a-tenant type

Whether or not a manager is naturally handsome, she can always appear neat, with a fresh shower and make-up, hair in place, shoes clean, clothing clean and trim. Jobs like vacuuming halls and cleaning apartments should be done in the morning, before most prospective tenants call. Even when cleanup is under way it is always possible to keep hair in bounds and work clothing changed regularly to present a passable appearance.

As important as appearance is a manager's attitude. A grumpy manager will discourage tenants from accommodations that answer every desire. A manager with a pleasing and inviting personality will encourage tenants to overlook items they may have considered paramount.

2. BE INVITING (ON THE PREMISES)

The steps of a contact naturally overlap somewhat. Many items under step 1, "Be Prepared," also fit into step 2, "Be Inviting." As part of his preparation, the owner should see that premises and manager are generally presentable. Then the manager should carry out the owner's policy, so that the prospect will be invited to become a tenant.

Prospective tenants keep evaluating a property from the moment of their arrival in the neighborhood until their departure. If the vicinity is run-down, the tenant may keep going to the next call on the list. If the front yard or the front of the building looks undesirable the tenant may not even bother to stop. It is of prime importance to keep up the front so as to present a good first impression.

The Wisters therefore have trimmed the shrubbery and freshly mowed the lawn. The front porch has been repaired and modernized with wide brick steps, transforming the former run-down eyesore. The front presents a fairly attractive appearance. It can be further improved chiefly by exterior paint, but that must wait till the weather permits.

After the prospect stops at the premises and appears at the front door, the next hurdle may be the lobby or the hallway or, in the case of the cottage, the rear yard. All approaches to the manager's door should be given priority attention, so that they will cause the tenant to continue rather than turn back.

The First Prospect Arrives

Mr. and Mrs. Allen ring the cottage doorbell at one thirty, just as the telephone rings. Mrs. Wister answers the telephone, and Mr. Wister greets the prospects with a cheery smile. "Good afternoon. Are you here to see the flat?"

"Yes, we're Mr. and Mrs. Allen. We expected to be a little earlier. We phoned—I guess your wife?"

"She's on the phone now. We're the managers. I am George Wister. Won't you come in?"

If the Allens had not volunteered their name, it would have been well to say at the beginning of the interview, "I'm George Wister. What is your name?" Referring to the prospect by name thereafter helps to put the interview on a more personal basis, which will aid in developing discussion.

When Mrs. Wister finishes her telephone conversation, she takes the opportunity, without appearing too obvious, to show that there are other good prospects. A cool prospect often turns hot as soon as a serious rival appears. The threat of competition must, of course, be handled with tact, as overdoing it will antagonize.

"There's another tenant wants to come right out," Mrs. Wister remarks to her husband. To the Allens, she may say, "Sorry for the delay. That phone's been ringing all day long."

3. FIND DESIRES (ON THE PREMISES)

In the inspection of the accommodations, the chief objective is to point out particular advantages. The main fault to avoid is making obvious generalities. I have heard some managers on a premises tour actually parroting, like a nursery rhyme, only the obvious that the tenant can already see:

"This is the living room. . . .
"This is the bedroom. . . .
"This is the kitchen. . .
"This is the bathroom."

Point Out Specific Advantages

To sell an apartment, some particular advantage in each room should always be pointed out. As Mrs. Wister guides the Allens through the flat, she mentions specific attractions.

"This furnace really throws out the heat in a hurry when you want it. You'll notice it doesn't smoke or smell because it has good venting.

It has a good heating capacity. Isn't it warm and comfortable today?
. . . The master bedroom is plenty large even for twin beds. And look how big these closets are. Lots of space for Mrs. Allen, with room to spare for Mr. Allen."

Mr. Allen remarks that he will certainly be thankful.

"Here is a spare wall bed in the living-room closet. You'll have loads of room for overnight guests, and for storage, too, with the extra bedroom in back. You can always make use of storage space, can't you?"

"Oh, sure," Mrs. Allen agrees. "We don't really need two extra beds, but as long as we have them they will come in handy when our two married children stay with us Christmas. They live out of town, you know. They visit the other side of their families Thanksgiving, and we always have our family reunion Christmas. There would be no objection to their staying overnight, would there?"

"No," says Mrs. Wister, "a short visit like that would be perfectly all right. It's good that you can make use of the beds. . . . Here in the kitchen the paint has just finished drying, so you don't have to worry about touching it. You can see there are quite a few cabinets, which always come in handy. There's a double outlet behind the refrigerator. And here are outlets on each side of the sink for your electric appliances. . . . On this service porch there's room for a washer and a dryer. Do you have both?"

Mrs. Allen says she has only a washer. She may be a bit old-fashioned, but she likes to hang her washing in the sun whenever possible.

"In that case you'll find this sheltered landing convenient. The pulley clothesline on this landing would be shared only with the tenant next door. Otherwise you have it to yourself whenever you want. Isn't that handy?"

By injecting occasional questions the prospect is encouraged to express his desires. Questions should be so worded as to encourage a "Yes" response, as with the last query. Every time a prospect agrees, his thinking is further conditioned toward complete agreement to renting.

By salient points like the foregoing the desirable features of the apartment can be sold. Questioning helps bring out how the apartment's attractions fit the tenant's desires.

4. GIVE SALES PUNCHES (ON THE PREMISES)

Sales appeals that will sell the apartment can be delivered in three different stages:

By pinpointing during the tour of the premises. Specific examples have just been covered in step 3.

By summarizing after the tour of the premises. The most attractive features can be summarized, including points previously overlooked.

By answering tenant's objections at any time during the contact.

Turn Objections into Sales Appeals

Selling can have marked effect when objections can be answered so that they will turn into appeals. Most salesmen are familiar with the three time-tested ways to answer objections:

The pass-up method
The boomerang method
The yes-but method

The Pass-up Method

This can be called the I-ignore-your-statement or I-don't-want-to-fight method, the most effective way to avoid an argument. Especially on what may be a ticklish matter, like a husband and wife asking you to arbitrate between them, the pass-up offers an easy retreat.

For example, in showing the master bedroom Mrs. Wister mentioned that the room was "plenty large even for twin beds." This innocent remark provoked an argument.

Mrs. Allen immediately pounced. "You know, that's a good idea, having twin beds. You can sleep without being disturbed every time your husband turns over." Then, to her husband, "As long as this would be large enough, don't you think now is the time to buy a twin-bed set?"

Mr. Allen replied, "We've been over that many times, dear. We'd have to put out the money for a new set, and you know I don't favor the idea of twin beds. A man might have to commute to work, but I can't see the object of commuting to my wife. Mrs. Wister, don't you believe it's best for a husband and wife to have a double bed?"

If the manager takes either side the argument will be prolonged, the arbiter will wind up with the blame, and the tenants will be lost. Here the pass-up calms the roiled waters.

(Pass-up) "I guess that just depends on how you sleep, and a lot of circumstances." (Switch subject.) "If you look out the window here you'll notice the secluded yard. See how the shrubbery shields it all around?"

The Boomerang Method

The boomerang reply can often be used to turn an objection directly into an appeal.

In the living room Mrs. Allen complains, "I don't think we'll like that furnace. We would much rather have central heating. It heats so much better. We used to rent a place with an old-fashioned furnace, and it never did give out enough heat."

(Boomerang) "It probably didn't have enough heating capacity. This is a very efficient circulating-type furnace that circulates the heat all over the flat. It has forty-five thousand BTU, more than you need to keep the whole flat heated. The big advantage is that it gives the most economical heat you can get. Your heat bills will be less with this, so you can save and still be plenty comfortable. Isn't it nice and warm now?"

Mrs. Allen agrees that the furnace seems to be doing all right now, and that maybe there is a difference in furnaces. If it saves on fuel bills, they can certainly appreciate that advantage.

In the kitchen Mrs. Allen objects, "We have a breakfast set and a dinette set too. We like to use the breakfast table when we don't have company. This kitchen is too small for a breakfast set."

(Boomerang) "A compact kitchen makes it easier to work in. You'd be surprised how many steps you save in a day by a compact, functional kitchen. And the previous tenant had a small breakfast set at the end, near the service porch."

Mrs. Allen agrees, "I guess that *is* a good place to put my breakfast table."

The contact progresses more smoothly if, after answering an objection, the manager proceeds to another subject, rather than waiting to prolong the discussion. In this case Mrs. Wister opens the door to the service porch and starts pointing out its advantages, some previously mentioned. "Notice how handy the service porch is to the kitchen. . . ."

The Yes-but Method

The easiest and most commonly used transition from an objection to an appeal is the Yes-but response. Here you first agree with the prospect to take the wind out of his sails. Then you use an appeal to counteract the objection.

When the fresh paint in the kitchen is mentioned, Mrs. Allen says, "This place looks all right inside, but what are you going to do about the outside? The front especially needs painting for sure."

(Yes-but) "I'm glad you mentioned that, because it certainly should be painted," yesses Mrs. Wister. "But you can't do a good outside paint job in cold weather. The owner plans to paint outside as soon as the weather is warm enough. Won't the front look attractive with all new colors?"

"Why, yes, that would be nice. How long would we have to wait?"

Mrs. Wister replies that it will probably be a couple of months, but it will definitely be done when the weather permits.

Most tenants' objections can be overcome by adequate salesmanship. At points in this contact with the Allens the objections could have been magnified if not properly handled, and the tenant lost. Thus far our contact is progressing smoothly, and we still have a good chance to gain the Allens as tenants.

Don't Draw Attention to Disadvantages

There is no object in drawing the tenant's attention to overlooked drawbacks. What may appear disadvantageous to the owner or the manager may not loom large to an individual tenant. The lack of a shower over the tub, for example, would prove decisive to many tenants and insignificant to others. If the prospect is legitimately interested in the apartment, he will bring out any particularly disturbing items.

"One thing I don't like is climbing up to the top floor," Mrs. Allen objects. "Then there's noise next door and below you. We would be waked up during the night every time somebody comes and goes."

(Yes-but) "Of course you don't want to be waked at all hours. But we have good steady tenants who don't keep late hours. We haven't been bothered a bit by that. And you'll find you won't get street noise at night with your bedroom toward the back of the lot like this. . . . Another thing you haven't looked at yet is the garage. You have only a few steps from the back door. Won't that be handy when you're shopping?"

"Oh, that's right," says Mr. Allen. "We haven't seen the garage yet. Let's take a look at it."

Cover Desirable Features

Depending on the tenant's reaction, a greater or smaller number of desirable points may be covered. No rental accommodation can be perfect in all respects, but most have attractive features which should be described. Among the major desirable features which should be covered where appropriate are those indicated in Chapter 5 under "What Do Tenants Want?"

> Good location
> Large rooms
> Ample closets and storage space
> Satisfactory laundry arrangements
> Convenient layout of rooms
> Adequate space for furniture in bedrooms
> Adequate working or eating space in kitchen

Another check list is provided in the previous chapter on advertising, under "The Attention Word" and "Other Essential Information." The items suggested for advertising will prove of interest to the premises visitor.

5. SAY "BUY" AND SAY GOODBYE (ON THE PREMISES)

The Allens have seen enough to enable them to feel a genuine interest. Prolonging the inspection may suggest other minor objections. It is wise at this point to guide the contact toward a successful termination, changing the prospect to a renter.

The accommodations may obviously misfit the tenant's needs; for example the sleeping capacity may be totally inadequate. Or the tenant may be obviously objectionable, like a wildlife lover who insists on keeping a pet leopard. In either case, the sooner the manager says goodbye and prepares for the next prospect, the better.

Always Ask a Good Prospect to Buy

The manager should never allow genuine prospects, like the Allens, to leave the premises without asking them to buy. Many a prospect leaves without renting merely because he isn't asked to. The prospect can be asked to buy by two methods:

The direct request
The "left-handed" request

The Direct Request

Some prospects are so eager they make a cursory inspection, then turn to the manager and say, "I'll take it."

Even most of the ready renters wait to be asked. If their approbation is quite apparent the manager may make the direct request, "Would you like to take the apartment?"

This of course is timesaving but, sad to say, often results in unnecessary failure. Many tenants like to spar before making up their minds. A direct request makes it too easy to say, "No," or "No, we haven't made up our minds yet." Once a prospect says no, it is much harder for him later to say yes.

The Left-handed Request

The easiest way to encourage a "Yes" response is by the "left-handed" or "contained decision" approach previously mentioned under "Selling By Telephone." The tenant is asked a question which does not require him to say he will definitely rent the apartment. His reply, however, contains the decision to rent. Thus a minor point gains his acquiescence.

Many categories of inquiry can be utilized for a left-handed request. Typical examples involve:

Alternate choice of accommodations
The moving-in date
Payment arrangements
Lease arrangements

ALTERNATE CHOICE OF ACCOMMODATIONS

An easy opening is presented where a choice of accommodations or services is available. If more than one flat were vacant, the tenant could be asked, "Which apartment would you prefer, Mrs. Allen?"

Where there is a choice of garages or of similar minor items, indicating a preference contains the decision to rent the entire accommodation. In this case there is one vacant garage plus the manager's garage which might be offered for a choice. "You could have either the garage against the wall or the one in the middle, Mr. Allen. Which would you prefer?"

If certain equipment or services are optional, these can be presented for the prospect's choice. "Would you want your apartment to include janitor service, or would you rather save the extra charge?" "Would you want us to furnish a refrigerator, or will you have your own?"

THE MOVING-IN DATE

If the accommodations are ready, as our flat is, you might ask, "Would you be able to move in right away?"

If an existing tenant is not moving till the end of the month, for example, you might try, "Would you like to move in on the first of the month?"

PAYMENT ARRANGEMENTS

Payment arrangements offer an especially effective means of encouraging an affirmative decision:

"Would you like to pay a deposit to tie up the apartment, or would you just as soon pay your first month's rent now?"

"Is the first of the month a convenient time to pay your rent?"

"Would you like to pay your rent by check or cash?"

LEASE ARRANGEMENTS

Tenants may ask about the lease before making a decision. Lease arrangements can sometimes be used to test interest, making a transition to a later, more definite request. Here are examples:

"Would you like to look over our lease, in case you have any questions?"

"We normally rent on a month-to-month [or annual, if customary] basis. We have all our tenants sign a lease and an inventory form so that they will be familiar with our house rules. Would you like to look over our lease now?"

As a rule the lease arrangements would not be discussed until after the tenant made an affirmative decision.

The Manager Proceeds with
a Successful Contact

Mrs. Wister selects the first example under "Payment Arrangements" and asks the Allens if they would prefer to pay a deposit or a full month's rent.

THE PROSPECT STALLS

Mrs. Allen replies, "That doesn't matter. But I want to look at more apartments before deciding for sure."

This is a common response for the many prospects who hate to get off the fence. The wide-awake manager will avoid giving a really interested tenant a chance to look further. Once a prospect leaves the premises he is usually lost, for he probably won't come back. The next manager, with no better accommodations, may be more persuasive and will consummate the rental. This thought should always be kept paramount when tenants like the Allens attempt to postpone a decision.

MRS. WISTER TRIES FOR ANOTHER LEFT-HANDED DECISION

Several left-handed requests may be needed to produce success. Mrs. Wister tries another tack. "It looks like this might fit pretty well what you are looking for. Is that right?"

"Well, yes, it looks all right," agrees Mrs. Allen. "But I have some more places on my list to look at before we make up our minds. If we don't find something else we like better, we'll be back."

MRS. WISTER GIVES SALES PUNCHES

It is better to press and lose than to let the tenant go without an aggressive attempt to complete the sale. Mrs. Wister Yes-buts into sales punches:

"Of course you might feel more satisfied that way. But while you're looking you might not find anything you like as well . . . with the space we have . . . as reasonable as this . . . in such a nice district. And by the time you came back I probably would have this place rented to someone else, as I have several very interested people coming this afternoon."

MRS. WISTER AGAIN ASKS THE TENANT TO BUY

It is timely to make another request to buy before the tenant gets restless. Women love to shop, while men avoid needless shopping. Since Mrs. Allen has agreed that the flat is acceptable, Mrs. Wister concentrates on Mr. Allen:

"As long as this flat is satisfactory for you, why don't you give me a deposit to hold the place, so that you will be sure not to lose it? Would fifty dollars be all right for a deposit, Mr. Allen?"

HOLDING DEPOSIT

"It's O.K. with me," agrees Mr. Allen. "Let's go ahead and give a deposit on this, dear. Then we'll be sure of having a place that suits us."

Mrs. Allen protests that she expected to look further, but if Mr. Allen wants, they might as well pay a deposit to hold the place.

Once a deposit is paid it would be very unusual for a tenant to continue shopping. While a prospect who leaves without putting money on the line seldom comes back again, a tenant who pays a deposit nearly always returns and pays a full month's rent. The Allens agree to return about six the next evening with the full month's rent.

Mrs. Wister gives a special "Holding Deposit" receipt in exchange for the $50. The paying of "earnest money" and the tenant's endorsement of the Holding Deposit's terms thus successfully conclude the sale.

RECEIPT FOR HOLDING DEPOSIT, APARTMENTS: Belvedere Apts. Receipt # 127

In consideration of $ 50.00 the undersigned manager hereby agrees to hold Apartment No. -4-,

3680 B Blvd. Street, Metropole, Columbia

for -1- days, to and including the 3rd day of October 19 65, for the undersigned tenant who agrees to accept said apartment on said date, at a rental of $ 110.00 per month, payable in advance on the said date

It is further agreed: 1. That the prospective tenancy is subject to the Owner's approval of the Tenant's credit and character references; 2. That the Tenant will sign and agree to the Owner's Standard Lease Form and pay the Owner's customary charges and deposits; 3. That in the event the prospective tenant does not take the said apartment and pay all charges on the said date, then the consideration herein mentioned shall be considered as and for the rental of said apartment and costs incidental thereto from the date of this receipt to the said 3rd day of October 19 65.

If the prospective tenant does take said apartment, then this deposit will be applied on the first month's rental hereunder.

Geo. W. Allen   Ailene Wister
PROSPECTIVE TENANT   MANAGER

DATED October 2, 1965   JOSEPH ENTERPRISE Owner

CREDIT AND CHARACTER REFERENCES

Mrs. Wister casually states, "With you, of course, it is only a matter of routine. But the owner requires that all tenants fill out an application form that includes character and credit references."

Usually with a couple only one person is asked to complete the form, but with separate breadwinners, such as two men or two women sharing accommodations, each is required to fill out the application. Mr. Allen completes the form as shown without protest. The tenant's business address and occupation, along with other listed information, should prove helpful in screening questionable prospects. It will also prove invaluable should action later be taken to collect delinquent rents or other damages, or in knowing whom to notify in case of death or serious illness.

TIME TO SAY GOODBYE

At this point it is well to cover any remaining business as swiftly as possible and say goodbye. As in the telephone contact, prolonged needless discussion may only throw cold water on a tenant who has already said yes.

The lease arrangements might be introduced, or they could be covered when the tenant returns to pay the full month's rent, or when he moves in. Usually the full lease arrangements should be reviewed at the time of paying the deposit. We are now ready for the next chapter's detailed coverage of effective lease terms.

It takes active selling to change a prospective tenant into a renter. Telephone callers must be encouraged to visit the premises, where they can be persuaded to become tenants.

TENANT APPLICATION TO RENT ACCOMMODATION
Character & Credit References & Specifications

Name ____Geo. W. Allen_____ Phone __837-9032__

Address ___6216 Angora Ct., Metropole_____

Number of Occupants ___2_____ Pets, specify ___None_____

Children _-0-_ Ages of Children: Boys_____ Girls_____

Have you formerly occupied rented accommodations? __Yes_____

Most recent rental __6216 Angora Ct._____ How long?__1 year__

Present Occupation __Engineer_____

Business Address __Metropole Electrical Products Corp.___

Spouse's employment __Housewife_____

Give 3 Credit References, including Bank:

Name	Address	Phone
Metropole Nat'l. Bank	2100 Broadway	822-5000
Bank Metro Prod. Credit Union	84701 Lucerne St.	410-8073
Ace Dept. Store	2550 Main	821-4411

Give 3 Character References:

Mother: Lucy Allen	516 Helvitia St.	827-4176
Nearest relative or friend Rev. Benj. Douthit	First Christian Church	821-3010
Pastor or other Church Reference Dr. Henry Ward	4020 Steele St.	457-6559

Accommodations wanted:____No. of Rooms_5__Furn.____Unfurn._X_Garage____X____

Do you have a TV?_X_Piano?_0_Auto?_X_Make_Ford_Type_4-Dr_Year_1964___

Drivers License Number: __XC1072394_____

Date accommodations wanted__At once_____

Date of this application__Oct. 2, 1965_____

Signed ___Geo. W. Allen____
Tenant Applicant

JOSEPH ENTERPRISE, AFFILIATED OWNER
NATIONAL APARTMENT ASSOCIATION
COLUMBIA APARTMENT ASSOCIATION

14. HOW TO PUT TEETH IN APARTMENT LEASES

Out of a hundred tenants ninety-nine are honest and respectable citizens who pay their rent on time and mind their own business. But the most careful screening may not prevent an occasional dead beat or troublemaker from worming his way into your building.

One Rotten Apple in a Bushel

I have known apartment houses where one malicious tenant has kept a whole building in constant turmoil, with resulting costly turnover. Like one rotten apple in a bushel of sound apples, one vicious or undesirable tenant can corrupt a wholesome apartment house and turn happy tenants into dissatisfied ones.

Contented tenants will eventually turn sour and vacate unless the rotten apple is thrown out. Once the troublemaker is removed, the remaining tenants will normally settle into a stable state of contentment.

To keep a smoothly running, full house you should operate with specified policies and house rules. Though few owners do it, it is highly desirable to gain a working knowledge of customary and legal practices. You may rent entirely through apartment managers, as I now do. Managers have more confidence if the owner possesses even a little legal know-how.

Where to Gain Practical Knowledge

Invaluable knowledge can be gained by attending public classes, as I have, in apartment-house management and in real-estate law. Both courses are available at many evening high schools, at trade or industrial schools, or in university extension courses. They are usually covered in one or two semesters by attending two or three sessions a week. For the greatest benefit these courses should be taken as soon as possible after you buy property and can apply the knowledge.

Real-estate-law courses are given chiefly for aspirants to a real-estate broker's or salesman's license, and for attorneys wishing to brush up on this speciality. Only a small percentage of owners or managers take the time to acquire this practical information, but it is recommended for all who plan the utmost development in real-estate investment or management. Accurate foreknowledge solves many minor legal problems which might otherwise have to be referred to an attorney. It forms a major protection against all troublemakers, especially the Philadelphia Lawyer tenant who loves to wrangle.

THE FIVE TROUBLEMAKERS

When troublemakers are found out, immediate action should be taken to correct their ways or evict them in order to keep peace in an otherwise contented family of tenants. There are five major categories of problem tenants:

1. The Philadelphia Lawyer, previously mentioned
2. The Professional Dead Beat
3. The Malicious Gossip
4. The Shady Character
5. The Bully

You may never encounter one of these characters in a lifetime of real-estate investment. Any may reside in your first building, particularly if it was haphazardly managed by the previous owner. All troublemakers spend their lives, with varying degrees of success, at making happy persons miserable. Examples of each, with effective weapons for counterattack, will be cited later in this chapter.

The two chief tools to cope with troublemakers are:

An ironclad lease
Enforceable legal notices

Details of various types of legal notices and the proper way to enforce them will be incorporated in the next two chapters. For the present we will deal with the chief foundation which empowers the owner to serve effective legal notices, namely a written lease.

AN IRONCLAD LEASE

The owner's greatest protection is an ironclad lease, which enables him to crack the whip over undesirables. Such a lease presents no difficulties whatever for the conscientious tenant. The recommended lease to be cited will refer where appropriate to provisions for dealing with obstreperous tenants.

WRITTEN LEASES SAFEGUARD THE OWNER

Oral terms concerning the rental of property are generally legal when handled on a month-to-month basis, and they may be binding up to one year, according to a typical state law. Leasing for more than a year, as with the sale of real estate, must be in writing to be binding.

Many property owners handle all rentals on an oral basis. Their only protection against undesirable tenants is the application of state or municipal laws. The more successful operator requires a written contract on each rental unit, even if cancelable on, for example, a month's notice. Besides providing a shield against undesirables, this insures that each tenant understands the terms of operation for the general welfare of all the tenants. Of course the written agreement will not insure against all eventualities, but it can guard against most problems and save much time and effort by blocking unnecessary disputes over minor matters.

Some mistaken owners disapprove of written agreements because they fear that additional rights are thereby granted to the tenant. The written lease clarifies the terms between owner and tenant, thus benefiting both. For the tenant it confirms for the most part the protection already provided by law. For the owner a judicious lease like the example to be cited confers safeguards over and above those granted by law.

AVOID CONFUSING PHRASES

Leases should be phrased as simply as possible. Many overlegalistic agreements are loaded with unnecessary terms like "party of the first part" and "witnesseth." These confuse and antagonize tenants and confer no greater legality. You will seldom find a ready-made lease which will adequately serve your purposes, and you may find it necessary to prepare your own. There are exceptions, like those provided by some apartment owners' associations, which in most cases will be tailored to legal customs of the area. Even with such lease forms you may find it advisable with experience to make some modifications to meet individual circumstances.

Most of the wording of the lease would be printed or mimeographed. The listed sample can be printed on one page of legal-sized, 8½-by-14 paper. In the following example the portions to be filled in by the manager will be underlined. The clarifying headings would not be included in the actual lease.

OPTIONAL TITLE of MONTH-to-MONTH LEASE

APARTMENT HOUSE
MONTHLY RENTAL CONTRACT and INVENTORY

NAMES of PARTIES and LOCATION of PREMISES

> *JOSEPH ENTERPRISE, Lessor in consideration of the agreements of Lessees, Mr. and Mrs. George W. Allen, set forth below, hereby leases to Lessees Apt. No. 4 in the Belvedere Apts., 3680 B Blvd. St., Metropole, Columbia.*

Start tenant relationships auspiciously by calling yourself where appropriate "Lessor," "Manager," or "Owner." Never take the name of "Landlord." Lordly titles in general are passé, and the New Deal fostered a bitter reaction to "Landlord." This title, not the position, creates resentment.

RENTAL STARTING DATE AND TERM

> *for the month commencing on the 2nd day of October, 1965, and monthly thereafter until this lease is terminated as hereinafter provided for. And Lessees in consideration of said leasing agree:*

THE STARTING DATE

The rent should start the day the tenant ties up the property, not the day the tenant's rent may terminate elsewhere. If the apartment is vacant the rent would normally start the day the lease is signed and the premises are reserved. If the apartment is occupied the rent would start the day after the present tenant moves out, unless there are repairs or other changes to be completed before the new tenant takes over. In the latter case the rent would start the day the premises are readied for occupancy.

DON'T BE A SLAVE TO THE "FIRST OF THE MONTH"

Some owners, like the Ballcryns, collect all rents the first of the month. If a tenant moves in during the month a prorated payment is collected, covering the balance of the month. Payment is afterward made on the first.

This may add to the owner's convenience, chiefly for banking and bookkeeping, but does not necessarily lend itself to the best operation of the property. There may be no vacancies for a period, then two or three may occur at once. Vacating tenants usually move on a rent termination date. If all rents are collected on the first and several tenants move out on the same date, there is more likely to be a delay before all vacancies are rented, resulting in a loss of rent. Also, more than one moving van in front of a building may generate unfavorable comment, such as "Something must be wrong with that building. Everybody's moving out." If collections are spread over the month, vacancies also will be spread, lessening adverse comment and making it easier to rerent each unit.

ADJUST RENT PAYMENT DATES TO PAYDAYS WHEN REQUESTED

The regular payment date should vary from the starting date only when the tenant prefers a change. For example, if Mr. Allen says he prefers to pay his rent on the tenth, a payday, it would be wise to make this the subsequent rent date. This helps insure rent payment when due. The first payment would be prorated accordingly, collecting for one month and eight days.

TERM OF TENANCY

This sample lease is drawn on a monthly basis, the most common form for apartments. Most business leases are made for a year or more, which is also the practice for apartments in some communities. In the latter case a one-year lease usually would read "for 12 months," a five-year lease "for 60 months." The length of the term should normally follow the common practice for comparable accommodations in the particular community.

Where the intended term is month to month, and there is no written agreement, tenants may claim they have an oral lease for up to one year. This is another disadvantage of oral rentals.

AMOUNT OF RENT AND ADVANCE PAYMENT

1. To pay as rental for said apartment the sum of $110.00 per month, payable monthly in advance commencing with the date last mentioned.

AMOUNT OF RENT

Once a fair market value has been established it is wise to hold all units in a building to a consistent level. It is better for a unit to stay vacant several days than to drop below the market in order to obtain a quick rental. Also a substantial rent concession to any particular tenant because of friendship or kinship will seldom fail to grapevine through an entire building and cause widespread dissatisfaction. Of course rentals may vary somewhat because otherwise comparable units may differ in accessibility, view, state of decoration, quality of furniture, and other value factors.

ADVANCE PAYMENT OF RENT

Where the lease is on a month-to-month basis one month's rent should be collected in advance with the signing of the rental contract. Where you lease for a year the first and last months' rents would be collected, and the tenant would forfeit one month's rent if he moved out before the expiration of the lease. An additional month's rent is usually collected for each year of the lease term. On a five-year lease, for example, a total of six months' rent would be collected in advance.

DON'T LET DEAD BEATS CIRCUMVENT ADVANCE PAYMENT

Where you rent on a monthly basis, Professional Dead Beats may seek possession without paying your requested month's rent in advance. Some tenants make a habit of never paying a full month's rent.

One, whose trail I have crossed several times in various apartment appraisals, was an alcoholic but otherwise exceptionally capable salesman. He was blessed with a winning personality, a demure wife, and two well-mannered teen-age daughters. As a bachelor he could not have got his foot past the door of the average manager. But his nice family paved the way for him.

His standard tactic was to appear with his entire family in answer to an ad. The premises would be inspected, and he would say it looked acceptable. His present quarters were too crowded, and that was why he wanted to move. In actuality he was always on the move because of evictions for nonpayment of rent.

When asked for a month's rent in advance he would say appealingly, "We've had quite a bit of sickness in the family, and my wife is just getting over an operation that cost us all our savings. Also, I have just changed companies to a better-paying job and haven't gotten my first full pay check. Couldn't you just let us move in, and I'll pay you ten dollars now and the rest next week?"

When the manager would say that the owner's rental policy required a full month's rent in advance he would praise the desirability of the apartment and the efficiency of the manager. Then he would offer a $20 advance payment, saying, "That will take ten dollars we were going to spend for groceries, but we will just skimp until payday. Next week I'll have a big enough check to buy groceries and pay you in full."

A $20 advance payment is the maximum rent he ever paid. After once moving in he would never pay another cent and would not give up possession until evicted. He would wait out legal eviction notices until just prior to the arrival of the sheriff to remove him by force. This process would take a minimum of one month. With a soft-hearted, gullible owner-manager who believed his continuing string of hard-luck stories, he might prolong eviction for three or four months. The only truth in his statements involved his obtaining new jobs, as he actually changed jobs continually to avoid garnishment of his wages.

With few exceptions the full month's rent should be collected before the tenant moves in. A tenant professing difficulty in paying his first rent will often stay in arrears, like the Professional Dead Beat, until evicted.

NUMBER OF TENANTS, CHARGE FOR EXTRA TENANTS, AND RESIDENCE USE

2. To use said apartment as living quarters for the residence of said named Lessees, being 2 adults and 0 children, and for no other purpose whatsoever, and to pay to the Lessor the sum of $10.00 monthly for each other person who shall occupy the apartment with said Lessee.

RESIDENCE USE

As specified, an apartment rented for a residence could not be used for business or professional purposes. In case other than residential use were later desired, the owner's consent would be necessary and a suitable additional rent could then be arranged.

NUMBER OF TENANTS AND CHARGE FOR EXTRA TENANTS

The number of adults and children should always be specified. A fixed sum, which might approximate 10 per cent of the base rental, should be charged for each additional tenant. This helps defray additional wear-and-tear and utility costs, and it pays additional revenue to the owner, as with extra guests in a hotel.

During OPA rent controls I inspected one desirable building where there were actually living in a 3-room apartment sixteen persons, composing the families of three brothers from Oklahoma. This high occupancy was contrary to city health regulations. Despite this, the OPA warned the owner not to raise the rents or evict a single tenant, because the owner had no written lease with an extra-tenant provision. Whether the unit is under rent controls or not, this tenancy clause permits the owner to apply an immediate additional charge for extra tenants.

CHILDREN MAY BE EXCLUDED

The phrase "for no other purpose whatsoever" also gives the owner the right to exclude additional tenants unless they are agreeable. Thus if the lease is written to show "2 adults and 0 children" the owner could refuse permission for children to be housed in the accommodation later. This circumvents parents who obtain apartments by subterfuge, claiming they have no children, and then after taking possession blossom out with a sizable family.

As far as policy is concerned, furnished apartments normally do not cater to children, because of the possibility of excessive damage. Unfurnished rental units may be made available to families with children without chancing so great a damage loss. In a particular building it is best to have either a rigid exclusion policy or a liberal policy permitting children. It causes dissension to have a few tenants with children and most without. Other parents sympathize when Baby cries in the wee hours or when older children make noise, but nonparents may vacate rather than suffer such annoyance. It should be noted that an apartment complex with more than one building lends itself to separate policies regarding children in each building.

An owner must consider the best policy for all tenants, modifying his policy with changing circumstances. He should rarely make exceptions from policy, as this is the chief cause of discontent. Tenants naturally react like employees in a business organization or children in a family. They accept impartial house rules which govern all for the benefit of all, but they resent favoritism or inconsistency.

CLEANING CHARGE

3. To pay for cleaning of said premises $15.00, *payable in advance.*

The normal practice is to assess a charge for having the quarters neat and clean. This charge is incurred only when the tenant moves. Otherwise the expense, like utility connection costs, would have to be prorated in the monthly rental charge. When the cost is assessed against the transient tenant who incurs it, the monthly rent can be kept accordingly lower for the tenant who stays put.

Some incoming tenants, in order to save the cleaning charge, would accept the conditions left by the outgoing tenant. Most tenants, however, refuse to rent a soiled apartment, preferring not to move into "someone else's dirt." They pay without undue protest a reasonable charge which compensates for the average labor cost for a janitor or a maid to clean the apartment.

Most owners figure a certain amount per room. The actual cost incurred in some cases will be less, in others more, but it is better to assess a fixed amount per apartment, according to size. As little as

$2.50 per room is charged in some houses, as high as $25 in others. Consideration should be given to actual labor costs and to prevailing practices for similar accommodations in the area.

IT IS BETTER TO COLLECT IN ADVANCE

Some owners collect cleaning charges in advance, together with the first month's rent. Others attempt to collect when the tenant moves out. It is easy to collect before the tenant moves in, often difficult or impossible when the tenant vacates. I know of otherwise honest tenants who have vacated surreptitiously, giving no advance notice or warning whatever, solely to avoid paying a cleaning charge due on vacating. They consider that paying to clean an apartment they are vacating is like paying to curry a dead horse.

Some owners collect a fairly large "cleaning deposit." The entire amount is returned when the tenant moves if the apartment is satisfactorily clean. Deciding whether or not the accommodation is "satisfactorily clean" often results in dissension. Unless absolutely contrary to prevailing practices in the area, the advance collection of a fixed overall cleaning charge is by far the fairest and easiest method to administer.

SECURITY AND DAMAGES DEPOSIT

4. To pay a security and damages deposit of $50.00, *said deposit to be refunded upon vacating* AFTER A MINIMUM PAID RENTAL OF SIX (6) MONTHS, *if there is no damage beyond ordinary wear and depreciation, and all rent and other charges are paid in full.*

The Security and Damages Deposit, refundable only after six months' paid rental, acts as a brake against short-term tenancy. Tenants subject to transfer object to a year's lease in many areas, but readily agree to pay a nominal security deposit. The amount usually runs between one-third and one-half of a month's rent. Forfeited if they fail to stay at least six months, this serves as a modified half-year lease. It is a fairly new rental arrangement that is gaining widespread practice among knowledgeable owners.

LEGAL COSTS TO BE BORNE BY THE TENANT

5. To pay all court costs and reasonable attorney's fees incurred by Lessor in enforcing by legal action or otherwise any of Lessor's rights under this lease or under any law of this State.

Unless this clause is included, attorneys' fees usually and court costs possibly would be borne by each party in a lawsuit, regardless of who wins the suit. Where the owner sues for nonpayment of rent, his legal costs might exceed the amount recovered. Making the tenant liable for all costs which the owner has incurred helps the owner collect the rent due him, without deduction of costs.

A SAFEGUARD AGAINST THE PHILADELPHIA LAWYER

This also serves as an adequate penalty to encourage the Philadelphia Lawyer tenant to pay before he is sued. If court action costs him nothing he may feel, Why worry about paying until they take me to court?

One such tenant, a frustrated accountant, made a practice of closely scrutinizing a lease before renting an apartment. He was happiest if there was no written lease at all. If asked to sign a lease he would make sure there was no provision for the tenant to pay legal costs in case of lawsuit. After gaining possession, he would claim a succession of uncommon "tenant rights" until refused. Then he would pay no rent because of being "denied his tenant rights."

His favorite claim was the weekly right to wash and polish his car in the common apartment driveway, blocking all traffic and spattering other tenants' cars. He loved to cause all the fuss and commotion possible, and he loved court action, as long as he wound up paying only the rent already owed.

Such a budding lawyer will be most discouraged by a lease incorporating as many clubs, like the foregoing, as possible. A Philadelphia Lawyer is a mental bully who may become a good boy if he loses but gets worse if he wins. If given any chance to win a point in an inconsequential matter, he will continually make life miserable for an owner or a manager, in addition to his family and acquaintances. Incidentally, my last report concerning this particular character stated that he was being sued for divorce by his third wife in five years for "incompatibility."

Some leases provide for double or triple damages in case of nonpayment of rent. Such a clause serves little purpose, since few courts will award punitive damages, even if provision for these is written in the lease. Contractual damages should cover actual rental or repair losses, plus actual court costs and attorney fees. Other damages may still be sued for in case of court action.

SPECIAL PROVISIONS: MORE TEETH IN THE LEASE

> *6. Not to sublet said apartment or any part thereof, nor keep any dog, cat or other animal or pet, nor use said apartment for any unlawful or immoral purpose, nor play any musical instrument or radio or television set before 8 A.M. or after 10 P.M. loud enough to be heard by other tenants, nor violate any regulations of the Board of Health, City Ordinances, or State Laws of whatever nature. Lessees agree that the covenants contained in this paragraph and in paragraphs 13 and 16 once breached cannot afterward be performed, and that in case of breach unlawful detainer proceedings may be commenced at once without any notice whatsoever.*

NO SUBLETTING: PROTECTS THE OWNER'S RIGHT TO CHOOSE TENANTS

The right to sublet would take from the owner the choice of succeeding tenants. It should be specifically provided that the tenant may not sublet, in order for the manager to screen desirable tenants.

NO PETS

The keeping of pets may be controlled as the owner sees fit, according to the type of rental and prevailing customs in the area. A dog or a cat may ruin the owner's furniture, whereas unfurnished property might not suffer undue damage except to the tenant's belongings. Certain animals are apt to commit a nuisance, from the standpoint of unclean and destructive habits and noise, while others, like canaries, might be acceptable. It is a common practice to charge an additional damages deposit, such as $50 for a cat or dog. A policy for each category of animal should be set for an entire building.

NO UNLAWFUL OR IMMORAL USE:
A PROTECTION AGAINST SHADY CHARACTERS

The specific restriction against unlawful or immoral use serves two chief purposes:

1. In case of criminal acts by a tenant within the building, the owner is better cleared of having permitted such acts.

2. It expedites eviction of Shady Characters who stay one jump ahead of the law and public scandal.

A manager should not challenge respectably behaving tenants who mind their own business. Scarcely a large apartment building fails to house at least one well-mannered couple wedded only by common law. Sensible apartment managers do not ask for an exhibition of marriage licenses, any more than would a hotel or motel manager. But where there are drunken parties or loud arguments annoying to other tenants, or openly flouted overnight entertaining of unlawful guests, a mere reference to this clause may cause the tenant to correct his disturbing ways or to move.

NO SECOND CHANCE: GIVES THE RIGHT
OF IMMEDIATE EVICTION

Whenever possible an offending tenant should be warned and given another chance. Often the first overt action of a tenant contrary to this paragraph will make it obvious you are dealing with a Shady Character whose retention would cause desirable tenants to move. The clause "once breached cannot afterward be performed" gives the owner the right to refuse keeping a tenant merely because he promises to "be good." The provision for commencement of "unlawful detainer proceedings at once" bypasses laws requiring, for example, a month's notice before eviction.

In one of my apartments a Bully, who fattened his ego by picking battles with weaker persons, beat his wife so that she ran screaming out in the hallway. The manager called the police and signed a complaint against the tenant for disturbing the peace. He was held in jail overnight. The wife then refused to sign an assault-and-battery complaint against her husband. Here was a clear-cut case where no second chance should be given for the tenant to perform the same or worse acts. The manager gave the tenant a notice to vacate within twenty-four hours because of breach of these lease terms. The tenant moved the following morning. Three weeks later at another location the Bully pistol-whipped his wife to death.

In a case like this, where the manager demands immediate eviction, a maximum of twenty-four hours should be granted to permit the offender to find other accommodations. Most tenants recognize the impossibility of screening out all undesirables. Other tenants seldom complain if housecleaning is accomplished within a day. They would have just cause to seek other quarters if obvious Shady Characters are permitted to remain much longer than one night after committing an overt unlawful act sufficient to warrant jailing.

OWNER'S RIGHT OF ENTRY VS. TENANT'S RIGHT OF PRIVACY

7. Lessor may enter said apartment at any time to inspect, repair and maintain same, or to show the property to any prospective buyer or loan or insurance agent, and in case either party has given notice of termination of this tenancy, to show the premises to any prospective tenant.

The owner has the right to rent his property to tenants he chooses. After the tenant takes possession, the premises should be considered his "castle" as much as a privately owned home. The manager should enter the premises only for good cause and should not seek petty excuses for snooping. It is most upsetting to tenants, and is apt to cause them to move, if, during their absence, a snooping manager enters their premises without reason.

SNOOPY MANAGERS CAUSE WRANGLING AND VACANCIES

Sad to relate, some managers go to unbelievable lengths to pry. Eventually their tenants are bound to find out. I inspected one building where ingenious booby traps were set for the snoopy, shrewish manager in reprisal, turning the apartments into a battleground.

I know of another 32-unit furnished-apartment building where the owner, a vinegary bachelor of sixty, also acted as manager. He was a professed misogynist, having been disappointed in love. He made a daily inspection of each apartment, making notes on the housekeeping. Had the rugs been vacuumed, the dishes washed, and the garbage wrapped neatly? Also he made a careful inspection to ascertain how many had slept in the apartment the previous night. Finally he would check the size of all light bulbs.

All rentals included utilities. To save on electricity he furnished undersized bulbs throughout, for example providing 25 watts where there should have been 60. Tenants would retaliate by buying their own 75- or 100-watt bulbs. The owner-manager on his daily rounds would take the large bulbs down, confiscate them, and replace them with smaller 15s. Some tenants would get 150-watters to purposely waste electricity and would hide the bulbs during the day so that the penny-pitching owner couldn't find them. Despite low rents this building was in constant turmoil, with wrangling tenants, high turnover, and many vacancies.

Believe it or not, this manager, who also owned considerable other property, slept in the boiler room. He said the furnace kept him warmer than a wife could and never talked back.

THE OWNER HAS BONA FIDE ENTRY RIGHTS

A manager should bend over backward to respect a tenant's right of privacy. However, a manager has responsibilities which a tenant should respect, and this point should be covered in the lease so that the right of entry will not be questioned. The premises should be inspected, for example, if—

1. Smoke, leaking water or other dangerous manifestations are noticed.
2. The tenant has not been seen on his regular rounds, and there is reason to believe the tenant may be critically ill or may have abandoned the premises without notice.

A prospective buyer, or a loan or insurance appraiser, who may wish to inspect the premises should always be accompanied by the owner or the manager. In case the tenant is home, permission should be asked before entering. It is unwise to antagonize the tenant by referring to lease provisions, unless inspection is refused. Tenants will appreciate a courteous introduction and explanation, such as, "This is Mr. Juster, from the insurance company. May we please take a quick look at your apartment?"

Some obstreperous tenants who are moving refuse to permit the premises to be shown to a prospective new tenant. If the accommodations are not shown till after the old tenant moves out, several days of lost rent may result. If the place is advertised and shown as soon as notice is given, it will normally be rented by the time the old tenant moves. This is an important safety device to offset turnover and helps cut the vacancy factor to almost nil in a well-managed building.

Some appraisers apply an automatic 10 per cent vacancy factor to all apartments. In many cases a percentage approaching this can be attributed to lack of control over vacating tenants, resulting in a time lag after one tenant moves out and before another moves in. The owner who protects himself by the foregoing clause, forcing the tenant to permit showing the premises, will add considerably to his net income.

No Waiver of Owner's Rights

8. All rights given to Lessor by this lease shall be cumulative and in addition to any other rights given by the laws of this State, and the exercise by Lessor of any right shall not operate as a waiver of any other rights. No statement or promise of the Lessor or Lessor's agents or employees with reference to altering the terms of this lease or as to any repairs or improvement of the premises, and no waiver of any rights of Lessor given by this lease or by law shall be binding unless specifically endorsed hereon in writing.

All legal rights are retained by the owner, whether or not they are covered by the lease. The requirement that any change in the lease terms shall be in writing helps to avoid misunderstandings or false claims.

Change or Termination of Lease

9. After one month's rental, this tenancy may be terminated at any time by mutual consent of the parties, or by either party by giving written notice to the other not less than fifteen (15) days before the date of termination. Any provision of this lease may be changed by Lessor in like manner.

Unless provided otherwise in the lease, state laws normally require that the length of notice required shall be the same as the period of rental payment. A rental by the month thus would require one month's notice. Some tenants will give a last-minute notice or move without notice, leaving the owner with a vacant apartment. Specific mention of notice requirements in the lease helps to enforce this proviso.

ADVANTAGES OF FIFTEEN-DAY NOTICE

Most owners incorporate a thirty-day-notice requirement to change a monthly lease. Consideration should be given to the advantages of a shorter term, such as fifteen days. It is often difficult to enforce more than fifteen days' notice on the part of the tenant, and it is to the owner's advantage to make changes or terminate the lease on fifteen days' notice.

Easier to Enforce

Since many tenants are apt to give less than fifteen days' notice, a fifteen-day requirement is easier to enforce than one of thirty days. If the tenant's rent is due and he gives notice to vacate immediately, he would be liable for fifteen days' rent. If he has paid a full month's rent and gives such notice, he would be entitled to a refund for the days beyond fifteen.

More Flexible for the Owner

With a thirty-day requirement, notice would have to be given on the rent payment date in order to take effect on the next rent day. But a fifteen-day requirement would enable the owner to raise the rent, change lease conditions, or give an eviction notice any time prior to fifteen days before the effective date.

In practice the notice would normally be given by the manager when the rent is paid, to take effect on the next rental date. It would still be legal, with a fifteen-day requirement, if the rent were paid a day or two past due. For instance, suppose the rent were due January 1, a legal holiday, and the tenant paid on January 2. Then a notice given January 2 could still take effect February 1, with any requirement of less than a full month. If a full month's notice is required, a notice given January 2 could not legally take effect February 1, and it might be postponed till March 1.

ALL TENANTS ARE RESPONSIBLE

10. The one signing this contract for Lessees agrees and warrants that he or she has authority to sign for all other Lessees.

This helps to enforce the lease if the signing party vacates and leaves one or more of the original tenants. For example, a husband who signs might later separate from his wife, leaving her as the tenant. The remaining tenants might claim they were not bound by the original lease, but the cited provision helps force them to honor it. Whenever such a change of tenancy occurs, however, the new or remaining tenants should be required to sign a new lease or to endorse the existing lease.

A PROTECTIVE CLAUSE AGAINST SHADY CHARACTERS AND DEAD BEATS

11. Any violation of any provision of this lease by any of the Lessees, or any person on the premises with the Lessee's consent, or any failure to pay rent upon the date due, shall result, at the option of the Lessor, in the immediate termination of this lease without notice of any kind, and Lessor may thereupon enter said premises and take and retain possession thereof and exclude Lessees therefrom.

This is a drastic clause which would seldom be enforced but which gives the owner remedy for unusual circumstances. Along with the teeth in paragraph 6, this provision would enable a manager to pressure a Shady Character who has committed an overt unlawful act to move at once without the customary notice.

The manager also can take immediate action against a suspected Professional Dead Beat who fails to pay rent when due, if she believes he plans to move without notice or otherwise evade payment.

ACCEPTING PARTIAL PAYMENT

12. The acceptance by Lessor of partial payments of rent due shall not, under any circumstances, constitute a waiver of

*any rights of Lessor at law or under this lease, nor affect any
notice or legal proceedings in unlawful detainer theretofore
given or commenced.*

This covers the instance in which a delinquent tenant has been
given notice to vacate and offers a partial payment of rent. Typical
state laws provide that acceptance of the partial payment would void
the vacate notice, unless this circumstance is specifically provided for
in the lease.

IF THE PREMISES ARE LEFT UNOCCUPIED

*13. If Lessees leave said premises unoccupied at any time
while rent is due and unpaid, Lessor may, if desired, take
immediate possession thereof and exclude Lessees therefrom,
removing and storing at the expense of said Lessees all property
found contained therein.*

Sometimes a past-due tenant will vacate without notice, leaving
some of his belongings to make it appear he is holding the apartment.
Unless protected by a clause such as this, the manager could not law-
fully take possession and rerent the accommodations except after the
delay and expense of legal proceedings.

PHYSICAL CONDITION ON WHICH TO BASE
POSSIBLE DAMAGE CLAIMS

*14. Said apartment and all of the furniture and furnishings
therein are accepted as in good condition; provided, however,
that if Lessees shall find any thereof not in good condition, or
that the inventory set forth below is incorrect in any particular,
a written statement of any objections shall be delivered to
Lessor within three (3) days after taking possession; otherwise
it will be conclusively presumed that said inventory is correct
in all particulars, and Lessees agree not to permit the premises,
including woodwork, floors, and walls, or any furniture, fixtures
or furnishings contained therein to be damaged or depreciated
in any manner, and to pay for any loss, breakage or damage
thereto. Lessees specifically agree that no tacks, nails, or screws
will be driven in the walls or woodwork. Lessees also are responsible for and agree to pay for any damage done by wind*

or rain caused by leaving windows open, and by overflow of water or stoppage of waste pipes.

The foregoing protects the owner from a tenant who moves into an apartment in good condition, causes damage, and then claims the damage was committed previous to his tenancy. Any noticeable damage at the time the tenant takes possession should be noted on the lease.

BAGGAGE LIENS: A POWERFUL COLLECTION WEAPON

15. The Lessor shall have the lien granted by law upon all baggage and other property of Lessees for their rent, accommodations and services, and the Lessees hereby grant to Lessor a lien upon all personal property brought into said premises, regardless of any provisions of law or whether or not the apartment is furnished, and Lessor may enforce said lien as provided by law or by entering said premises and either taking possession thereof and the belongings contained therein for safekeeping, or by removing said property therefrom and storing the same at the expense of the Lessees. Said lien may be enforced whenever rent is due and unpaid and regardless of whether or not a three- (3) day notice to pay rent or quit shall have been served, and enforcement of the lien shall not operate to waive any other rights of the Lessor in unlawful detainer or otherwise. If rent is still due and unpaid thirty (30) days after the enforcement of said lien, then the Lessor may sell any or all personal property taken possession of as herein provided, and may apply any monies received against the unpaid rent, and against any storage charges and any other costs and fees as designated in paragraph 5, provided that any monies received in excess of the total amounts due shall be turned over to the Lessees.

TO THWART THE PROFESSIONAL DEAD BEAT

The baggage lien is the strongest weapon against the congenital dead beat who is out to steal the owner's livelihood. Many state laws grant liens similar to this on baggage and personal property. Some laws govern only baggage, to the exclusion of other personal belongings. In some cases the law exempts necessities such as a stove and a refrigerator. Some laws cover only hotels. Others cover only hotels, motels and furnished apartments, excluding unfurnished accommodations.

The inclusion of specific lien rights in the lease clarifies the owner's rights of recovery in case of nonpayment of rent. In most cases of nonpayment a three-day notice to pay or move would normally be given before any action to take possession of personal property. The right of immediate possession without notice further protects the owner in the event it appears the tenant is attempting to evade payment by moving surreptitiously.

If Tenant Removes Furniture or Baggage

16. If Lessees should remove from said premises any furniture or baggage without the agreement of the Lessor, said removal shall constitute at the option of the Lessor an abandonment and surrender of the premises, and the Lessor may take immediate possession thereof, and exclude Lessees therefrom, removing and storing at the expense of said Lessees all remaining property found therein.

Unless this clause is inserted the tenant might remove part of his belongings at a time, intending to move without notice. With this paragraph the manager could immediately take possession of the premises and any remaining personal property. Sometimes a tenant, moving without notice, may leave some worthless personal property in the apartment. Whether done in spite or not, this might legally bind the owner to leave the premises vacant till the end of the term of rental, or until after a legal notice has been posted. Clause 16 would enable the owner to rent the premises to a new tenant at once.

No Storage or Damage Rights

17. No right of storage is given by this lease, and the Lessor shall not be liable for nondelivery of messages or for any loss of property by fire, theft, burglary or otherwise from said premises or building, nor for any accidental damage to person or property in or about the leased premises or building resulting from electric wiring, or water, rain or snow, which may come into or issue or flow from any part of said premises or building, or from the pipes, plumbing, gas, sprinklers, or any electric connections thereof, or that may be caused by the negligence of Lessor or Lessor's employees or by any other cause whatever, and the Lessees hereby covenant and agree to make no claim for any such loss or damage.

NO STORAGE RIGHTS

Whether storage space is available for tenants or not, it is well to stipulate that use of such space is a special courtesy subject to cancellation, and not a right. This would protect the owner in case he later wished to utilize the space for house storage or other purposes, such as additional apartments or garages. Once a tenant possesses an unqualified right like storage, he will oftener move than give it up.

NO INSURANCE AGAINST TENANT'S LOSS

The owner normally does not insure the tenant's property. It is well to cover this contingency in the lease so that there is no question but that the tenant wishing coverage against loss should carry his own insurance. The clause "to make no claim for any such loss or damage" helps to discourage the Philadelphia Lawyer from suing over imagined or inconsequential damage. However, in case of real damage there is no way of preventing court action. In fact, it is likely to be inevitable. Any such claims against the owner should be covered by the owner's liability insurance.

It should be mentioned that while a tenant's personal property would usually be excluded from an owner's fire insurance policy, the belongings of a manager or other employee can be included at little or no additional cost if the owner so requests.

GARBAGE HANDLING

18. All garbage must be enclosed or wrapped in paper before disposal.

Unless instructed otherwise some tenants may carry wet garbage dripping down hallways in open boxes or pails.

No Running Children

19. Children will not be permitted to run or play in halls, entrances, and stairways, or on the roof, porches or fire escapes.

Whether children are accepted as tenants or not, they may be in the building as guests. It is wise to restrict their activities which may be dangerous or disturbing to other tenants.

No Washing Machines or Aerials

20. No washing machines may be installed in the apartment, and no outdoor radio or television aerials of any kind may be installed by Lessees.

The use of washing machines should be prohibited where there is a community laundry and no individual laundry space. Some flats provide space and adequate plumbing for individual washers, in which case this clause would not be required. If individual facilities are not provided, the use of a washer in kitchen or bath will clog drain lines not intended for such usage. Also, slopping is apt to cause serious damage to floors, and to ceilings below.

RADIO AND TV AERIALS

Radio aerials are now comparatively uncommon, but apartment houses suffer damaged roofs and unsightly appearance by permitting tenants to install outdoor television aerials. A tenant may promise to repair the roof when he removes an aerial. Such a promise is often difficult to enforce. A vacating tenant entertains no worries about the owner's roof. Any amateur patching, even if conscientious, will more than likely leak within a year or two.

Merely walking over a roof to install, adjust, or remove an aerial will often cause damage. In most metropolitan areas modern TV sets do not require outdoor aerials, with the availability of improved indoor aerials and built-in reception. In outlying locations good reception may demand outdoor aerials. In this case both owner and tenants would benefit by the owner's installing cable-TV or a master antenna and charging interested tenants a nominal monthly hookup charge to amortize the cost.

ALWAYS MAKE AN INVENTORY

In both furnished and unfurnished rental units there will be some items of furnishing which should be inventoried when the tenant moves in. When the tenant vacates there would then be no question regarding what the accommodation should contain. The inventory should normally be a part of the lease, appended at the end. Following is a sample inventory list, with blank spaces for miscellaneous items.

LIVING ROOM	LIVING ROOM	BEDROOMS	MISCELLANEOUS
__ Sofa & Chair	__ Bookcases	__ Sofa Bed &	8 Light Bulbs
__ Occasional	__ Dividers	__ Mattress	__ Complete
__ Chairs	1 Wallbed &	__ Bedframes	__ Traverse Drapes &
__ Coffee Tables	__ Mattress	__ Headboards	__ Rods
__ Corner Tables	1 Heater	__ Dbl. Dressers	6 Curtains
__ End Tables		__ Triple Dressers	6 Rods
__ Occasional		__ Chests	3 Drapes
__ Tables		__ Desk	8 Shades
__ Table Lamps &	KITCHEN &	__ Bkcase	__ Air-Conditioners
__ Shades	DINING ROOM	__ Dbl. Mattresses	__ Shower Curtains
__ Pole Lamps &	1 Stove & Broiler	__ Twin Mattresses	2 Apt. Keys
__ Shades	__ Pans	__ Dbl. Box Springs	1 Mail Box Keys
__ Floor Lamps &	1 Refrigerator	__ Twin Box Springs	__ Planter & Flowers
__ Shades	2 Ice trays	__ Mattress Covers	__
__ Desk & Chair	__ Table &	__ Spreads	__
__ Pictures	__ extension leaf	__ End Tables	__
1 Mirrors	__ Chairs	__ Chairs	__
__ Rugs or w/w	1 Iron Board	__ Tbl Lmps & Shds	__
__ Carpets	__ Metal Shelf Unit	__ Mirrors	__
	__ Waste Bskts	__ Pin-up	__
	__ Garbage Can	__ Pole	__
		__ Vanity	__
		__ Rugs or w/w	__
		__ Carpets	

Deposit of $3.00 for 3 keys will be refunded when keys and receipt are turned in.

BOTH PARTIES SHOULD SIGN

Executed and entered into this 3rd day of October, 1965.

JOSEPH ENTERPRISE, Owner
by Ailene Wister   Geo. W. Allen
_____   _____
MANAGER OR AGENT   FOR LESSEES

KEY DEPOSIT

The list includes three keys, with a deposit of $1 for each. Key deposits should be nominal. Unless some charge is made tenants often lose keys or move out without turning them in.

The lease and inventory should be prepared in triplicate and all copies signed by both parties in order to be binding. The manager should keep the first copy, give the second to the tenant and the third to the owner. This protects both owner and tenant from corrections not acceptable to both. Any subsequent changes should be noted on all copies and the manager's and the tenant's copies initialed by both parties. If changes of a major nature occur, like a husband moving out and the wife retaining the premises with a sister, for example, a new lease should be executed, as previously mentioned.

The Allens give the lease a cursory examination, and Mr. Allen agrees to sign without quibbling.

How About Existing Tenants?

In taking over the management of a building it is advisable to prepare leases for all tenants, unless there is an adequate lease already. At the B Boulevard flats we find no written agreements of any kind. We introduce the lease by referring to the inventory listed at the end. We say that for the tenant's protection it would be desirable to account for all the furniture so that there will be no misunderstanding. All furniture involved is inventoried with the tenant, the seller, and the new owner present, so that any controversies can be settled as to what belongs to the tenant and what belongs to the building.

After checking the furniture, we state that we have a written rental agreement that goes with the inventory. We are making the same arrangement with all the tenants to cover the desired operation of the building for the mutual benefit of all.

ONE TENANT OBJECTS

Three of the four tenants readily sign the Inventory and Rental Agreement. Only one tenant protests, saying they have got along all right without signing a lease and see no reason for having one now.

The tenant is told, "We have written agreements for all the tenants so that there will be a clear understanding by everyone. This gives you protection as well as the owner, especially regarding the furniture. Let's check the furniture and see how it comes out."

The tenant remarks that one arm of an upholstered chair is frayed and was that way when she moved in. She is happy to have this noted on the inventory. The remaining furniture is inventoried to the satisfaction of all parties. Then, without further objection, the tenant signs the agreement along with the inventory.

If the tenant refused to sign the agreement, the inventory could be signed separately. As long as the tenant is already in the building the existing oral agreement could be continued. I have never known of a case where a tenant refused to sign a written agreement, as long as it was requested before the tenant moved in. Such a refusal of a properly presented agreement, or an attempt to strike out pertinent provisions, would indicate a tenant apt to be a troublemaker. The owner is better off not to take a tenant who will not sign a rental agreement as presented.

FILE LEASES BY APARTMENT NUMBERS

The owner should keep all leases filed by separate properties, and by rental units at each property, rather than by tenants' names. In case questions later arise, it is advisable to retain leases at least one year after a tenant moves out. A tenant's liability for damage might not be discovered until after the tenant moves, or the damage may be apparent but payment unsettled. Past leases may also be useful in case of possible rent controls.

Keeping leases by apartments also serves as a check on turnover in each unit. Excessive turnover would indicate a need for modifications or improvements. For instance, frequent turnover in a unit adjacent to a laundry room would alert the owner to correct an offending situation. If night noise has been disturbing, the laundry room might be closed at an earlier hour, and notice posted stating the new hours.

If the noise of a laundry room, boiler room, or garbage chute could not be controlled otherwise, soundproofing might be installed on adjacent walls. If incinerator odors are objectionable, as another example, additional gas or oil firing or perhaps a taller chimney might solve the problem.

The thought to keep in mind is that excessive leases for a particular unit point the finger at a problem which should be corrected. Once the owner is alerted he can usually find a solution which will encourage tenants to stay.

For most tenants a lease is needed only to establish house rules and inventories.

The provisions of an ironclad lease may never have to be enforced in any of your rental properties. Incorporating real teeth in a written lease protects the owner and makes the manager's job easier, just in case an unco-operative tenant comes along.

15. HOW TO COLLECT RENTS WHEN DUE

This chapter and the next in large part will show how to utilize and enforce lease terms cited previously. This chapter will deal with information on rent collections, including the giving of legal notices to enforce payment.

Income rental operations demand full rent collections in advance when due. It is better to leave an apartment vacant, eating up no wear-and-tear and utility costs, than to coddle a tenant who does not pay his rent. Operating apartments must be construed as purely a money-making investment rather than a charity.

Any tenants actually deserving charity can find ample aid from government relief sources, city, county, state and federal, and from various philanthropies. An owner who yields to charity appeals from nonpaying tenants cannot meet his own operating and loan costs and will wind up bankrupt.

USE EFFECTIVE COLLECTION FORMS AND NOTICES

Rents will be collected more effortlessly and efficiently if consistent collection steps and proper notices and forms are utilized, and a modicum of legal knowledge is acquired. Effective collections and legal notices, to be covered in this chapter and the next, tie together to a great extent. Though real-estate purchases and rentals both involve many legal forms, the average attorney may know little about the handling of property. Some attorneys, happily, specialize in real-estate law. If you familiarize yourself with the particular aspects of real-estate law that apply to your operations, you will find that in most matters you will have greater knowledge on the subject than the non-specializing attorney.

Use Clear Rent Receipts that Leave No Questions

Some owners invite problems merely by giving no receipts, or by using receipts with ambiguous phrases. The wording of a rent receipt may mean the difference between an argument and a clear-cut understanding. For example, many receipts read: "Rent for one month, from October 1 to November 1."

In common business practice this means the rent starts October 1, includes the full month of October, but does not include November 1. However, many tenants not familiar with business practices would maintain that the rent is paid to and including November 1. This type of rent receipt was the cause of the argument with the Goldens when they moved from the Number 4 flat at B Boulevard.

Such provocation can be eliminated simply by using a rent receipt that states: "Rent for one month ending October 31."

There are myriad workable forms of wording a rent receipt, many of which embody a specific house rule or two that the owner wishes to emphasize. On the next page is a special example, covering the rental to the Allens described in the lease in the previous chapter.

It will be noted that the rent terminates here on November 1, because it starts October 2. This type of receipt avoids the confusion that might otherwise result when the rent starts on a date other than the first.

Always Give a Receipt

Failure to give a rent receipt invites more arguments than a poorly worded receipt. A tenant may pay by check, sometimes in a hurry on the way to work, and say, "Don't bother with a receipt. My canceled check will be sufficient."

Many owners accept statements such as this as an easy way to save the little time and expense of preparing a receipt. Here is a rather obvious example of being penny wise and pound foolish, as arguments will often arise later regarding the term covered by the check, and whether a payment has actually been made.

RECEIPT   DATE___October 3_____19_65_   **014113**

RECEIVED FROM_____George W. Allen

FOR RENT OF_____Apt. 4 at $110.00 monthly

One hundred twenty-eight & No/100------- DOLLARS $ 128.00

FROM   Oct. 2, 1965 ENDING Nov. 1   BAL. DUE   TO PAY BY

S-D Dep.	50.00	Total, Extras	68.00	How Pd.		JOSEPH ENTERPRISE (Owner)
Key Dep.	3.00	Pre. Bal.		Check	X	7070 Paradise Rd. Suburbia
Cln. Chrg.	15.00	Rent	60.00	Cash		Columbia Phone 233-4127
Late Chrg.		Total Due	128.00	M. O.		RENTS TO BE PD. IN ADVANCE
		Amt. Pd.	128.00	Voucher		By____Ailene Wister
Total, Extras	68.00	Bal. Due		Tr. Ck.		☐ m Thank You !

Where owners gave no receipts, I have known of tenants who paid by monthly check for a year or more, then claimed they were paid a month ahead. Other tenants who became delinquent claimed they were actually paid up. With no consistent receipt plan, and no duplicate receipts on file, their claims threw the owners on the defensive. If you always give receipts, and maintain a duplicate file, you place squarely on the tenant the burden of proof to show his receipts whenever there is a dispute over the payment of rent.

Receipts should always be prepared at least in duplicate, and the original given to the tenant. Thus if the tenant should alter the receipt the duplicate on file will show how it was actually prepared. The duplicates should be kept for a minimum of one year in case of questions.

Some owners require a triplicate, so that they can maintain a file in addition to the manager's duplicate file, chiefly as a means of insuring the manager's fidelity. This is seldom necessary with monthly rentals. There are other adequate methods of supervision, as will be covered in detail in a later chapter. With weekly or daily rentals, however, such as in a motel or a transient rooming house, it is highly recommended that the owner insist on triplicate, numbered receipts. Utilizing books of consecutively numbered receipts is desirable in all cases, both to check questioned receipts with tenants, and for supervision of the manager.

Avoid Mistakes by Preparing Receipts in Advance

Mistakes will be avoided, and tenants when in a hurry will appreciate the time saved, if you have all receipts prepared in advance. For example, before the first of the month the manager could prepare all receipts for the coming month, leaving off only the date of payment and the signature. This proves a great help if payment is tendered when the manager is busy, perhaps speaking on the telephone or showing an apartment to a prospective tenant. If the receipt is filled out under the pressure from such interruptions, mistakes are easy to make. Common mistakes involve the wrong name or apartment, misspelling the tenant's name, incorrect rent, and incorrect term. The prepared receipts could be kept by apartment number in a card file.

Always Collect in Advance

I know of many examples of tenants who could tell the most believable falsehoods, like the alcoholic in the previous chapter, to avoid paying a full month's rent in advance. Very few lived up to their promises, if they were unable to pay to start with. It is a fairly hard rule that he who cannot or does not pay when he moves in will seldom catch up afterward. The foolish owner who fails to observe this rule will be derided as a skinflint rather than thanked for charitable impulses when later attempts are made to enforce collection.

Smooth-talking dead beats cajole many susceptible managers into allowing them to move in while paying little or no rent. The nonpayers who get the most rent for the least money are those, like the alcoholic, who have families. The most efficient of all in this regard are those with pregnant wives. Here is a typical example:

A PLAUSIBLE DEAD BEAT OUTSMARTS
A GULLIBLE OWNER

A sympathetic widow, a Mrs. Spynthy, advertised for rent the vacant half of her duplex house. She worked days as a telephone supervisor, and she lived in the other part of the duplex. Since the unit was completely furnished, she planned to rent only to adults, but she failed to include this stipulation in her ad.

On a Tuesday evening a pleasant-appearing woman of about thirty-five, obviously several months pregnant, answered the ad. She was soft-spoken and obsequious in manner and said that her name was Muggs and that she was desperately anxious to find a place to live. She had just arrived from out of town with her husband and their two small children. Mr. Muggs, a skilled cement finisher, had gone to work the day before with a contractor who promised steady employment. They were living temporarily in a cramped motel and were anxious to move into a permanent home.

Mrs. Spynthy protested she would like to take in the family, but her place was nicely furnished and she did not think she could chance the children's causing damage.

The prospective tenant told a convincing story of how careful they would be. "We're not the kind of ordinary tenants who cause damage. We used to own our own home till we had a bit of bad luck and lost it. Being experienced owners ourselves, we know what it means to look after your property, and we'll give you no cause to worry. We'll be extra careful. I can tell we would like to live here, because we'll have such a nice, understanding landlady."

Against her better judgment, the widow promised to rent to the family. Then she asked for the monthly rent of $85.

"Oh, we haven't any money right now. We're dead broke after the expense of moving and all. But just let us move in, and we'll pay you the full month when my husband gets paid this Friday. He makes good money, and we can pay it with no trouble at all."

The owner could see that, if the family was actually penniless and had to pay for groceries and other necessities, it was obvious there would be little chance of obtaining a full month's rent from only one week's pay. She restated her policy of not letting any tenants move in until they had paid a full month in advance.

Mrs. Muggs admitted they might be pressed to pay all the rent that Friday, but she said the contractor had taken a liking to her husband

and would advance what was needed over his pay to pay the rent in full. She named a well-known contractor.

Mrs. Spynthy said that as soon as they got the rent the Muggses could move in, but she couldn't let them in before. By this time she was becoming dubious as to whether she should rent to the family at all. She said she couldn't hold the property without a deposit and would have to rent to the first one who put up his money.

THE TENANT OFFERS JEWELRY AS SECURITY

At this Mrs. Muggs presented her ace in the hole. "I want your place so bad. It's just what I've been looking for. I tell you what, I'll give you my rings, my wedding and engagement rings, to hold it. They're worth several hundred dollars, with this big solitaire, and you know I wouldn't part with them for the world."

Mrs. Spynthy reluctantly agreed to take the rings as a deposit to hold the unit. The tenant then argued that the rent should start Friday when they moved in. The clincher to the owner was an agreement to start the rent that same day, Tuesday, when the place was tied up. Thus no further rent would be lost. Mrs. Muggs agreed to move in Friday and at that time redeem the rings by paying a full month's rent.

Thursday evening the whole family arrived, driving a dilapidated pickup truck. A boy about five and a girl of three were riding in back, atop a bundle of bedding. Quilts, sheets and blankets were piled helter-skelter over kitchen utensils, groceries, a crib, and other belongings, exposed through the slatted sideboards of the pickup.

The little boy ran to the owner's door and asked for the key. Mrs. Spynthy told him to have his mother and father see her about the rent. Both parents then came to the door. Mr. Muggs explained he would lose a day's pay if he waited to move in the next day, so they thought they ought to move in tonight.

"Have you the rent money?" demanded Mrs. Spynthy. "Your wife promised to pay the rent before you moved in."

"We'll have it tomorrow for sure," assured the husband. "My boss has promised me a little extra so's I can pay you the whole eighty-five dollars. You're still holding on to my wife's rings, so you've got nothing to worry about. We moved out of the motel, figuring you wouldn't mind us moving in tonight, long as you've got plenty of security. My wife said she gave in to starting our rent last Tuesday, and we don't want to pay double rent any longer. Can't you see your way clear to let me and my little family move in, ma'am? I'll bring you the money the first thing when I get home from work tomorrow."

The unexpected, well-planned assault overcame Mrs. Spynthy's objections. She was persuaded to give up the keys without receiving a cent in cash.

Mr. Muggs came home from work about six the next evening. Mrs. Spynthy waited expectantly for two hours, but nobody approached her. After eight o'clock she rang the Muggs's doorbell and asked for the rent.

"We ran into a little snag," alibied the husband. "The contractor had to hold up my pay until next week account of some trouble with the union. But it'll all be straightened out the first of next week. Now, you've got those rings for security, so there's no need for you to worry."

A Sad Awakening

Day by day the tenants procrastinated with one excuse or another. After two weeks with no rent payment, Mrs. Spynthy phoned the contractor. This, of course, in view of the dubious circumstances, she should have done before allowing the family to move in. The contractor said he had advanced Muggs $25 above his wages to help pay his rent on the first Friday payday. He had seen nothing of the worker since. He did not know where the fellow was working now and would like to get hold of him.

Mrs. Spynthy confronted her tenants with this story. Caught in their web of fabrication, the wife became brazen. "Well, we had to use the money to pay some of our other debts, so we had to tell you something. Anyway, we've got the money for you now, and I'll just give you a check."

Mrs. Spynthy was skeptical about taking a check, especially one drawn, as it developed, on a bank in an adjoining state.

Mrs. Muggs guaranteed the check to be good as gold. She said all their pay checks had been mailed to their home bank to keep up their account. She had expected Mrs. Spynthy to return her rings on receipt of the check, but if it would make her feel better the landlady could continue holding the rings until she was sure the check had cleared.

With these assurances, Mrs. Spynthy accepted the check, retained the rings, and gave the Muggses a receipt for the month's rent. The check was deposited in the owner's account. A week later, her bank mailed it back, stamped "Insufficient funds."

Mrs. Spynthy now confronted the Muggses with the returned check. Mrs. Muggs said there must be a mistake, and she offered to write a new check in exchange for the old one. The owner decided she would agree to nothing which could prolong her tenants' rent-free stay, so she demanded the rent in cash.

Mrs. Muggs said they didn't have any cash. Mrs. Spynthy asked where the husband was now working. The tenants refused to tell where the husband worked.

The widow said she would find out from the union and have her lawyer garnishee the wages if the rent remained unpaid. "Either pay me the money you owe, or I'll have you put out."

"You can't put us out while I'm pregnant," shrilled Mrs. Muggs. "No judge in the land would allow that, seeing I just might have a miscarriage. Then you'd be responsible, and I'd sue you for everything you've got. We're not budging an inch till we get a legal notice."

What to Do When a Tenant Fails to Pay Rent

In desperation Mrs. Spynthy called the Apartment House Association, to which, fortunately, she belonged. On the advice of their business manager, she turned the whole affair over to one of their attorneys. He was not so dismayed as she over the miscarriage threat.

"Next thing you know, you'll be blamed for inducing the pregnancy," laughed the attorney. He instructed his secretary to fill out a "Pay up or move out" notice. The secretary typed in the blank portions of a commonly used printed form, preparing three copies.

Many state laws forbid anyone but an attorney to prepare a legal notice for another person for gain. However, owners or managers may normally fill out legal forms such as the one following for their own operations, once they have ascertained the proper form, and if they observe certain principles. Printed forms applying to the situation in your locality can be obtained from various sources, including the local apartment owners' association, stationery departments or stores, banks, title companies, and Real Estate Boards.

Fine legal points vary in different states. The object of the notice is to force the tenant to pay or move. It warns the tenant, giving him a chance to make good. Major requirements include:

1. Tenant's name
2. Address of the rental unit
3. Amount of delinquent rent
4. Date of serving notice
5. Name of individual on whom notice is served

A THREE-DAY NOTICE TO PAY OR MOVE

APARTMENT HOUSE ASSOCIATION OF
METROPOLE COUNTY, INC.
Member

NOTICE TO PAY RENT OR QUIT PREMISES

TO: Mr. and Mrs. Mansfield M. Muggs
ADDRESS: 10410 Boyd Street, Apt. 2
Metropole, Columbia

NOTICE IS HEREBY GIVEN, that there is due and unpaid rent required by the written agreement dated May 24, 1965 under which you hold possession of the above described premises as follows:

The monthly rental on these premises is $85.00; making due and payable rent in the total amount of $85.00; for the period from May 24, 1965, ending June 23, 1965.

WITHIN THREE DAYS, after service on you of this notice, you are hereby required to pay said due and payable rent or quit and deliver up possession of said premises to the undersigned or the undersigned will institute legal proceedings against you to receive possession of said premises, to declare a forfeiture of said agreement and to recover TREBLE RENTS AND DAMAGES, ATTORNEYS FEES AND COSTS.

The undersigned elects to and does declare a forfeiture of the agreement if said due and payable rent is not paid within three (3) days.

DATED: June 13, 1965

OLIVIA L. SPYNTHY, OWNER

By: Olivia L. Spynthy
OWNER

In order to save her the cost of a professional process server, the attorney advised Mrs. Spynthy on how to serve the notice. He told her to give the original to the Muggses, to note the duplicate and the triplicate and to return them to him. The duplicate would be required in conjunction with court action, if that became necessary. The triplicate would be a spare file copy. At the bottom of the duplicate and the triplicate he had his secretary type the information he wished Mrs. Spynthy to give. She filled this in on delivery that evening:

Date delivered to tenant June 13, 1965
Time delivered to tenant 6:30 PM
Person delivered to Mrs. Mansfield M. Muggs
Delivered by Mrs. Olivia L. Spynthy
(Title)   Owner

This information was subscribed in case of question if the case went to court. The same items should be noted by owners or managers who deliver similar papers on their own initiative.

OUT MOVE THE MUGGSES

Mrs. Spynthy stayed up till midnight the third day to keep an eye on the Muggses. Observing no overt actions, she turned out her lights and retired. The next morning the Muggs family had disappeared, leaving the rental unit filthy.

The kitchen was strewn with garbage. Papers and dirt, torn boxes and debris were scattered over the rest of the apartment. The sofa was heavily blotched with grease, and a large hole had been burned in one arm by a cigarette. One mattress used by the children was yellow from bed-wetting. The damage exceeded $200, and Mrs. Spynthy had not received a cent in rent.

Glad that she at least had been wise enough to hold the Muggses' rings as security, the owner took them to a jeweler for appraisal. He laughed at her. The engagement "diamond" was only paste. Although a fairly good imitation, he said, the set could be duplicated at any costume jewelry counter for less than $5.

The Apartment House Association recommended Mrs. Spynthy's turning her claim for rent, damages, and attorney's fees over to a collection agency. The latter quoted a fee of 25 per cent of the amount collected if no court action were required, and 50 per cent if court action were necessary. However, they failed to earn either percentage, as no trace of the Muggses ever was found.

This sad experience with wiles and stratagems of a typical dead beat caused Mrs. Spynthy to make some firm resolutions, which any rental owner might well consider:

1. Don't permit a tenant to move in unless he pays his full rent in advance.
2. Don't accept security other than cash or a check in payment of rent. (This does not preclude taking a tenant's valuables to enforce rent payment after he moves in.)
3. Don't take checks from delinquent tenants, prolonging their delinquency. (Checks are acceptable from all but suspect tenants.)
4. Don't rent furnished accommodations to families with children unless a substantial damages deposit is collected.
5. Don't delay in taking legal action once a tenant proves delinquent.

Steps to Take When a Tenant Is Slow in Paying Rent

The foregoing case history, embodying a series of dead-beat tricks, covers an unfortunate mistake in judgment in renting to the Muggses at all. What steps should be taken when a tenant pays his rent on moving in but later deteriorates into a "slow pay"?

I mentioned emphasizing on both the monthly rental contract and the receipt that the rent should always be paid in advance. Most tenants expect to pay their rent faithfully on the due date as a primary obligation. For those of slovenly payment habits, and particularly for such who are new tenants, certain educational steps usually prove effective.

Give Prompt Reminders When Rent Is Overdue

If the rent is due on the first, for example, no action should be taken until the following day, as the tenant may be planning to pay the rent in the evening. However, on the morning of the second the manager should contact the overdue tenant and inquire if he is ready to pay the rent, as she must get all rents promptly collected and turned over to the owner. If the tenant is out, a note should be left under the door requesting him to call at the manager's office or apartment.

When tenants respond by paying the rent, some may question such prompt reminder action. In a firm but friendly manner the manager should explain that rents due on the first must be collected by or on the first. If that is inconvenient for the tenant, she will be glad to change the rent date, and they can prorate the rent to adjust for the change.

If a tenant fails to appear by a reasonable hour the second evening, the manager should contact him at his apartment and say she has come to collect the rent. If the rent is then paid, the tenant should be thanked and requested to bring it to the manager thereafter when due.

LEAVE A SHORT, URGENT NOTE

If the tenant is still out, a second note should be left, asking him to contact the manager. For example: "IMPORTANT. Please see Manager at once."

If no response is received within three days, or an evasive tenant pays no rent and gives no definite commitment, then a three-day notice should be served. This notice to pay or move should be served after only one day's delinquency to a tenant who has habitually been in arrears.

Of the few tenants who are at first slow in paying, most will respond to the educating reminders cited. If there is a remaining tenant, it is very seldom that the legal phraseology of a three-day notice, given in no uncertain terms, fails to produce results. Either the tenant will secure the money to pay or he will move within the three days. Not one slow-paying tenant in a hundred will await actual court-ordered eviction. For the dead beat who waits out the last minute of grace, it may take two to four weeks to have the tenant ejected by a constable or a deputy sheriff. The recalcitrant who stretches the limit of the law will usually move just before the arrival of the sheriff.

How to Get the Sheriff to Evict
a Nonpaying Tenant

If the tenant does not move within three days, pay rent, or make firm arrangements to pay, how do you get the sheriff to evict? The sheriff takes such action by court order, so the case must now be filed in court. A copy of the three-day notice is submitted as a basis for action, making it important that the notice be properly prepared and served. Otherwise a new, correct notice would be necessary, and the procedure would be delayed till after its delivery.

Usually an attorney is required to plead the case in court. In some states an owner or a manager may present the case in a small-claims court, where no attorney is permitted. Although the actual amount owing may be more, the small-claims court may be utilized where the amount claimed does not exceed the maximum, between $100 and $300 in various states. Not all small-claims courts have the power to enforce evictions for nonpayment. In any event, with the time required for the case to be heard and for judgment to be rendered and ready for execution, it will take from two to four weeks before the sheriff appears at the tenant's door with power to evict.

How About the Tenant Who
Promises to Pay Later?

Some tenants may say that they haven't the money now but will pay later. What action should be taken? If the tenant is new and untried the owner should normally be firm in demanding immediate payment or quittance. If the tenant has established a good payment history, the manager should be more lenient, making allowances for extenuating circumstances, such as the loss of a job, death in the family, or illness.

In any case the manager should require a definite promise of a specific date when the rent will be paid. General statements, such as "We'll take care of it as soon as we can," should not be acceptable. For example, if the rent is due on Monday special action might be postponed for a tenant who says he will pay on Friday. The proffered date should be firmly established, with an implied threat of immediate action if the promise is not kept. The manager could say, "As long as you will definitely pay your rent this Friday, I'll hold up collection until then."

If the tenant fails to keep such a definite promise, a three-day notice should be served the following day. Further time might be granted if partial payment—half the rent, for instance—is made, with a new commitment to pay the balance within a reasonable time, such as another week.

DOES PARTIAL PAYMENT INVALIDATE A THREE-DAY NOTICE?

As mentioned in Chapter 14, if a three-day notice to pay or move is given and the manager accepts a partial payment, in many states this would invalidate the notice. In the case of the Muggses, where $85 was due, accepting $5 on account might have legally canceled the three-day notice.

This would be especially undesirable if all steps have been taken to evict, and possibly several weeks have elapsed from the date of giving the notice. The owner would thus be required to start the process all over again, losing more in further nonpaid rent than the small amount tendered. With such alternatives, the owner would be wise to reject the offered partial payment.

The owner should be in a position to take all monies offered. For possible protection on this point include as part of the lease the provision in paragraph 12, "The acceptance by Lessor of partial payments of rent due shall not, under any circumstances, . . . affect any notice or legal proceedings . . ."

FOLLOW-UP ACTION

The manager might vary collection practices, according to circumstances, for slow-paying tenants who have been subjected to the foregoing education and are still not prompt in subsequent months. An obstreperous tenant should be given a three-day notice the day following the rental due date, instead of three days later. If the tenant appears merely forgetful, a tactful reminder notice left under the door often results in prompt payment.

Taking a Tenant's Personal Property

As cited in Chapter 14, one of the owner's strongest clubs to enforce rent payment is the right to take, hold, and sell a delinquent tenant's personal property. This right is commonly called the "baggage lien law" and is operative in most states. Pertaining to hotels and inns, it has been a part of the common law for centuries. This right is usually extended to cover furnished apartments, and it may or may not by right of law be extended to other dwelling units, such as rental houses and unfurnished apartments. All your rentals will be protected, however, by inclusion of the lien right under paragraph 15 of the lease.

Where it becomes obvious that a delinquent tenant will not pay, the owner should act as soon as possible to hold sufficient valuable property to offset the amount due. If such action is delayed, other creditors may take possession of the personal property before the lessor, even though he may legally have the prior claim. Also the tenants may move out their belongings surreptitiously as did the Muggses.

Many state laws specifically exempt from lien provisions certain property essential to livelihood, such as a cookstove, or a workman's trade tools. Usually a TV set is the most obvious object of value which may be taken. Most tenants possess one and will do their utmost to redeem it, even more than for an "essential of livelihood." In the case of the Muggses, the owner could have held a valuable TV set.

The owner or manager should be careful to avoid personal injury or a possible damage suit. Use no force in the taking of a tenant's property. Although the owner has the right to hold the property, he has no right to inflict personal injury on the tenant in order to take it. Some tenants might give up on demand sufficient property to guarantee rent payment. Professional Dead Beats, like the Muggses, would seldom give up anything of value without a fight.

The only way of taking the property then would be doing it when the tenant is out. In this event the manager or owner should always be accompanied by a witness. A written inventory of the property taken should be countersigned by the witness, to forestall the possibility of the tenant's claiming that more was held.

How Long Should the Property Be Held?

Some laws provide that such property must be held six months or a year before sale, giving the tenant plenty of time to redeem it. A delinquent tenant usually moves away and is seldom heard from again, unless he has especially valuable property to redeem. Of course if the tenant makes conscientious arrangements for later redemption, the manager should extend the holding period. If no such arrangements are offered, a lease provision such as in paragraph 15 enables the owner to sell the property after thirty days. This expedites the release of storage space and the collection of sale proceeds to pay for delinquent rent.

Most tenants put rent at the head of their payment lists and pay their bills when due.

Consistent collection practices and proper notices and forms make rent collections easier and more efficient.

16. HOW TO HANDLE
RENT RAISES AND EVICTIONS

Exploring further how to utilize and enforce lease terms, this chapter breaks into two main subheadings:

How to Raise Rents and Change Other Lease Terms
How to Evict Undesirable Tenants

How to Raise Rents and Change Other Lease Terms

The raising of rents is handled the same as the changing of any other condition of tenancy. As stated in Chapter 14, changing a condition of tenancy is subject to state laws unless controlled by a lease. A typical state law requires, before a change of rent, the same notification period as the rent payment period. A month-to-month continuing rental is subject to a month's notice, a weekly rental to a week's notice. Annual or longer leases, with definite expiration dates, may be changed only when they have expired.

As previously covered, changing the provisions of a rental due the first of the month requires giving notice on or before the first of one month in order to effect a change on the first of the following month. If the first is on a Sunday or a holiday and the rent is paid on the second, the tenant may not be available for notification until the second. The change cannot then take effect on the first of the following month. In most states it may still take effect on the second day, but this is awkward where the rent is paid on the first. In some instances the notice is not legal unless it takes effect on the rent payment date.

Having a fifteen-day clause, as in our cited lease, gives the owner a more flexible opportunity to make changes. It also appeals to the tenant, because he may give notice of vacating fifteen days ahead instead of a month.

TIME TO RAISE RENTS AT B BOULEVARD

After improving the landscaping and painting the halls, the Enterprises review their rent schedule in relation to adjoining rents. The previously remodeled Number 2 flat rents for $125, the Allens' newly rented Number 4 flat for $110, and the remaining two flats for $90. In view of the comparative ease of renting to the Allens for $110, it appears that the two $90 flats should also rent readily for $110. They would need only painting and possibly other minor changes, including the removal of undesirable furniture.

The Enterprises therefore decided to raise the two $90 tenants to $110 each. They will be given notices of the raises on their January rent payment dates, to become effective on their February due dates.

In Metropole it is not necessary for an owner to explain why he is raising the rent. Regardless of whether he expects to operate at a modest or high profit, his long-term rent schedules must be based on fair market values for comparable rentals in a comparable district. But it eases the tenant's pain if an explanation is given, and normally this is advisable in order to obtain the tenant's co-operative agreement.

It could be explained that some rents are being raised to equalize the rent schedule. In this particular case there has been much publicity in recent issues of the local newspaper concerning major increases in local property taxes. The Enterprises therefore advise Mrs. Wister to tell the tenants that raises are necessary chiefly because of a considerable increase in taxes.

A Sample Raise Notice

A notice is given by Mrs. Wister to each of the two $90 tenants, similar to the one following, which is presented to the tenant in the Number 1 flat:

CHANGE OF TERMS, APARTMENTS: Belvedere Apts.

To Tenant: Homer McIntosh

You and each of you will please take notice that the terms of the agreement under which you hold possession of the premises known as Apt. No. 1, 3680 B Blvd. Street, Metropole, Columbia will be and the same are hereby changed effective the 1st day of February 1966, as follows: From and after said date the rent for said premises will be $110.00 per month, payable in advance on the 1st day of each calendar month.

Other terms are changed as follows: None.

Dated this 2nd day of January 1966, Metropole, Columbia.

The remaining terms of said tenancy will remain as before.

Ailene Wister

MANAGER

JOSEPH ENTERPRISE, OWNER

Notices of rent raises should always be given in writing. Many owners give such notices orally, thereby inviting criticism and controversy. A written notice carries finality.

Mixed Reactions

Being next door to the $125 flat, Mrs. McIntosh says that she and her husband have been expecting a raise, as they know they have been paying low rent. She is thankful the raise isn't more than $20, as they can easily pay this.

The tenant in Number 3, adjacent to the Allens' $110 rental, grumbles. She says it will be difficult to pay the increase on her salary as a teacher, and with her mother to support. Both the teacher and her mother complain of the injustice of the raise, and they threaten to move to where they won't have to climb so many stairs.

Paired and separately they shop other rentals diligently in the same and other neighborhoods. By the end of the month they reluctantly agree they are not getting a bad rental bargain. Both the Number 1 and Number 4 tenants pay their raised rents when due in February.

OTHER CHANGES IN LEASE PROVISIONS

Other conditions that might be changed and would merit the giving of a written notice include:

1. Increased rental on garage, storage space, or other accommodations
2. Increased charges for maid, janitor, or other services
3. Taking away of garage or storage space, perhaps for remodeling
4. Taking away maid, janitor, or other services that prove uneconomical
5. Changing from owner-paid to tenant-metered utilities, whole or in part (this would effect a rent raise, of course, if no offsetting reduction in rent were granted)
6. Changing of amount of rent for additional tenants
7. Changing the rental period to daily, weekly, or monthly (this might be effected by a new lease, which would be necessary in case of a change to an annual or longer tenancy)
8. Changing from free to metered launderette service

HOW TO EVICT UNDESIRABLE TENANTS

It is judicious to clean your house of undesirables who fail to heed warnings and are obviously incorrigible. Some unwise owners boldly padlock out or forcibly eject an unwanted tenant, thus subjecting themselves to personal injury, criminal assault charges, and civil suit for damages. Other owners judiciously practice a so-called "constructive eviction," causing tenants to move by shutting off utilities, such as heat, light and water. Evictions can be handled in three legitimate ways:

1. Thirty-day notice to vacate
2. Notice of rent raise
3. Emergency one-to-twenty-four-hour notice to vacate.

1. THIRTY-DAY NOTICE TO VACATE

The most obvious legal form of eviction is a simple notice to vacate. This in effect changes the tenancy by a notice of termination. On a month-to-month rental, the notice is normally given one month in advance and is commonly called a "thirty-day notice." Where the lease provides for a fifteen-day notice, a notice to take effect the first of the month may be given any time up to fifteen days prior to the eviction date.

The thirty-day notice is normally used when there is no controversy involved, as in remodeling where it is desirable to vacate the premises. Except under rent controls, no reason is required in order to make the notice effective. The owner may require a tenant to vacate whenever he sees fit. It may be because the tenant is a troublemaker, because he entertains questionable company, or for any other reason.

However, where the reasons are other than controversial, it is a recommended courtesy to state the reason, such as "because of plans to remodel the premises." Under rent controls any notice normally requires a reason to be given, such as "violation of city ordinances," or other permitted basis for eviction.

SAMPLE THIRTY-DAY NOTICE

Here is a sample notice, which may be used by Mrs. Wister if it is desirable to ask a tenant to move because of remodeling:

NOTICE to VACATE PREMISES
TO CLAIR LARSEN, TENANT in POSSESSION:

You are hereby required to vacate the premises hereinafter described, and which you now hold possession of, and deliver up possession of the same to me within one month of this date as provided by law and the terms of the lease governing said premises.

This notice is given because of the necessity to vacate the premises in order for the owner to remodel same.

Said premises are situated in the City of Metropole, County of Metropole, State of Columbia, and are described as follows:

Apartment Number 3, a five-room flat at 3680 B Boulevard, commonly known as the Belvedere Apartments.

Dated this 10th day of February, 1966.

JOSEPH ENTERPRISE, OWNER

By <u>Ailene Wister</u>

MANAGER

Court-Ordered Dispossession May Be Delayed

Where there is no controversy, especially if a good reason is given, the tenant will nearly always move without court action. If the tenant holds out for court-ordered dispossession, a minimum of thirty days after termination of the notice, sixty days from the date given, would be required. Sometimes six months to a year may pass before a court order is obtained.

Sympathetic judges have postponed indefinitely or denied completely the execution of a vacate notice where the tenant has pleaded a plausible hardship, such as a complicated pregnancy or illness, whether feigned or not. This even though the law clearly states that the owner has the right to require possession of his premises when he so desires. Where such may be the possibility, the easiest enforceable eviction is accomplished by simply raising the rent.

A stiff raise may effectively be added to the 30-day notice as a penalty for staying over. Replace the second paragraph of the Clair Larsen notice with:

You are hereby notified that should you remain in possession of said premises after one month from this date your rent shall be twenty-five dollars ($25.00) per day, starting March 10, 1966.

2. NOTICE OF RENT RAISE

Many experienced owners handle evictions of average troublesome tenants through the device of raising regular monthly rents slightly above the market level. The form of notice is then the same as previously shown for changing the terms of a lease.

The amount of the increase should be judiciously chosen, sufficient to cause the tenant to move rather than pay the raise, and not so exorbitant that it invites adverse comment. Doubling the rent, for example, would make it too obvious that the raise is given in order to effect a vacating of the premises.

In the case of the Number 3 flat, where the market level is about $110, the rent could be raised to $125. This should cause the tenant to move, but it could be defended as reasonable because the remodeled Number 2 flat in the same building is already renting for $125. The tenant could be advised orally that the owner is planning to make certain rent raises and that on this particular Number 3 flat he has decided to rent for $125.

ADVANTAGES OF EVICTION BY RAISING RENTS

The advantages of a regular rent raise over a straightforward vacate notice are many. They include the following:

1. The tenant's pride is not hurt.
2. It is harder for a tenant to fight a raise.
3. Eviction will be easier to effect.

THE TENANT'S PRIDE IS NOT HURT

Because his pride is not hurt, as it would be by a vacate notice, the tenant will co-operate better. He feels he has merely been given a raise and can tell his friends he prefers to move rather than pay it. It is like giving an unsatisfactory employee a chance to resign in preference to being discharged. An eviction notice, like a discharge notice, implies something is wrong with the person involved.

IT IS HARDER FOR THE TENANT TO FIGHT A RAISE

The tenant's natural defense against an above-market raise is to move. There is not much else he can do, except not pay the raise. In the latter case he is subject to a three-day notice to pay or move.

A tenant with whom the manager has had difficulties will fight a simple vacate notice in self-defense. Some managers make the mistake of telling the real reason why the notice is given, such as "because you're always complaining and you're too hard to get along with." Tenants then may prolong the agony by justifying or alibiing, may call the owner or an attorney, may promise to do better, ad infinitum. Where previous warnings have been given, the tenant fails to cooperate, and the manager decides the only step is to get the tenant out of the building, the easier this can be accomplished the better.

Common examples of tenants' inviting eviction by the rent raise route are the malicious gossip who is continually stirring up trouble and the neurotic complainer who unceasingly makes accusations against innocent tenants. I know of one frustrated spinster with a noise complex, who caused a succession of desirable neighbors to move by daily upbraiding them for the minutest pin drop. The flush of a toilet or the squeak of a bedspring would cause her to pound on the floor in a spasm of rage. An inexperienced manager failed to pinpoint the problem until the spinster made a vigorous complaint about how noisy the tenants below her had been all the previous night. The manager knew the tenants in question had left two days before for a week's vacation. On checking, she found that nobody had been in the apartment.

When a questionable tenant causes good tenants to move, the manager should take action. A friendly warning should be given, emphasizing the spirit of "live and let live." If tenants prove incorrigible, the wise manager takes the rent raise steps which will remove them as quickly and easily as possible.

EVICTION WILL BE EASIER TO EFFECT

Considerable delay may ensue in case a tenant fails to heed a regular vacate notice. But if a tenant fails to heed a rent raise, a three-day notice can be given for failure to pay rent. Eviction will then be much speedier and easier to enforce.

Among thousands of rental cases studied, I can cite many instances of tenants' fighting an eviction notice. I know of many raises given for eviction purposes, and not one such case where the tenant failed to move peaceably.

Sometimes the tenant may actually pay the increased rent for a month or so until he finds suitable accommodations within a more reasonable range. If the rent has not been raised sufficiently and the tenant continues to pay the increased rent, he can be raised again, preferably after two or three months' delay.

3. EMERGENCY 1-TO-24-HOUR NOTICE TO VACATE

The emergency notice would be given only in the unusual instance of a tenant's flagrantly violating municipal or state laws or house rules. Though seldom used, this type of notice should be kept in mind and enforced without hesitation when appropriate.

A FLAGRANT CASE

I know of one unusual case involving an eviction even under the restrictions of rent controls. This happened in a quiet, highly respectable apartment house in a desirable neighborhood. A well-mannered couple, whom we shall call the Frohlichs, a Navy lieutenant and his attractive honey-blond wife, rented an apartment. A month later the husband was transferred to Pacific sea duty, leaving the wife alone. Mrs. Frohlich obtained a supervisory position in a Navy procurement office.

She acted decorously for several weeks. But when her husband had been gone two months she held a wild party one Saturday night, including a boy friend and another couple. The party got noisy about 11 P.M. The manager asked them to quiet down and said that the guests would have to leave shortly.

By midnight the party grew louder. The manager advised Mrs. Frohlich that all her guests would have to leave at once. Otherwise the manager would have to call the police. A few minutes later the four participants thundered down the stairs into the lobby and stormed out the front door. Before climbing into a waiting cab all four turned and thumbed their noses toward the manager's apartment, which adjoined the entrance.

About 1 A.M. Mrs. Frohlich returned to her apartment. Her girl friend of the evening followed in fifteen minutes or so and pressed continuously on the apartment buzzer at the main door. The tenant refused to admit her. Another incoming tenant then let the girl friend into the lobby.

The next thing the manager heard was a loud crash of breaking glass. The girl friend had smashed in with her purse and fist a panel of frosted glass on the upper portion of Mrs. Frohlich's apartment door. The girl's hand was streaming with blood. She told the manager that her boy friend was two-timing her and had sneaked back into Mrs.

Frohlich's apartment and she was going to break in and scratch their eyes out.

The girl friend refused to leave until the manager called the police and had her forcibly removed for disturbing the peace. Mrs. Frohlich denied there was anyone in the apartment, saying that her friend was just insanely jealous. No search was made by the police.

The manager said she would not press charges or ask that the girl friend be jailed if she promised not to return, and if she and the tenant both guaranteed payment to cover the damages.

The manager left her door open a crack so that she could see the hall. Shortly thereafter a man slipped out of Mrs. Frohlich's apartment, down the hall, and out the rear exit. In a few minutes the tenant left by the front door and stepped into a waiting taxi.

About 2:30 A.M. Mrs. Frohlich returned in another taxi with a new companion. She brazenly ushered him to her apartment, talking loudly all the way. The manager had wakened on hearing the discussion involved in paying the taxi fare. She phoned the police again and advised them of what had occurred. Then she dressed and went to the tenant's door.

Mrs. Frohlich answered only after repeated ringing. The manager told her it would save a lot of trouble if she got rid of her company at once, because the police were coming.

The inebriated tenant told the manager to go to blazes, she was just an old snoop, and there was nobody in the apartment. "You can kiss my foot," she said, "but brush your teeth first."

When the police arrived Mrs. Frohlich told such a convincing story of injured innocence that they almost left without searching the apartment. The manager insisted she had seen a visitor enter. The police glanced through the apartment halfheartedly and came out, saying they had found nobody.

The manager said she knew the visitor had not left. She accompanied the police when they agreed to re-search the apartment. The man was found cowering behind the shower curtain in the bathtub.

He said Mrs. Frohlich had met him at a bar and had bought him a drink. When the bar closed she invited him to her apartment "to help fix her plumbing."

The police wanted the manager to press charges against both the visitor and the tenant. But the manager would not sign a complaint against him, since he had obviously come invited. A formal complaint was made against the tenant, however, and Mrs. Frohlich was lodged in jail overnight.

She was out on bail the next morning, Sunday. The police phoned the manager and said that a court hearing would be held at 3 P.M. Monday. The manager thought the tenant would want to leave the premises immediately, out of shame, but Mrs. Frohlich said she would not give up her apartment.

AN EMERGENCY NOTICE TO VACATE

The manager returned an hour later with the following notice:

24-HOUR NOTICE to VACATE PREMISES

TO MRS. HORTENSE FROHLICH, TENANT in
   POSSESSION
APT. No. 131, HILLCREST MANOR APARTMENTS
6060 MORNINGSTAR WAY
METROPOLE, COLUMBIA

You are hereby required to vacate the premises hereinafter described, and which you now hold possession of, and deliver up possession of the same to me within 24 hours of this date and time, as provided by law, and the terms of the lease governing said premises.

This notice is given herewith because of your violation of legal regulations and of the terms of the lease governing said premises.

Said premises are situated in the City of Metropole, County of Metropole, State of Columbia, and are described as follows:

Apartment Number 131, a three-room apartment located at 6060 Morningstar Way, commonly known as Hillcrest Manor Apartments.

Dated this 7th day of December, 1952, at the hour of 1:00 P.M.

HILLCREST MANOR APARTMENTS

By <u>Althea Armstrong</u>
MANAGER

THE TENANT IS OBSTINATE

The notice purposely does not state specifically what legal regulations have been violated. More specific accusations can be handled orally if necessary. The tenant may infer that there are more charges contemplated. Although a specific charge of "disturbing the peace" was made in order to jail the tenant, other charges could be made, involving public morals, property damage, and damage to the reputation of the apartment house. The latter could be made the basis of a civil suit after the tenant had been found criminally guilty. Such a suit would seldom be worth mention except as a further club to force the tenant to move.

In this case the manager gave the notice to the tenant, stating she was being allowed twenty-four hours to find another apartment, although she was not entitled to any notice in view of the circumstances. Mrs. Frohlich proved to have the fiery nature that attempts to justify obvious error by fighting. She declared she had no intention of moving. She would get an attorney to fight eviction.

The manager said it would be a good idea for Mrs. Frohlich to consult her attorney before she got into more trouble. Any conscientious attorney looking out for her best interests would advise her to leave immediately to avoid further difficulties.

Even though it was Sunday the manager received a phone call from the tenant's attorney an hour later. He attempted to bluff Mrs. Armstrong by saying that her notice was in violation of rent control regulations; she should get the rent control office's consent and wait at least ten days before giving any kind of eviction notice.

THE MANAGER PURSUES THE
THREAT OF CRIMINAL CHARGES

The manager said she didn't know whether Mrs. Frohlich had explained all that had actually happened. In view of what had occurred the tenant was subject to eviction with no notice whatever. She could be required to move out immediately. She was being granted twenty-four hours, which would give her till noon the next day. If she co-operated by moving, the manager could co-operate by agreeing to probation or a dismissal of the charges. If Mrs. Frohlich was not out of the building by the deadline, the manager would press charges to the utmost to see that the tenant received all she had coming to her in the way of a jail sentence and a fine.

To forestall countersuit and the possible collapse of an attempted eviction such as this, it is highly important that this type of notice be given only when there is ample evidence of criminal action, sufficient to land the tenant in jail.

The attorney said he had learned enough to know that his client would not want any publicity at the Navy procurement office, where she held a responsible job. She would not like her husband and friends to find her out. He agreed to advise Mrs. Frohlich to move. Then he asked if she could be granted a few days to enable her to find another apartment.

Since the court hearing was slated for 3 P.M., the manager reiterated, she would appear in court to "tell it to the judge" in detail if the tenant had not moved before 1 P.M. If the tenant were out she would not press the matter further.

At this the attorney agreed to advise his client to move immediately without fail. Mrs. Frohlich packed and piled her belongings into a taxi later that afternoon. She said she was moving to a hotel, where she would stay until she found an apartment.

This example is cited in detail to indicate the prompt and decisive action which the manager should take in this type of case. However, most managers and owners are not apt to have a similar experience in a lifetime of investment.

CAPITAL VALUE ALREADY INCREASED $9,000

Information will be cited in later chapters regarding additional knowledge which will improve operations, such as income-tax and finance considerations.

Thus far the B Boulevard capital value has already been increased by $9,000. This is arrived at by adding the two $20 monthly raises to the increased monthly earnings of $20 from the Allens' apartment and $15 from the manager's house. The total monthly increase of $75 results in an annual increase of $900, with no added operating costs. Multiplying the increased net annual revenue by our yardstick of 10 gives us a $9,000 increased capital value.

The Enterprises have still to make a major jump in value by modernizing the three other flats along the lines of the $125 Number 2 flat. We are now ready to turn to the further progress of the Enterprises. You will see how their experience surpasses our formula, which will make you a millionaire.

Unique case histories, cited for your guidance in handling tenants, I have gleaned from literally thousands of interviews with owners, managers, tenants, realtors, bankers, attorneys, judges and law enforcement officers.

PART SIX

BUYING YOUR THIRD PROPERTY

17. SHOPPING FOR A $150,000 INCOME PROPERTY

All contemplated improvements of the B Boulevard property have been completed by July 1, 1966. This, within eleven months after purchase, appreciably steps up our average turnover allowance of two years. We are ready to proceed with the next major pyramiding step, the exchange of our apartments for a larger property.

As with the move from A Avenue to B Boulevard, we will seek the largest income property that our accumulated resources can buy on a sound financial basis. To estimate the realistic range in value of the property we should buy, we will first determine our equity in the Belvedere Apartments. Our equity, of course, comprises the present value, less outstanding loans. What is the present value?

SUMMARY OF IMPROVEMENTS

Before assessing a value we will briefly summarize the improvements that have been made to increase value. Details of exterior and interior improvements at the A Avenue house were covered in Part Three. Since similar improvements were required at our B Boulevard Apartments, it will not be necessary to cover them thoroughly as we did on the A Avenue property. The completed work essentially matches that outlined in Part Four when the Belvedere Apartments were appraised.

The three remaining flats have been modernized, with modifications as previously cited, to conform with the already remodeled Number 2 flat. All hallways and stair wells have been painted. The front of the building has been stuccoed to present an entirely new and attractive appearance, along with sprucing the landscaping and painting the balance of the exterior. The exposed rafters have been ceiled.

ONE MASTER CONTRACT SPEEDS THE WORK

We previously estimated that all recommended improvements would cost about $6,000. All this work could have been handled in stages, as at A Avenue, if necessary because of financing. However, the contractor who handled the porch repairs at A Avenue gives us an over-all bid of $6,375. He includes the Belvedere porch foundation repair in this contract and says that he could arrange to finance the entire amount at once. Before doing the work we check two other contractors. Both bid higher than the first, so we give him the job.

Through his loan contacts we were able to secure a new mortgage to cover the cost of all improvements, plus paying off the existing loans. After the work was completed we were able to add the $430 porch reserve to our account. Since details of financing for both improvements and purchases will be dealt with in later chapters, we will not further explore the loan ramifications at present.

During the construction period all tenants remained. They were not greatly inconvenienced, and their flats were undergoing continuing improvement with no change in rents. On July 1, however, the teacher gives notice that she will move August 1.

RAISE RENTS AFTER MODERNIZATION

This saves giving her notice of a rent raise in line with current levels. With the completion of improvements a raise from $110 to $130 is given to the other two lower-paying tenants. The Wisters are raised from $90 to $120, and their management allowance increased from $30 to $40. The Number 2 tenants are raised from $125 to $140, including furniture. All raises are effective with the August rent dates.

The Allens give notice that they will move in August, rather than pay the increase, which they say exceeds their budget. The teacher is the only one who does move. After shopping for comparable accommodations the Allens decide to raise their budget and advise the manager they will stay.

The Number 3 apartment, in spick-and-span, completely modernized and decorated condition, readily rents for $130 before the vacating tenants move, although the teacher has been highly skeptical that her flat could rent for that much. The change in tenants resulted in a gain rather than a loss in rent.

NEW INCOME SCHEDULE

To be used as a basis for appraisal and sale value, the following rent schedule is in effect by August 10, 1966:

Apt. No.	Monthly rent
1	$130.00
2	140.00
3	130.00
4	130.00
5 (House)	120.00
4 Garages @ $5	20.00
TOTAL MONTHLY INCOME	$ 670.00
	× 12
ANNUAL GROSS INCOME	$8,040.00

FIGURING THE PRESENT VALUE

Present fixed expenses for taxes, water, scavenger service, hall lights, and fire insurance amount to $71.46 monthly. Adding the manager's allowance of $40 makes total monthly fixed expenses $111.46, or $1,337.52 annually. Deducting this amount from our gross income of $8,040.00 leaves a net income of $6,702.48. Multiplying by 10 gives us a new capital valuation of approximately $67,000. This is $6,800 more than we estimated when appraising the property for possible resale value.

FIGURING OUR EQUITY AND NET WORTH

Our three loans when we bought the property totaled $26,750. Payments on principal have offset new financing and escrow costs, plus a net amortization of about $400. Deducting the $400 and adding the improvement contract cost of $6,375 gives us an outstanding loan balance of $32,725 on August 10, 1966.

Deducting this amount from our capital valuation of $67,000 gives us an equity of $34,275.

In addition the Enterprises have added the $430 porch reserve plus $1,440 to their August 5, 1965, bank balance of $1,389, bringing their account to $3,259. The $1,440 addition has been augmented by $50 monthly personal savings, plus an average of $70 net in-pocket income from the Belvedere Apartments. The $70 has been netted after paying fixed expenses, loan payments, minor sundry expenses, and repairs and improvements not covered by the master contract.

Adding the current bank balance of $3,259 to the Belvedere equity of $34,275 shows that the net worth of the Enterprises' investment has mushroomed to $37,534.

In Three Years We Approach
Our Eight-Year Goal

Taking stock of our progress to date, we find that it is only two years and eight months since the A Avenue house was bought December 4, 1963. We have four months in which to find and consummate a trade for our next property and still realize our second turnover within three years.

How does this time and money-making performance compare with our Chapter 2 formula to make you a millionaire in twenty years?

Checking our formula, we find that step 6 gave us a four-year goal of $11,575. Step 8 set a six-year goal of $21,681, and step 10 an eight-year goal of $39,363. Within three years we have already arrived at a net estate considerably surpassing our six-year goal and approaching the eight-year target.

Not Unusual Results

The results at A Avenue and B Boulevard are not at all unusual. Many deals are consummated with smaller results, but many incorporating our suggestions produce better results. Both examples serve to show that my formula in Chapter 2 leaned toward the conservative.

Results like the individual steps set forth in the formula can be earned on a hit-or-miss basis of operations, with little long-range planning. With fair luck and ability you can readily match our A Avenue and B Boulevard accomplishments. With foresight and superior luck and ability you can expect to surpass these two examples.

I know of many more productive cases. On one recent turnover six 5-room flats were bought with $5,000 down for $33,500. The flats were modernized, and four were transformed to four 3-room and four 2-room apartments, all at a cost of $12,500, which was financed 100 per cent. Net income with the ten resulting apartments was increased within twenty-two months of the purchase date to $9,250. The sale price of $92,500 doubled the combined purchase and improvement costs. The $41,875 net profit, after 5 per cent sales costs, multiplied the net worth to over eight times the initial investment.

If you see in this rewarding field a goal that fires your imagination and courage, and if you keep at it with sustained investment, improvement, and turnover, you can conservatively expect to make the million dollars set in our formula.

HOW BIG A PROPERTY CAN WE BUY?

We will prove the market value of our B Boulevard property, as with A Avenue, when we sell or exchange it for a larger property. Figuring on 75 per cent financing, as before outlined, we multiply our $37,534 net worth by 4 to estimate how big a property we can buy. This gives us $150,136 as a target price. Allowing approximately 20 per cent leeway would give us a rounded range between $120,000 and $180,000 for our target purchase price.

Since we expect to buy for as much as 25 per cent less than the asking price, a maximum listed-price ceiling of $200,000 might be considered where financing and other factors are especially favorable.

Considering the foregoing figures, the probability of buying for less than the asking price, the desirability of buying soundly and winding up with a small reserve, we round out a median target of $150,000 for the value of the property we seek.

HOW TO FIND A $150,000 PROPERTY

We bought property in the $10,000 and $40,000 brackets through newspaper ads. In a current weekday issue of a metropolitan newspaper we find six columns of ads under "Rental Dwellings," listing sixteen interesting properties apparently in the price range which we now seek. Seven of the ads list apartment houses that invite further investigation. The other nine ads, although in the approximate price bracket, do not suit our mode of operations. All the ads, however, may lead to brokers who handle the type of property we are looking for.

The property buyer can be likened to the hunter in search of game, whose chances of success can be many times increased by using a pack of dogs. Different types of dogs, such as setters and deerhounds, are trained to help bag particular types of game. So it is with efficient property hunting. Some realtors specialize in homes and smaller income properties. Some concentrate on industrial and commercial buildings, some on motels and hotels, and others on apartment houses.

Large realty offices may adequately handle all types of listings, but they will have certain salesmen who specialize. To utilize to the utmost the invaluable aid of the realtor in "bird-dogging" the kind of property you want, time should be concentrated with brokers who have many listings in your field of interest. In most cases the best lead to these particular agents will be through newspaper ads listing property similar to what you seek.

In our first purchase we developed the physical appraisal of advertised properties. In our second purchase we explored special economic factors. Now that we are ready for larger property, we will concentrate on examining another important aspect, the Statement of Income and Expense, which realtors normally provide. This statement reveals the net income, the yardstick on which to base values. The experienced buyer can glance over such a statement and in five minutes know whether the property should be rejected or may be of further interest. I always refuse to look at a property until given such a statement to analyze. The difference between consistent success and possible disillusion lies in the ability to recognize favorable aspects and to spot fateful omissions.

As with our first two purchases we will first examine the most obvious rejects. We will compare ads that appear to be in the sought-for price range; then we will evaluate income and expense items, including complete statements.

THREE BARREN ADS FAIL TO GIVE THE PRICE

A good buy might be found from an ad which failed to list the price. However, unless there is some particularly intriguing feature the experienced shopper seldom wastes much time on such coyness. If the price is fair it normally would be in the ad. Failure to price usually means overpriced. As a check we phone three of the unpriced ads.

A DOUBLE-PRICED AD

OUTSTANDING 12-unit stucco apartment building; Class "A" basement garages. Off Monte Avenue, above Eisenhower. Income over $22,500; $40,000 handles. (Luffmeier) Profit with

THE EARTH SELLERS
Realty and Finance Co.
5320 7th Ave. Phone 323–0404

The "Class 'A' basement garages" means steel-reinforced brick or concrete construction. This is required by most building codes to fireproof garages which are in the same structure as dwellings.

A phone call reveals a $22,500 scheduled gross income, on the basis of 100 per cent occupancy. Fixed annual expenses are listed at $10,800, leaving a scheduled net income of $11,700. Without checking the figures for discrepancies or omissions a sale valuation of $117,000 is indicated.

The salesman says the asking price is $225,000, ten times the gross instead of ten times the net income. This asking price is close to double the market value. It is obvious that there is no object in checking further.

A BLUE-SKY AD WITH NO FIGURES AT ALL

MOST TERRIFIC VALUE IN
AREA
16 1-bedroom, 8 2-bedroom, some with 2 baths, beautiful
setting with swimming pool. Fantastic return.
GOODER REALTY CO.
8150 ELM
Phone 525–1751 or 368–6170

This ad gives no figures whatever. The total of 24 units might be in our price range. A phone call shows that a vacant building is being advertised. It is a luxury type, built in an outlying subdivision area that caters to low-income buyers. The "fantastic return" is based on the following schedule of projected rentals:

16	1-bedroom apts.	@	$250	monthly	$4,000.00
5	2-bedroom apts.	@	325	monthly	1,625.00
3	2-bedroom apts.	@	350	monthly	1,050.00
	TOTAL MONTHLY INCOME				$6,675.00
					× 12
	TOTAL ANNUAL INCOME				$80,100.00

The salesman says that expenses are estimated at $10,000, about 12.5 per cent of the estimated gross income. This would leave a net annual income of $70,100, making the property worth $701,000. The owner is selling at a sacrifice, as he is asking only $600,000. The building has been completed for eighteen months. It is being kept vacant so that the new owner can pick his own tenants.

APPLYING A RULE-OF-THUMB ESTIMATE FOR EXPENSES

It is obvious that the foregoing statements are highly deceptive, that the building is being left vacant because actual attainable rentals in this area would be about one half of the schedule. A maximum gross would approximate $40,000 annually. On a property of this size 25 per cent fixed expenses are normally figured as the minimum in the absence of actual cost experience. Where utilities are provided by the owner, fixed expenses can be expected to average about 35 per cent, depending on the services included. Deducting $10,000 for fixed expenses, the 25 per cent, realistically estimated minimum, would leave a net of $30,000. This means an approximate market value of $300,-000, half the asking price.

The only figures given by the salesman with any degree of accuracy were the expenses. Here his amount was about right, but his percentage was considerably underestimated. It is difficult to visualize why any seller would attempt to overprice a property to such an extent. About his only chance to consummate a sale would be on a trade where the other party is trying to dump an overpriced lemon, like a money-losing resort.

A THIRD INFLATED AD WITH UPGRADED RENTS

New Listing

GREAT BOULEVARD DISTRICT. Close to shopping center and Express transportation; 5-year-old modern; 17 units, 12 2s, five bachelor, completely furnished; shows excellent income with 100% occupancy; reasonable terms. Owner will consider part trade. Mr. Bludgeon, Phone 254–8320; evenings, 628–8080.

BONNY WORMSETT CO.

This ad might have an appeal because of the willingness to trade. However, we anticipate no difficulty in effecting a trade.

The five "bachelor" units turn out to be not apartments but single rooms only, with no kitchens. "Shows excellent income with 100 per cent occupancy" would indicate the building is 100 per cent occupied. A check of the existing rental shows that all five bachelor units and seven of the 2s are vacant. The owner is asking $110 monthly for the bachelor rooms. Their market value in the area would not exceed $75. He is asking $145 for the 2s where the market value would be about $95. The few tenants he gets are quick turnovers from out of town who leave after a month or two.

The schedule on a realistic basis is thus overpriced $175 on the bachelors and $600 on the 2s, a total monthly inflation of $775, or $9,300 annually. Multiplying by 10 would lessen the sale value by $93,000.

The salesman, Mr. Bludgeon, shows a scheduled gross of $27,480, annual expenses of $8,170, and a net of $19,310. Ten times the net would give a theoretical market value of $193,100. He says the asking price is $179,500, "which is a darned good below-the-market buy."

True rental values would drop the gross $9,300 to $18,180. Deducting the listed expenses of $8,170 would leave a net of $10,010. This would give a market value closer to $100,000 than $180,000. The listed expenses normally would not change, despite a change in the rent potential. In this case they are exceptionally high, approximately 45 per cent of the realistic gross, and apparently could be reduced.

A PERSONAL EXPENSE FACTOR

The manager's salary is shown at $150 monthly, plus an apartment. With an operation of this size a competent manager could be readily obtained for a salary of $25 monthly plus an apartment. It develops that the manager is a widowed aunt of the owner, a personal item which would not be reflected in a new owner's operation. Reducing the manager's salary $125 monthly would result in a $1,500 annual saving. This would increase the sale value $15,000 to approximately $115,000, still only two thirds the asking price.

NEVER TAKE FIGURES FOR GRANTED

The foregoing three ads show why considerable elimination can be made without taking the time and effort for on-the-ground appraisals. These unpriced ads give a warning which cannot be overemphasized: Never take a salesman's figures for granted.

A salesman usually accepts the figures given him by the owner, seldom checking their accuracy. If a property fails to interest you, of course it is time-wasting to check further. But on any building that arouses your interest, never take a salesman's or owner's income schedule at listed value. Always check each individual apartment with the manager. How many are vacant, and how many occupied? What is the actual rent being collected from each occupied apartment? It is essential also, especially when you are warned by excessive vacancies, to check comparable rentals in the neighborhood to establish the probable rental level at which the building will stay reasonably full.

It should be mentioned that grounds for a damage suit are established if you can prove substantially inaccurate the figures given you as a basis for buying income property. Having a legal claim and collecting, however, are not the same. A real-estate broker who leaves his office open to suit is apt to be unable to pay damages. The seller may dissipate assets before suit is accomplished.

In the case of a trade the court may order a return to the status prior to the exchange, which would put you right back where you started. The loss of time and effort would be compensated only by your added education.

Most income-and-expense statements presented to you will prove fairly accurate on examination. But the property you choose to buy might be the one misrepresented by a completely misleading statement. You will avoid regrets and safeguard your success, therefore, if you make it a cardinal rule never to take figures for granted.

FOUR ADS INDICATE OVERPRICED NEW CONSTRUCTION

Four of the ads cover apparently brand-new construction. Three apartment houses have just been completed, and one is not yet finished. Together they comprise a cross section of what might be found in the new construction field.

As mentioned in previous chapters, we are seeking buildings which are basically sound but in need of improvement. Obviously the latter are less apt to be found in new construction. New apartments may pay off well costwise for the initial builder. But they are almost invariably priced to the next buyer at a substantial profit over the cost of building.

TWO NEW CONSTRUCTION GIMMICKS
THAT DISTORT RENTALS

Some new apartments being sold by unethical builders and other speculators show income ballooned considerably above realistic rentals, and yet no vacancies. One new 20-unit apartment house I inspected showed a net income of approximately $30,000, and a sale price of $295,000. The sale value based on market level rents was about $120,000. Expecting to sell before 3 months elapsed, an unscrupulous builder filled his apartments at double the market rents by including free groceries, chargeable to his account, for 3 months. Of course by then the tenants would move unless they received halved rents or continued free groceries.

Another speculator filled his 24 efficiency apartments at a $150 rent schedule when their market value was only $100. He signed up all tenants on one-year leases at $150 monthly, giving them credit for $900 to cover the first and last 5 months' rent. They paid only $300, however, and thus received the last 4 months' rent free. Although on an annual basis they actually paid $100 monthly, on paper their rent was $150. This juggling increased the speculator's net rental statement by $14,400 annually, and he thereby upped his sale price by $140,000 above the realistic value.

Such cases of showing a full building at over-the-market distorted rents are peculiar to new construction, baited for the unwary by only a few fly-by-night speculators. They can be guarded against if you heed any one of the four following precepts:

1. Avoid paying more than the cost of construction, which you can duplicate
2. Verify the present rentals and terms with the manager and some tenants
3. Check against prevailing neighborhood rentals
4. Avoid new construction until you gain experience

Since you may duplicate good profits on initial building, you might well consider this field after you gain experience, as we also suggested previously. But here is a field where it is easy to make grievous mistakes. Until you have experience, it is well to stay in the field of existing older construction, generally at least three years old, where the rents are proved and where you can find room for improvement.

As additional checks, however, we will cite two new-construction ads to indicate other particular items to watch for.

AN OVERPRICED "JUST BUILT"

NEW 16 UNITS, NEAR RIVER: swimming pool, $24,000 income. $195,-000. Evenings. Phone 929–5709.

Investigation reveals that the listed number is for the residence of a general contractor who has built the apartments for speculation. The building has been completed for two months. It is located in an outlying industrial area. Within a quarter mile are a tannery and an equally obnoxious fiberboard plant.

Four of the units are rented, and twelve are vacant. The scheduled income is based on monthly rentals of $125, which would be about right for a 3-room apartment in a desirable suburban area. These units are all 2s.

THREE MAJOR MISTAKES

The contractor has made three major mistakes:

1. He has built in an undesirable neighborhood, no doubt because the land was cheap. Cheap land is costly when the resulting plant loses money.

2. He has built efficiency 2s, with no bedrooms, in a suburban area which normally holds tenants with a minimum of three rooms. Twos rent well when close in, but most tenants willing to rent in the suburbs demand at least one bedroom. Suburban dwellers expect more spacious living, with bigger quarters and outdoor areas. The builder who skimps space in the country will experience heavy turnover and vacancy losses.

3. He has built expensive features, like the swimming pool, which will not pay off in this neighborhood. Small apartments in this area would be rentable only if they offered unusually low rents. This could be done by building essentials and omitting costly de luxe items.

The contractor has estimated the annual expenses, since he has only two months' operation as a guide. He lists expenses at $6,500, leaving a net, even with the inflated $24,000 gross, of $17,500. Without checking the accuracy of the expenses, the correct price on the basis of the listed figures should be $175,000.

But the units could not be kept rented approaching a full-house basis for over $95, at the maximum, in their location. This would lower the gross by $4,800, lowering the net by a like amount to $12,700. The market value would be reduced to $127,000, a long way from the asking price of $195,000. These apartments are a typical example of unproved rents.

Discussion with the contractor divulged that he had been the general contractor on a building with an identical floor plan for an investor in a choice location closer downtown. The investor had quickly filled his apartments, so the contractor figured he would save architects' fees and make money by using the same plans to build for himself in another location. The contractor wasn't taking in enough rents to pay off his loan and expenses. He had to sell the building or lose it.

AN OPTIMISTICALLY PRICED "NOW-BUILDING"

> OFF GARY BOULEVARD: now building 18 de luxe garden-type apartments. You select your own colors. $176,000. (Napes or Colon) Today is filled with buying, selling and exchanging income opportunities.

Ask the HOLLANDAISE
Realty and Finance Co.
10410 Broadway. Phone 668–6574

Here we run into a new gimmick. "You select your own colors" means you pay for putting them on. The price is within bargaining range for the eighteen 3-room apartments in a desirable locality. However, the rents are figured on the basis of having the buyer completely furnish all apartments, besides paying for the interior and exterior painting, and also the landscaping.

A rough estimate of these costs would include $14,000 for furniture, $6,000 for interior and exterior painting, and $2,000 for landscaping, making a total added cost of $22,000.

It turns out that a speculative builder has died and his heirs are attempting to dump the property in an unfinished state. Such incomplete construction is dangerous for investment. Frequently contractors' liens for unpaid work will be found recorded against the property. Often the finished work has exhausted potential financing, and the balance has to be done mostly for cash, or with subsidiary loans financed at high premiums.

TIME TO CHECK THE ADS WHICH LOOK GOOD

Among the seven ads which look good enough for thorough investigation, we first select one advertising "Almost New."

A JERRY-BUILT "ALMOST-NEW"

Almost New Faraway Meadows. 14
attractive 3-room units, each with
dining area. Complete, modern decor
throughout; landscaped inner court;
wall-to-wall rugs; individually metered.
Superb rental location. Excellent financing available; $129,500.
M. C. Loudermilk Co.
Phone 533–2097: evenings 252–7504.

The broker, Mr. Loudermilk, shows us a statement which indicates that $129,500 is a low price for the listed annual net income of $14,068.44. There are many ways in which a statement of income and expense can be set up. Here is the one submitted by Mr. Loudermilk.

FARAWAY MEADOWS APARTMENTS
71410 Meadowbrook Lane
Metropole, Columbia

One-story ranch-type 14-unit apartment house, all 3-room. Fine "homelike" apartments. Lovely inner court and garden setting. Large rooms. Ample closets.

All apartments except four are furnished.

Equipment: Gas-fired individual heaters. Gas stoves (new O'Keefe and Merritt table top). Electric refrigerators. Incinerator. Easy-to-clean linoleum halls. Apartments have wall-to-wall rugs.

Building erected: 1942.
Area of Land: 100.09' × 146.47' more or less.

Six blocks from Metropole transportation. Six blocks from shopping area. A few blocks from river. This is a first-class residential and apartment neighborhood where new building is expected.

Garage space: 9 cars.
Offers considered at $129,500.00
Minimum cash payment   32,500.00 (25%)
Monthly loan payment   750.00 (Incl. 6% interest)

ANNUAL SCHEDULED INCOME $17,184.00

Income Schedule, June 1, 1966:	* 1966 Fixed Expenses:	
2 Unfurnished apts. @ $89.00		
2 " " @ 90.00	Manager's Salary	$600.00
4 Furnished apts. @ 97.50	Electricity (halls)	106.16
1 " " @ 99.00	Water	340.06
1 " " @ 100.00	Telephone	51.48
4 " " @ 120.00	Taxes	1,603.96
	Insurance	233.88
	License, scavenger	
	and miscellaneous	180.02
	* Total expenses	$3,115.56

Monthly Income $1,432.00

* Maintenance expenses vary from year to year with different types of management, and are omitted.

SCHEDULED NET INCOME$14,068.44

While we believe the above information to be correct, it is not guaranteed, and is, in its entirety, subject to change without notice.

M. C. LOUDERMILK COMPANY
8363 15th Street, Metropole, Columbia
Phone 533–2097

JUNE 1966

A Brief Check of the Statement

Each of the items listed can, with experience, be recognized as being within reason or as being out of line and warranting detailed checking. Under INCOME, in any case, we will check the actual rental of each apartment. Under EXPENSES we will check whether any items which should be listed are omitted, and if any of those listed are incorrect.

UTILITIES

If the owner provided utilities these expenses, including electricity, fuel, and power, would be considerably higher. If the tenants actually pay for their own utilities the expenses listed seem to be in line. Any time there is doubt about an expense, it is always wise to ask for the previous year's bills, which will be presented without protest by an honest owner.

TAXES AND INSURANCE

These charges seem in line, but again the bills may be asked for if you are in doubt.

MISCELLANEOUS

Small fixed items like license fees and scavenger service are sometimes listed separately, sometimes grouped under "Miscellaneous."

ITEMS NOT COMMONLY LISTED ON A REALTOR'S STATEMENT

Three common expenses which are not normally listed on such an expense statement for apartment houses are:

1. Capital items which are a depreciation expense
2. Supplies and sundries, such as stationery and office and janitor supplies
3. Vacancy factor

All have to be taken into account by an appraiser and by a buyer. In a well-run building without major capital expenses they should be covered by 4 per cent of the gross income, leaving an actual net of 6 per cent in place of the 10 per cent fixed net.

It should be mentioned that these three items are normally included in a business property listing, such as a motel.

MANAGER'S FREE APARTMENT SHOULD BE SHOWN AS EXPENSE IF LISTED AS INCOME

The salaries of manager, janitor, gardener, elevator man, maid, and other employees should be listed. Often owners and brokers fail to list these salaries, either as a whole or in part. In a 14-unit building like this there normally would be only one employee, the manager, who would also take care of any janitor and gardening work.

Duties of an employee should always be fully checked. What work does the listed employee handle? Such questioning often reveals undisclosed expenses, such as payments to a gardener or a janitor, which have not been listed.

In this example the manager cleans vacated apartments without additional compensation. The listed expense of $600 annually, $50 monthly, for a manager is obviously low. This amount might be about right for a cash payment, but could not include the value of an apartment, normally given to a manager in addition, in an operation of this size.

The common practice is to include in the gross income the value of the manager's apartment or other employee quarters. The same rental value should then be shown as part of the expense. Sometimes the employees' quarters are omitted from the income statement, and in this event their value would properly be omitted from the expense.

The net income is falsely inflated when the value of the manager's apartment is shown under income and not under expense. We ask Mr. Loudermilk if the manager occupies one of the fourteen listed apartments or an additional one which is not indicated. He says the manager lives in one of the fourteen apartments. We ask at what rental, and he says the one listed at $100 monthly.

FIXED EXPENSES ARE UNDERSTATED BY $1,200

This falsifies the annual fixed expenses by $1,200. Adding to the listed $3,115.56 would increase fixed expenses to $4,315.56. Deducting the new total from the listed rentals of $17,184 would leave a revised net of $12,868.44.

The capital value would be reduced to $128,684 instead of the $140,684 previously arrived at. Thus, correcting one misleading item transforms the asking price of $129,500 from a fair bargain to a slightly overpriced buy.

However, "Offers considered at $129,500" indicates that a considerably lower price might be obtained. If the rest of the statement stands up, and the building looks good on inspection, we might pursue the possibility of making an offer.

BOTH BUILDING AND STATEMENT FALL TO PIECES ON INSPECTION

The "almost new" in the ad proves fanciful, unless you take the slant of newness in London, where guides tell you anything under five hundred years old is considered "modern."

JERRY-BUILT WAR HOUSING

Investigation reveals that the previously considered fair buy is a rank white elephant. The building has been cheaply slicked over in an attempt to cover up the fact that it was built as temporary wartime housing and was marked for destruction at the end of the war. That is why the rambling barrackslike, one-story structure was erected on mudsills, with no foundation. The exterior walls are composed of thin plasterboard, which has been kicked through with large holes in many places. The holes have been patched over and painted with a rough-surfaced stucco paint in an amateurish attempt to camouflage.

Cheap cotton-tufted carpets have recently been tacked over inside halls, living rooms, and bedrooms to cover the crumbling dry rot in floorboards and underpinning. The apartments are located in the middle of a marshland, which, the neighbors say, usually lies under several inches of water when it rains. There are a number of vacant lots, and a few fairly new low-cost homes adjoining. The area is fairly close in, but it is surrounded by heavy commercial enterprises, such as warehouses, a dairy plant and office, and a power company pole yard.

BUILDING FACES CONDEMNATION

A later check at the City Hall shows that no condemnation notices have yet been posted. The owner has been warned in writing that the building will be condemned unless substantial foundation, wall, and plumbing alterations are made to bring the structure up from its substandard condition.

No lending institution would loan a dime on the apartments in their present state. The building was erected by the government without cost to the owner and was turned over to him free and clear after the war. In order to dump the property, the owner is willing to carry back almost any kind of loan, which explains the "excellent financing available."

There are too many profitless headaches involved to warrant further consideration. As a guide to later appraisals, however, we might as well audit the accuracy of the statement with the manager while we are on the premises. Starting with apartment 1, we ask the manager what each apartment is renting for, and whether it is tenanted or vacant. It develops that the four apartments listed at the highest price of $120 are vacant.

The highest actual rent being collected is $97.50. This rental includes a garage, which is figured at $5. All seven tenants who pay $90 or above have a $5 garage included in the rent. There are no vacant garages. The manager occupies one, and the ninth is needed for a workshop and for storage. This indicates that the market level for the four empty apartments, which could not be provided with garages, would be not over $100 each. The total rents that could actually be collected would be reduced $80 monthly less than the amounts listed.

This $960 annual reduction from the last revised annual net of $12,868.44 would leave a new net of $11,908.44. The capital value would be lowered to $119,084 without further investigation, a value which could be considered only if the building were in fair condition.

THREE GIMMICKS TO CATCH THE UNWARY

The foregoing warns of three common gimmicks which falsify the net income and are designed to catch the unwary:

1. Omitting the value of the manager's apartment as an expense
2. Inflating rentals by listing vacancies higher than their market value
3. Showing present rentals higher than they actually are

We have found several disillusioning properties. Although they have been selected from one day's actual newspaper ads for your guidance, you might shop the market for a long time before you could match them. We know there are on the market many desirable apartments which will meet our requirements. As long as you have a good picture of the kind of property you are looking for, and of the income and expense items that warrant special attention, you can proceed without hesitation. We are ready for further appraisals of provocative ads to find our building in the $150,000 price range.

THREE MORE ADS ARE QUICKLY DISCARDED

Of the six remaining ads, three develop into fair buys and three lead to quick discards. We will briefly review two of the discarded ads, as a further guide to what to avoid.

AMONG THE CHICKENS AND TURKEYS

A Better Selection at
NORTHEASTERN
Realty & Finance Co.
SELL
OR
TRADE
15 APARTMENTS, plus 5 stores. Battersea. $2,033 monthly income. $160,-000. Evening, Phone 429–5618.
NORTHEASTERN
Realty & Finance Co.
8210 Main—Phone 474–0055.

We find a run-down, four-story apartment house in a formerly elegant part of town that has degenerated into a produce district. There is a poultry distributor on each side of the building. One house specializes in chickens and eggs, the other in turkeys.

On the ground floor the advertised building has five stall-like "stores," each with a ten-foot frontage. There are three stories of walk-up apartments above the stores.

The apartment rents are as low as $95 monthly. In this noisome atmosphere there are still six vacancies. The income shown on the statement includes a $75 monthly rental for each store, but three are vacant. Across the front windows of the two occupied "stores" there is an admonition crudely lettered with red paint:

BLOOD OF THE LAMB Repent Your SINS TODAY	FAITH MISSION Be SAVED INSIDE

The church uses one store as a meeting place and the other as the residence of a Reverend Chauncey P. Osgood, his wife and eight children. The total rent collected for both stores is $75. The manager says the owner figures a $75 rent for the use of one store for a residence. The Faith Mission is shown on the books as a $75 rental and a $75 donation. Such a bookkeeping practice serves no useful purpose except to distort by $900 the annual gross income. The latter is used as an appraisal guide by most buyers and lenders, multiplying by 6.5 to 7.5 as common apartment factors.

Checking actual income against scheduled expenses leaves an approximate net of $9,000 annually, lowering the capital valuation to $90,000. For income, for location, and for the age and condition of the building, the poultry-surrounded apartments are distress merchandise.

A RABBIT-WARREN ROOMING HOUSE

A—GIBRALTAR
For over a quarter of a century offering sound and substantial
INVESTMENT OPPORTUNITIES
For Sale or Exchange
CORNER. Mayfield—Stucco. 24-unit apartment. Liquidating. Income $25,-

000. Sacrifice, $125,000. Terms. (Rick-
enmayer.)
GIBRALTAR
Realty and Finance Co.
4750 42nd—Phone 827-2490

This ad indicates a money-maker, but inspection reveals another headache-maker. The "24-unit apartment" turns out to be a rooming house, converted from an ancient mansion. The front has recently been camouflaged with stucco, but the sides and rear still reveal the original cedar-shingle exterior popular about fifty years ago.

The original mansion had three regular stories, plus an attic and a basement, making five floor levels. All five floors have been jammed with small rooms. Various types of makeshift cooking devices, some gas and some electric hot plates, have been installed to make "housekeeping rooms." By stretching the imagination, one might call these units apartments.

To produce the rent schedule shown, the rooms are completely furnished, including nondescript dishes, cooking utensils, and bedding. Most of the rooms have single cots, as there would scarcely be enough maneuvering space to permit a double bed.

WEEKLY RENTS ARE A RED FLAG

The rents are all collected on a weekly basis, which is a red flag for the wary investor. Desirable apartments rent by the month or year. An owner who rents by the week usually does so only because his accommodations attract none but transient tenants. This means high turnover, heavy vacancy losses, and costly labor and maintenance expense in cleaning up after outgoing tenants and getting ready for new ones. After figuring actual rents, vacancies, and expenses, the resulting net is insufficient to keep up loan payments.

Here is another example of a bad buy. When we were looking for our first purchase in the $10,000 bracket at the beginning of the book, I mentioned that you should always seek basically sound property that appears originally designed for its present use. Difficulties will nearly always be found where a building has been converted from its original purpose in a haphazard manner such as this.

THREE FAIR BUYS LEAD TO A BARGAIN

We are ready to cover the three ads which describe properties listed at a fair price.

A POSSIBLE GOOD BUY, BUT FINANCING TOO TIGHT

> OWNER LEAVING. 18 excellent
> units. Corner, close to Lake Con-
> stance, hardwood floors, 18-car con-
> crete garage, $25,000 yearly gross.
> Marcia Evans. Phone 223-3172.
> MacBride Realty Company
> 9850 Grant Street
> Phone 422-6591.

Previously we cited three barren ads in which the prices were not listed. This is the only ad without a price tag which turns out to be a fair buy. The omission here might be because of feminine coyness, as Mrs. Evans is the only female agent contacted in the particular group of ads.

Mrs. Evans says the asking price is $160,000. The "$25,000 yearly gross" turns out to be fairly realistic. The rent schedule, which is considerably below the market level for the area, develops an annual gross of $24,800. Fixed expenses, apparently complete, are shown as $9,300, leaving an annual net of $15,500. A capital value of $155,-000 is indicated. Leaving room for bargaining, the asking price is not out of line.

Mrs. Evans says the owner is a college professor who is taking over a higher-paying post as dean at a university some distance away. His wife has been managing the apartment house. He prefers not to operate as an absentee owner and is anxious to sell. The professor would probably consider a reasonable offer, but he wants all cash down to the present first mortgage of $62,800. The highest commitment for a new first mortgage is $90,000. The owner will not listen to a trade or to taking back a second mortgage, as he is violently opposed to both.

The apartments are in tiptop condition and in an excellent rental location. Although little opportunity is offered for the physical improvement we particularly seek, there is a good chance to make a substantial capital increase in value merely by raising the rents.

Only bargaining would reveal the lowest selling price. If the property could be bought for as low as $145,000, the lowest probable price in view of the circumstances, it would represent a good buy for a buyer with plenty of cash. But the $55,000 required in cash would represent about $17,500 more than our equity. With other owners who refused to trade, a solution could be attempted by working out a three-way trade, selling our property to a third party. It would still be necessary for the owner to take back a second mortgage of $20,000 or so, depending on the net proceeds from selling our B Boulevard apartments.

If the professor were remaining in town, some kind of transaction might eventually be worked out. Since he is leaving, all the signs point to a high improbability of consummating a deal with the equity financing we have in mind.

Fair Buys with Little Room to Increase Values

The next two ads lead to similar conclusions, so we will cite only the choicer of the two, which offers better financial arrangements. Both ads represent fair buys but offer little opportunity to increase values.

> **$25,000 DOWN**
> Abrams Blvd. 16 units, 3 story, full
> concrete basement. 8–3's, 6–4's, 2–2's,
> excellent condition. Close Lakeshore
> and downtown Metropole. $135,000.
> **A. J. KETTEBEC CO.**
> Phone 623–0749; evenings 459–5284.

Both the price and the financing look good. The building is attractive and in a good rental area. The gross income, with rents close to the market level, comes to $22,600 annually. There is only one vacancy, indicating a realistic rent schedule. Fixed expenses, including all normally shown, total $9,100. This leaves a net of $13,500 and gives a capital valuation of $135,000. The property has been priced at exactly its factual capital value to show a 10 per cent net on the basis of scheduled income and fixed expenses.

Mr. Mansfield, the salesman who answered our call to the Kettebec office, states that the price is pretty firm. The rents are lower than they could be, the building is in good condition, and the owner is offering unusually good financing.

"That all may be true," we protest, "but surely you expect to sell for something less than the asking price. What is the lowest you think the owner would take?"

The salesman says he will not state a lower price. If we want to try for less it is up to us to make an offer. When pressed, he says that the owner might take as low as $125,000, but he would not be too sure. The owner has previously turned down an offer of $120,000.

All indications are that here is a fairly good buy for a prospective owner who is looking purely for sound income rather than for an opportunity to increase capital value. There is little of the opportunity we seek to make improvements which will increase values.

After you gain experience, a few minutes spent in examining a statement of income and expense will tell you whether a property is worth further consideration.

Thus you can reject most undesirable listings with little expenditure of time, saving your physical appraisals for properties with attractive financial statements.

18. CHOOSING YOUR THIRD PROPERTY

We tell the salesman our conclusions and mention that the kind of property we prefer would be basically sound and in a good location, like these sixteen apartments on Abrams Boulevard. To meet our requirements the property should be more run-down, in need of painting and other improvements.

Mr. Mansfield says he advertised just such a building in the previous Sunday's paper. He has received a number of replies, but everyone who looked at the advertised property was afraid of it. Maybe it needed too much work. If we're interested in looking at the property, he'll take us to his office to pick up the financial statement on it.

On the Trail of a Real Bargain

Mr. Mansfield has a copy of the Sunday paper in his car, and he shows us the following ad:

A SPECULATOR'S DREAM
"1966 Special," 24 modern stucco apartments, close in. Needs paint, paper. Out-of-town owner priced it sensibly. Consider trade. Try $25,000 down. Tomorrow might be too late. Sam Mansfield, Phone 623–0749.
A. J. KETTEBEC CO.

At his office Mr. Mansfield shows us the following statement, which indicates we are on the trail of a real bargain.

CYNTHIA COURT APARTMENTS
THREE-STORY STUCCO-FRAME
APARTMENT BUILDING

LOCATION: 4440 Cynthia Court, Metropole, Columbia

LOT SIZE: 70′ × 150′ more or less

IMPROVEMENTS: 3-story stucco-and-frame building, divided into 24 units, 3 3s, 21 2s; 51 rooms; 95 per cent furnished. Building approximately 25 years old. Fireproof garage for 20 cars.

ANTICIPATED INCOME:

Apt.				Apt.				Apt.			
101	3 rm.		$105.00	201	3 rm.		$105.00	301	3 rm.		$105.00
(Mgr.) 102	2	"	80.00	202	2	"	80.00	302	2	"	80.00
103	2	"	80.00	203	2	"	80.00	303	2	"	80.00
104	2	"	80.00	204	2	"	80.00	304	2	"	80.00
105	2	"	80.00	205	2	"	80.00	305	2	"	80.00
106	2	"	80.00	206	2	"	80.00	306	2	"	80.00
107	2	"	80.00	207	2	"	80.00	307	2	"	80.00
108	2	"	80.00	208	2	"	80.00	308	2	"	80.00

TOTAL MONTHLY INCOME $1,995.00

TOTAL ANNUAL INCOME $23,940.00

FIXED EXPENSES, ANNUAL:

Taxes	$2,105.39
Sanitation	180.00
Water	452.52
Gas and electricity	1,867.02
Manager Apt. 102	960.00
Manager salary	600.00
Insurance	229.00
License	41.25
	$6,435.18 6,435.18

ANNUAL NET INCOME $17,504.82

LOANS: First loan: $71,711.00, 6%, $600.00 per month
Second loan: $33,789.30, 6%, $375.00 per month
$105,500.30

REMARKS: Central refrigeration disconnected. Installed 24 new Westinghouse refrigerators at a cost of $4,725.00, payments approximately $200.00 per month on chattel mortgage. Balance June 1966 approximately $4,500.00.

PRICE: $150,000.00
Note: The above information was obtained from sources we believe to be reliable; however, it is not guaranteed and the A. J. Kettebec Co. assumes no liability for omission or error.

The rentals seem reasonable for the general area, and the fixed expenses appear realistic. Thus the net income of $17,504.82 reflects a factual capital value of $175,000. The asking price of $150,000 seems unusually low. We must be wary of hidden detractions.

We check with Mr. Mansfield regarding two points in his ad, "try $25,000 down" and "consider trade." By adding the $105,500 in outstanding loans to the $25,000 suggested down payment we come up with a total of about $130,000. Did Mr. Mansfield mean that the owner would accept a trade equity of approximately $25,000 for his equity in the property?

THE ASKING PRICE DOES NOT
INCLUDE THE NEW REFRIGERATORS

The salesman says, "It isn't as simple as that. The owner is asking $150,000 without the twenty-four new refrigerators. They had an original chattel mortgage of $4,725, reduced now to about $4,500. The price including the refrigerators would total $154,500, as the owner will let them go for their loan balance.

"The owner got a good buy at wholesale through a fellow-Italian friend in the appliance business. It would pay to take the refrigerators over, as the former central system has been completely junked. Otherwise they would be released back to the chattel mortgage holder, and you would have to buy new ones."

The matter of the refrigerators and the chattel mortgage we let drop for the present while we explore further. We mentally tuck away three possible choices if a deal gets into the home stretch:

1. Squeeze the refrigerators into the deal without additional cost to us.
2. Take them over and assume the chattel mortage.
3. Let them go, and buy new refrigerators.

THE PRESENT OWNER IS ANXIOUS TO SELL

Mr. Mansfield says, "The owner, Mr. Giacolini, is offering a real sacrifice, as he paid $210,000 for the property. He bought it from another Italian friend. That price showed up good incomewise when he bought the building and it was full at higher than the present rents. It also was considerably under the replacement value, which I figure at about $250,000.

"The second mortgage was taken back by the previous owner in selling to Giacolini. The second loan also includes a chattel mortgage on all the furniture except the new refrigerators. The owner is now having a lot of trouble with a run-down building and too many vacancies. He isn't making enough on the property to meet expenses and pay all his loans, and he's plenty anxious to sell."

Mr. Mansfield displayed a title guarantee policy in the amount of $210,000 to bear witness to the previous sale price. He said that "consider trade" and "try $25,000 down" referred to two separate items. The owner's price of $150,000 was rock bottom, and he therefore had an equity of $45,000. He wanted $25,000 down in cash. The balance of $20,000 he would accept in trade for an equity in a smaller building.

Mr. Giacolini would not sell without some cash, needed to pay pressing obligations plus the real-estate commission, which would amount to $7,500. He did have other income from a railroad pension and from other property in an adjoining city where he lived. He had been phoning Mr. Mansfield daily to tell him how anxious he was to sell the Cynthia Court Apartments.

THE BUILDING LOOKS SURPRISINGLY GOOD OUTSIDE

Mr. Mansfield suggests a visit to the property, which turns out to be in a desirable rental area. The exterior makes a surprisingly good first impression. The building is of fairly modern design and has been recently painted. The only discordant note is a weather-beaten wooden

"Apartment for Rent" sign two feet square, hanging from the fire escape over the front door. The sign is in black letters painted over a much-besmudged white background.

We remark to Mr. Mansfield that his previous discussion and the ad reference "needs paint, paper," gave us the preconceived idea that the place would look much more dilapidated. The only paint needed on the front of the building was on the sign. The salesman says it is quite run-down inside, as we shall see, but the exterior was painted only two months before and a new roof has been installed.

Inspection by way of a rear stair well shows a completely new tar-and-gravel roof. Inside, the central hallways on the second and third floors have fairly new carpet displaying giant white roses, two feet across, against a wine-red background. The main-floor carpet, which would give the first impression to a prospective buyer or tenant, is worn threadbare for its whole length, with large holes at the thresholds.

Mr. Mansfield states, "Mr. Giacolini installed the third-floor carpet two years ago, right after buying the building. The second-floor carpet was put in last year. Carpet for the main floor was planned for this year, but the owner got discouraged and decided to sell the building without putting out any more money."

A SHOCKING DETERIORATION INSIDE

An inspection of the individual apartments reveals fairly new, modern furniture. The interior paint and wallpaper, however, are terribly dilapidated. The ad reference, "needs paint, paper," was no exaggeration. Many apartments have large, dark splotches, several feet across, on plaster walls and ceilings. Some rooms have two- or three-foot holes in the plaster. The bedrooms are decorated with wallpaper, much of it torn, dirty, and disfigured.

The salesman explains the unbelievable deterioration. The roof was not replaced, nor was the exterior sealed and painted, by the previous owner in the twenty-three years he owned the building. He kept patching up obvious holes in the roof and did nothing to preserve the exterior walls.

The heavy rains of the previous winter leaked through the roof into many apartments. Also, cracks formed underneath the gutters and windows, causing considerable damage from that source when the wind blew rain directly against them. The present owner was forced to put on a completely new roof, as it was far beyond further patching.

He also had all exterior wall cracks sealed. Then the only way to cover up the patchwork was to paint the entire exterior.

These misfortunes were followed by the collapse of the refrigeration system, requiring extensive repairs. Instead of making the repairs the owner had the old system removed and bought the twenty-seven new refrigerators on time payments. After going this far he refused to spend another cent on the building and let the damaged interiors go unrepaired.

The owner had a fixation about interior decorating, according to Mr. Mansfield. He owned several small stores on leases where the tenants paid all expenses. His only other dwelling rental was a duplex house in his home city. During rent controls he got by with forcing the duplex tenants to do all their own painting. He still expected them to, and he demanded the same of his tenants at the Cynthia Court Apartments. The fact that eight vacancies resulted could not alter his stand.

MORE TROUBLE, THIS TIME WITH AN UNBONDED MANAGER

A single man of about sixty-five, a Mr. Bandy, lives in the manager's apartment. When we say there are a few questions we would like to ask, he says he doesn't know much about the previous history of the building. He is only pinch-hitting, at Mr. Mansfield's request, until a new manager can be hired.

It develops that a middle-aged couple previously managed the building. The husband ran away with one of the tenants, an attractive divorcee who had been working as a restaurant cashier. The divorcee took about $500 in restaurant receipts, and the manager's husband outdid her with a month's rentals, close to $1,300. The restaurant owner's loss was covered by a bond. The manager was not bonded, so the apartment house owner had to stand his full loss.

THE RENT SCHEDULE STANDS INSPECTION

We verify the rent schedule with the manager, apartment by apartment. Eight are vacant. Five apartments—301, 302, 304, 307, and 308—are on the third floor, where the damage is worst. Also vacant are 204 and 205 on the second floor and 101 on the main floor. The rents applied to the vacancies are in line with those of the rented apartments.

All the other apartments are renting according to the schedule except 105, which rents for $75 instead of the $80 shown. The manager says he has been told that all 2s have been renting for $80 from rent control days until recently. When the previous 105 tenant moved out the place needed painting so badly they had reduced the rent to $75 to obtain a new renter. It is difficult to get $80 under present conditions, even though garages are included at this rental.

The garages were charged for at a differential of $2.50, also the old rent control price, says the manager. The 3s previously all rented for $105.00, including garages. The amounts shown on the apartment schedule include the garage rentals.

ANOTHER COSTLY OWNER FIXATION

"New tenants are hard to get," continues the manager. "The only advertising is the 'Apartment for Rent' sign in front. I suggested putting an ad in the paper, but the owner is too set in his ways. The owner says the place has always kept full before with a 'For Rent' sign, and he isn't going to approve any new ideas that will cost him money."

REPLACEMENT VALUE HOLDS UP

Continuing our physical inspection, we look at the basement, which appears in sound shape. There is space for twenty cars. A large storeroom is filled with discarded furniture. There is a workroom and a vacant refrigerator room. The boiler room has a newly equipped furnace. Apparently the steam heating plant originally had an oil furnace, which was recently converted in a workmanlike manner to gas, a desirable improvement.

There are 6,600 square feet per floor, 19,800 square feet for the three floors. New replacement cost for this finished interior would be $12 per square foot. Depreciating to as low as $7.20 per square foot gives a depreciated replacement value of $142,560. The 6,600 square feet of garage, storage and utility space, entirely enclosed in concrete, could not be duplicated for less than $8 per square foot. Depreciating this basement area to $4.80 brings the total depreciated building valuation to $174,240.

Twenty-four apartments of furniture and equipment would average $500 each, depreciated, adding $12,000. The lot value is probably about $25,000. Lot and depreciated building and furniture values would total approximately $211,240. At $210,000 the present owner paid a fair price replacementwise. Evidently he did not consider a realistic net-income value and did not deduct the cost of the repairs and improvements he was forced to make.

ESTIMATING RENOVATION COSTS

The interior halls and all apartments could be completely painted, and wallpapered where desired, in top shape for an average of about $175 per apartment, or $4,200. This could be increased to $5,000 to allow a safe margin. The other required major expenditure would be a new carpet on the main-hall floor, for which a $1,000 allowance would be ample.

The immediately required expenditure of $6,000 should be deducted from the replacement appraisal of $211,240, leaving $206,-230. From a replacement view, a sale price in the neighborhood of $150,000 represents a real bargain. If the potential income value approaches the replacement value, and potential headaches are not overwhelming, here is a property worth considerable further pursuit.

POTENTIAL INCOME VALUE IS HIGH

We estimate the potential income with the halls and apartments painted attractively, and with a new carpet on the all-important main floor, which gives prospective tenants their first impression of the interior. The three 3s should rent readily for $125 monthly, a total of $375. The twenty-one 2s should rent for $95, bringing in $1,995. The twenty garages could be raised to $7.50 each in this area where parking has become very tight, making a garage income of $150.

In addition a coin-operated launderette could be installed on a concession basis in the abandoned refrigerator equipment room. Besides helping to attract tenants, the launderette should gross $3 per apartment, or $72. A 25 per cent estimated net return to the owner would make $18.

Adding the four items would total a new gross income of $2,538 monthly,. or $32,994 annually. Deducting the $6,435 fixed expenses, which should not change appreciably, would leave a new net of $26,-559. The resulting new capital value would be approximately $265,-000, which would become the potential resale price.

WHAT MAY BE THE OVER-ALL COST?

To obtain the over-all cost we add our estimated purchase price to the cost of renovation. Mr. Mansfield said the owner was firm on his price of $154,500, including the refrigerators. Probably the price cannot be reduced to a major extent of 25 per cent or so, as with many asking prices. Patient and persevering negotiation should win a reduction of at least 10 per cent, however. This would bring the purchase price down to the neighborhood of $140,000.

Adding our estimated equity of $34,275 in the B Boulevard apartments to the outstanding loans of $105,500 would make a total of $139,775. This means that we may be able to trade on a basis of equity for equity. Our present equity may be sufficient to consummate a purchase without our giving cash or taking an additional loan.

The $6,000 renovation cost added to the $140,000 estimated purchase price would make an over-all cost of $146,000.

WHAT ARE THE POTENTIAL RESALE PROFITS?

Deducting the estimated over-all cost of $146,000 from the potential resale price of $265,000 leaves a gross sales profit of $119,000. Deducting a 5 per cent sales cost of $13,250 gives a net profit of $105,750. A safety margin of $25,750 could be deducted and still would leave $80,000 net profit.

Here is an opportunity to more than triple our net estate in this single turnover. The potential increase is over eight times the conservative turnover goal of a 25 per cent gross profit, outlined in Chapter 2, which will enable you to make a million dollars in twenty years.

POTENTIAL HEADACHES ARE NOMINAL

Sometimes the potential profit picture looks rosy, but the potential headaches are too overwhelming to be worth tackling. Examples of the latter are the previously appraised apartments, like the Faraway Meadows wartime housing, discarded in the previous chapter.

With the Cynthia Court Apartments the potential problems are negligible compared to the estimated profits. Chief management measures are:

1. Hire and train a new manager.
2. Start advertising that will fill the building.
3. Negotiate painting contracts.
4. Negotiate carpet contract.
5. Arrange to finance new carpet and painting.
6. Raise rents to the projected schedule.

Mechanics for points 2 and 6 have been covered previously. Subsequent chapters will cover details of the other points with which you should be familiar for most efficient operation.

A NOT TOO UNUSUAL EXAMPLE OF STYMIED OPERATIONS

As we progress with our appraisal, it seems almost unbelievable that an owner would fail to take the steps that are so obvious and can be accomplished for comparatively little cost. There are many properties like this awaiting imaginative buyers. It would seem that such a bargain would be snapped up as soon as it was put on the market, but Mr. Mansfield said that several prospects had already looked the property over and discarded it. Most prospective buyers overlook the inherent opportunities awaiting in a limitless number of deteriorated or mismanaged properties. Most prospects are willing to pay a premium for property already in top condition and drawing top rents.

Just as familiarity breeds contempt, it also induces blindness. As time dulls observation an owner often gets used to overlooking shortcomings and eventually cannot even see them. Or he may have them pointed out and refuse to make corrections because of lethargy or obstinacy. As a new owner seeking improvements which produce capital gain, you can readily identify money-losing factors which you can remedy and transform into money-makers.

WILL INCOME PAY FOR EXPENSES AND LOAN PAYMENTS?

Since the building has eight vacancies, the required renovation must be completed immediately, at least in the vacant apartments, so that they can be readily rented. Financing will have to be worked out accordingly. For the property to pay for itself, a more nominal vacancy factor like the national average of 2 per cent for comparable rentals must be approached.

Assuming that our plans for a full house work out satisfactorily, will the present income schedule pay for fixed expenses and loan payments, cover vacancies, repairs and sundries, and leave a safe margin? We could rent redecorated vacancies according to our new schedule. For at least two or three months we would not raise present tenants. Our calculations for initial operations should therefore be based on the present schedule.

The present income-and-expense schedule shows an annual net of $17,504.82, which is approximately $1,459 monthly. From this we deduct the mortgage loan payments of $975 monthly, leaving $484 monthly. We next deduct for vacancies, repairs, and sundries 4 per cent of the $1,995 monthly gross, amounting to approximately $80. This gives us a remainder of $404 for an in-pocket net and a safety margin to cover emergencies.

The new schedule should be in full operation within six months, producing a scheduled annual net of $26,559, approximately $2,213 monthly. This would be $754 higher than the present schedule, almost tripling the in-pocket net and safety margin to approximately $1,158.

It should be emphasized that the above mentioned 4 per cent estimate for nonfixed expenses is realistic for our operations but can be maintained only with efficient management. Major repairs could not be included and are covered in our program as a part of capital improvements, separately financed for the most part, rather than paid for from operating income.

OPENING TENTATIVE NEGOTIATIONS

We ask Mr. Mansfield if he thinks he can work out a direct trade, so that we will not have to sell our property to raise cash. He says, "That is absolutely impossible. The owner insists on receiving a minimum of

$25,000 cash. He will not deviate from this stipulation. He has already turned down two good trade offers where the smaller properties were reasonably priced and would have given him his full asking price. But no cash would have been involved, so he spurned the offers, even though the smaller buildings would have been easier to sell to produce cash. Mr. Giacolini is the kind who will not change once he gets a fixed idea, just as he made up his mind to leave the interiors unpainted unless the tenants did the painting. He suffered eight vacancies as a result, but he would not change his policy even if the building emptied out.

"If you're interested in buying the Cynthia Court Apartments," continues Mr. Mansfield, "the only thing for you to do is put your building in my hands to sell. If enough cash can be raised to make a deal, you can then make an offer."

ANOTHER DILEMMA

This brings us to the dilemma which we faced when seeking to trade our A Avenue house. We can't buy the larger property until we sell the smaller. We don't want to sell the smaller until we have a larger good buy in hand. By the time we sell the B Boulevard property, the Cynthia Court Apartments would very likely be sold to another buyer.

In order to resolve the dilemma, we will have to negotiate an arrangement to keep the Cynthia Court Apartments tied up until a third party is found to buy our property. This can be handled by a three-way trade. The intricacies involved and the negotiations which will induce even a skeptical seller to participate in such a trade will be described in the next chapter.

As an investor seeking deterioration and mismanagement which can be improved to produce high resale profits, you will be prospecting for limitless opportunities which most buyers overlook.

19. HOW TO MAKE A
THREE-WAY TRADE

An owner may often tell his broker unequivocally, "I will not trade," or "I will not sell unless I get $25,000 in cash."

Later the owner may agree to exactly the opposite, consenting to a trade with no cash involved. Circumstances may change before a legitimate offer is received. Perhaps time alone may wear away resistance so that the owner will be receptive to a transaction previously considered anathema.

Regardless of how a broker may quote an owner, there is no harm in making an offer along the lines most desirable to you. If your initial offer is rejected you can always change. If you consider it best to initiate a direct trade, as we worked out with our A Avenue house and the Belvedere Apartments, then you should make an offer accordingly.

With the Cynthia Court Apartments, apparently advantageous trades have been offered and rejected. The owner seems unusually obstinate. Therefore, although we still expect to trade, our negotiations should be handled indirectly, eventually working up to our objective.

FIVE STEPS TO A THREE-WAY TRADE

The three-way, or multiple, trade offers the solution which enables you almost always to trade your property when you prefer not to sell outright. In nine deals out of ten a trade will eventually be consummated according to your designs if you take the following five steps:

1. You offer to buy the desired property "subject to the sale of your property."
2. You negotiate an agreement acceptable to you and the seller.
3. The broker obtains a buyer for your property.

4. You consummate a paper trade, exchanging the deed to your property for the property you buy.

5. The seller of the property you buy takes the proceeds from the sale of your traded property.

Control, Price, and Tax Advantages

Handling the transaction along these lines has three major advantages:

You keep the desired property under control.

Your net cost is less than if you sold outright and bought outright.

You retain the tax advantage of trading.

If the transaction is handled properly you will be liable for no income taxes on the increased value of the property you trade. If you sold your property and bought in separate transactions, you would be liable for a capital gains tax on the property sold. You would be taxed on the difference between your depreciated cost and your net sales price.

Tax ramifications will be amplified in Chapters 25, 26 and 27. The first two preceding items will be developed in this chapter under the five steps to a three-way trade.

1. MAKING A "SUBJECT TO SALE" OFFER

An offer subject to the sale of your property can be handled either as a purchase or as a trade agreement. Normally an exchange agreement would be made, subject to the sale of your property. As obdurate as the Cynthia Court owner appears, it would be psychologically advisable to use a Purchase Agreement form.

The agreement would be written substantially the same as our offer in Chapter 6 to buy the A Avenue house. We will therefore omit details which would be similar and will cite only major new features.

Establishing the Purchase Price

As far as the seller is concerned we are making an outright offer to purchase. Thus our offered price can be cut as low as the estimated lowest cash price. We previously set a tentative purchase target of $140,000. It would be unusual for this price to be accepted if offered initially, so we must determine an offering price to start bargaining.

Our chief clue is a request for $25,000 cash, out of which it is presumed a $7,500 commission would be paid. We could cut the requested cash 20 per cent, to $20,000. It is probable the broker would take a note for all or part of his commission, and this would reduce the amount of cash needed by the owner.

Adding the $20,000 in cash to the $105,000 in loans would make $125,500. This could be rounded to $125,000 for an offering price, an amount approximately 20 per cent less than the asking price, including the refrigerators.

Pulling Down the Salesman

We tell Mr. Mansfield the place is in a lot more terrible condition inside than we had thought possible. We are interested in the property only if it can be bought at a sacrifice.

Mr. Mansfield reviews many of the good points and then asks what figure we have in mind. We say we are prepared to offer $125,000.

The salesman is shocked. He says, "Such a price is, of course, impossible. However, let's go back to my office to see if we can write up an offer."

On the way in his car, Mr. Mansfield attempts to raise our sights. We emphasize that with the place in its present deplorable condition and losing money as it is, we will offer $125,000 and no more.

Deposit

In the office, as we discuss the various items, Mr. Mansfield writes them down on a Sales Agreement form. First, we suggest a deposit of $1,000. The salesman says that this is small for such a large property, but it shows our earnest intention. It will be acceptable, since we are tying up our own property for sale in the bargain.

We give Mr. Mansfield a $1,000 check, made out to "A. J. Kettebec Co. Trust Account." If other than a well-established realtor were involved, we would make out the check to the Metropole Land Title Insurance Company. Thus the broker could not cash the check, but would hold it until the seller accepts the offer, then turn it over to the title company.

Description of Property

In describing the property, it is essential to mention all furniture and equipment, which would include the refrigerators. After giving the legal description of the Cynthia Court Apartments we add the phrase, "including all furniture, furnishings and equipment now on the premises used in conduct of the business."

Total Purchase Price

Mr. Mansfield attempts to get us to at least add the $4,500 cost of the refrigerator loan. We insist on $125,000 as the total purchase price.

Time to Consummate

The salesman agrees with us that we should tie up the Cynthia Court Apartments as long as feasible without antagonizing the present owner. We decide on a ninety-day time limit, after acceptance, to consummate the transaction.

Down Payment

With a total purchase price of $125,000 and outstanding property loans of $105,500, the down payment is designated as $19,500.

Financing

Included is the statement, "This offer is subject to the buyer's assuming the following existing loans: (1) first mortgage of $71,711, payable $600 monthly, including 6 per cent interest, (2) second mortgage of $33,789.30, payable $375 monthly, including 6 per cent interest."

The printed part of the agreement provides: "Title is to be free of liens and encumbrances other than those specified." This means that any loans not specifically mentioned, including the refrigerator loan, must be paid off by the seller.

Subject to Sale

In covering the factor of selling our property, the price we seek could be omitted, merely stating, "This offer is made subject to the buyer's selling his property, described as follows . . ."

However, there might be a question of our being forced to sell if offered a lower price than we wish to take. For this reason, and also to establish a high price in case subsequent negotiations develop an outright trade, it is wise to establish a sale price on our property. We previously figured $67,000 as the fair market value, so we add approximately 10 per cent to make $75,000.

The offer is written to include: "This offer is made subject to the buyers' selling their property at 3680 B Boulevard, Metropole, Columbia, commonly known as the Belvedere Apartments, for the sum of $75,000."

Time to Accept

The date we write up the offer is September 12, 1966, about one month after we started shopping for a $150,000 property. Mr. Mansfield suggests giving the seller fifteen days to consider our offer. We specify seven days. The owner is anxious to sell, we know. But if too much time elapses another improvement-minded buyer may enter the picture.

Exclusive Listing and Commission on Our Property

After completing the terms of our offer, Mr. Mansfield brings up the subject of selling our property. He says that getting an acceptance will depend on his convincing the other owner that our place can be readily sold close to our price range. The Cynthia Court owner would not agree to tying up his apartments if our chances of selling and paying him cash were virtually hopeless.

With this introduction to his purpose, Mr. Mansfield asks, "Will you give me an exclusive listing on your property? And will you pay a 5 per cent commission on your sale price?"

On a "subject to sale" offer such as this, it is advisable to give the broker an exclusive listing. His listing helps to establish your price with the other owner. The broker can be expected to apply diligent advertising and sales effort, as he will earn a commission from both properties if the deal is consummated.

If the broker obtains your full asking price, you should be glad to pay the full commission he has earned. But if your eventual sale price is adjusted to less than you expect, you can always dicker on an adjustment of the commission.

We advise Mr. Mansfield that we will give him an exclusive listing on the Belvedere Apartments as soon as he secures acceptance of our offer. We also agree to pay a 5 per cent commission on our property. We give the broker a complete operating statement on our apartments, then take him on a personal inspection.

After checking our statement and our premises, Mr. Mansfield suggests that a cash sale price more in the range of $65,000 than $75,-000 can probably be realized. Will we give him a listing on the lower price? We answer that of course we would consider a cash offer lower than our asking price, but we want to leave room for negotiation. The listed price stays at $75,000.

2. NEGOTIATING AN AGREEMENT ACCEPTABLE
TO BOTH PARTIES

It is seven days later, on the date our offer expires, when we hear another word from Mr. Mansfield. We are beginning to wonder if the whole affair has bogged down so far that the agent is discouraged from pursuing it further. On the seventh day he phones and asks if we can come to his office to discuss the status of our offer.

At the salesman's office he introduces us for the first time to his broker, Mr. Kettebec. The latter says he happens to be in the office and would like to sit in on our conference "to see if there is any way I can help out." It appears obvious that Mr. Kettebec is present for the purpose of pressuring us into accepting a counteroffer, which may or may not be to our advantage.

An Attractive Counteroffer

I know of offers similar to the one presented on which considerable bargaining was expected. In some instances bargaining continued for six months or so before an agreement was reached. One recent transaction involving out-of-town owners took fourteen months to complete. In a few cases the original offer was accepted immediately.

Mr. Mansfield presents a counterproposal which at first glance appears like hardly any concession at all from the Cynthia Court owners. But a little analysis suggests that he has worked out a short cut to the goal we are seeking.

The salesman says, "I've spent considerable time with the owners of the Cynthia Court. Mr. Giacolini's first reaction to your offer was that he would not consider it under any circumstances. However, he consented to humor me by inspecting your Belvedere Apartments.

"Mr. Giacolini was impressed with their tiptop condition and the fact that all the units were rented for their listed prices. He thought maybe it wouldn't do any harm for his wife to see them.

"The wife didn't want to waste her time. But after her inspection she wanted their four married children to look the property over. Considering their misfortune with the Cynthia Court, they were all most impressed with the condition and the 'no vacancy' factor at the Belvedere."

Equity for Equity

Mr. Mansfield has been making daily trips to the neighboring city, and he has participated in numerous family discussions. The family came to the conclusion we had a nice property that would sell not too far below our asking price. However, they felt the disparity between what we expected to receive and what we expected to pay was ridiculous, especially in view of our having only five units and their having twenty-four units.

The salesman finally worked them up to the following counteroffer: The Giacolinis would agree to tie up their building, subject to our selling ours, if they received as much for their equity as we asked for our equity.

Deducting our approximately $33,000 loan from our $75,000 asking price would give us an asking equity of $42,000. If we added this equity to their property loans of $105,500, we would have a purchase price of $147,500. The Cynthia Court owners would agree to this proposal, providing we assumed the $4,500 refrigerator chattel mortgage.

On the surface it appears that the Giacolinis are lowering their asking price by only $2,500. They probably will also concede the refrigerator chattel mortgage. But it looks as if there is quite a way to go, percentagewise, for negotiations to produce the $140,000 target price we are shooting for.

The key to this counteroffer is not the amount mentioned in dollars, but the evidence that the Giacolinis are already thinking in terms of trading equity for equity. This is a possible goal we considered in the previous chapter. Our realistic equity of $34,275 added to their $105,500 in loans would make $139,775, our target just about on the nose.

Protracted bargaining can be bypassed if we seize this opportunity to immediately switch into an exchange offer, "subject to sale of our property."

We Counter the Counteroffer

We tell Mr. Mansfield that the suggestion of trading equity for equity seems fair. However, we insist that the Cynthia Court equity include paying off the $4,500 chattel mortgage.

The agent evidently has expected this, as he agrees without protest to submit our proviso. He immediately phones the Giacolinis in our presence to see if they will agree.

Mrs. Giacolini answers Mr. Mansfield's call, and he explains the revised proposal to her. She then puts Mr. Giacolini on the line, and the salesman repeats the whole matter. Husband and wife hold the phone while they discuss the proposition.

Finally they tell Mr. Mansfield, "The deal is O.K. if you can sell the Belvedere for $75,000."

Switching the Burden to the Giacolinis

We are almost positive the Belvedere will sell closer to our valuation of $67,000. The sale price would probably approximate that figure if we are prepared to wait a few months. To sell within the next month or so, an offer between $60,000 and $65,000 would doubtless be the highest to materialize.

Adjusting our new agreement similar to the existing purchase form, we would be contracting to buy the Cynthia Court for $147,500 and expecting to sell the Belvedere for $75,000. If we then considered a lower offer on the Belvedere, the burden would be on us to attempt to lower the Cynthia Court price accordingly. Otherwise we would receive less for our equity than we would be paying for the Cynthia Court equity.

Taking Off the Price Tags

We had not expected to transfer the burden to the Giacolinis until a month or two had elapsed after tying up their property. As long as they propose setting the prices on the basis of trading equities, we are in a good position to drop the price tags immediately.

We suggest to Mr. Mansfield and Mr. Kettebec that a new Exchange Agreement be prepared, arranging to exchange our equity for the Giacolinis' equity. We would trade our property subject to our mortgage in exchange for the Cynthia Court, subject to its two property mortgages. All other mortgages or liens would be paid off, including specifically the refrigerator chattel mortgage.

Instead of the provision, "subject to sale of the Belvedere Apartments for $75,000," we propose the following revision: "Subject to sale of the Belvedere Apartments by the A. J. Kettebec Co. at a price acceptable to Second Parties (Giacolinis)."

The change in the form of the agreement takes us out of the middle in any jockeying. The burden is put on the Giacolinis in case circumstances condition them to accepting a lower price for the Belvedere. Regardless of their selling price for the Belvedere, we will wind up owning the Cynthia Court on an equity-for-equity trade.

The Exchange Agreement replacing our Purchase Agreement eliminates the proviso for a $1,000 deposit. Mr. Mansfield returns our $1,000 check, which his firm had held pending acceptance of our offer.

3. THE BROKER OBTAINS A BUYER FOR THE BELVEDERE
APARTMENTS

The broker heavily advertises the Belvedere Apartments. Mr. Mansfield shows the property to a number of prospective buyers. In the next month he receives several trade offers approaching the asking price. The highest initial cash offer is $50,000, which he is able to raise to $55,000. The Giacolinis turn this down without equivocation.

In the beginning the Cynthia Court owners would consider nothing but a cash deal on the Belvedere. However, they perceive there is no longer any interest by other buyers in the Cynthia Court, as we have succeeded in taking it off the market. As time goes on, the Giacolinis become more receptive to the thought of taking in a smaller property plus cash in selling the Belvedere.

Another Trade Enters the Transaction

By October 15 Mr. Mansfield finally works out another trade, which on paper gives the Giacolinis close to the $75,000 asking price. Involved is a third property the salesman did not dream the Cynthia Court owners would consider. An elderly retired couple make an initial offer of $60,000 and come up to $70,000 as a purchase price for the Belvedere, with the following provisions:

1. They trade in a free-and-clear furnished mountain-resort summer home, "Dunroamin," with one and a half acres of forest land, at a value of $15,000.
2. They assume the Belvedere loan, which is estimated at approximately $32,500 by the tentative closing date of November 1.
3. They will pay the balance of $22,500 in cash.

Mr. Mansfield has obtained a supplemental agreement from the elderly couple, the Whitmores, to pay his office a 10 per cent commission of $1,500 on Dunroamin. Ten per cent is the usual commission for resort property in the area.

The Giacolinis at first express a complete lack of interest in the resort property. The deal might still be consummated by Mr. Mansfield's selling Dunroamin to a fourth party, making a four-way trade. Then the four married Giacolini children hear about the possibilities of free summer vacations for their families. They persuade their parents to accept the mountain home.

The Giacolinis Get $20,000 in Cash

The Giacolinis tell Mr. Mansfield they don't mind accepting the summer home, and the rest of the deal as worked out, but they must have a minimum of $20,000 in-pocket cash. If they receive the Whitmores' $22,500, they can spare only $2,500 cash toward paying off the refrigerator chattel mortgage and the broker's commission. How can he work this out?

Mr. Mansfield has already obtained an agreement to receive a $1,500 cash commission from the Whitmores. If the transaction collapses he will not receive a cent. He does not mind taking back notes in part payment, so he is willing to compromise on the amount of cash received. After reviewing the various possibilities, Mr. Mansfield presents a revision of the financial arrangements, which all parties accept. The basic consideration is not changed for us and the Giacolinis. The broker winds up with his full commissions but he receives only $3,000 in cash.

The broker says the commission from the Giacolinis is $7,125, which is 5 per cent of $142,500. The latter is figured as the sale price of the Cynthia Court by adding the sale equity of $37,500 received from our property to the approximately $105,000 now outstanding in Cynthia Court property loans. The Giacolinis have an obligation for the $7,125 commission, plus approximately $4,500 to pay off the refrigerator loan, making a total of $11,625. Deducting the $2,500 cash they will release in escrow leaves $9,125. The broker takes a note and a first mortgage for the latter amount on the Giacolinis' newly acquired summer home.

Our 5 per cent commission obligation on the $70,000 sale price of the Belvedere would be $3,500. The broker credits our escrow account with this amount, plus a $1,000 cash bonus, as an even exchange for our taking over the approximately $4,500 refrigerator loan.

4. WE CONSUMMATE A TRADE OF THE BELVEDERE FOR THE CYNTHIA COURT

The refrigerator loan by the time of closing is paid down to approximately $4,250. This means we wind up $250 ahead as compared with paying the $3,500 commission and taking the refrigerators free and clear. Also our in-pocket cash is increased by $1,000.

In the title company office we deed the Belvedere Apartments to the Giacolinis, and they deed the Cynthia Court to us. The transfer of necessary papers is consummated November 5, 1966.

On the Cynthia Court we receive guaranteed-title insurance in the amount of $143,000, our purchase price on paper. Our Belvedere Apartments have sold for $70,000 to the Whitmores. The net receipts to us for our Belvedere equity can be figured by deducting the $105,-000 in Cynthia Court loans from the $143,000 purchase price, leaving $38,000. This becomes our new paper equity in the Cynthia Court.

Taxwise we are liable for no gain in the increased value of our estate. As with the trade of our A Avenue house for the Belvedere, to all intents and purposes we have merely maintained a continuous real-estate investment.

5. THE GIACOLINIS TRADE THE BELVEDERE FOR THE DUNROAMIN SUMMER HOME

After taking title to the Belvedere, the Giacolinis take the next step of trading it for the Whitmores' Dunroamin summer home. They give the broker a first mortgage of $9,125 on Dunroamin.

The Giacolinis do not fare so badly on taking in the summer home. They offer their four married children a full share in its use, providing they pay the loan payments to the broker. This loan is amortized at $100 monthly, including 6 per cent interest, thus making each child liable for $25 monthly.

THE TITLE COMPANY PAYS US $2,053.79

The transaction could have closed November 1, but we held off until November 5 in order to receive additional cash from the proration of rents. The Cynthia Court rents were all collected on the first, giving us a credit of twenty-five thirtieths of the $1,230 in actual rents, or $1,025.

We also receive a credit of $731.04 on the Cynthia Court taxes, representing the Giacolinis' liability from July 1 to November 5. This will of course be offset by our making the first-half payment of $1,052.70, which is due December 10.

The Giacolinis pay the Cynthia Court escrow and title guarantee charges, and we pay these charges on the Belvedere. After deducting our portion of the escrow costs, and the proration of rents and taxes on the Belvedere, the title company also credits us for our paid insurance retained at the Belvedere. Our net proration credit is computed at $1,053.79. In addition, we receive the $1,000 cash bonus for taking over the refrigerator loan.

We have advanced no cash in the closing of the escrow. Yet we receive a check from the title company in the amount of $2,053.79, after consummating a transaction which considerably enhances our opportunities.

NEW POLICIES ARE PLACED
WITH OUR INSURANCE BROKER

The Whitmores have retained our fire insurance on the Belvedere, for which we received credit. We cancel existing coverage on the Cynthia Court, ordering completely new policies from our Apartment Association insurance broker. The latter arranges a "survey" to determine adequate coverage for our expanded operations.

We follow our broker's resulting recommendation to order a three-year "Blanket Apartment House Policy," with the premiums billed annually. Discounted rates result from including all the following coverages in one policy:

1. FIRE INSURANCE
   Amount $144,000. Ninety per cent average clause. Surveyed cost of replacement, less depreciation, less noncombustibles. Includes Extended Coverage, Vandalism and Malicious Mischief, and one year's Rental Income Loss.
   One-year premium $229.50
2. COMPREHENSIVE LIABILITY INSURANCE
   Amount $50/100,000. $50,000 coverage for single claim, $100,000 coverage for multiple claims. Premium subject to annual audit, automatically protects against added liability risks.
   One-year premium   85.64
3. BURGLARY AND ROBBERY INSURANCE
   Amount $1,000. (This amount is sufficient, as the manager will be instructed to bank receipts before they exceed $1,000.)
   One-year premium   18.75

4. FIDELITY BOND ON MANAGER
   Amount $1,000. (A sufficient amount for the same
   reason as above.)
   One-year premium   15.00
       TOTAL PREMIUMS $348.89

PROTECT YOUR ESTATE THROUGH
A COMPETENT INSURANCE BROKER

The above statement will help serve as a guide to recommended insurance coverages. Rather than explain in further detail, I strongly urge that you discuss any insurance problems with a competent broker who specializes in business and investment property insurance.

The only reason for property insurance is to protect against loss. An experienced insurer not only knows how to obtain adequate coverage at less cost but, when claims arise, he also knows how to secure the fullest payoffs with the least conflict.

Our insurance broker gives the title company a binder which states that the fire insurance is ordered and the building and contents are covered, the policy to follow later. We receive a statement following the close of escrow, and the bill is payable within sixty days.

After paying for all the policies and reserving $1,052.70 for taxes due December 10, we still have a cash balance of $652.20 from the escrow credit. Adding this to our August 10 bank balance of $3,259 and the intervening three months' accumulation of $780 from savings and net rentals gives us a November 5, 1966, cash balance of $4,691.

Now we are ready to hire a competent new manager who will take over most of the day-to-day operating duties. Then we will arrange for financing the improvements which will help pyramid the value of our newly acquired 24-unit Cynthia Court Apartments.

In nine deals out of ten you can negotiate a three-way trade in place of a sale and purchase. This saves income taxes, besides enabling you to buy lower and sell higher.

PART SEVEN

MANAGING YOUR APARTMENTS

20. HOW TO HIRE YOUR APARTMENT MANAGER

If the manager of newly bought apartments appears fairly competent and is willing to continue, it is wise to retain the same manager on a trial basis. If the manager is obviously unsuitable it pays to put in a new one the day you take over. Any compensation for lack of ample notice, customarily thirty days, would thus be the obligation of the outgoing owner. Once you accept a manager you take over the obligation for notice and compensation.

With the Cynthia Court Apartments, the bachelor occupying the manager's quarters said he was only filling in temporarily as a favor to the real-estate salesman, Mr. Mansfield. Therefore our first concern before we take any other major action is to secure a competent manager to replace the temporary one. We place an ad under "Furnished Apartments for Rent" in the *Metropolitan,* to help fill the vacancies. We arrange with the acting manager to stay till the end of the month, then turn our attention to hiring a new manager.

PLENTY OF GOOD MANAGERS TO CHOOSE FROM

Many owners become panicky at the thought of replacing a manager, perhaps because the manager may know more than the owner about the operation of his property. For this reason they may permit an incompetent or unco-operative manager to remain in their employ. There should be no reason whatever for retaining an undesirable manager. You will soon learn that there is a wide field of good managers to choose from whenever you need a replacement.

THE TEN CHIEF ATTRIBUTES OF A GOOD MANAGER

Before proceeding with the hiring of a new manager, it would be well to list the chief attributes we are seeking:

1. Willingness to follow instructions without quibbling
2. Pleasing personality
3. Ability to take responsibility
4. Neatness in personal appearance and housekeeping
5. Forthright honesty
6. A husband handy at minor repairs
7. Willingness to perform apartment housekeeping duties
8. Appreciation of the type of opportunity offered
9. Willingness to stay at home
10. Experience

1. WILLINGNESS TO FOLLOW INSTRUCTIONS WITHOUT QUIBBLING

The most important attribute of all is an attitude of willingness. Unusual situations are bound to arise which will necessitate asking the manager to perform duties never previously mentioned, some of them unpleasant. Included might be serving a dispossess notice, or cleaning a hallway after a vomiting drunk.

The labor-lawyer type of employee will protest any task not outlined in black and white at the time of hiring and will demand extra compensation or will refuse to do the work at all. A desirable manager and her husband must be willing to handle responsibilities that arise, without quibbling, the same as a couple would with their own home.

2. PLEASING PERSONALITY

The manager you select should possess an outgoing, pleasing personality that will attract new tenants and please all. Such a personality will help keep a building full and fill vacancies when they occur.

Beware of the sour personality as you would the plague. Some repellent managers turn prospective tenants away and cause otherwise happy tenants to move. I know of one 36-unit apartment house, bought in 1955, where there were nine vacancies, chiefly because the manager was an unkempt, hypochondriac harridan of sixty who had been thrice divorced. One of her many phobias was the fear of rape, and she suffered nightmares, according to her story, in dread of being taken advantage of by a male tenant. Because of this she refused to show vacant apartments to male prospects. She would open her door, secured by a burglarproof chain, only a crack, poke the key out, and tell the prospective tenant to look the apartment over alone. This was selling in reverse.

There was a continual wrangling between the manager and her tenants. Often she would knock loudly on a tenant's door late at night and demand admittance so that she could make an inspection and make sure there was "nothing going on that shouldn't be." It is no wonder that there was a continual turnover and heavy vacancies, even at low rents.

The outgoing owner was advised that his manager would be replaced on the day of title transfer. The new manager, a sweet-tempered housewife with a cherubic three-year-old daughter, was a marked contrast to the ejected slattern.

The building was filled within two weeks after changing managers. Within ninety days the rents were increased $360, an average of $10 a unit. On the basis of ten times the annual net, this increased the property value by $43,200.

Subsequent improvements further raised the rents to produce a total increased valuation of $85,000. Merely installing a receptionist-type manager with a "Welcome" personality gained half the total increase in value. This was the most spectacular improvement. It cost no more than a "Help Wanted" newspaper ad and a little time and judgment in making the selection.

3. ABILITY TO TAKE RESPONSIBILITY

One of the main reasons for having a manager is to take all the day-to-day interruptions and problems off your shoulders, leaving only policy decisions for your personal attention. This can be accomplished if you delegate as much authority as possible to the manager. The manager by temperament and ability must be capable of handling the authority you are willing to give her.

4. NEATNESS IN PERSONAL APPEARANCE AND HOUSEKEEPING

Nothing is more repelling to a prospective tenant than a slovenly manager. As personal housekeeping is apt to match personal appearance, such a manager's apartment will detract from the whole building. A tenant will judge apartment potentialities from the appearance of the manager's quarters.

Some women find it impossible to look neat even when they are doing nothing. Others appear attractive regardless of the kind of work they do. It is essential that the manager present a neat appearance, even when vacuuming the halls or cleaning an apartment.

5. FORTHRIGHT HONESTY

Honesty is, of course, absolutely essential. As long as you cover your manager's honesty with a fidelity bond, you should have little to worry about in this regard.

6. A HUSBAND HANDY AT MINOR REPAIRS

You are chiefly hiring a wife as apartment manager. Except, in larger buildings, where a separate janitor might be employed, it is essential to hire a couple who together can handle janitor work and minor repairs. An owner can lose a major portion of his net income by calling a skilled mechanic every time there is a minor repair job.

With a 24-unit building like the Cynthia Court, the husband would normally be expected to have a full-time job elsewhere. He should have enough spare time to take care of the minor repairs, such as changing a dripping washer, which a householder expects.

7. WILLINGNESS TO PERFORM APARTMENT HOUSEKEEPING DUTIES

If the manager chooses to use her salary to hire labor for vacuuming halls and cleaning apartments, it might seem no concern of the owners. However, in most cases you will keep a much more satisfied and permanent manager if she increases her in-pocket income by performing these duties herself, or with the help of her husband, as a regular practice.

If there is a competent manager already employed who always hires this work, you could authorize continuing the arrangement. In hiring a new manager for up to 40 units, however, make it a practice to reject anyone who does not expect to perform these duties most of the time. Any manager faced with sudden peaks, like several apartments at once being vacated and needing cleaning, would be expected to hire the excess work.

8. APPRECIATION OF THE TYPE OF OPPORTUNITY OFFERED

A satisfied manager who really appreciates the opportunity you offer will work willingly with you and will maintain a harmonious manager-tenant relationship. An experienced manager may take for granted or may belittle a salary offered at the prevailing level. You could hire an inexperienced employee for considerably less. I advocate giving first preference to eager applicants, even though inexperienced, and still paying the prevailing rate.

In this way you will be able to select a manager who really appreciates the opportunity offered, and who will go out of her way to do a good job. You can choose the very best type of employee—one who, after she is hired and trained, will remain loyal to you, rather than covet greener fields.

9. WILLINGNESS TO STAY AT HOME

An apartment manager's job allows for a great deal of freedom. For the most part she can call her time her own. When her presence is needed, to show a vacancy or collect rents, for example, it is important that she be on the job. Some wives like to gad about, and some like to stay home. The happy manager, like many a happy housewife, expects to spend most of her time in her home.

You should be especially skeptical of anyone who is overconscious of the hours spent in the building and who tends to consider all at-home hours as working hours. An ideal attitude of expecting to remain at home is common with the mother of a young child. Many owners reject managers with children, but these parents usually prove the most appreciative and conscientious stay-at-homers.

10. EXPERIENCE

Experience is helpful, but to an efficient owner it is the least important of the ten desirable attributes. Of course there are numerous top-notch experienced managers whom you would be glad to hire. Many will take up more of your time trying to correct their inefficient methods of operating than it would take to train someone completely inexperienced.

WHAT SHOULD YOU PAY YOUR MANAGER?

Before hiring a manager you should establish the pay. The salary might later be adjusted by circumstances and by the response you have to advertising, as with the hiring of a manager for the Belvedere Apartments. This might be particularly true in a smaller operation like the Belvedere, where you offer a rental allowance. With a 24-unit building like Cynthia Court, a free apartment plus cash would be the normal arrangement.

Cash salaries for managing a similar number of units may often vary considerably. If the manager's free apartment has a high rental value, this would usually be offset by a lower salary. If the owner retains the cleaning charges he should pay his manager a higher salary. Other operating procedures, such as the specified duties required of the manager, would influence the amount of cash.

After we conclude the purchase of Cynthia Court, Mr. Mansfield, the real-estate salesman, tells us, "The manager who absconded was paid $100 monthly plus a free apartment. You will probably have to pay the same amount to get a competent manager. The present bachelor is receiving only $50 monthly, but he is in charge only on a temporary basis. It would be more efficient to hire an experienced couple."

THE SALESMAN'S ADVICE

The operating statement when we bought Cynthia Court showed a free 2-room apartment plus $50 cash monthly for the manager's salary. If we follow Mr. Mansfield's belated advice and have to pay $100 in order to get a good manager, this will decrease our net income by $600 annually. The sale value, in turn, would drop $6,000.

Further discussion reveals that the previous manager cleaned vacated apartments without additional compensation, whereas we plan to add the cleaning charges to the manager's pay. Most real-estate salesmen are not too sharp on operating practices. Rather than take Mr. Mansfield's word for it, we should check other sources on the prevailing levels for comparable jobs.

SOUND SOURCES OF INFORMATION

There are two chief sources of information as to prevailing salary levels. One is the Apartment Owners Association, or a similar organization. The other is an examination of comparable operating statements, such as those we looked over in previous chapters.

A check of fifty operating statements on buildings ranging from twenty-one to thirty-six apartments shows some managers receiving a free apartment only, with no cash salary. A few receive as high as $100. Several range from $25 to $75. The majority pay $50, so this is the basic salary we plan to pay if the new employee takes the present manager's 2-room apartment.

This decision is confirmed by the Metropole Apartment Owners Association, whose office manager says that the prevailing cash salary for a 24- to 30-unit building is $50 where the manager retains the cleaning charges. The Association representative also advises they maintain a free employment service for apartment managers. They have several experienced managers listed who would be glad to take over our building at the $50 salary.

When asked if she would especially recommend any, the office manager says, "No, my last real good manager has just been hired for a 60-unit deal. I've had some jewels that have taken our training, but they usually get snapped up fast. The ones I have left are so-so, none especially good. But they wouldn't be on my list unless they could do the job."

The managers now listed by the Association might well be considered. They no doubt would measure up to average standards of competence. It might not be amiss to interview employees available here, along with others. To a great extent, however, the remaining Association-listed managers may turn out to be chiefly floaters or the castoffs of efficient owners. The chances are remote at present, in view of the office manager's comments, that this source will produce as good a manager as can be found elsewhere. We will therefore concentrate our efforts on the open market, where there are normally plenty of good managers to choose from, who will come closer to filling all ten of our sought-after desirable attributes.

THE BEST WAY TO SECURE A GOOD MANAGER

Like securing tenants, the best way to secure a wide choice of managers is through a newspaper ad. There might be a question as to the classified heading under which we should advertise—"Help Wanted—Female," "Help Wanted—Male," "Help Wanted—Couples," or "Apartments for Rent."

In a tight rental situation, as under rent controls, and where help is hard to get, more response might result from advertising under "Apartments for Rent." Many owners advertise under "Help Wanted—Female," since they want to hire a woman as manager. Since you want a couple, the best results will be obtained by emphasizing this and advertising under "Help Wanted—Couples."

With the foregoing in mind, we place a one-week ad in the *Metropolitan:*

> Apartment plus salary. Handy, reliable manager. Bondable. Metro Box P112068.

OMITTING ADDRESS AND TELEPHONE NUMBER

Many owners, and especially owners' representatives such as realty agents with management contracts, list an address or a telephone number for the prospective manager to contact. This is needlessly time-consuming, unless a manager must be hired on short notice, as scores of obviously unqualified prospects can be expected to appear or phone. It also fails to screen out the poorly educated who may present a good appearance but can hardly read or write.

Any apartment manager ad offering a salary should receive a heavy response, and a lot of time will be saved by listing a box number for the applicant to write to. When we examine some of the replies, we will see that most of the applicants can be readily screened out, and several desirable prospects can be chosen for further investigation.

SCREENING A HEAVY RESPONSE

The second day after the ad appears fifteen replies are received. In the week before the ad expires there is a total of seventy-two replies.

This includes sixty-three letters, eight postcards, and one telephone memorandum left at the newspaper office.

As the replies arrive we screen them into three appropriate categories, noting the following symbols on the envelopes or cards:

> G—Good. Those which appear very good. There are twenty-two of these.
>
> F—Fair. Twenty-four replies. These are not irrevocably eliminated, but they are not on a par with the Goods. In case no Gs pan out, we can dip into the Fs, although we expect never to touch the Fs when there are twenty-two Gs to consider.
>
> P—Poor. Twenty-six replies. This includes those who give little or no information and the obviously misfit who would be time-wasters to advertisers giving addresses or telephone numbers.

We will interview only the Goods, from whom our manager should be hired. First, we will cite examples of the various replies, quoting actual responses verbatim except for names. The three categories will be covered in reverse order, starting with the summarily rejected Poors.

Ps, or Poor Prospects, 26 Replies

Into this category we throw the memo, the eight postcards and three reproduced form letters. If the applicant does not feel the job important enough to warrant writing an individual letter, he is not the person we want to hire. Of course, if the one applicant who phoned had stated that a letter was to follow, we could wait and judge the application by the letter. However, he had left only his name and address, which were written by the *Metropolitan* ad clerk on a slip of yellow paper.

With a lot of very good prospects available, this applicant isn't worth the time to explore. Even if intriguing information had been left, there is no telephone number to call. It would be too drastic to say that a telephone response would never be considered, but the information left would have to be highly meritorious to warrant investigation.

A few of the postcards are not too bad, but there is insufficient space, of course, for any to give much information. They show an inclination to want a job without taking the trouble to cite their qualifications. This will probably prove they are lacking in qualifications or in willingness to be co-operative. Why waste time with those who want the compensation without working for it, when there are plenty of applicants who are anxious to give full information?

Typical of the postcards is the following:

> *Gentlemen*
> *am putting*
> *in my application*
> *for the opening*
> *you have as*
> *Manager am*
> *From So Metro*
> *a hastey reply,*
> *will be appreciated*
> *Resp*
> *Theo C Cantler*
> *4306 Merrimac Ave*
> *Metropole, Colum*

This exemplifies the postcard replies and also the letter replies which we reject. There is absolutely no information regarding the qualifications of the applicant. The card indicates only that the applicant is crudely educated and in haste to get a job.

The signature "Theo" might represent either a single man or a husband. Since the wife will be the key employee, a reply from the woman would be preferred. However, male replies should not be eliminated without consideration, as some capable wives leave all business arrangements to their husbands. Again there is no telephone number. In any event Theo's reply is not worth exploring.

MORE POOR PROSPECTS GIVE NO INFORMATION

We throw into the "Poor" pot all letters giving no information about the applicant. One reject, handwritten on a half sheet of paper, merely states:

> *I would like some infro-*
> *Mation about the Appartment*
> *Manager job you have in the*
> *Metropolitan.*

If interested please write or
call 541–0014
Mrs. Ruby Hummingstone

Another example of a no-information reject emphasizes employee demands rather than a willingness to work. It is typed at the very top of an 8½-by-11 sheet of paper:

Sirs;
    Your ad appeals to me and Mrs. Charleton and myself would like to talk with you so we can make an appraisal of things and come to satisfactory terms. 1 would not waste your time if 1 felt 1 was not capable of filling the bill.
    Shall be ready and able to see you at once.
                                            Sincerely
                                            Thomas Y. Charleton

A third letter with no information is also handwritten on a half sheet of paper:

Dear Sir.
    Saw your ad in
    the Metropole Metropolitan &
    am applying for the
    position.
        Awaiting your reply,
                    Sincerely
            Mr & Mrs B Victor

OTHER POOR PROSPECTS REVEAL
THEY ARE UNSUITABLE

Three of the rejects are widows living alone, who answered our ad although we specified "couple." They appeal to our sympathy, but obviously they would be unsuitable for our type of operation.

Others give statements which show they might be capable but would not fit our pattern. Some ask for full-time jobs for both husband and wife. Naturally, unless they are pensioners, their expected compensation would be more than we can pay.

Of the rejects not willing to perform the work we have in mind, one writes:

> *I (or we) have had a number*
> *of years experience in*
> *both Apt & Court managing*
> *Have been bonded: We are*
> *not interested in Apt cleaning*
> *when a vacancy occurs.*

Fs, or Fair Prospects, 24 Replies

The Fairs give no indications of being poor managers. They reveal enough to show they could possibly be suitable, but they fail to prove of real interest. Many merely state they have had experience as managers, giving no details. If interviewed, several of these would no doubt turn out to be good potential managers.

As mentioned we would dip into the Fairs if no Goods are hired. With twenty-two Goods to choose from, the chances are very remote that we will need to spend any time exploring the Fairs.

Gs, or Good Prospects, 22 Replies

Outstanding replies, giving details of various abilities, come from all age groups, in three main divisions:

1. Settled Elderly Couples. Half of the satisfactory replies, eleven, come from elderly couples. Typically the husband is over sixty, is retired, has a pension, and expects to spend most of his time puttering around as a handy man. The children are married, and the family home has been sold or is in the process of being sold.

This group forms the majority of acting managers, and a good portion are highly satisfactory. Chief shortcomings to watch for are that they may be too set in their ways, too sickly to be dependable, or too refined to work. In the last instance the husband may appear ideal for his portion of assigned duties, but the wife may not expect to do anything.

2. Ambitious Young Couples. The second largest group, with seven replies, is made up of ambitious young couples in their twenties or thirties, anxious to get ahead by saving their rent. Many have young children. The mother wants to remain at home and yet be a breadwinner. An apartment manager's job is ideal to meet this combination of desires which are otherwise often impossible to reconcile.

3. Home-Loving Middle-Aged Couples. The third group, comprising the remaining four of the desirable prospects, consists of middle-aged couples between forty and sixty. The husbands have steady jobs, ideally with more leisure time than the average. One is a railroader, another a postal employee.

In most such cases, the wife has worked at office and other jobs and is now anxious to stay home. She wants to have dinner ready, the laundry finished, and the living quarters in neat condition when her husband arrives from work. She wants to be a more complete housewife and still be a breadwinner and make a little pocket money she can call her own. Here again, an ideal solution is found by managing an apartment where a salary is included. No wonder there are so many replies to our ad.

THE MOST OUTSTANDING REPLY

The "Good" letters in various degrees cite capabilities and a willingness to work. Many express appreciation for being considered. One is most outstanding, the answer to an owner's dream, well covering the information desired:

> BOX P112068
> Metropole *Metropolitan*
> In answer to your classified ad concerning the exchange of services for an apartment and small salary, we will endeavor to describe our capabilities in hopes of a reply from you. We have been watching for an opportunity such as this for quite some time since my husband is a postman and does not earn a sufficient salary to meet today's prices. He returns from his work at 3:30 P.M., and has one day off and Sunday, to perform any necessary duties. I do not have an outside job. We are both in excellent health, he is 41 years old and I am 28. I am listing the things we are able to do below.
> My husband has had experience with and does well:
> Plumbing and heating repairs,
> Carpentry,
> Plastering repairs,
> Electrical repairs,
> Painting and redecorating with economical cost,
> Gardening and yard maintenance,
> Furniture moving.

I have had considerable experience, and am able and willing to do:

General household cleaning, waxing, vacuum cleaning and window washing,
Drapery making, seat covers, and reupholstering,
Furniture painting,
Cooking,
Collection of rents and interviewing prospective tenants,
Accurate bookkeeping and typing.

We would be most happy to come for an interview if you wish. We are quiet, enjoy staying at home and do not drink. The amount of salary is not important to us providing it is commensurate with duties, since we are most interested in saving the amount we now pay for an apartment. We are bondable and will provide references. Thank you for considering our application.

Sincerely,
MR. AND MRS. DAVID WARD

INTERVIEW SELECTED PROSPECTS IN THEIR HOMES

Although more time-consuming, it pays in the long run to check the prospect's housekeeping by visiting the present residence. The manager's apartment, being on constant display, will serve to enhance or detract from the attractiveness of the entire building. A naturally sloppy applicant might present a false front in a personal appearance. The normal condition of a prospect's home is more difficult to cover up and more apt to reveal a true picture.

From the fifteen replies received the first day, there are six rated "Good." Mrs. Ward does not give a telephone number, and if the letter were not so outstanding we would bypass it. As it is, we will make this contact unannounced. We call each of the five others to make appointments.

Over the telephone we say that the applicant's answer to our ad has been received and that we would like to come for an interview. One respondent says she has already accepted another job. One does not answer. Thus we wind up with four interviews to make, including three appointments and the Ward contact. We will cover the interviews chronologically.

ONE PROSPECT STINKS

One letter is short, shows a lack of education, yet reveals experience and a willingness to handle required duties. The prospect might prove a diamond in the rough.

> DEAR SIR:
> I am answering your add. My husband and I have run or managed apartments for over 10 years and he does all maintenance work for the apartment and we took care of cleaning and renting the apt. too.
> He does all electric painting carpenter plumbing work for the places we took care of. Hoping to hear from you.
> Sincerely,
> MRS. OLGA FLORSON

A ROUGH VISIT

The prospect turns out to be in the rough, but no diamond. The residence is a three-room cottage at the rear of a larger home. Mrs. Florson opens the door. She is about sixty, with a beer-bloated face and a beer-barrel figure of about 260 pounds to match. Her hair has been peroxided some time previously and later hennaed, and it now shows a mixture of red and blond at the fringes and a mixture of black and gray at the roots. She is dressed in a soiled gingham wrapper and smells sourly of sweat.

The living room smells musty. One third of the dumpy sofa is covered by a curled-up shaggy English sheep dog. The balance is covered by dog hair. We are invited to be seated but can find no place not covered by hairs. A stale, rancid smell wafts from the kitchen.

The husband is skinny as a rail, but strong. He is an Army pensioner, is willing to paint and handle repairs, and is a prodigious worker and a prodigious talker. Husband and wife are both talkative and interrupt each other, voicing strong opinions on just how an apartment house should be run.

If they were hired, the physical work would be handled but desirable tenants would eventually move out of the building. All their experience has been in skid-row flophouses. They have held many jobs, but have never operated more desirable apartment buildings. They have been collecting unemployment insurance since they left their last job, but now it has run out and they are anxious to get into a nice building. They might prove suitable for another flophouse, but they could not possibly be hired by an owner with an ounce of discrimination. Chances are they would only work long enough to qualify for more unemployment insurance.

AN ACCEPTABLE MIDDLE-AGED
PROSPECT LACKS ENTHUSIASM

Another "Good" letter gives more information, some essential, some inconsequential:

> DEAR SIR
> My husband and I are interested in the position which you have to offer. I am sure we can qualify for the position. We are 55 years of age, very neat no drinkers, do not have any wild parties, we are Catholic, & very hard workers in any job we do. I am a neat housekeeper.
> My husband is an all around good maintenance man. Have our own furniture. My husband is employed & has been at his present job 10 years in April. We have live in this same residence for 8 yrs. We would like to change jobs We have the best of referencies
> We have had 10 yrs experience in apt house work. for our selves & other apt houses.
> Would like very much to have an appointment with you. so you could see our referencies & see us in person. Our Telephone No. is 712–3614.
> Thank you
> MR & MRS RANDALL CLAREMORE

A SATISFACTORY VISIT

The Claremores live in a house at the rear of a large suburban estate which takes up a quarter block. Both appear responsible and are dressed conservatively and neatly. The house is immaculate. The husband's main employment is as a city gardener. He also does the gardening for the estate in exchange for free rent plus $60 monthly.

They are anxious to move closer in. The wife would like to have something regular to do. She has previously managed apartment houses up to 12 units in size, and at one time a 6-unit building of their own. She now works part time at house cleaning and baby-sitting at $1.75 per hour.

The Claremores impress us as a conscientious couple who would make dependable managers, far better than the run of the mill now operating many buildings. They are somewhat disappointed at the $50 base salary, saying they would be taking smaller quarters and a $10 cut from Mr. Claremore's present part-time job. However, they are still interested and would like to look the apartment over.

REVIEW ESSENTIAL RESPONSIBILITIES

There is no object in reviewing specific responsibilities with a prospect you have no intention of hiring. With any potential applicant worthy of further consideration, it is wise in the screening interview to cover essential duties. This often will eliminate some prospects previously thought good and will avoid later controversy. Considering the Claremores favorably as possible managers, we try to bring out most of our requirements naturally during the interview as an owner's normal expectations:

1. Does the wife expect to stay in the building most of the time? The wife's essential duties of keeping the building full and collecting rents require her presence when apartments are vacant and when rents are due.

2. Do the wife and the husband expect to keep the halls and yard clean as part of their duties?

3. Do they expect to clean vacated apartments for which they will receive the cleaning charges? If they plan to hire all this work for 24 apartments like the Cynthia Court, you would normally reject them as unsuitable.

4. Does the husband cheerfully expect to perform handy work such as lighting the incinerator, policing garbage cans, and minor repairs such as changing washers? The husband's lack of experience is not essential, but willingness to perform is most essential.

5. Will the husband be responsible for mowing the lawn, trimming shrubbery, and moving furniture when necessary? Duties such as these may often create dissension if not reviewed in detail before hiring.

If expected duties are not spelled out, it may also happen that an apparently willing and able couple simply cannot perform. Perhaps the husband has a slipped disk, a chronic strained back, or some other disability which prevents his doing heavy work, regardless of how occasional, like moving furniture. If the prospect cannot or is not willing to do the work required, the sooner this is found out the better.

A LACK OF APPRECIATION

Our chief adverse reaction to the Claremores is that they show little appreciation of the opportunity offered. Soon after we take the trouble to train them in our way of operation, they are apt to bounce from our apartment house to another with a higher salary.

They appear capable, and we might not find a more suitable couple. We therefore give them a note to the present manager of the Cynthia Court, asking him to show the manager's quarters and the apartment setup in general.

We tell the Claremores we have several other applicants to interview before making a final decision. They can look the apartment over in the meantime to see whether they are still interested. If we decide on hiring them, we will contact them within a week.

AN EAGER HUSBAND AND A WEAK WIFE

Another letter reveals a willingness to work, and several hours' available time for the husband. The couple are no doubt unusually eager because they have a ten-month-old baby. We will observe the discipline, neatness and quietness of the child. If the baby is overloud or demanding of attention, the family might not be so likely to work out.

> To WHOM IT MAY CONCERN
>
> I am writing you concerning your ad in the Metropole Metropolitan. I feel that I have the qualifications necessary to furnish you with the kind of help you need.
>
> I am employed with the Metropole Metropolitan and go to work at 1:40 P.M & get off at 6:30 P.M. so I do have a lot of spare time in which to do the necessary work, my wife is also equally handy in every phase of work.
>
> Our ages are both in the twenties (27–25) so in case of hard or tedious work there would be no drawbacks.
>
> We do have a ten months old daughter, which you might not want children but at her age, I feel she will not bother anyone.

If you feel that our qualifications are what you are looking for, I would greatly appreciate your getting in touch with me at your convenience.

Thank you
MURRAY JACKSON

I can furnish you the best of references.

THE VISIT INDICATES A JELLY-WILLED WIFE

The Jacksons live in a five-room white house. A woman of about fifty-five opens the door. Her hair is bleached white. We ask for the party who answered our ad. She calls her son, who comes from the rear with a baby in his arms.

It develops that ever since their marriage the Jacksons have been living in the husband's mother's home. They are most anxious to move to a separate residence where they can save the rent and earn an extra income, as with an apartment manager's job. Their obvious unexpressed desire is to fly from the mother's nest.

The baby sits quietly in her father's lap, appears neat and unusually well behaved. Her living in the manager's apartment should present no problem.

The chief family problem is the mother-in-law, the typical domineering comic-strip type. She persistently injects her experiences and desires into the interview. "I am a widow and, now that my son has answered your ad, would like you to consider me for an apartment manager's job—that is, if you know of another opportunity besides this one for my son. I could use the extra money I would be able to make from renting out my house . . . ."

Of course the mother-in-law should not become too much our problem if she does not live in our apartment house. The son is employed as a *Metropolitan* circulation supervisor, a job which gives him considerable free time. He is willing to do any kind of work asked of him. He has done all the repair jobs for his mother's home and feels he could easily handle the work at the apartment house. The eager husband gives the impression of being an ideal prospect for a handy man.

The wife looks demurely into the folded hands in her lap most of the time and doesn't have much to say. She would no doubt blossom out away from the domination of the mother-in-law. She seems to be willing enough and is a good housekeeper according to all appearances. The husband says his wife takes care of all the housework and he does the handy work, in exchange for free rent from his mother. The wife appears to have all the necessary qualifications as far as handling the labor is concerned. However, her retiring personality seems such that the tenants would probably tell her how to run the building, instead of her acting with the determination and force of character needed to gain their respect, prompt rent payments, and obedience to house rules.

A Comparison with the Claremores

The husband impresses us as being more co-operative and willing than the previous husband, Mr. Claremore. Mrs. Jackson, however, would probably be a much poorer manager, temperamentally, than Mrs. Claremore. And the key employee is the wife, who will be responsible for keeping the building full and the rents collected. The Jacksons might be considered only tentatively as in reserve for further exploration if no better prospect develops.

We prefer the Claremores as a couple and expect to interview additional applicants who will please us more than the Jacksons. Therefore we do not waste time—or overencourage them—by giving them a card to the Cynthia Court manager. We tell them where the apartments are located and the employment conditions, including wages; then we say that we may be getting in touch with them if we so choose. A parting admonition comes from the hopeful mother-in-law, who tells us, "Don't forget me if you hear of anybody that needs a good woman."

The Best Letter Writer
Proves the Best Prospect

Next we are ready to visit the Wards, who wrote the outstanding letter cited earlier. Sometimes a top-notch letter may come from completely unsuitable applicants, like the Florsons. Usually a good letter leads to a good prospect, and this proves to be the case with the Wards.

The Wards also live in a small house in the rear of a large one. Their bell is answered by a little boy of two, who comes running in his pajamas and opens the door for us. His father, in the living room, puts down his newspaper, and his mother comes dashing out of a bedroom.

At the door the mother apologizes for her son's being in his pajamas and explains that she was getting his bed ready. She has a pleasing smile and a peaches-and-cream complexion. She is taller than average, about five feet seven, and is of a strong build, but well proportioned, weighing about 150. She is dressed in a trim blue skirt and a neat white blouse.

The husband is of about equal height and smaller build, weighing about 140. He is slim-waisted, with a heavy chest development, and appears wiry and athletic. He says he is a home delivery postman, required to carry a pack on his back. He enjoys good health and is very handy and willing to do anything asked.

The little boy has unusually large eyes and is naturally inquisitive. He doesn't want to miss anything by leaving the room. However, he obeys when his mother takes him into the bedroom and orders him to stay there.

The house, small but tastefully furnished, is clean and neat as a pin. Mrs. Ward is evidently a good housekeeper.

The couple know the Cynthia Court area, which they like, and they are both most eager to get the job. They have just bought a suburban home on a GI loan. In order to build up a nest egg for future investment, they have decided to rent the house and try to get an apartment manager's job.

After the expected duties are reviewed, they express surprise that the guaranteed salary will be $50 plus the free 2-room apartment and all utilities. Also the manager will retain the cleaning charges and be paid $1.65 hourly for painting and other improvement work. Mrs. Ward says frankly, "That seems very generous. We really hadn't expected as much, being that we are inexperienced in that sort of thing."

We emphasize that there is a lot to learn but experience is not a major factor. As long as they appear generally satisfactory, we are chiefly interested in their attitude. Are they willing to do whatever is asked of them? And will they not be fazed by minor but innumerable demands upon their time and patience?

The couple assure us they are most anxious to do whatever is asked. They would be highly appreciative if they are given a trial.

We feel that we have found ideal manager material and that there is no use exploring further. We expect several more letters in answer to our ad, but we have no additional appointments. We tell the Wards to look the apartment over and then let us know what they think of it. Unless they are fully satisfied with the place and anxious to take the job, we prefer not to hire them. Of course their employment would be on a trial basis until they proved themselves. But we would like to know that they expect to be fairly permanent if hired.

The Wards assure us they will be satisfied and will take the job without looking the apartment over, as they already know the district. However, we insist that they inspect their prospective new home, so that there will be no question about its fitting into their plans. They can go over the next afternoon when Mr. Ward is off work, then phone and tell us if they are still interested.

Mr. Ward phones early the next evening. As with the interview in their home, he is refreshingly frank. He says, "We are real happy with the apartment house. It is nicer than we expected. We'll be happy to take the present manager's 2-room apartment. But with three in the family we'd appreciate a 3-room apartment with a bedroom. We'll gladly pay the difference. Would it be okay?"

We say the present rent schedule shows a difference of $25 between the manager's 2-room and an adjoining 3-room apartment. We'll be glad to adjust this to a $20 differential, making the basic guaranteed salary $30, including a free 3-room apartment.

"The wife and I would be tickled pink with that kind of a deal. We're ready to move in as soon as you want us."

We ask if they can come to our home that evening to sign the customary management contract. There will also be other papers and matters to discuss. The Wards agree to come at once.

An apartment manager's job enables a housewife to remain at home and yet be a breadwinner. A desirable manager must be willing, without quibbling, to handle any responsibilities that arise.

There is a wide field of good managers to choose from whenever you need a replacement.

21. HOW TO SUPERVISE YOUR APARTMENT MANAGER

In a quarter century of apartment ownership I have developed a supervisory system that insures maximum efficiency and yet requires a minimum of time. Comprehensive supervision has a three-fold purpose:

> To delegate to the manager as much responsibility as possible
> To eliminate irritations and interruptions for the owner
> To promote honesty and discourage infidelity

Some supervisory considerations were mentioned in the screening of ad replies and in the initial interviews with selected prospects. Further steps will develop immediately with the hiring interview, which will lay a foundation for future smooth relationships.

TWELVE MAJOR SUPERVISORY FACTORS

Twelve major supervisory factors, along with special tools where appropriate, will be covered in this chapter:

1. Management agreement and contract
2. Payroll Tax information
3. Fidelity bond application
4. Burglary and robbery insurance considerations
5. Liability insurance considerations
6. Transfer of management
7. Monthly reports
8. Duplicate rent receipts
9. Triplicate leases
10. Bank deposits
11. Payment of bills
12. Periodic supervisory visits

1. MANAGEMENT AGREEMENT AND CONTRACT

Many owners bumble along without written inventories and leases. Even more invite needless controversy by failing to utilize a written contract with their managers. To formalize the delegation of authority to the manager, and to help avoid misunderstanding, it is essential that there be a written management contract.

Normally the manager would also be a tenant, as with the Cynthia Court. In this case an inventory would also be prepared, covering the items of furniture in the manager's apartment. The management contract, however, would supersede and take the place of a tenant lease or contract.

The contract prepared for hiring the Wards will be cited in full, with appropriate explanations:

AGREEMENT AND CONTRACT REGARDING
APARTMENT MANAGEMENT
JOSEPH ENTERPRISE, OWNER

THE UNDERSIGNED MANAGERS agree to perform the services such as are usual for Apartment House Managers to perform at the Cynthia Court Apts., located at 4440 Cynthia Court St., Metropole, Columbia in exchange for the full monthly rental charge for one apartment. Such services include the showing and renting of apartments (tenants to be subject to the approval of the Owners): faithful collecting, accounting and banking of rents, with Managers to be responsible for any bad-check losses due to giving cash for change or refunds; the maintenance of peace and quiet and assembling and moving furniture on the premises, except that no tenant or furniture shall be moved from one apartment to another without the specific approval of the Owners and that no act shall be permitted or performed by any of the tenants therein contrary to Federal, State, County or Municipal Laws.

In this type of operation it is advantageous to allocate separately the pay for management and for custodial work. In this case a natural division is to charge the apartment value to management, and the cash salary to maintenance.

The reference to the tenants' being subject to the approval of the owner establishes the owner's right to determine the type of tenant and to accept or reject given tenants. However, the owner would seldom interfere with the selection of individual tenants, confining approval to broad determinations, such as whether or not children or pets would be allowed.

Many bad-check artists have talked apartment managers into giving substantial change, then skipped. Our manager is authorized to accept checks for rent, but not to give change.

CUSTODIAL AND GARDENING DUTIES

Further, said Managers agree to maintain the apartment buildings and yards in a clean and orderly condition, with particular reference to the halls, garbage disposal, laundry facilities, store-rooms, garages, porches, garden, pool, walks and driveways, wherever any of the foregoing are situated on the premises; and in exchange for these services the Owners agree to pay the following:

Two Per cent of the gross rental receipts, with a minimum guarantee of $30.00 monthly.

Sometimes a separate gardener or janitor may be hired, depending on the size of the building and of the grounds, in which case the contract would be adjusted accordingly. With the Cynthia Court the Wards will handle all garden and janitorial work.

Avoid the word "janitor" in discussions with the manager. A higher-class manager can be hired by referring to the dirty work as "maintenance" or "custodial." This compares with hiring a top-caliber church custodian by giving him the title of sexton rather than janitor. Many a college graduate would not mind telling his friends he is an apartment manager but might shun being referred to as a janitor.

In one large apartment house employing both a manager and a handy man, the owner was unable to find a satisfactory replacement for the latter during a labor shortage. All advertising had been for an apartment janitor. I suggested changing the title to Assistant Manager, and the owner was snowed under with satisfactory applicants.

In each case the duties were fully explained, so there was no question of misrepresenting the work. Chiefly involved was the preservation of the employee's dignity, an important factor in all supervisory relationships.

CLEANING OF APARTMENTS

Further, said Managers shall arrange to clean each apartment that is vacated; and shall retain as a bonus after cleaning and renting each apartment the following authorized cleaning charges that are approved by the Owners and paid by the incoming Tenant along with all other required charges and deposits, including a full month's rent: The cleaning charge shall be for a Studio Apt. $10.00; 1-bedroom Apt. $12.00; 2-bedroom Apt. $15.00; 3-bedroom Apt. $20.00. The foregoing amounts shall not be changed except with the specific approval and agreement of the Owners.

Many owners retain the cleaning charge as income, in some cases compensating the manager by increasing the monthly salary, in others with no additional pay at all. The most equitable way of handling this item is by allowing the manager to retain the full amount as earned.

Vacancies are hard to predict. There may be none for months, and then there may be several at once. The cleaning charge should be considered neither slave wages nor a windfall. It should be sufficient to compensate fairly for the average cost of cleaning at prevailing hourly janitor rates in the area. If the manager gets swamped with work, she could arrange to hire some of the cleaning and pay the wages out of her fixed fee.

In some cases the apartment may be left in perfect condition by a proud housewife. An hour or so of attention to minor items may take care of the cleaning. Other housekeepers may leave filth that will cost more to clean on an hourly basis than the fixed compensation. Regardless of the condition left by the outgoing tenant, the fixed average amount assesses the same charge to each incoming tenant for being able to move into a clean apartment.

The time to collect is when the tenant moves in. A vacating tenant will often try to evade payment, but an incoming tenant seldom complains about a cleaning charge, if it is reasonable. Unless the charge is clearly specified, a manager will sometimes increase the amount without consultation with the owner. If given a free hand, a manager may be more inclined to charge more than tenants are willing to pay.

Some owners wonder why they suffer long vacancy periods when their accommodations should be readily rentable. Often it is because the manager discourages desirable prospective tenants by demanding an excessive cleaning charge, which she expects to pocket. The manager may be encouraged to such practices where there is no written provision, as in our leases, showing the owner what the tenant pays.

Obviously it is in the owner's interest to secure tenants as easily as possible by holding the cleaning charge down, as long as it is reasonable and compensates the manager fairly for the required labor.

TERMINATION

> *This Agreement and Contract with associated apartment rental may be terminated by a written notice of not less than 30 days from the Managers or not less than 15 days from the Owners, or by mutual agreement.*

Unless specified the manager may feel free to leave on short notice. I know of managers, operating without benefit of contract, who have left after giving a twenty-four-hour notice, or no notice at all. This might force the owner to take over on an emergency basis until he could secure a new manager. Such short notice is apt to be given if the manager becomes miffed at the owner or is anxious to move to a higher-paying position.

A contract helps to enforce a more reasonable notice period. With thirty days there should be ample time to secure a competent replacement. The owner may set a termination date that fits his schedule by reducing the time to as little as fifteen days.

DATE, SIGNATURES, AND SOCIAL SECURITY NUMBERS

AGREED AND SUBSCRIBED TO this 22nd day of November 1966 at Metropole, Columbia, with responsibility to start December 1, 1966.

OWNERS:	MANAGERS:
Joseph Enterprise	*Mrs. Jeanette Ward*
	SOC. SEC. # 266–40–9011
Mary Enterprise	*David Ward*
	SOC. SEC. # 545–08–2167

After reviewing the items of the contract, both owners and managers sign two copies. The original is retained by the owners, and the duplicate is given to the managers.

2. PAYROLL TAX INFORMATION

The next step is to have each employee fill out a U.S. Treasury Department Form W-4, Employee's Withholding Exemption Certificate. This will determine the number of exemptions to be computed in the owner's payroll preparation. Although the husband will also be helping with the handy work in this operation, his payroll report would only reflect extra labor, such as painting. The wife would usually be considered the chief employee for payroll purposes, and would be credited with the manager's salary plus the adjusted value of the free apartment.

After discussion, Mr. and Mrs. Ward elect to claim one withholding exemption each for their Cynthia Court wages.

THE MANAGER ENJOYS AN ATTRACTIVE
INCOME TAX PROVISION

At this point it is timely to point out to the Wards that the commonly accepted practice for payroll purposes is to show the value of their free apartment at approximately two-thirds the market value. A rental valuation of $70 will be included as compensation for Social Security, unemployment insurance and disability insurance payroll taxes. However, the lodging value will not be subject to income tax, since, in a building with seventeen or more apartments, a resident manager is required by state law. There can be no question that the use of quarters within the building is a mandatory, and therefore tax-free, condition of employment.

3. FIDELITY BOND APPLICATION

The use of a fidelity bond relieves the owner of considerable reference checking and worry over shortages. The value of the bond is as much psychological as practical. A manager under bond will be more apt to hew to a straight and narrow line of conduct moneywise. An owner might be lenient in case of discovered peccadillos, but it is common knowledge that a bonding company may make an example of an offender by pressing charges to the limit to discourage similar offenses.

A BONDED MANAGER IS MORE TRUSTWORTHY

An owner operating without a bond might feel it necessary to make a detailed check of references as to honesty. With a bond, the owner can safely leave much of this to the judgment of the bonding company, which is most experienced in this field. I have known unbonded managers to resign when asked by a new owner to fill out a bond application. Such resignations prove that either their present or past operations could not stand an audit. On the other hand, a manager who cheerfully fills out a bond application and is accepted by the bonding company should automatically win the owner's trust.

Regardless of the accounting procedures used, an apartment manager entrusted with rent collections is in an easy position to abscond with collected funds, as did the former manager's husband at the Cynthia Court. If the manager in this case had been bonded, the bonding company would have reimbursed the owner in full for his loss, up to the limit of the bond.

The use of a bond also influences banking procedures. Many owners hire a resident manager for custodial purposes but have someone else, either the owner or a designated agent, handle the rent collections and subsequent banking. This is a needless waste of time and expense. From the standpoint of convenience to owner and tenants no one is in a better position to handle both rent collections and bank deposits than the resident manager. The owner should have much less worry about mishandling of funds if there is a bond and if he uses other safeguards described in the following pages.

Two copies of a fidelity bond application are given to the Wards. The original will be sent to our insurance broker. The duplicate will be retained by the owner, attached to his copy of the manager's contract for reference purposes.

We fill out the portion with which the owner is familiar. The balance is to be filled out by the Wards, ready for delivery to the owner not later than the day they take over Cynthia Court.

On pages 362–65 is the bond application completed by Mrs. Ward, with the portion filled in by the owner capitalized.

4. BURGLARY AND ROBBERY
INSURANCE CONSIDERATIONS

After discussing any fidelity bond aspects that may need clarification, it is timely to review other insurance considerations, including burglary and robbery coverage. Point out that the owner will be reimbursed by insurance for burglary and robbery losses up to $1,000. The manager should feel relieved of any obligation to defend the owner's funds. The rents in hand should never be permitted to exceed $1,000. (Of course this limitation also insures that the fidelity bond coverage will not be exceeded.)

Rent funds should be kept in a concealed location. Robberies or burglaries of apartment houses may be rare. But if a burglary should occur on the premises, or if the manager should be held up on the way to the bank, no attempt should be made to resist. That might invite personal injury or death. Instead, the manager should try to be calm and hand over the funds without resistance. The manager's records will show the amount of money involved, and the insurance company will reimburse the owner. Even if a loss is never sustained, the little cost of burglary and robbery insurance is well compensated for by the resulting peace of mind of both owner and manager.

5. LIABILITY INSURANCE CONSIDERATIONS

The manager should be advised that the owner carries liability insurance. If anyone is injured on the premises, the owner should be immediately notified, so that he can advise his broker. If the owner cannot be reached, the manager should contact the broker direct. The insurance company instructs owner and manager not to divulge that there is liability insurance coverage. Any claims or suit will be brought against the owner. However, the insurance company will represent the owner and will assume liabilities up to the amount of the policy.

6. TRANSFER OF MANAGEMENT

An inexperienced manager taking over an apartment house as large as the Cynthia Court may approach her new assignment with as much trepidation as a timid virgin her bridal chamber. Fear of the unknown will be relieved by understanding and patience. On the day that a new and untried manager takes over it is most important for the owner to be on hand to give assurance and answer questions.

The outgoing manager should teach the new one most of the day-to-day operating procedures, such as the use of certain equipment. Included would be routine practices like daily checking of garbage collection areas and the water level in the boiler. The new manager should also be briefed on the rent schedule, the names of the tenants, any pertinent information about individual tenants, the amount of rent due from each apartment, and the dates that rents are due.

The outgoing manager will usually be fully co-operative in breaking in the new manager. But the owner is the one the new manager must look to for authority, and he should always be on hand on the take-over date. The owner can review any items not covered by the vacating manager and correct any misinformation handed out. By actively participating in the transfer, the owner in effect lifts the mantle of responsibility from the departing manager and places it on the shoulders of the new one.

The manager should be impressed that she is hired to operate the building as the responsible agent of the owner, not as a representative of the tenants, nor as a mediator between owner and tenants. Often, however, the manager will serve well as a buffer to bear the brunt of tenant demands.

In discussions with tenants the manager should be encouraged to use the third person when referring to the owner or house policy. "I will not let you do thus and so" may incur personal enmity on the part of the tenant. The tenant's wrath would easier be turned by the more impersonal "The owner does not permit dogs in the apartment house," or "The house rules do not allow loud music."

Along with a current monthly statement covering all tenants, rents and due dates, the manager's lease file should be turned over. In addition there may be a card file set up chronologically by rent payment dates. By using a comprehensive monthly report, the manager may, in many circumstances, dispense with the card file.

7. MONTHLY REPORTS

A sound monthly report sheet is absolutely essential for proper accounting. It can be utilized to serve five major purposes:

1. The manager's ready reference of rents due
2. The manager's accounting of rents collected
3. The manager's report to the owner
4. The owner's auditing of the manager
5. The owner's income tax report on rents received

The previous owner and manager of the Cynthia Court had used no regular reporting system. The former manager and the present temporary one both made up a monthly tally sheet, showing only the total number of apartments occupied and the total rents collected. As unbusinesslike as this may seem, it is not too uncommon a practice.

I know a national management organization whose monthly report covers only the following:

Apt. No.	Amount collected
1	$90.00
2	90.00
3	90.00
4	90.00
TOTAL	$360.00

CONFIDENTIAL

APPLICATION FOR FIDELITY BOND

BOND NO. _____

AMOUNT $ 1,000.00

INDIVIDUAL FIDELITY

Agent ___ACE INSURANCE COMPANY___   Address ___1110 MAIN ST., METROPOLE, COLUMBIA___

(The Applicant must answer fully all questions asked. Confidence must be reposed in the Company, if confidence is expected in return.)

AILENE WISTER
Show name of person replaced by Applicant

I hereby make application for fidelity suretyship in my behalf and in favor of my Employer, in amount and in form satisfactory to my Employer, and for the continuance or renewal of, or any substitution for, such fidelity suretyship at any time thereafter in such form and amount as my Employer may require.

1. Applicant's name in full ___Mrs. Jeannette V. Ward___   Social Security No. ___266-40-9011___
   (Print or typewrite the FULL NAME)

2. a. Present Home Address of Applicant ___1440 CYNTHIA COURT, METROPOLE, COLUMBIA___
   (Street and No.)   (City, Zone No. and State)

   b. Previous Home Address of Applicant ___1780 Hays St., Metropole, Columbia___
   (Street and No.)   (City, Zone No. and State)

   c. Nationality ___U. S.___   Born at ___Park Rapids, Minnesota___   Birth Date ___Dec. 7, 1938___

3. a. NAME OF EMPLOYER to whom bond is to be given ___JOSEPH E. ENTERPRISE___
   (Give Employer's FULL NAME including firm name, if any)

   Address with Zone No. ___7070 PARADISE ROAD, SUBURBIA, COLUMBIA.___

   b. Nature of Employer's business ___APARTMENT OWNER___   Date of employment ___DEC. 1, 1966___

   c. TITLE OF YOUR POSITION ___APARTMENT MANAGER___   Where located? ___1440 CYNTHIA COURT, METROPOLE___

4. a. Marital Status: ☐ Single; ☒ Married; ☐ Divorced; ☐ Widow(er)

   b. Number of persons supported: ___Wife___   Children _____   Others _____

   c. Spouse's Name ___David Edward Ward___   Occupation ___Letter Carrier___   Address ___1440 Cynthia Court___

   d. Father's name ___Henry Boronson___   Occupation ___Telephone Mgr.___   Address ___Chicago, Ill.___

   e. Mother's name ___Mrs. Tina Marie Boronson___   Address ___Teacher,___   " "
   (If parents are deceased, give name and address of nearest male relatives)

5. a. Have you ever been bonded? __No__ By what surety company? _____

b. Has your application for bond always been accepted? _____ If not, give full facts _____

6. Has a shortage ever occurred in your accounts? __No__ If so, give full facts on separate sheet.

7. Give present value of your property holdings: Real Estate $ __12,000__ Jeannette V. Ward umbrances or mortgages
   8,517.60
   (In whose name)
   thereon $ __2,882.40__ Personal property, including stocks, bonds, mortgages, etc., $ __3,000__
   Liens or incumbrances thereon $ __None__
   (State to whom pledged and for what purpose)

8. Give amount of all other debts, in addition to those listed above $ __700__ When due __1968__
   To whom due __Postal Credit Union__ How incurred? __Auto Purchase__

9. a. Do you carry any life insurance? __Yes__ b. Total amount $ __2,500__
   c. To whom payable __David E. Ward & David E. Ward,Jr.__ Nature of Policies __Endowment__

10. a. If ever engaged in business on your own account, give reasons for discontinuance _____
    b. Have you ever failed in business? __No__ Give complete facts _____

11. IN THE POSITION FOR WHICH THIS BOND IS REQUIRED:
    a. If you have authority to sign checks, state for what amount $ __NONE__ Is countersignature required _____
    (Yes or No)
    b. Do you receive goods, merchandise or other property on consignment? __NO__
    c. What salary will you receive? __$100 MO.__ e. If commission, how and when paid? _____
    d. Do you make regular outside collections: __NO__ ? If so, the amount
    of your daily cash $ _____ , checks $ _____
    12. Have you any other income? __Yes__ From what source? __House Rental__ Amount $ __1,440 Yr.__

General Fidelity Application for Officers and Employees of Banks, Corporations, Railway Companies, etc., and for Employees Generally of Firms, Associations and Individuals

0409 R3 6457

PREVIOUS EMPLOYMENT

Give in sequence, beginning with the name of your last employer, the names and addresses of previous employers over a period of ten years, positions occupied, time engaged with each, reasons for leaving each, and also give periods, if any, during which unemployed. This data is important and replies must be full and complete.

FROM Month Year	TO Month Year	NAME AND ADDRESS OF EMPLOYER (with Zone No.)	EMPLOYMENT LOCATION	Name and Present Address (with Zone No.) of Person Under Whom You Then Worked	WHAT POSITION DID YOU HOLD?	WHY DID YOU LEAVE?
11 1962	12 1966	Self	Metropole		Housewife	
7 1962	10 1962	University of Columb.	Metropole	L.T. Hazeltine Toll Supt.	Laboratory Asst.	Family need
3 1962	7 1962	Columbia Telephone Co.	Metropole	Franklin St.	Operator	Illness
10 1961	3 1962	Montgomery Ward & Co.	St. Paul Minnesota	Mail Order Mgr.	Order Filler	Seasonal Layoff
1 1958	10 1961	Self	St. Paul		Housewife	
9 1956	1 1958	University of Minn.	Minnesota		Student	Could not afford to continue
9 1952	6 1956	Minneapolis High School			Student	Graduated
19	19					
19	19					
19	19					

REFERENCES OTHER THAN FORMER EMPLOYERS OR RELATIVES

Give at least three. Write clearly and distinctly. Be sure to furnish complete and proper addresses.

NAMES OF REFERENCES	OCCUPATION	P. O. ADDRESS IN FULL (WITH ZONE NO.)
Charles Robertson	Branch Supervisor	U.S. Post Office, Metropole, Columb.
Mr. & Mrs. Daniel Herrold	Pharmacy Owner	Suburbia, Columbia
Branch Edwards	Store Manager	Super Stores, Inc. 1550 E. Galway St. Metropole, Columbia

Please Give References for any Period of Self-Employment (companies dealt with, Rental Agencies, Trade Name)

In consideration of the execution by the GENERAL INSURANCE COMPANY OF AMERICA, (hereinafter called Company) of the suretyship herein applied for, I hereby agree: *First*, to indemnify the Company against all loss, liability, costs, damages, attorneys' fees and expenses whatever, which the Company may sustain or incur or become liable for thereunder through my acts; *Second*, that the voucher or vouchers or other evidence of the any payment, settlement or compromise of such loss, liability, costs, damages, attorneys' fees and expenses shall be *prima facie* evidence of the fact and extent of my liability in any suit hereunder; *Third*, that the Company shall have the right and is hereby authorized, but not required, to adjust, settle or compromise any claim, demand, suit or judgment upon said suretyship, unless I shall request the Company to litigate such claim or demand or defend such suit or to appeal from such judgment, and shall deposit with the Company collateral satisfactory to it in kind and amount; *Fourth*, that the Company shall have the absolute right to decline to issue said suretyship, or, if issued, to cancel same at any time, and the Company shall be under no obligation to disclose its reasons therefor or give any information in connection therewith, the provisions of any law to the contrary being hereby expressly waived.

Signed, sealed and dated this ___1st___ day of ___December___, 19 _66_

WITNESS: __(Signed) Joseph E. Enterprise__   __Mrs. Jeannette V. Ward__ (SEAL)

(Applicant sign FULL name here)

PHYSICAL DESCRIPTION OF APPLICANT

Age _28_ Height _5'7"_ Weight _150 lbs._ Complexion _Olive_ Color of Eyes _Brown_

Color of Hair _Brown_ Color of Mustache _____ Color of Beard _____ Race or Color _Caucasian_

Birthmarks, prominent scars or other distinguishing features _None_

NOTE — Agent will please see that the physical description of Applicant is filled up, and all questions answered in detail, and application properly dated and signed.

If the building is 100 per cent occupied, then the manager turned in one rental for each apartment, apparently a foolproof procedure. However, in one of this organization's 28-unit properties which I studied as a prospective buyer, on one month's report I found a windfall of three months' rent, amounting to $204. The owners had no inkling of these extra rents, which the manager pocketed.

HOW A MANAGER POCKETED THREE MONTHS' RENT

Three military tenants, who paid their rents on the first, the fifth, and the tenth of the month respectively, all received, on the eighteenth, rush transfer orders to move on the twentieth. Under the state law they were required to give thirty days' notice and were liable for the days between their paid-up period and thirty days from the eighteenth, when they gave notice. When the manager pointed this out to them, all were grateful that they were not to be so charged and gladly gave up all thought of a refund for the unused portion.

By the twenty-seventh new tenants had rented all three vacated apartments, which thus earned double rents for the calendar month. The manager retained all the excess rents under the reporting procedure in practice. If the reverse circumstance occurred, and no rent was collected from a particular unit during the month, the manager would report "Vacant" under the apartment number. This might happen where, for example, a rent was due on the twenty-fifth, the old tenant moved out, and the apartment was not rented until the following month.

The foregoing exemplifies the deficiency of this slipshod reporting system. Yet the aforementioned company has been operating under the same procedure for over thirty years.

THE CYNTHIA COURT MANAGER COMPLETES
OUR DETAILED MONTHLY REPORT (see page 368)

Since there has been no detailed report of any kind at the Cynthia Court, we instruct the outgoing manager, Mr. Bandy, to fill out our regular form for the month of November. The incoming manager will then complete the same reporting form for each month hereafter.

The report shows all rents collected during the calendar month, although the rents due November 1 were all credited to the previous owner and then prorated as of November 5. The first eight apartments showing rents due later than the first were vacant on November 5 when we took the building over. In addition, apartment 305 was vacated November 13 and rented to a new tenant November 18, earning two rentals for the month. All vacancies had been rented by the twenty-fourth at $10 over the prevailing schedule through appropriate advertising and by promising incoming tenants that their apartments would be painted and the main hall newly carpeted as soon as feasible.

8. DUPLICATE RENT RECEIPTS

The preparation of a rent receipt and the recommended form to use were explained in Chapter 15. Adequate supervision also requires the use of duplicate, numbered receipts. The original should be given to the tenant and the duplicate retained for the time being by the person signing the receipt.

Many owners, even of large rental holdings, collect all rents personally, chiefly because they do not trust managers with the handling of funds. This is a needless assumption of a purely routine task which can safely be delegated to the manager with the checks and balances outlined in this chapter.

With our apartment operation, the manager will collect the rents and turn the duplicate receipt over to the owner each time an accounting is made. With hotels, motels, and any accommodations where the rents are collected daily or weekly, it is a common practice to prepare triplicate receipts. In this event the third copy would be retained by the manager in case of question by the tenant. For monthly rentals, as at the Cynthia Court, no triplicate receipts will be needed. The manager's duplicate copy of the monthly report will show her how rentals stand.

The fact that the owner has duplicate, numbered receipts helps to insure that no receipts will be issued of which the owner is not aware. Since the owner can always compare his duplicate with the original given to the tenant, the manager is not so apt to report rentals at variance with actual collections.

HOW ANOTHER MANAGER PURLOINED EXCESS RENTS

I know of another manager of a 24-unit building who pocketed considerable excess rents during several years following decontrol when rents were generally subject to heavy raises. The owners seldom

JOSEPH ENTERPRISE OWNER   MONTHLY INCOME REPORT

Address   Cynthia Court Apts.   Month Ending November 30 1966

APT. NO.	RENT	GAR.	NAME	NO. TEN-ANTS	DATE DUE	DATE REC'D	NEXT DUE	LATE AND EXTRA CHGS.	DEPOSITS AND OTHER	DUE	PAID	BAL. DUE
101	115.00	X	James C. Kulle	3	Nov. 20	Nov. 20	Dec. 20		**KD 53.00	168.00	168.00	
102	—	X	Henry Bandy, Mgr.	1	—	—				—	—	
103	80.00	X	Vaughn Earnest	1	Nov. 1	Nov. 1	Dec. 1			80.00	80.00	
104	80.00	X	Gabriel Sultan	1	Nov. 1	Nov. 3	Dec. 1			80.00	80.00	
105	75.00		Susan Percival	1	Nov. 1	Nov. 1	Dec. 1			75.00	75.00	
106	80.00	X	Glenn Utterbach	2	Nov. 1	Nov. 1	Dec. 1			80.00	80.00	
107	80.00	X	Chas. Burchard	1	Nov. 1	Nov. 2	Dec. 1			80.00	80.00	
108	80.00	X	Agnes Valentino	1	Nov. 1	Nov. 1	Dec. 1			80.00	80.00	
201	105.00	X	Everett Robinson	2	Nov. 1	Nov. 1	Dec. 1			105.00	105.00	
202	80.00		Cecil Bowlby	2	Nov. 1	Nov. 1	Dec. 1			80.00	80.00	
203	80.00	X	Clinton Andersen	1	Nov. 1	Nov. 1	Dec. 1			80.00	80.00	
204	90.00	X	Beverly Beauchamp	1	Nov. 12	Nov. 12	Dec. 12		KD 28.00	118.00	118.00	
205	90.00	X	Ross Taylor	2	Nov. 10	Nov. 10	Dec. 10		KD 28.00	118.00	118.00	
206	80.00		Evelyn Meers	1	Nov. 1	Nov. 1	Dec. 1			80.00	80.00	
207	80.00		Margaret Bain	1	Nov. 1	Nov. 1	Dec. 1			80.00	80.00	
208	80.00		Trent Evans	1	Nov. 1	Nov. 2	Dec. 1			80.00	80.00	
301	115.00	X	Florence Hoover	1	Nov. 24	Nov. 24	Dec. 10		KD 53.00	114.28	114.28	pro-rated
302	90.00	X	James Russell	2	Nov. 22	Nov. 22	Dec. 22		KD 28.00	118.00	98.00	20.00
303	80.00		Richard Bohn	2	Nov. 1	Nov. 1	Dec. 1			80.00	80.00	
304	90.00	X	Constance O'Brien	1	Nov. 12	Nov. 12	Dec. 12		KD 28.00	118.00	118.00	
305*	80.00		Colin Billings	2	Nov. 3	Nov. 3	*(Moved Nov. 13)			80.00	80.00	
306	80.00		Laura Humphreys	1	Nov. 2	Nov. 2	Dec. 1			80.00	80.00	
307	90.00	X	Joe Scoggin	1	Nov. 14	Nov. 14	Dec. 14		KD 28.00	118.00	118.00	
308	90.00	X	Roger Schulte	2	Nov. 21	Nov. 21	Dec. 21		KD 28.00	118.00	118.00	
305	90.00	X	John Waugh	1	Nov. 18	Nov. 18	Dec. 18		KD 28.00	118.00	118.00	

**KD—Key & Damages Deposits

Page Total   2,308.28
Grand Total   2,308.28
Refunds   3.00
Net Received 2,305.28

Henry A. Bandy
(Signed) Manager

Mary Enterprise
Auditor.

MONTHLY REPORT FOR CYNTHIA COURT

appeared on the premises, were as asleep to changing times as Rip Van Winkle, and failed to authorize an increased rent schedule. Leases were not used at all, so there were none for the owners to check. No duplicate receipts were prepared. The manager merely noted the rental paid on a stub, which she retained only till the next payment and then destroyed.

The manager raised the rents on a gradual basis to an average of 55 per cent over the owners' schedule. She continued to report the original price-control rentals to the owners and purloined the balance. Incidentally, the owners in this instance were partners who were feuding because neither wanted to put out more supervisory effort than the other. Consequently both lost thousands of dollars in rent.

The property was sold at cost, which was considerably below the market value, in order to break up the partnership. Strange as it may seem, both partners must have believed they had an excellent and trustworthy manager, as they recommended her highly to the new owner. This was chiefly because she never bothered them with calls, taking full charge of rent policies, banking, and the ordering of repairs and supplies.

THE MANAGER SKIPS

The new owner, at my suggestion, belatedly instituted more businesslike operating procedures. Toward the end of the month he gave the manager a fidelity bond application to fill out and turned the form in to the bonding company. The manager waited until after the first-of-the-month rent collections and then disappeared one night with $1,200 in receipts. Subsequent attempts to claim unemployment insurance revealed that she and her husband, a construction worker, had skipped across the border into Mexico.

The insurance company reported back that the manager was not bondable, as she had a previous record of pilfering funds while clerking in a department store. The bond application was therefore not accepted, and the owner was not insured against fidelity loss pertaining to the absconding manager. Luckily only $280 of the $1,200 was in cash. The owner arranged with the tenants to stop payment on all checks and wound up with a $280 loss.

His small misfortune was more than counterbalanced by a major stroke of good fortune. He had bought the building on a discounted basis and on the yardstick of the partners' rent schedule. After checking with each tenant, he found the unusual circumstance of over-all rents, being 55 per cent greater than represented, increasing his market value accordingly.

9. TRIPLICATE LEASES

The lease form to be used at the Cynthia Court is the same as the one we used at the Belvedere, explained in Chapter 14. Mr. Bandy and the Wards are advised that we require all leases to be prepared in triplicate. The original is to be retained by the manager, the duplicate by the tenant, and the triplicate by the owner. Of course the tenant should have a copy and the manager should have a copy for ready reference. But why a copy for both owner and manager?

A MEANS OF ELIMINATING TEMPTATION

The use of triplicate leases is one of the most foolproof means of eliminating the temptation of a manager to falsify rents. When the owner receives a copy of the lease signed by the tenant every time there is a change in the terms of a tenancy, he can keep up to date on the actual rental paid. He will know not only the new rental amount but also the date the new rent starts, thus establishing a check on double rents in the calendar month, as previously covered.

A copy of the lease in the owner's file also aids in the quick settlement of controversies. Although such instances seldom arise, a tenant may call the owner direct, or the manager may call for emergency reasons, like a tenant's claim for damage to his furniture. The lease also expedites the settling of routine matters like the date that rent starts or terminates.

10. BANK DEPOSITS

Some managers are instructed to collect rents and then turn the funds over to the owner for banking. In addition to consuming the owner's time needlessly, this practice also delays deposits. Usually the manager can conveniently bank receipts at a neighborhood branch of the owner's bank, so that his central account will be credited.

Since we wish the Wards to both collect and deposit rents, we review the banking procedure we have already established with Mr.

Bandy. Checks are to be made out to the owner, Joseph Enterprise. So that nobody can cash them, all checks are to be endorsed immediately on receipt with our bank deposit stamp:

FOR DEPOSIT ONLY
JOSEPH AND MARY
ENTERPRISE

Bank deposit slips are also to be prepared in triplicate. The original is taken by the bank, and the duplicate by the owner so that he will have a record of the actual amount banked. The triplicate is to be retained by the manager as her receipt.

The amount banked should always equal the total rents collected less authorized disbursements. All rents collected and deposited would be shown on a monthly report. However, the monthly report would not correspond with the banking report, as there would be several deposits during the month, and some deposits might cover portions of two months' collections. As an example of the latter, a deposit made on the third might include receipts from the twenty-fifth to the third.

BANKING REPORT

For ready checking, the manager should prepare a banking report showing details of receipts and disbursements. The receipt information should be copied from the duplicate rent receipts, and the disbursement claims from paid bills. On periodic supervisory visits the owner can check receipts and bills against the items listed by the manager, correcting discrepancies on the spot.

Auditing of arithmetic can be made on the premises if desired. Like many owners, I prefer to check arithmetic later, in my office, where it is more convenient to tally all rent receipts and bills by adding machine.

Below is a copy of the Cynthia Court banking report, covering rents collected from November 10 to November 24. Mr. Bandy has prepared this report according to our instructions, and we use the same as an example for the Wards to follow. The check-marks show that the entries have been checked against duplicate rent receipts, paid bills, and the bank deposit slip. The deposit balance is not certified "O.K." or "Correct," since the arithmetic will not be audited until later.

BANKING REPORT:

JOSEPH ENTERPRISE OWNER INCOME RECEIVED LESS CASH EXPENDITURES

Address Cynthia Court Apts.   Period Ending November 24 1966

APT. #	RENT	RECEIPT #	GAR.	NAME	DATE DUE	DATE REC'D	LATE AND EXTRA CHGS.	DEPOSITS & OTHER	TOTAL DUE	PAID	BAL. DUE
205	90.00	251	X	Ross Taylor	Nov. 10	Nov. 10		**KD 28.00	118.00	118.00√	
204	90.00	252	X	Beverly Beauchamp	Nov. 12	Nov. 12		KD 28.00	118.00	118.00√	
304	90.00	253	X	Constance O'Brien	Nov. 12	Nov. 12		KD 28.00	118.00	118.00√	
307	90.00	254	X	Joe Scoggin	Nov. 14	Nov. 14		KD 28.00	118.00	118.00√	
305	90.00	255		John Waugh	Nov. 18	Nov. 18		KD 28.00	118.00	118.00√	
101	115.00	256	X	James C. Kulle	Nov. 20	Nov. 20		KD 53.00	168.00	168.00√	
308	90.00	257	X	Roger Schulte	Nov. 21	Nov. 21		KD 28.00	118.00	118.00√	
302	90.00	258	X	James Russell	Nov. 22	Nov. 22		KD 28.00	118.00	98.00√	#20.00
301	115.00	259		Florence Hoover	Nov. 24	Nov. 24		KD 53.00	*114.28	114.28√	

* Pro-rate rent 61.28 to Dec. 10
** Key & Damage Deposits
# Will Pay Dec. 5

Totals:
Collected: 1,088.28
Paid Out: 4.82√
Balance to Bank: 1,083.46√

	DATE	ITEM	APT. #	AMOUNT
	11–15	Notebook		.26√
	"	Carbon paper		.52√
Paid Out:	11–13	Key deposit refund 305		3.00√
	11–20	Box washers		1.04√
		TOTAL		4.82√

Above is complete report
of Collections to date listed
Henry A. Bandy
(Signed) MANAGER

Above checked as to amounts listed
(subject to further audit) date:
Joseph Enterprise
(Signed) OWNER   11/25/66

11. PAYMENT OF BILLS

Some owners insist on paying all bills, regardless of how small. Others authorize their managers to pay all bills, including major repair and supply accounts. A compromise between the two extremes proves most efficient.

THE MANAGER SHOULD PURCHASE MINOR ITEMS

Minor items, like the notebook and other small purchases shown, the manager should be authorized to pay for, using rent funds in hand. The owner will save a great deal of time if the manager is encouraged to buy such obviously needed items without consulting him. Thus, none of the owner's time is wasted in discussing the authorization, making the purchase, and making payment.

Some owners have a petty-cash fund for this purpose. While this is a customary business practice, a petty-cash fund involves unnecessary bookkeeping in most apartment operations. The manager nearly always has some rent funds on hand from which she can pay small bills. Otherwise she can pay from her own funds and reimburse herself from the next cash rent collection.

At first this might seem to encourage a mixing of the owner's and the manager's funds, a phrase which causes auditors to throw up their hands in horror. It does not create a problem if the cardinal principle is enforced that at all times the manager's cash is subject to audit. She should have either a bank deposit slip, receipted bills, or cash on hand to offset every cent collected.

MAJOR EXPENSES SHOULD BE BILLED TO THE OWNER

The Wards are given a list of all major contractors and suppliers from whom we regularly purchase. In emergencies the manager can call our plumber or electrician, for example, and the charges will be billed direct to the owner. If there is no emergency, the manager is instructed to contract no major charges except with the owner's specific approval.

We have wholesale accounts from which major recurrent supplies and fixtures can be ordered by the manager. Included are items such as electrical fixtures and light bulbs by the case direct from an electrical supply distributor and pipe fittings, water faucets, and toilet seats from a plumbing supply house.

Establishing regular accounts billed to the owner enables him in many cases to buy at wholesale or factory prices instead of at retail. This also bypasses the possibility of the manager's padding bills or maneuvering a kickback system, both widespread practices where managers are authorized to pay all bills.

12. PERIODIC SUPERVISORY VISITS

We tell the Wards to phone us in any emergency or, particularly now while they are just starting, any time there is a question about operations which they feel needs an immediate answer. We emphasize that, besides the obvious emergencies such as a tenant's falling downstairs and breaking a leg, we consider a real emergency the case of a tenant's moving without notice and leaving an apartment not drawing rent.

In such an event we want to be notified immediately, so that we may inspect the apartment and decide what steps should be taken. While we are developing the Cynthia Court, we wish to appraise each vacancy to determine whether to change furniture or decorate, and what rent to charge. Later the manager will have sufficient experience with our operations to make most such decisions demanding immediate attention. We anticipate there will usually be ample notice from outgoing tenants, so such matters can be discussed during our periodic visits, which will be regularly made on a weekly basis.

REGULAR VISITS SAVE TIME

Making regular weekly visits will prove a considerable timesaver in the long run, as it will be found that the manager seldom needs to contact the owner otherwise. Checking of books and other routine matters can usually be handled in a few minutes. A complete owner-manager apartment review will normally take between one and two hours. In this time the owner can keep abreast of problems that affect income and expense and can insure that the employee is following the owner's up-to-date policies, rather than veering off on a tangent or failing to heed instructions.

Especially while they are being broken in, and at any time major repairs or changes are under way, we expect religiously to contact the Wards on the premises on a regular weekly basis. With the building undergoing improvement, this practice will normally be continued unless we are kept away by a vacation trip or other matter. We stress that we are delegating to the manager authority to continue with day-to-day operations on her own, and she will seldom have to contact us between visits. Most problems we expect Mrs. Ward and her husband to work out themselves, holding major decisions until our visit.

ENCOURAGE MANAGER TO ACCEPT RESPONSIBILITY

Giving the manager as much authority as possible increases her feeling of importance and encourages her to accept responsibilities. The manager should be impressed that in making decisions she will not be criticized for an occasional mistake. If action is taken contrary to the owner's wishes, he will point it out and give her an opportunity for correction.

A manager, like any other employee, is anxious at all times to know where she stands. In a close relationship with the owner, she may be especially sensitive to a lack of commendation, which may be interpreted as silent censure. The more intelligent your manager, the more sensitive she will be to the absence of approbation. Therefore, tend toward the lavish in praise of commendable decisions and actions.

As long as the manager is doing an over-all satisfactory job, overlook minor points that do not really matter. Do not expect every decision to be made exactly as you would determine it. Bear in mind that no two people will take the same action on every problem, any more than they will write identical letters.

In a properly conducted owner-manager relationship, the manager should welcome, rather than resent, the owner's supervisory visits. Their chief purpose is to keep abreast of current trends and to amicably solve any problems. All my managers, I am sure, will honestly tell you they are genuinely glad to see me. I know of many managers, on the other hand, who dread the appearance of the owner because he habitually pours out criticism with no leavening of praise. Some owners feel that the purpose of supervision is to keep the manager on her toes by probing for picayunish points to criticize. This creates resentment, results in a poorer job, and induces manager turnover.

If two or three vacancies happen to occur at the same time, don't blame the manager, as long as she stays on hand to show the apartments. If you display confidence, she will be more confident. A mentally relaxed manager will rent apartments, whereas one driven panicky by the owner may press too hard and drive prospective tenants away.

The more confidence the manager has, the more responsibility she will take, leaving you with scarcely any decisions to make. Although it pays to keep abreast of your apartment operations by periodic visits, a manager whose confidence is built up can carry on satisfactorily for months without supervision. My wife and I recently enjoyed a three-month vacation in Europe, leaving our managers in complete charge. We left forwarding addresses where they could contact us, but no problems arose which they could not handle completely on their own.

ENCOURAGE MANAGER TO MAKE SUGGESTIONS

The manager is the eyes and ears of the owner on the premises and she should be encouraged to make suggestions for improvement of property or operations. An alert manager, in rapport with the owner, will bring to his attention many profitable ideas which he might not have considered.

For example, I know of one manager who suggested to the owner that if he replaced some of his dilapidated sofa sets with new, modern pieces, she could raise the rents enough to repay the cost in one year. In fact, she had already obtained the agreement of two tenants to accept such raises in exchange for new sofas. Naturally, the manager's suggestion was adopted. The owner's wholesale cost was paid for by slightly under ten months' rent. This gave him a 120 per cent return for the particular investment.

To encourage rather than discourage zeal, it is important for the manager to realize that the owner appreciates her continuing to bring to his attention any ideas she may have in mind, although all suggestions cannot be carried out. The manager should never be answered with a gruff dismissal of a rejected brain child, even though many suggestions may be turned down completely and others deferred because of factors such as cost in relation to resulting income.

Under normal operations, biweekly visits may be sufficient after a competent manager is well trained. Sometimes you may be tied up and may substitute a telephone call for a periodic visit. Or you may make a visit in a hurry and dash away after a few minutes' routine checkup. As a regular practice it is important to allow time for a friendly visit and discussion. This is where the regular supervisory visit may develop valuable recommendations. Often a productive mood can be induced by asking questions about personal or building problems.

WHY ENCOURAGE LITTLE THINGS TO DRIVE AN OWNER CRAZY?

With the owner-manager relationship that is recommended, the owner can practically eliminate unexpected calls from managers or tenants. But it is surprising how lackadaisical supervision can encourage distracting interruptions over picayunish problems.

When I was a telephone employee, one of my co-workers took up most of his spare time talking with the resident manager and tenants of his 24-unit building. He did not trust his manager with the rent funds, and he collected the rents from the individual tenants. This involved a special trip, and sometimes several call-backs, to the apartments every time a rent was to be collected. By establishing a personal contact between the owner and each of his tenants, he had encouraged them to call him direct instead of referring to the manager for all problems, major or minor.

This owner had inherited the property from his father, and his only supervisory experience was as an Army sergeant. He castigated the manager unmercifully if she made a mistake, regardless how minor, or spent a cent which he had not specifically authorized. As a result she called him at least once a day at his office, and usually again at night after he was comfortably ensconced at home. She would phone, for example, to get an O.K. to spend ten cents for a note pad. Many of the calls were for the purpose of asking the owner to referee arguments between the manager and the tenants. Ninety-nine per cent of them could have been handled by the manager herself or held until a regular weekly meeting.

The unhappy owner remarked that although I owned more apartments, I apparently never received calls from my managers or tenants during the day. How did I train them to wait and call me only at home?

I replied that apartment calls came very infrequently to my home. This owner could have been induced to sell his building at a sacrifice, but instead I outlined my supervisory procedures, described for your guidance here. I recommended that he bond the manager, have her collect rents and bank them, authorize her to make minor decisions and purchases, and arrange for a regular weekly supervisory visit. He should give her a chance to institute the changes. If she still proved unsatisfactory, he had better hire a new manager.

OWNER AND MANAGER TRANSFORMED

Since the owner was encouraged by the example of my own comparatively unfettered supervision, he unhesitatingly accepted all my recommendations. The previously frustrated manager so appreciated the opportunity to work under a system of freedom and recognition that she was transformed into a very desirable employee. She was able to hold almost all problems requiring the owner's decision for his regular weekly visit. He scarcely ever received calls any longer at his office or his home.

He usually went over to his property for an hour or two Saturday morning. If he was going on a trip or golfing, his visit would be made on a weekday evening. After the new system was in operation for a while, if he had something special to do on Saturday he would phone the manager and eliminate the weekly checkup altogether.

After advising the Wards of our desires from the standpoint of giving them authority and holding up major decisions until our next weekly supervisory visit, we turn the Cynthia Court over to them. Now we are ready to contract for the badly required renovation and to arrange for the necessary financing to pay for it.

Businesslike procedures and a bond help keep a manager trustworthy, relieving the owner of worry over fidelity losses. Comprehensive and understanding supervision encourages the manager to take responsibility, insures maximum efficiency, and yet requires a minimum of time.

Build up the manager's stature as the owner's representative. Then you can devote your attention to major policy decisions, and you will find apartment ownership more a stimulating challenge instead of a chore.

PART EIGHT

FINANCING YOUR PYRAMIDING

22. HOW TO BORROW MONEY

"For whosoever hath, to him shall be given . . . ; but whosoever hath not, from him shall be taken away even that he hath," said Jesus.

The popular colloquialism restates this as "Them that has, gets."

Fitting many phases of life, both spiritual and material, these precepts nowhere are more true than in the field of finance and credit. If you need money desperately and have no credit, you cannot borrow a cent. A bank does not loan on the basis of need, only on your ability to repay. Like the miserable servant who hid his talent, he who fails to use his resources to develop credit will find he has no credit when he wants it.

If you have all the money you need and have credit, then it is easy to borrow in order to make more money. Spectacular big-time promoters like the Metropolitan Life Insurance Company, Scheuer, and Stevens normally have ready access to all the money they want to plan and complete major redevelopment projects. Their talents have already pyramided their resources into multimillions.

Fortunately, even though you may have only meager resources, you can be like the industrious servants in the parable, who, while their master was gone on a journey, pyramided their talents fivefold and tenfold. Through the cultivation of credit, you can keep pyramiding, to millions, if you aspire to.

EACH DIGIT ADDS A MEASURE OF CREDIT

The accumulation of capital pyramids on a rising scale, faster and easier at each stage of progress. Bankers like to measure your net worth in digits. Each digit constitutes an escalator to a higher credit plateau.

I overheard a newlywed tenant say, "We've only been married three months and already have a four-figure savings account." It developed that her bank balance amounted to $55.36. Despite the bride's boast, her banker will tally only dollars in measuring the size of her account.

Below $1,000 you have a lowly "three-figure account." Your credit is practically nil, limited to $100 or so. You will probably need a cosigner or security to borrow. When your net worth passes the $1,000 mark you become a "four-figure man," due a modest amount of credit. You will still be limited essentially to conventional financing.

After you reach $10,000, your "five-figure net worth" entitles you to deference from the bank's assistant manager. Your credit is much more substantial, stretching beyond the conventional. You will be able to borrow $1,000 or more on your signature alone. This might be sufficient to make a down payment on your first income property, like the A Avenue house.

INTO THE STRATOSPHERE

Over the $100,000 plateau you are a magic six-figure man, eligible to deal with vice-presidents and major branch managers. You may borrow $10,000 or $15,000 on your signature whenever you have a sound need. You find it easy to stretch financing when you want to buy property. You can close deals without putting in much of your own money or property.

Atop the $1,000,000 peak, you are a seven-figure magician, on easy terms with bank presidents. A whole new world of fabulous opportunity opens before you. You may borrow $25,000 to $100,000 on your signature alone. You can buy all the property you want at substantial discounts without throwing in a penny. You are able to finance spectacular buys you previously might have forgone for lack of sufficient credit. You can virtually write your own ticket on how far and how fast you want to go into the multimillion-dollar stratosphere.

DISNEY MEASURED SUCCESS BY DEBTS

The imaginative multimillionaire businessman Walt Disney, when asked if he was making a success of his enterprises, responded, "I must be successful. I owe seven and a half million dollars!"

100 PER CENT FINANCING BY A
SYNDICATE OF FIVE SPECULATORS

I know of one recent real-estate transaction where a syndicate of five speculators bought a $2,500,000 parcel of apartment buildings with 100 per cent borrowing. Each borrowed $10,000 on a six-month commercial note, making a down payment of $50,000. The balance was raised by maximum individual mortgages on each of the twenty-eight pieces of property.

Within two years they resold all the properties and repaid their notes, which had been renewed every six months. They realized a total net profit of close to $1,000,000, earning almost $200,000 each without putting in a cent of their own. The original $10,000 each, of course, was borrowed on each speculator's individual credit, rather than on the property.

A LONE WOLF'S 100-PER-CENT-PLUS FINANCING DEAL

Another transaction involved an investor with a net worth of over $1,000,000. For $160,000 he bought a block of four warehouses with a market value of $250,000. The entire purchase price was financed against the property, and he wound up with $8,000 in-pocket cash. He arranged a $125,000 first mortgage with his bank, gave the seller a $35,000 second mortgage, and gave the broker an $8,000 third mortgage to cover his commission.

The secret of this $90,000-under-the-market purchase was that the seller was on a financial limb through failure to refinance a speculative subdivision. His credit had been shot, so he had been unable to borrow more than $45,000, which now was the outstanding balance on his warehouse properties. He was forced to sell at a loss to a buyer with sound credit.

The $45,000 mortgage was paid off out of the $125,000 new bank loan, leaving cash proceeds of $80,000. Since the broker agreed to take back, from the buyer, a third mortgage for his commission, which was the seller's obligation, the buyer pocketed $8,000 in cash, which he received from the seller. The seller realized $72,000 net cash, enabling him to stave off bankruptcy, re-establish his credit, and start afresh to recoup his losses.

KNOWING HOW TO BORROW IS IMPORTANT

Big real-estate operators with financial know-how do not hesitate to borrow to the hilt on individual transactions. The income from their large holdings cushions against losses, permitting them to handle speculative property where there is no present income, or where there may even be a net loss. Experience enables them to convert such properties into money-makers which can be resold at phenomenal profits. As previously mentioned, skilled improvement of operations may enhance values as much as or more than physical improvements. The larger investors usually expect to make a minimum of 20 per cent net on their commitment of pledged funds.

Lacking a big cushion, the smaller investor hesitates to borrow heavily and is restricted to property that will pay for itself. A loss of income could cause foreclosure. Yet the beginner is most in need of borrowed money in order to get started. For maximum expansion a general knowledge of how to borrow is as important as credit standing. What profit credit if you don't use it? This and the next two chapters will outline accepted mechanics which will help you to finance a pyramiding ownership of real estate.

FIVE GUIDEPOSTS FOR BORROWING MONEY

Principles which will be considered in this chapter include the following:

1. Figure complete financial requirements before you borrow.
2. Borrow the highest repayable amount, with the lowest possible payments.

3. Determine the highest loan potential on the property.
4. Contract to spend money only after finances are firmly committed.
5. Prepare a financial statement.

1. FIGURE COMPLETE FINANCIAL REQUIREMENTS BEFORE YOU BORROW

You may be forced to compromise and handle planned improvements piecemeal, as we did at A Avenue. It is better to plan over-all needs and attempt to finance them in one loan project if possible, matching our stepped-up achievement at B Boulevard. This will speed your progress immeasurably, as will soon be seen again with the refinancing of the Cynthia Court. Often the most desirable financial arrangement proves easier to secure than borrowing in extended little bites. Also, a single loan project facilitates master contracts, as with the Belvedere Apartments, simplifying the supervision of improvements.

Cost of Improvements

Painting is the major requirement at the Cynthia Court. Before we ask for bids, we want to determine how much painting is required, including the planned launderette. We check with three companies furnishing automatic washing machines and dryers on a concession basis. One offers 20 per cent of the gross revenue, one 25 per cent, and the highest 40 per cent. All agree to provide modern equipment and connect necessary gas for the dryer, and water, electricity, and drain lines. Only the 20 per cent company is willing to take care of painting the converted refrigerator room. We select the 40 per cent company and plan to include this painting in our master contract.

An Amazing Spread of Bids

We ask for bids from six contractors, specifying workmanlike patching and two-coat painting throughout all halls and apartments and in the converted laundry room. The highest bid of $12,500 comes from a coast-to-coast advertiser who offers to arrange all necessary financing through an "improvement loan." This is an example of the high premium you might pay for a contractor's securing your financing, on which he often collects a heavy brokerage fee.

The general-contracting firm we employed at B Boulevard bids $9,600. This includes a heavy contingency allowance and a 15 per cent premium for taking the bid and then subcontracting it to a painter. This bid proves that the low bidder on one contract, as at the Belvedere, may be far from low on another project. Such a disparity is especially likely where the contractor is skilled in one craft and makes a bid covering another. In this case the general contractor was a skilled carpenter.

One local paint contractor with a large crew bids $6,000. Another bids $5,200. Both of these contractors and the general contractor are listed in the classified telephone book and in the Metropole *Apartment House Magazine.*

One painter, who works alone except for a single helper, is contacted from his ad in the Metropole *Metropolitan.* He bids $4,800. The lowest and winning bid of $4,200 comes from the painter who did the work at our A Avenue house. Although we were inclined to call on him first, it is always best to secure several competitive bids. Most experienced owners figure on a minimum of three for any major expenditure.

The foregoing illustrates the wide variation that may sometimes develop in bidding, and the importance of not letting contracts without securing several bids. Most bids include overhead and profit allowances which may be heavily padded upward, or shaved downward. The same contractor may figure one job excessively if he is busy and may discount nearly all the padding on the next if he becomes hungry for work.

Beware of Mechanic's Liens

Besides guarding against inferior material and workmanship, the chief shortcoming to watch for is a possible failure on the part of a contractor to pay his bills. A painter might bid $4,200, for example, slap on $2,000 worth of paint, collect in full from the owner, and then skip the country without paying for the material. Some contractors have collected from unsuspecting owners and then gone into bankruptcy before paying material bills. Unpaid bills for paint or any other material applied to a property can be made a lien against the property. The same is true of unpaid labor or subcontractors' bills. The property owner is still liable for such unpaid bills regardless of whether he has paid a middleman such as a general contractor.

This liability can be guarded against in several ways. Where there is any doubt as to reliability, the contractor should not be paid until after one or more of the following precautions have been taken:

1. File notice of completion with the County Recorder. (A typical state law provides that the owner is liable only for claims made within thirty days thereafter.)
2. Require the contractor to post a bond.
3. Require that all material bills be paid for directly by the owner.
4. Pay the contractor only after he shows that his bills are paid.
5. Verify the contractor's reliability with his bank, supply houses, and retail-credit or contractors' association.

Beware of Cost-Plus Gimmicks

The paint contractor making the $6,000 bid says, "I loaded my estimate pretty heavy in order to protect myself from any unforeseen patching and scaling. Probably I could do the work for a lot less if you would let me take over on a cost-plus basis. I would just bill you for the actual cost of labor and material, plus 5 per cent for overhead and 10 per cent for profit. Many of my regular customers have done business with me this way and have been able to save a good deal of money, since I cut out all the padding. With good luck I might even get the job done for as little as $3,000. Wouldn't you like to save money by making such a deal?"

Many contractors love cost-plus contracts, but such arrangements are sucker bait to be wary of. The fact that this contractor's bid is higher than three others shows that he is not a particularly economical worker. Cost-plus contractors often put on their slowest and most inefficient workers to spread out the job. Why not dawdle when the more the cost the more they make? On small repairs, of course, you can instruct a competent mechanic to go ahead without a contract, but on any major project like the painting of the Cynthia Court you should avoid proceeding without a firm, written contract. When you have several bidders, the lowest can usually be depended on to cut corners down to the least possible cost to you.

A Double-Cost-Plusser

One fast-talking general contractor on a modish remodeling job induced an owner to accept a cost-plus deal. Another contractor had bid $15,000. The cost-plusser said he would have to give a bid in that range if firm, but he could probably do the work on a cost-plus basis for around $12,000. The owner agreed to his blandishments and then gave his eight tenants dispossess notices to make way.

The contractor tore the building apart and then went off uranium hunting while he left an unsupervised, makeshift crew of two on the job. The owner found, by the time the contractor returned, that he had been paying the latter's uranium-hunting expenses. When the work was completed the total bill came to $33,000, more than double the firm $15,000 bid from a reputable contractor. In addition the owner lost three months' rent on eight apartments, as the cost-plusser took six months. The other contractor had promised to complete the work in three months.

Other Improvements

New carpet on the main-hall floor comprises the only other major improvement. We discuss with carpet contractors and other owners the replacement possibilities, including wool, cotton, nylon, viscose, and various combinations. We decide on a medium-quality nylon, which has displaced wool as by far the most popular material for new carpets. With identical specifications we obtain three bids.

We previously estimated an allowance of $1,000. The lowest bid of $750 comes from a carpet discount house advertising in the Metropole *Apartment House Magazine*. The second bid is $900 from a selected advertiser in the Metropole *Metropolitan*. The third is for $1,200 from a display advertiser in the telephone book.

Furniture Replacement

The furniture generally is in good condition. There are only minor items which warrant replacement, including a dozen floor lamps, a dozen cocktail tables, and one sofa set. All can be bought for $300 through wholesale suppliers advertising in the *Apartment House Magazine*. The more important factory outlets often advertise in such publications, sometimes giving the apartment owner or builder lower prices than the cost to a neighborhood dealer.

Some owners make a practice of buying secondhand rather than paying retail prices for new furniture. You can buy new, modern furniture direct from factory or distributor for little more than the cost to secondhand retail buyers. Most distributors consider the apartment owner a wholesale customer whose volume buying entitles him to substantial discounts. Besides household furniture and appliances, factory prices can often be obtained on other major cost items such as paint, wallpaper, and electrical and plumbing equipment.

Terms and restrictions vary from time to time. At this writing, for example, General Electric requires a minimum of ten appliances per initial order to qualify for factory prices. The manufacturers of Wedgewood stoves restrict factory sales to initial orders of at least five. GE, Wedgewood, Frigidaire and Kelvinator will sell a single item, such as a refrigerator or a stove, per supplemental order, with the proviso that it must be delivered to an apartment house address.

Refrigerators

Our twenty-four apartments have the 8-cubic-foot refrigerators bought by the previous owner for $4,725. What will new refrigerators cost?

In the *Apartment House Magazine* are ads of Frigidaire, General Electric, Kelvinator, and Westinghouse, all quoting factory prices to Owners Association members. All display an approximately 10-cubic-foot box as the new standard apartment size, replacing former standard 6- to 8-cubic-footers. All sell in the same price range of $127 f.o.b. the local factory warehouse. Optional are a one-year service guarantee charge of $3.50, and delivery and setup charges of $6.00. This makes a total of $136.50, delivered and guaranteed, for a refrigerator that retails at $209.50.

Multiplying $136.50 by 24 gives us a figure of $3,276, which is $974.00 less than the $4,250 outstanding balance on the twenty-four older 8-cubic-foot refrigerators! This is a fair measure of the "bargain" given the previous owner by his countryman.

The Most Favorable Terms

Although varying to some extent, there is not a great deal of difference between one major-name refrigerator and another in regard to cost, appearance, convenience, and serviceability. There is a difference, however, in credit and financing policies. Of the various refrigerator supply houses shopped at this time, all but Kelvinator usually demand cash on delivery or within a maximum of ten days from delivery. Such drastic policies have been caused by poor credit experience with contractor-builders and retail appliance and auto dealers.

Only Kelvinator as a standard practice recognizes the credit ratings of apartment owners as investors distinguished from risk-taking business operators. Kelvinator offers thirty days for payment without financing charges and will arrange financing for as long as five years. Their representative says that they will not only finance their own equipment, but also, where a kitchen is completely equipped by Kelvinator, they will include all new furniture and equipment in an apartment, up to one and a half times the value of Kelvinator purchases. Although in this instance we expect to pay cash from other financing, we select Kelvinator because of its more liberal payment policies. It is well to look to the future in establishing our purchase relationship, in the event that we may later wish to buy on extended credit.

Total Financing

In figuring our complete financial requirements we plan to release the twenty-four old refrigerators to the chattel mortgage holder, and buy twenty-four new ones for $3,276. Adding this to the $300 for furniture makes a new furniture-and-equipment cost of $3,576. The $750 carpet bid and the $4,200 paint bid bring the total projected capital expenditure to $8,526. In addition we obtain a low bid of $325 for modern landscaping to replace the old-fashioned shrubbery in front of the building, making a total financial requirement of $8,851.

When you plan improvement financing, it is desirable to add 10 per cent or so for contingencies. In this case we add $1,000, making a new total of $9,851, which we round out to $10,000. Here we are considering the desirable minimum to seek in negotiating for additional financing. If we become cramped for funds because our goal is cut, our plans will be modified to handle necessities. Some projects, like buying new refrigerators, might be dropped or postponed.

2. BORROW THE HIGHEST REPAYABLE AMOUNT, WITH THE LOWEST POSSIBLE PAYMENTS

Here we have two dovetailing factors to consider, as indicated in the heading: (a) Borrow the most you can, limited to the amount you can pay back, and (b) keep payments as low as possible.

The Highest Repayable Amount

The more money you can borrow, the faster you can pyramid. On each major financing campaign, borrow up to the hilt. You will seldom be able to borrow more than you can repay, but that should be your only limitation to keep resulting payments safely within your net income. While you are getting started, this limit should normally apply to each individual property. As you expand, your borrowing may be circumscribed only by over-all loans and income. For example, you might borrow more on a building in the process of remodeling than its present income would warrant. You would make the payments from other income and expect the property to be self-supporting after development.

Inexperienced investors have a tendency to borrow less than they actually need to cover planned repairs and improvements. They then may be forced to throw in reserve funds, or to complete financing by short-term, high-cost personal loans. Others borrow close to the exact amount required, even when their loan potential is much higher. Both are shortsighted, as the more you borrow at any given time the more you have to work with for further expansion.

As an example, if you should be fortunate enough to borrow an extra $10,000 in refinancing the Cynthia Court, you could use that amount to start another pyramid at the Belvedere level. A factor like this alone, enabling you to work on two pyramids instead of one, might cut in half, from twenty to ten years, your target time to a million dollars.

The Lowest Possible Payments

The lower the payments the more will be left for expenses, emergencies, and in-pocket income. The latter can be built up in a reserve fund until you are ready to commit it for further expansion. Besides the amount of the loan, the payment size is governed by the interest rate and the payoff period.

The Lowest Interest

The lower the interest the smaller the over-all cost of financing, of course. In addition, the lower the interest the larger the portion of each payment which will be credited to principal. This reduces the amount required for each payment.

The Longest Term

The longer the term of the loan, naturally the lower the payments. At 6 per cent interest, the monthly payment on $100,000 for twenty years, for example, would be $43 *less* than on $90,000 for fifteen years, although you would receive $10,000 additional cash. Many cash buyers who dip occasionally into financing strive to pay off their loans as quickly as possible, so that they will owe nothing. I know an accountant who rejected an offered twenty-year loan, taking only ten years to refinance his 4-unit fourplex house.

This would be a fine aspiration if you have reached your financial goal and want to rest on your laurels. But while you are building an estate, take the longest term you can get to pay off your loans. You may expect later to sell or trade a refinanced and developed property anyhow. What matters is to stretch out the payments so that they may be kept low and may leave you with maximum in-pocket income for further investment.

3. DETERMINE THE HIGHEST LOAN POTENTIAL ON THE PROPERTY

To determine the highest loan potential, we go back to our appraisal before buying the Cynthia Court, in which we projected the anticipated gross income and expenses after renovation. This projection gave us a net annual income of $26,559, with a resulting capital valuation of $265,000.

Borrow on the Basis of Improved Income

Here is one precept for maximum borrowing: When you are contemplating improvements and rent increases, borrow on the basis of the improved income, rather than on the past or present income. Prepare a detailed supporting schedule, covering fixed expenses and individual apartment rentals. Such a schedule should be made up similar to the statement used by the salesman, Mr. Mansfield, in selling the Cynthia Court. Instead of PRICE it is advisable to show NEW CAPITAL VALUATION, $265,000. So that there will be no question that the income projection is based on anticipated rather than present rents, always include a heading such as INCOME SCHEDULE AFTER RENOVATION.

Some lenders accept such a schedule without further question. Others will demand a detailed present schedule in addition. The more experience you have, the more such an estimated-income projection will bear weight. With no experience to back you up, such a projection will be examined more fully, but it will still be accepted if it is realistic.

A Percentage Estimate for Borrowing

With maximum primary, or partial secondary, financing, you should be able to borrow approximately two thirds of the new capital valuation. This would give you $176,667. In a tight money market the first-mortgage limit might be about 50 per cent, or $132,500. Any balance needed would have to be financed through other loans, such as a second mortgage or a chattel mortgage.

It should be mentioned that borrowing potentials on refinancing may be higher dollarwise than the potential on purchasing, because of improvements, higher income and resulting higher capital valuation. The borrowing potential percentagewise, however, will normally be less when you are refinancing. When you are buying, owners and brokers will take back subsidiary loans, giving you from 75 to 100 per cent financing in order to consummate a sale.

Examining Present Loans

With the foregoing loan potentials in mind, we should examine the present financing. Should we attempt to extend the present loans, or should we look for entirely new financing through insurance companies, banks, or other mortgage lenders? Maximum financing can usually be arranged through new lenders after improvements are completed and rents fully raised. We will therefore postpone this major pyramiding step if we can obtain sufficient funds from present lenders to pay for improvements.

We plan to drop the refrigerator loan, now reduced to $4,250, and pay for the new refrigerators with long-term financing if possible. The payments on the present refrigerator loan are $200 monthly. The payments on $4,250 would be reduced to a maximum of $56.17 monthly on the poorest long-term loan we would arrange, which would be for ten years at 10 per cent.

We have assumed $105,000 in real-estate mortgages, reduced approximately to a $71,400 first loan and a $33,578 second loan. The first mortgage was originally $82,500, and the second $37,500. If we could raise the first mortgage to the original amount, plus the $10,000 estimated for improvements, we would have a new first mortgage of $92,500 and would pick up $10,600 cash. We will tackle this simplest solution to our financial problem, after reviewing other loan considerations, including the acquiescense of the second-mortgage holder.

4. CONTRACT TO SPEND MONEY ONLY AFTER FINANCES ARE FIRMLY COMMITTED

Regardless of how favorable the financing may look, do not contract to spend money until you have it in hand or firmly committed. Investors who violate this rule and go ahead with substantial projected work because they expect to get necessary financing when needed are inviting bankruptcy. This has happened particularly with subdividers who have contracted large expenditures on the basis of previous easy financing and then run against a tight money market after a project was started. This was no doubt the major cause of the abnormally large number of contractor bankruptcies in 1956 and 1957, for example, involving contractors turned speculators rather than investors.

Even the Astors Could Not Take Financing for Granted

Many experienced builders used to start major construction projects with no committed funds. They were always able to obtain money when it was needed, often arranging for necessary financing after a project was well under way. They experienced little difficulty obtaining additional funds as work progressed. Such on-the-spot progressive financing is now difficult to obtain.

All lenders, like lovers, are allergic to being taken for granted. They are reluctant to commit funds for a major construction project unless they are consulted in the initial planning stages. Some lenders confine their loans to specific areas or neighborhoods. Institutional lenders are apt to have pet stipulations they wish to incorporate in any plans. Some insurance companies, for example, will loan only on apartments with a minimum of two bedrooms. Others will settle for at least one bedroom, ruling out "efficiency" apartments. Some favor furnished units, while others refuse to make loans on furnished apartments. Some insist on conventional bathtubs, while others will accept stall showers.

One builder spent $5,000 for a beautiful set of plans for a building of sixty apartments. The plans had to be considerably altered before he could secure financing, because his best loan source insisted that the bathroom entrance be from the living room rather than the bedroom. On another project the builder was forced by the lender to incorporate a central hallway not contemplated in the original plans.

A spectacular 1957 denouement involved multimillionaire Vincent Astor. With two Columbia Broadcasting System executives, he started a $46,000,000 New York office-building project without firm financing. Millions were invested to buy and tear down old buildings on a choice Park Avenue location. Normally 5 per cent money would have been easy to obtain on this kind of project if a lending agency had been consulted in advance. Astor offered 5½ per cent interest ex post facto, and still found no takers. At year's end he was still seeking financing to proceed with erection, while contemplating a big hole in the ground which was eating up overhead and interest, with no offsetting income.

Astor's chief shortcoming was his failure to secure long-term leases in advance. On constructing a commercial or office building it is now next to impossible to borrow any sizable amount until after a major portion of the space is signed up in advance on long-term leases by established tenants with A-plus credit ratings.

This is a further example of the comparative soundness of apartments from an income standpoint. It is customary to loan on new apartment-house construction with no committed tenants whatever.

Get Your Loan Commitment in Writing

A loan commitment should be considered as a bid to lend money. Like any other contract proposal, it should always be required in writing. Lenders will usually give you a firm written commitment, with a certain time limit, like thirty days. Within that time limit you may seek better financing and may come back to the offered plan if it is still the most favorable.

Often you may receive a preliminary oral commitment. The wisest course is to await written confirmation before burning your bridges behind you. I know of many an oral commitment, even from reputable concerns like banks and insurance companies, that has been reneged entirely or modified before being finalized. This happens when a loan officer approves a loan within the scope of his authority and then a superior or a loan committee makes a change because of a shift in policy or because of unpredictable adverse reactions.

5. PREPARE A FINANCIAL STATEMENT

In addition to the statement of projected income and expense on the Cynthia Court, most lenders would demand a complete financial statement showing your total income, assets, liabilities and resulting net worth. Although all seek the same basic information, each agency, such as a bank, an insurance company, or a building and loan association, uses a different type of form. Usually other lenders, and credit raters such as Dun & Bradstreet, will accept your duplicate bank statement, rather than require the completion of their particular forms.

The proper preparation of a financial statement is one of the most important acts you will perform in seeking credit, and it will exercise a critical effect on the rapidity of your expansion. We will therefore cite the complete form filled out by the Enterprises for their bank and will include appropriate explanations and suggestions. Like many other forms, a financial statement as a whole may first appear somewhat complex. It is easier to digest when studied item by item.

The average financial-statement form, like that shown on pages 395 and 398, is printed on both sides of a sheet of 8½-by-11 paper. The first page usually consists of a general summary, the second of corroborating details. A banker always examines the first page before he turns to the second. However, you cannot complete the first page until after you have prepared the other. The two pages are therefore cited in the order in which you would prepare them, beginning with the second page.

Objective

In preparing a financial statement for the purpose of borrowing money, the objective is to present as optimistic a picture as possible, within reasonable bounds. Comments to follow are intended to show the accounting procedures resulting in the best picture which will be accepted on appraisal.

EXPLANATION OF FINANCIAL STATEMENT, PAGE 2, SCHEDULE 6, REAL ESTATE OWNED

Under this heading all real estate owned on the date of preparing the statement should be included. The Enterprises list their suburban home in addition to their newly acquired Cynthia Court Apartments.

MONTHLY INCOME

The gross scheduled rental on the statement date is shown. Included is the rental value of the manager's apartment.

ESTIMATED PRESENT VALUE

The total present value must first be estimated before breaking it down into LAND and IMPROVEMENTS in the two previous columns. Since you are here valuing only the real estate, the value of personal property, including furniture and equipment, should be deducted and shown on page 1.

In this example the present net of $18,813 multiplied by 10 gives a total income-property valuation of $188,130, which we round to $188,000. From this we deduct our furniture and equipment valua-

Schedule 4 Readily Marketable Securities and Other Investments — **Financial Statement** — Page 2

No. of Shares or Bond Amounts	Description	AMOUNT AT WHICH CARRIED ON THIS STATEMENT	LISTED SECURITIES MARKET VALUE NOW		UNLISTED SECURITIES		
			PRICE	TOTAL	VALUE NOW PRICE	TOTAL	YEARLY DIVIDEND
	TOTAL ON THIS STATEMENT						
	IN WHOSE NAME ARE THESE SECURITIES CARRIED?						

Schedule 5 Life Insurance

INSURED	BENEFICIARY	FACE AMOUNT	CASH VALUE	LOANS
Joseph Enterprise	Wife, Mary	7 000	1 200	
TOTAL		7 000	1 200	

Schedule 6 Real Estate Owned

Parcel No.	LOCATION AND TYPE OF PROPERTY	TITLE IN NAME OF	Monthly Income	VALUATION ON THIS STATEMENT LAND	IMPROVEMENTS	ESTIMATED PRESENT VALUE
1	24 Furnished Apts., 4440 Cynthia Court, Metropole	Joseph & Mary Enterprise	2,119	25 000	151 000	176 000
2	6 Rm Home, 7070 Paradise Rd., Suburbia	"		3 500	14 000	17 500
3						
4						
5						
6						
	TOTAL		2,119	28 500	165 000	193 500
	LESS RESERVE FOR DEPRECIATION				4 000	
	TOTAL ON THIS STATEMENT			28 500	161 000	

Schedule 7 Real Estate Mortgages

ON PARCEL NO., SCHED. 6	TO WHOM PAYABLE	HOW PAYABLE			INT. RATE	MATURITY DATE	AMOUNT
1	Monarch Life Ins. Co.	$ 600	per	month	6%	1978	71 400
2	Citizens National Bank	$ 105	per	"	6	1981	10 638
2 1	Ronald Biggsworth	$ 375	per	"	6	1973	33 578
4		$	per				
5		$	per				
6		$	per				
	TOTAL ON THIS STATEMENT						115 616

FOR BANK USE

This is a copy of an original signed statement in the credit files of this office.

_____ MANAGER

Date _____

JOSEPH ENTERPRISE

November 25, 1966
DATE SIGNED

(Signed) Joseph Enterprise
By

tion of $12,000 to arrive at a real-estate value of $176,000. On the Enterprise home the value shown indicates the present market value, which is $2,000 above cost.

THREE DIFFERENT VALUATIONS

In your accounting there should be three distinct valuations, each valid for a different purpose. It is well to review them in order to choose the proper valuation for a particular purpose.

1. Cost. This represents your actual out-of-pocket cost—the original cost plus all improvement costs, including labor and material. Do not overlook improvements if the lender asks for your cost, as many lenders will. Included should be major sprucing-up costs like painting, even though, for income tax purposes, this may be shown as a repair item.

2. Book Value. The book value will be the valuation on your books for income tax reporting. The book value will reflect the actual cost of capital items, less depreciation. On property held for a length of time the book value may be next to nothing because of depreciation, while the market value may still be substantial. Noncapitalized expenditures, which have been taken as an annual expense, would not be reflected in the book value. An example like painting and decorating might be capitalized under over-all improvements, or it might be shown as an annual expense.

3. Market Value. The valuation which you give to the bank to reflect your net worth should be the fair market value on the statement date. This is the value at which the property could probably be sold within a reasonable time without forced sale. On the apartments the common denominator, 10, multiplied by the annual scheduled net on the statement date would give the normal market value. In some cases the market value might be less than cost, as with the Cynthia Court apartments under the Giacolinis prior to their sale. The same apartments under new ownership show a market value in excess of our cost, even though recently bought. The fact that you have bought property with a definitely scheduled improvement program immediately enhances its value. In addition you take credit for making a shrewd buy.

VALUATION OF LAND

In our original appraisal we estimated the apartment land value at $25,000, which was confirmed by comparable recent sales in the area.

VALUATION OF IMPROVEMENTS

This is arrived at merely by deducting the land values from the total real-estate values in the last column.

RESERVE FOR DEPRECIATION

The depreciation taken for income tax purposes would not necessarily be shown on the financial statement. The figure should be reasonable, like the approximately 2½ per cent figure of $4,000. Depreciation will be added to liabilities on page 1, thereby reducing the net worth. To make the net worth as high as possible and still acceptable, the depreciation should be neither excessive nor unrealistic.

SCHEDULE 7, REAL ESTATE MORTGAGES

Requested information involving all real-estate loans is shown. This excludes any loans not recorded against the property, such as the refrigerator chattel mortgage.

EXPLANATION OF FINANCIAL STATEMENT, PAGE 1

ASSETS

Total assets of $218,527 are arrived at by including CASH, CASH SURRENDER VALUE OF LIFE INSURANCE, REAL ESTATE, and PERSONAL PROPERTY. This figure shows how rapidly an estate can accumulate for an apartment investor who three years previously owned total assets of a home equity and $2,500 in the bank.

Schedule 1, Cash

The cash balance includes savings and commercial accounts, and cash on hand. With an apartment owner the latter is often sizable, including all unbanked rentals collected by managers. In this example $1,083 in net rentals, collected between the November 5 escrow clos-

| Personal Financial Statement | | TO: CITIZENS NATIONAL BANK | Office METROPOLE | Page 1 |

Name ___ JOSEPH ENTERPRISE ___ ☐ Single ☒ Married. Spouse's given name ___ MARY

Address ___ 7070 Paradise Road, Suburbia, Columbia

Employed By ___ Columbia Utilities Co.

Statement of ☐ my or ☒ my and my spouse's Financial Condition on ___ November 25 ___ , 19 66

ASSETS	OMIT CENTS		LIABILITIES	OMIT CENTS	
Cash (Schedule 1)	6	827	Accounts Payable		
Collectible Accounts Due Me			Installment Contracts Payable	4	250
			(Apts. refrigerators loan)		
Good Notes Receivable & Mortgages Owned (Sched. 3)			Notes Payable - Banks (Schedule 2)		
Other Receivables			Notes Payable - Others		
Readily Marketable Securities (Schedule 4)			Income Taxes Payable		
Other Investments (Schedule 4)			Other Taxes Payable	1	053
Cash Surrender Value of Life Insurance (Schedule 5)	1	200	Loans On Life Insurance (Schedule 5)		
Real Estate Owned (Schedule 6)	193	500	Real Estate Mortgages (Schedule 7)	115	616
Other Assets (describe) Personal property:			Other Liabilities (describe)		
Furniture, fixtures & equipment	15	000	Depreciation reserve	4	000
Auto	2	000	TOTAL LIABILITIES	124	919
			NET WORTH (Total Assets less Total Liabilities)	93	608
TOTAL	218	527	TOTAL	218	527

ANNUAL INCOME			PLEASE ANSWER THE FOLLOWING	CONTINGENT LIABILITIES	
Salary	7	200	Have you ever gone through bankruptcy or compromised a debt? ☐ Yes ☒ No	As Endorser	
Dividends				As Guarantor	
Fees or Commissions			If this is a statement of you and your spouse are any assets spouse's separate property? ☐ Yes ☒ No	On Damage Claims	
Rentals Net	18	813		For Taxes	
Other			Are any assets pledged or debts secured except as shown? ☐ Yes ☒ No	Other	
TOTAL	26	013	Have you made a will? ☒ Yes ☐ No	Total (Indicate if none)	NONE

Schedule 1 Cash

SVGS.	COML.	CASH BALANCE ON ABOVE DATE	Where carried (Name of Bank)
☒	☐	3 530	Citizens National Bank
☐	☒	3 197	" " "
☐	☐	100	Cash on hand
☐	☐		
☐	☐		
☐	☐		
		6 827	Total on this statement

Schedule 2 Notes Payable—Banks

AMOUNT OWED ON ABOVE DATE	INT. RATE	METHOD OF BORROWING (UNSECURED, COLLATERAL, GUARANTY, ETC.)

Schedule 3 Notes, Mortgages, and Trust Deeds Owned

NAME OF DEBTOR	TOTAL AMOUNT DUE	MATURITY DATE	HOW PAYABLE	DESCRIPTION OF SECURITY
			$ per	
			$ per	
			$ per	
			$ per	
			$ per	
			$ per	

51-034 (1-66)

Please Complete all Applicable Schedules and Sign on Page 2

ing date and the November 25 statement date, has been banked. The inclusion of negligible amounts such as a householder might have on hand for personal expenses would be optional. Mary Enterprise's personal household account could be included, but it is not shown here.

The $6,827 cash balance reflects the $4,691 in the bank at our November 5 accounting, plus the $1,083 banked November 25, plus the $1,053 tax reserve. Taxes have not yet been paid, but we have mailed the $348.89 insurance check.

Collectible Accounts

This would normally be a major item for a business concern. For an apartment owner rents are usually collected close to the due date, leaving a negligible amount collectible and past-due.

Schedule 6, Real Estate Owned

This is the total ESTIMATED PRESENT VALUE of $193,500 from page 2. Depreciation is not deducted here, as it will be listed on the other side of the page as a liability.

Other Assets

Frequently overlooked in a financial statement are valuations for personal property, including autos and home furniture. To the $12,000 in apartment furniture and equipment we add the $3,000 market valuation on the Enterprises' personal property, excluding autos. The market value of autos, trucks, and trailers should be shown as a separate item.

LIABILITIES

Included under LIABILITIES are all loans, real-estate and otherwise, taxes payable, and the depreciation reserve.

Accounts Payable

The average business would have a significant amount to include under ACCOUNTS PAYABLE, as with ACCOUNTS COLLECTIBLE. Where all accounts are paid when received, or within a maximum of thirty days, the normal practice of the Enterprises, it is not necessary to show this as a liability item.

Installment Contracts Payable

Included here would be all installment loans other than real-estate loans. This would encompass chattel mortgages and personal loans. The chattel mortgage on the refrigerators is the only such item for the Enterprises.

Income Taxes Payable

This should be shown if any sizable amount will shortly be due.

Other Taxes Payable

The December 10 installment of real-estate taxes has not been paid on the statement date.

Schedule 7, Real Estate Mortgages

The $115,616 total for all real-estate loans is taken from page 2.

Other Liabilities

For the Enterprises the only figure under this heading is the DEPRECIATION RESERVE. This item might be large on a property owner's statement and small for many business enterprises.

NET WORTH

As indicated on the statement, the NET WORTH is arrived at simply by deducting total liabilities from total assets. Of the $93,608 total, $6,862 is represented by the Enterprises' equity in their home. Other personal assets shown in cash, life insurance, auto and other personal property total $6,200.

This leaves $80,546 as the portion of net worth which has developed in three years from $2,500 available for initial investment, plus additional savings of $50 monthly.

ANNUAL INCOME

To Joseph Enterprise's $600 monthly salary we add the present scheduled net income from the Cynthia Court. Here it is important, especially for an investor bent on expansion, to show scheduled income on present holdings rather than the income for the preceding twelve months. This shows the income in relation to the listed assets and liabilities. Figuring current income schedules against current mortgage payments and other obligations gives a balanced picture.

The accumulation of capital pyramids on a rising scale, faster and easier at each stage of progress.

A bank does not lend on the basis of need, only on your ability to repay.

Borrowing money is a highly rewarding art at which you can become adept through study and practice.

23. HOW TO REFINANCE YOUR APARTMENTS

In this chapter we will handle the refinancing of conventional real-estate loans on the Cynthia Court Apartments. This involves the existing first and second mortgages and presents three major considerations:

1. How to Make a Successful Loan Request
2. First Mortgages and Deeds of Trust
3. Subsidiary Mortgages

1. How to Make a Successful Loan Request

Like the preparation of a financial statement, the proper presentation of your loan request can have a major influence on borrowing money. Some would-be borrowers with a sound case invite a cold turndown by presenting their requests in such a haphazard manner as to make their business ability questionable. On the other hand, borderline requests may meet with full approval because of a thoughtful, businesslike presentation. Cold figures and physical appraisal of properties will of course be the controlling factors, but presentation will also have an important determining influence.

A loan presentation may often be brief. Its sole purpose is to sell the lender on loaning you money. It should be planned as carefully as any major sales contact. To effectively cover essential points, we will break the contact into proven successful steps, similar to our previously covered steps for renting an apartment:

1. Be prepared.
2. Introduce yourself.
3. Get to the point.
4. Ask for your specific desires.
5. Say goodbye.

BE PREPARED

Before making your contact it is most important to organize a complete picture of your improvement and financial plans. All papers should be in order and typed for legibility and a businesslike appearance. In this case you have prepared:

List of planned improvements, including contract and unforeseen-contingency costs increased to a healthy $12,500
Financial requirements and amount to be requested, $95,000
Projected and present income-and-expense statements on the Cynthia Court
Financial statement, showing obligations and ability to repay

Where is the best place to apply for a loan? In this case we have determined first to contact the insurance company that has the present loan on the property. We are seeking the longest possible term, a feature normally best obtained from an insurance company. Second in line for maximum financing would usually be a building or savings and loan organization, third a bank, and fourth a private lender.

INTRODUCE YOURSELF

We telephone the local office of the present first-mortgage holder, the Monarch Life Insurance Company. We ask for the name of the loan supervisor, and we are given the name of Riverbanks.

Make an appointment

We ask to speak to Mr. Riverbanks and give him our name and the address of the Cynthia Court Apartments. We say we would like to arrange for a larger loan to pay for needed improvements. We have our cost and income figures all ready. Would tomorrow be satisfactory for an appointment to discuss the matter more fully?

Mr. Riverbanks is noncommittal, agrees to an appointment the next morning.

Always try to find out the responsible person to contact, then make an appointment if possible. After you reach the proper party, get to the point as rapidly and clearly as possible. Nothing exasperates a busy loan representative, or any other businessman for that matter, more than an applicant who hems and haws before stating his business.

In person

Calling in person after an appointment insures that you will be given ample time to present your case. Give thought to personal appearance. It is not necessary to be overconservative, but it is essential not to be loud or garish in dress, appearance or conversation. The man who can turn down or approve your loan is not the proper one to whom you should show off your Bermuda shorts or Hawaiian sport shirt.

If you should call unannounced, state your purpose immediately after introduction. Don't weaken your contact by lame clichés like "I was in the neighborhood and thought I would drop in and see you."

A sad example

I actually heard that identical phrase used at an adjoining desk, while I was applying at my bank for $15,000 to pay for apartment improvements. The speaker was a stocky man of thirty asking for a $1,000 personal loan with which to start a health studio. His loan officer asked many searching questions, quickly developing the obvious information that the applicant knew nothing about the business he proposed starting.

The applicant's chief qualifications as presented were that his father belonged to the same Masonic Lodge as the loan officer, that he and the officer had played football at the same state university, and that he was completing his fifth year of business experience, working as a used-car salesman.

When I left the bank with my requested five-figure check, the loan officer was still courteously explaining some of the reasons why he could not lend the would-be health studio operator a single dollar.

Be confident

An attitude of confidence may have as important a result as your figures. A calm, confident approach often wins favor even in borderline applications. In reverse, giving a first impression of hesitant uncertainty or jittery desperation may start a chain of negative responses that will lead to ultimate rejection.

A lender wants to loan money

The youthful swain may hesitate to declare himself to his beloved because he is wary of rejection. Not until he has been married for some time does he realize that the object of his love may be as anxious as he.

So it is with borrowing money. The beginning investor may hesitate to ask for a substantial loan for fear of rejection. But the banker loses money on idle funds, and he is as anxious to put his money to work as the borrower is to use it. You have only to convince the lender that your purpose is sound and that you will be able to repay without raising the red flag of delinquency.

GET TO THE POINT

Your lender wants to know what the money is wanted for and whether you will repay it. Stress the soundness of your request from the standpoint of increasing or solidifying your income and, therefore, your ability to repay the loan. Since you must build up your ability to repay, never mention need, regardless of how direly you want the money. If your lender senses you are aquiver with anxiety, he may fear your stability and refuse your loan.

Dramatize the specific improvements you have in mind, not only the physical but also the operational improvements. The latter will impress the lender that you know your business and can be expected to develop the property to the utmost. When seeking a loan increase from an existing lender, point out the extent of the property's deterioration, which might have produced a money-loser on which they would be forced to foreclose except for your taking over. Any lender naturally caters to a borrower who will transform a distress property into a valuable money-maker.

Be frank in answering questions. If you don't know the answer, say so, and offer to get the requested information.

ASK FOR YOUR SPECIFIC DESIRES

After you have presented your case, come to the point about your loan desires. Ask specifically for the loan you have in mind, or for somewhat better terms if you think your request is apt to be modified. In this contact you ask for a $95,000 loan, at 6 per cent interest, for twenty years. Mr. Riverbanks had indicated during the discussion that his company was making some 7 and some 7½ per cent loans for ten-to twenty-year periods. We ask for 6 per cent, the present interest, hoping this will continue. We ask for a twenty-year term, in hopes this will induce approval of at least fifteen years, as at present.

Mr. Riverbanks appears receptive and asks for copies of the improvement contracts, which we give him. He says he will make an up-to-date appraisal of the property and take some snapshots of the building and the surrounding neighborhood. His company probably will not grant the full amount requested. In fact he is not too optimistic about their exceeding the previous loan limit of $82,500. They may hold the term to fifteen years, and they will probably settle for 7 per cent interest. He is in sympathy with our request, however. If his appraisals bear out his present feelings, he will present our proposal to his company as submitted.

Mr. Riverbanks gives us a Monarch loan application and a financial-statement form to fill out. He says his company requires completion of their special form and will not accept our bank statement, even though the information desired is almost identical.

SAY GOODBYE

Once an agreement has been reached, say goodbye and exit as rapidly and gracefully as you can. This is no time to be gabby. A tangential conversation may drop a tidbit of information that arouses the lender's natural conservatism. He may then lower his already committed sights. As in any effective sales contact, once you have made your point, put on your hat and get out!

2. FIRST MORTGAGES AND DEEDS OF TRUST

While waiting for Mr. Riverbanks to obtain his company's response to our loan application, we can examine some of the aspects of real estate first mortgages.

The type of loan on which you can always get the best terms, the lowest payment and interest and the longest period, is the first mortgage, or deed of trust. The term *first mortgage* designates the loan which is first recorded against a particular piece of property. Otherwise, first priority can be obtained only by agreement, commonly called *subordination,* a term to be explained later under "Subsidiary Mortgages."

Whenever there is a possibility of financing through a first mortgage, that should be the first avenue to explore, whether you are seeking funds for improvements or for other purposes. To finance improvements, many investors automatically look to subsidiary loans, which cost them higher interest and payments. Make it a precept to try securing the most favorable terms through a new first mortgage, as with our application to refinance the Cynthia Court.

DEEDS OF TRUST

Many state laws favor the deed of trust over the mortgage form of loan. Either may be used on a first loan or on subsidiary loans. A deed of trust is designed to give greater control, in most cases, to the lender. A typical state law permits consummating a deed-of-trust foreclosure in three months, whereas a year is allowed after foreclosure action to redeem a mortgage. Trust deeds are often commonly referred to as mortgages, both being recorded loans against real estate. We will speak of mortgages throughout, although a deed of trust might be the loan form required by a lender in a given state.

INTEREST RATES

On new first mortgages for apartment houses between 1966 and 1968 the usual interest rates ran between 6 and 7½ per cent, with 7 per cent becoming increasingly common. On loans advanced by building and loan associations for new construction, the prevailing interest rate has been increased to 7 per cent, with 7½ per cent being not uncommon.

CONSTRUCTION AND TAKE-OUT LOANS

A combination of *construction* and *take-out* loans is often used to handle new construction. Where the Monarch Life Insurance Company is able to consider an additional loan based on improvements, they cannot legally advance the money to pay for the work. They can give a written commitment to make a loan when an improvement or major construction project is completed according to their approved specifications. This is called a take-out loan.

Advance funds, called a construction loan, would have to come from other sources. Banks and building and loan associations are usually willing to make construction loans where there is a firm take-out commitment. The advantage of using both loans is that the bank normally would not advance as much money unless backed up by a take-out loan and would not give as favorable rates or terms as the ultimate lender.

AN EXAMPLE OF CONSTRUCTION FINANCING

A builder of eighteen new apartments needed $100,000 to complete financing. An Eastern insurance company offered the full required amount at 6 per cent for twenty years, making the payments only $716.50 monthly. The builder's bank, on the other hand, was willing to lend only $70,000 at 7 per cent for ten years, making the payments $812.80 monthly for $30,000 less funds. The balance of the required money would have had to be raised on even more costly subsidiary financing.

A building and loan association on the same new construction offered $85,000 at 7½ per cent for fifteen years, making their monthly payments $788. The bank commitment was $30,000 short, and the building and loan association $15,000 short. Yet their payments would have been higher than on the insurance company loan for the full $100,000. It is no wonder that the double loan arrangement is a common practice in new construction.

Being for a short time, averaging between six and twelve months, construction loans usually involve a bonus payment of 1 to 10 points, 1 point representing 1 per cent. In the above example the building and loan association demanded a 5-point and the bank a 2-point bonus. Although willing to lend only $70,000 on a regular loan, the bank advanced the $80,000 needed to complete construction, charging 7 per cent interest plus a 2-point bonus. The insurance company deposited a letter of commitment in escrow, making their $100,000 available after completion of construction and the expiration of a thirty-day mechanic's lien period. The $80,000 bank loan was then paid off. The balance of $20,000 went to the builder for his profit and to pay final bills and accumulated interest and escrow charges.

MR. RIVERBANKS MAKES SOME STIPULATIONS

December 5, ten days after our loan application. Mr. Riverbanks receives the decision of the Monarch Insurance Company's loan committee. Here are the terms offered:

1. Total loan to be $92,000, instead of the $95,000 requested.
2. The amount of $82,500 to be advanced immediately after satisfactory title search.
3. Balance of $9,500 to be advanced thirty-five days after completion of projected improvements. This additional loan amount to be canceled if the improvements are not completed within ninety days.
4. Interest to be 7½ per cent.
5. Period to be seventeen years, making monthly payments $772.50.
6. Penalty of 5 per cent of unpaid balance if paid off within two years, and 2 per cent of unpaid balance if paid off thereafter.
7. Appraisal fee of .2 of 1point, $184.
8. December 10 tax installment to be paid before closing.

We are most happy with the loan granted, as all the terms are customary for the time of application. The required improvements can be paid for from the $82,500. The $9,500 additional loan can be used to start a new pyramid, or, if necessary, to partially pay off the second-mortgage holder.

EXPEDITING THE CLOSE OF ESCROW

The insurance company already possessed a title report and appraisal from the closing of the escrow November 5, when their loan was transferred from the Giacolinis to the Enterprises. At the time of our new loan application, the title company was advised to prepare a new title search. A new preliminary report was sent to the Monarch Insurance Company's office, with copies to Mr. Riverbanks and to us. The title company was thus ready to close with little delay, rather than wait for the usual two or three weeks after receiving a loan commitment.

As soon as we settle with the second-mortgage holder, the new loan arrangement can be consummated. Within another week all new papers, including new notes and deeds of trust, can be signed, notarized, and recorded. The title company proceeds should be ready for distribution December 15. Even though all commitments are firm, however, we wait until the transaction is closed in the title company before letting any contract.

WAIT FOR CLOSING BEFORE SPENDING

It is unwise to jump the gun in starting improvements, as many things can happen to delay a closing. I know of one instance where a contractor secured a $90,000 bank commitment to build a 12-unit apartment house and started construction before the escrow was closed and the mortgage recorded. The bank loan supervisor drove by the site and saw the foundation work in progress. He knew the mortgage was still being processed, so he instructed the title company to hold up the loan.

Even though this was the contractor's first investment venture, he should have known that any institutional lender would take this step. The usual loan application provides that all liens shall be satisfied before any money can be advanced. As soon as any labor or material is used on a construction project, an automatic cause for mechanic's lien exists. For this reason, banks, insurance companies, and other lenders insist that no work shall start until their mortgage is recorded.

In this instance the contractor had insufficient assets and insufficient credit to raise funds to pay for the work already started. He had lost money building a block of eight houses, as he had bid too low to offset his rising costs for labor and material. His personal credit was already stretched to the limit and he was hoping to recoup his losses by building his own apartment house. Against this blind credit alley, the bank could not advance a dollar toward their loan commitment until the started work was paid for and the mechanic's-lien period had expired.

This one miscue was the deciding factor which forced the contractor into bankruptcy. Here was another example to show that a new investor should be especially chary of new construction until he gains experience in already built apartments with proved income.

WHAT IF LOAN APPLICATION WERE UNSUCCESSFUL?

Before proceeding further, we should explore the next logical steps in case our loan application were unsuccessful or so drastically cut as to prove unsatisfactory. In a borderline case, for example if the total granted were $77,500, helping but not solving our problem, we might hold the loan in abeyance pending further exploration. Usually thirty days would be allowed in which to accept.

If the loan response were completely unacceptable, we should contact:

1. Other insurance companies. Term commonly fifteen to twenty years; 1968 interest rates 6½ to 7½ per cent. Maximum apartment house loan 70 per cent, as with New Jersey–chartered Prudential. Some companies, for example Equitable in New York, have a maximum of 66⅔ per cent.
2. Building and loan or savings and loan associations. Term commonly ten to twenty years; 1968 interest rates 7 to 7¾ per cent. Maximum apartment loans vary with different institutions between 66⅔ and 90 per cent.
3. Commercial and savings banks. Term commonly ten to twenty years; 1968 interest rates commonly 6½ to 7¾ per cent. Maximum loans in practice vary from 50 to 66⅔ per cent.
4. Loan brokers. May handle loans for any of the foregoing, or may handle private loans, which might be highly flexible.

In favorable circumstances the term of a loan may run longer than those shown above. For example, some building-and-loan associations grant loans for twenty-five to thirty years on new apartments. The terms indicated, however, are usual for 1968.

LOAN BROKERS

Failing to obtain satisfactory results from any of the first three sources, we should next turn to loan brokers. They handle increasingly larger percentages of mortgages, especially when there are considerable construction funds in demand in a tight money market. Often they have access to large pools of money which you could not otherwise tap. Banks and some other lenders, like Prudential Life, usually handle their own loans. But many large financial institutions, for example Aetna Life and Massachusetts Life, designate certain loan brokers as their principal agents, or correspondents. This has proved more productive at less cost, in many instances, than maintaining expensive branch loan offices.

Besides being the sole representative of certain companies, the average successful loan broker keeps abreast of the fluctuating policies of other regular lending agencies. Often the loan broker has many money sources up his sleeve, including:

Private pension and trust funds
Union pension funds
Other trust funds
Corporation surplus funds
Individual loan funds
Syndicate mortage funds

One loan broker I contacted revealed that his portfolio included the following available mortgage money:

$40,000,000 from one insurance company
$3,000,000 from an individual who had sold a large supermarket
$250,000 from a syndicate of ten doctors and lawyers
$150,000 from a retired farmer who had recently sold his last farm

LOAN FEES

This broker charged a flat 1 per cent for his services in bringing a lender and a borrower together. He was not interested in financing which involved less than $50,000. Another broker, who handles only large union pension funds, will not consider a loan of less than $250,-000. His fee is also 1 per cent. The fees of most legitimate brokers handling larger loans will usually be in a reasonable 1 to 2 per cent range, in which case they are worthy of hire. There may be no loan fee where a regular correspondent is paid by his company.

It is always good business to learn in advance the cost of loan brokerage. Some fringe brokers charge exorbitant fees, compounding hardship when they know a borrower is desperate for money. Some brokers ask for large advance fees. They should not be paid more than nominal appraisal or "stand-by" fees except from actually secured loan proceeds. Some legitimate loan brokers ask for a 1 per cent stand-by fee, for example, as a guarantee that you will take the loan if granted as applied for. Otherwise this fee is returned.

LOAN BONUSES

From more unorthodox moneylenders, like the syndicate and the two individuals in the portfolio just mentioned, you often will be required to pay a bonus in addition to the loan fee. The broker retains the fee, and the lender gets the bonus. On first mortgages this bonus will usually be nominal, seldom going over the 5 per cent asked by the previously mentioned building and loan association on a construction loan.

The $3,000,000 supermarket seller asked no bonus, but he would lend only first mortgages on first-class apartment or commercial property. His loans were restricted to 60 per cent of current market value, at 6 per cent for fifteen years. The syndicate of professional men asked a 5 per cent bonus, the retired farmer a 2 per cent bonus. Both funds were available only for first mortgages, which could go as high as 75 per cent of current market values, at 7½ per cent for not over fifteen years, with ten to twelve years receiving preference.

3. SUBSIDIARY MORTGAGES

Except from a seller, or a realtor handling a sale, second and other subsidiary mortgages can usually be obtained only through a loan broker. Fees and bonuses on secondary loans are often extremely high. In one state where the maximum legal interest rate is 10 per cent, I know of a borrower paying $10,000 in costs for a $10,000 loan. He gave a $20,000 second mortgage, due in five years and at 10 per cent interest, in exchange for the $10,000 he needed to complete financing of a 12-unit apartment building already started. The lender put up $12,000, receiving a 66⅔ per cent bonus of $8,000. The loan broker received a 20 per cent cash fee of $2,000.

THERE MAY BE ANY NUMBER OF MORTGAGES

Commonly called secondary financing, there may be third, fourth, or any number of subsidiary mortgages. Their priority depends on the order of recording unless there is an agreement to the contrary. If many mortgages in one escrow are recorded on the same date, they would be recorded in the order previously agreed on. We already have a second mortgage from the original owner of the Cynthia Court. There are no other real-estate mortgages. It would have been perfectly feasible, however, for the selling Giacolinis to have taken back a third mortgage, and for the realtor to have taken a fourth mortgage in lieu of a cash commission. Both the seller and the realtor took back subsidiary mortgages, you may recall, when we traded our A Avenue house for the Belvedere.

WHAT OF FORECLOSURE?

It is a common misconception that a subsidiary mortgage holder is forced to pay off the mortgages ahead of him in order to foreclose. The holder of a second mortgage, for example, would have to pay off the first mortgage. This is not true under ordinary circumstances. Usually the second-mortgage holder can foreclose and merely assume the payments on the first mortgage, rather than have to pay it off.

RECORDED IMPROVEMENT LOANS

FHA Title I improvement loans are as a rule not recorded, since the government insures them against loss. This type of loan will be covered more fully under "Unsecured Loans" in the next chapter. Improvement loans are mentioned here because they may be recorded as an additional protection for the lender. This is more apt to happen if the amount is in the 1968 maximum range of $15,000. If recorded, the improvement loan becomes in effect a subsidiary mortgage.

OPEN-END LOANS FAVOR IMPROVERS

The open-end loan is coming into wider usage by major lenders like the New York Life Insurance Company. Under this type of loan the borrower may obtain up to the amount he has amortized, without a new recording. The monthly payments and the interest rate would remain the same, the life of the loan merely being extended. In the case of the Cynthia Court open-end loan, the Monarch Life Insurance Company could advance the $11,100 difference between the original $82,500 and the present balance of $71,400.

Open-end loans are especially favorable for improvers, as open-end funds are ordinarily advanced for repairs and modernization, such as planned at the Cynthia Court. The Mortgage Bankers Association estimates that open-end loan volume jumped, for example, in the ten years between 1948 and 1958 from a hundred million to approximately one billion dollars, and this trend continues to expand.

SUBORDINATING THE EXISTING SECOND MORTGAGE

If our refinancing were not in excess of the original amount and a new recording were not necessary, the existing second mortgage would not be affected. The new $92,000 loan will have to be recorded, however, automatically moving the present second mortgage into the position of a first mortgage. The $92,000 mortgage would drop to second position, a contingency which the insurance company would not sanction. A *subordination agreement* has to be obtained from the second-mortgage holder, agreeing to leave his loan in a subordinate position.

Subordination agreements are most common where vacant lots are purchased. For example, a $50,000 lot was bought by a builder who paid $10,000 down. The seller took back a $40,000 first mortgage which contained an agreement to subordinate to a construction loan. The builder obtained a $200,000 insurance company loan, financing on a 100 per cent basis his cost for twenty-four apartments. The lot loan dropped to a second mortgage by virtue of the subordination agreement. This device enabled the builder to secure total financing of $240,000 with his initial investment of $10,000. Within a year he resold for $325,000, netting a $65,000 capital gain after paying sales costs.

Not being already committed by a subordination agreement, as in the foregoing example, the second-mortgage holder of the Cynthia Court, Mr. Biggsworth, may not consent to an increased first mortgage without inducement. Among the possibilities we consider before contacting Mr. Biggsworth are the following:

1. Most optimistically, he may subordinate to a $92,000 loan with no other inducement than the increased soundness of his loan because of the planned improvements.

2. The most pessimistic possibility is that he may not consent to subordinate under any circumstances, demanding that we pay him off in full if we wish to place a new loan. In this event we might have to hold the first-mortgage increase to the open-end limit of $82,500, or else seek a new first or second mortgage.

3. He is most likely to agree to subordinate if he receives concessions like:

Higher interest
Larger payments
Reduction of the principal by a cash payment
A bonus penalty added to the outstanding loan

WE CONTACT THE SECOND-MORTGAGE HOLDER

We plan our contact to conclude a new loan arrangement with Mr. Biggsworth as carefully as we planned the interview with Mr. Riverbanks regarding the first mortgage. We have plans ready to show how the Cynthia Court will be improved, so we can point out how this will increase the value of the property and thereby enhance the soundness of the second mortgage. The new first mortgage will be increased only $9,500 over the original amount. We will be spending more than this on the property, plus improving operations. In addition, Mr. Biggsworth's loan is paid down close to $4,000 below its original $37,500 amount when the $82,500 mortgage was in effect.

Mr. Biggsworth proves to be a retired man of about seventy. He mentions that he owns mortgages on several other properties which he has sold. He is in no need of cash and is primarily interested in making all he can on his money. "I like your plans and would like to go along with you. If I agree to subordinate I ought to receive a little more interest on my money, or some kind of bonus. Ordinarily I would want at least 8 per cent on a new second mortgage, plus a 5 per cent bonus. Also on new seconds I'm making the term only five years and am including an acceleration clause.

"I don't want to be unreasonable with you, since I'd like to encourage you to build up the property. In this case I'm not advancing any new money, so I'll do you a special favor. I'll settle for 7 per cent interest, plus a 1 per cent bonus, which will cost you only about $350. You don't have to put out any money, as this can be added to the loan. The monthly payments can be left at $375. However, I want a five-year due date on the note, with an acceleration clause."

BEWARE THE ACCELERATION CLAUSE

Many sharp lenders insist on an *acceleration clause,* so called because it accelerates the due date to any date there is a change in ownership or in loan arrangements. In case of sale the loan would become immediately due, thus protecting the lender from having the property fall into the hands of an unscrupulous bleeder. If the lender disliked a prospective buyer's looks, he could refuse to continue the loan.

Acceleration-minded lenders also expect to pick up extra bonuses. Whenever a loan is renewed an additional bonus payment can be demanded. Since the acceleration clause puts the lender rather than the owner in the driver's seat, it may often prevent the owner from making a profitable resale.

BEWARE THE SHORT-TERM NOTE

Short-term notes, running from one to seven years, are frequently used on subsidiary mortgages. They result in either high monthly payments or a final balloon payment. In case of reversal the property might not readily be refinanced when the note becomes due. The mortgage holder could demand a high bonus, with the alternative of foreclosure. This harks back to the loan practices of the depression years, when pay-out loans were not common, as they are now.

The acceleration clause and the short-term note are an additional protection to the lender. The wary investor should shun both for other than small loans, unless absolutely unavoidable in order to consummate an otherwise desirable deal.

BARGAINING ON TERMS

Whereas an institution may observe fixed loan policies, many private lenders are apt to deviate considerably. We point out to Mr. Biggsworth that we prefer to secure $92,000 in order to handle the plans we have in mind. Rather than pay both a bonus and increased interest, we could forgo improvements entirely, or else take insurance-company open-end mortgage funds only up to $82,500. After all, this involves merely a change in Mr. Biggsworth's loan, and it is not the same as his advancing new funds.

However, we have other investments in mind on which we could use additional cash. Perhaps he would be receptive to increasing the loan back to the original $37,500? In that event we would feel warranted in paying a 1 per cent bonus on the entire amount.

After some discussion, Mr. Biggsworth agrees to subordinate his second to a new $92,000 first mortgage on the following terms:

1. He will advance $3,922 in cash to bring the outstanding $33,578 loan back up to $37,500.

2. We will pay a 1 per cent bonus, $336, on the outstanding loan, and approximately 2 per cent, $80, for the new money.

3. The total bonus of $416, rather than being discounted, will be added to the $37,500. This will increase the new loan to $37,916.

4. The payments, including interest, will be $400 monthly or more

until paid, rather than having the note due in five years. The "or more" clause permits payoff, for example to refinance, without penalty.

5. Interest will increase from 6 to 7 per cent.
6. There will be no acceleration clause.

SKIPPING A PAYMENT

The last payments on both the first and second mortgages were made November 1. No payments were necessary during the customary grace period between December 1 and December 15 while the loans are in escrow. Since the old loans will be paid off with new mortgages, we have a customary forty-five-day period in which to start new payments. We select January 5 for the second-mortgage payment, and January 15 for the first, thus skipping December payments entirely. The interest that normally would have been paid in December will be added to our loan accounts.

Skipping payments for one month credits $975 to our cash account. This gives us $407 net cash after offsetting the $568 total out-of-pocket escrow and loan fee costs. Such an opportunity to increase cash funds is often overlooked, although it is nearly always available when one is renewing or replacing a loan. It should be kept in mind when making a loan application or giving escrow instructions, at the time you select your payment date.

$14,000 CASH FOR FURTHER INVESTMENT

The new second-mortgage agreement with Mr. Biggsworth gives us close to $4,000 cash to use for expansion beyond our plans at the Cynthia Court. We have already arranged for a new first mortgage which will pay for planned improvements and give us an additional $9,500 or so in cash. Refinancing these two loans, including the $407 netted from skipping payments, gives us approximately $14,000 in cash which we can use for further investment pyramiding.

The securing of additional funds from both the first- and second-mortgage holders is a fortunate, but not too unusual, circumstance. The results emphasize the advisability of emulating Oliver Twist, whenever you renegotiate loans, and always asking for more.

The effective presentation of your loan requests can have a major influence on your ability to borrow money.

You have only to convince lenders that your operations are sound and that you will repay, and you will find them as anxious to make loans as you are to borrow.

24. MORE WAYS TO BORROW MONEY

As there are "more things in heaven and earth than are dreamt of in your philosophy," so it is with borrowing money. There are more ways to borrow than the average investor has ever dreamed of.

In the previous two chapters we have covered conventional mortgages. It would take several volumes to describe all the various ways to borrow, particularly if we wished to explore fully the fields of consumer credit, and of small business, government, and corporation finance. We will confine ourselves to major additional ways to borrow which you may find helpful to know, as an investor primarily in real estate.

$44,000,000,000 A YEAR AVAILABLE

Your major borrowing will be in mortgage loans secured by real estate, enabling you to share in the biggest available money source. According to a study by the Federal Home Loan Bank Board, $22 billion in new real-estate-mortgage money was expected to be available, for example, in 1968 alone, and recaptured funds would double the total available to over $44 billion. Mortgages already outstanding in January 1968 totaled $369 billion.

Although they are of secondary importance, you will normally have occasion also to utilize unsecured and chattel loans to some extent, as with the refrigerator chattel mortgage when we took over the Cynthia Court Apartments. We will therefore separate our additional loan information into two major divisions:

Real-Estate Loan Considerations
Loans Not Secured by Real Estate

REAL-ESTATE LOAN CONSIDERATIONS

In the previous chapter we covered (1) first mortgages and deeds of trust, and (2) subsidiary mortgages. Our discussion has involved for the most part conventional and commonly known real-estate financing. Now it is timely to review more advanced aspects of real-estate financing:

1. Blanket mortgages
2. Hypothecated mortgages
3. Assigned mortgages
4. Transferred mortgages
5. Contracts of sale
6. Purchase-and-lease-back transactions

1. BLANKET MORTGAGES

A loan covering more than one piece of property is commonly called a *blanket mortgage*. This is a device to extend credit beyond the ordinary limits obtainable from financing properties individually. By having such properties under one loan, the lender spreads his risk, which justifies heavier financing. Blanket mortgages may be primary or subsidiary, or a combination of both. The same mortgage might be first on some properties, and subsidiary on others.

In one of Roger Stevens' exploits, individual first mortgages were obtained on twenty-seven buildings, which were purchased from several syndicates in one transaction. Four million dollars additional was needed to complete financing. Two and a half million dollars was borrowed from J. P. Morgan sources on a blanket second mortgage. The balance of one and a half million was raised from a blanket third mortgage advanced by a loan association which Stevens controlled.

More common is the application of a blanket first mortgage. Where several properties are bought in one transaction, all may often be financed under one first mortgage. For example, on a purchase of five warehouses leased to one corporation, all five properties were financed by a single bank loan, secured by a blanket first mortgage.

Blanket mortgages are often used on subdivisions. A subdivider may blanket a block of lots under one mortgage, or several houses may be built under a blanket construction loan. What happens when it is desired to sell an individual property covered by a blanket loan?

Release Clause

In the latter case a release agreement must be obtained. With subdivisions a *release clause* is normally included as part of the loan terms, providing that a piece of property may be released from the blanket mortgage upon a stipulated payment. If there is no release clause, then negotiations to satisfy the lender would be necessary.

2. HYPOTHECATED MORTGAGES

Hypothecating a mortgage is a loan device which puts up a mortgage rather than property as security. Sometimes there may be considerable advantage from the standpoint of:

Tax savings where a gain is involved
Retaining rather than selling a desirable mortgage

Tax Savings Where a Gain Is Involved

Tax angles will be discussed more fully in the next three chapters. The point to bear in mind when considering financing is that a transferred loan constitutes about the same as cash to the seller in figuring current income taxes. If you raise cash by mortgaging a property and then transfer the mortgage to a buyer, the cash so raised is included in computing your tax liability for the current year. If you raise cash by taking back a mortgage from the buyer and hypothecating this mortgage to your bank, your taxable gain can be spread over the life of the loan.

In one example of this type a retired couple took back a $120,000, fifteen-year, 7½ per cent first mortgage on a profitable apartment-house sale. They then signed a hypothecation form whereby their bank took the mortgage as security for a $90,000 cash loan at 6½ per cent for fifteen years. The bank was authorized to make the collections and credit the excess to the seller's account. In hypothecating, the mortgage remained in the seller's name. He was still responsible to the bank for his payments, and for collection from the buyer, in case of the latter's default.

Retaining Rather than Selling a Desirable Mortgage

In another case, where no tax advantage was involved, a farmer sold a desirable dairy and took back a $70,000 first mortgage, due in five years, and with interest at 8 per cent. He wanted to raise $25,000 in cash. He could have refinanced in order to obtain this amount or more, as the acreage involved was in the path of subdivision. However, he wished to keep the 8 per cent interest earnings. He thus retained control by hypothecation, putting up his mortgage as security for a $25,000 bank loan at 6½ per cent.

3. ASSIGNED MORTGAGES

Mortgages may be sold by assigning all right and control. Outright sale should be avoided, in favor of hypothecation, where the mortgage has been taken back on property sold at a profit. Any taxable gain deferred by the mortgage would become due upon its sale.

Where no tax angle is involved, mortgages are assigned freely to effect a sale. Assignment may be utilized to save escrow charges. In a typical case without tax implications, a bank put up an $80,000 construction loan to build a church. At the end of construction the loan was taken over by a national church-building society at face value. Rather than require a new mortgage, the building society accepted the bank's assigned mortgage. Thus the church saved the customary title and escrow charges which would otherwise have been involved in refinancing.

4. TRANSFERRED MORTGAGES

An assigned mortgage changes the mortgage holder but retains the same borrower. A *transferred mortgage,* on the other hand, changes the borrower and retains the holder. A property with an existing mortgage is usually sold, as with our taking over the Belvedere and Cynthia Court apartments, subject to the buyer's assuming the outstanding loan obligation. In most cases assuming a loan is synonymous with transferring a loan, but not always. When a loan is transferred, the former borrower is relieved of any further responsibility.

Deed May Transfer and Seller May Still Be Held Responsible for Loan

The deed may change hands and the buyer may contract to assume existing loans. Yet the seller may still be held responsible unless he has been released by the lender. A modified type of acceleration clause might enable the lender to hold both seller and buyer responsible if he so demands.

Transfer of the mortgage might be considered a routine matter and be overlooked by the seller, who might think he has been released while all the time he is still held jointly responsible. I know of cases where responsible title companies have neglected making such transfer arrangements. Usually such an omission would be rectified when discovered. In some states the seller of property subject to a purchase money mortgage cannot be held personally responsible. But if the transaction is completed, the lender in some cases may continue to hold the seller responsible for payment in the event that the buyer defaults. It behooves the seller to keep in mind on every sale the transfer of any obligations which the buyer contracts to assume.

5. CONTRACTS OF SALE (often called "LAND CONTRACTS")

When it is desirable to sell property without transferring deed or loans, a *contract of sale* may be consummated, and the deed held by the seller. Possession of the property, but not the deed, may be delivered to the buyer. This form of real-estate transaction is commonly used for two chief purposes:

To avoid disturbing existing loans
To offset the buyer's lack of money or credit

To Avoid Disturbing Existing Loans

In the case of the five warehouses mentioned under "Blanket Mortgages," the tenant offered to pay a bonus to release one warehouse, which was no longer needed, from his lease. The owner found a prospect who preferred buying to leasing and was willing to pay a good profit to take over this one building. There was no release clause, and the bank refused to release the property from the blanket mortgage. The owner had to pay off the loan and refinance the other four buildings, or keep the existing blanket mortgage and sell the one building on a contract of sale. Loans with some acceleration clauses might have prevented this, but with the bank mortgage there was no acceleration clause.

The multiple owner continued to make his regular payments to the bank on the blanket mortgage. The new buyer of the single warehouse made payments on his loan to the seller. The contract of sale called for delivery of the deed when the existing loans were completely paid off at the end of ten years.

To Offset the Buyer's Lack of Money or Credit

Where a lender refuses to transfer a desirable loan because of a buyer's poor credit, the loan might be retained by selling on a contract of sale. The buyer might assume loan liabilities if he buys one entire property covered by a loan, but the seller remains responsible to the lender in case of default. A contract of sale may be recorded or not. The deed might not be transferred until the property is paid for in full, as with the warehouses. The usual practice is to deliver the deed after a certain amount is paid, according to the terms of the contract.

A contract of sale gives the seller greater control where the buyer has little to pay down. In a typical example, a house was sold for $10,000, with only $100 down. The contract stipulated that the deed would be transferred after the buyer had paid $1,000 on the principal, reducing his obligation to $9,000. The loan payments were set at $100 monthly, including 7 per cent interest.

There was an existing insurance company first mortgage of $7,500, payable at $60 monthly, including 6 per cent interest, for which the seller was still responsible. The contract provided that the buyer would take over this first mortgage upon transfer of the title. The seller would then take back a second mortgage, payable at $40 monthly, for the difference between $9,000 and the remaining first-mortgage balance.

6. PURCHASE-AND-LEASE-BACK TRANSACTIONS

The *purchase-and-lease-back transaction,* coming more and more into use, comprises a sale followed by a lease. This is one real-estate tool which often results in 100 per cent financing for the ultimate buyer. Following are the advantages it offers to the sellers, the buyer, and the lender respectively.

Advantages to Seller

Sellers may prefer this form of transaction because of resulting income tax advantages. Large commercial buildings and service stations on expensive midtown sites are most often handled by this type of deal. For example, Standard Oil buys a lot and builds a service station. They sell the improved property to an investor and lease the station back for a long term of twenty to ninety-nine years. The latter is the maximum lease period permitted by law.

A large department store like Macy's follows a similar pattern, building a store to suit themselves, selling to an investor, then leasing it back. Macy's and Standard Oil in these cases gain the tax advantage of deducting their entire lease payment as an annual expense. If they retained ownership they could only show offsetting interest payments and depreciation of improvements. Payments on principal would not be deductible, nor would any depreciation be allowable on the land, proportionately very costly in a hundred-per-cent-retail location. Lease payments to cover land costs are deductible in full.

In cases where a sale is made to a tax-free foundation, the property might not even be taxed. The annual costs would thereby be reduced so that lease payments to compensate the tax-free buyer would be considerably less than loan payments by a taxed commercial owner.

Advantages to Buyer

In a case like the previous one involving the foundation, the latter would normally expect a smaller return—ranging from 5 to 6 per cent —than customary on other types of property. The buyer's chief advantages in such a case would be complete freedom from operational problems. There would be no rent delinquencies. The tenant in such an arrangement would customarily arrange and pay for all upkeep, repairs, and improvements.

Private buyers enter this type of transaction because of favorable financing. On a long-term lease, a deposit is often customary to cover terminal months of the lease. In a lease of ten years or more, there might be a deposit equal to one year's rent, which would be offset by a rent-free year at the end. Often such a lease deposit will be sufficient for a buyer's down payment. By financing the balance of the down payment he is able to take ownership of the property without putting up a cent of his own money.

A deal of this kind can usually cash out the seller, inducing him to sell at a substantial discount. On the Macy's and Standard Oil type of transaction, the same firms erect the improvements they desire, sell, and lease back. On another type of transaction, used on large apartment houses and supermarkets, for example, the buyer or the original builder uses the purchase-and-lease-back formula purely for advantageous financing, in most cases 100 per cent.

Advantages to Lender

Money sources forbidden by law to make mortgage loans can often put their funds to work at good interest through the purchase-and-lease-back arrangement. Some union and other trusts, for example, may not be permitted to lend money on property, but they may use their money to purchase and then lease back on mortgage terms. Besides swollen union trusts, certain banks and other financial institutions have surplus trust and other funds they would like to invest in long-term mortgages, which are unlawful for them. In some cases they are also restrained from buying property for investment. These banks and others legally deposit their intended mortgage funds in an investment trust, which then buys property on a purchase-and-lease-back basis.

A TYPICAL TRANSACTION

On a typical transaction of this type, a desirable supermarket in a fast-growing area showed a $65,000 annual net and was listed for sale at $750,000. The owner said he would not sell for less than $650,000 net, which meant exclusive of commissions. This was the nominal market value. Other business ventures, including a disastrous venture as a new-car dealer, pushed the owner out on a limb. He became desperately in need of $100,000 cash in order to salvage his business. All his holdings were financed to the hilt, including a $350,000 maximum loan on the supermarket.

Putting Trust Funds to Use

An established investor with a top credit rating was approached by a loan broker, who said he thought the property could be bought for $500,000 cash, because of the owner's financial straits. The entire half-million-dollar suggested purchase price could be obtained from union trust funds. Trust restrictions vary according to the purposes of the trust and the state laws under which they are governed. This particular trust provided that no money could be invested in mortgages. Purchases were legal only if there were long-term leases to tenants with outstanding credit. Here were the conditions proposed:

1. No deal involving less than a half-million dollars would be considered. The trustees wanted a minimum of servicing for each dollar invested. They were anxious to put piled-up funds to work in fairly large chunks.

2. The investor had to own two points of net assets for each point

of funds advanced. In other words, he had to show a net worth of one million dollars in order to secure a half million.

3. The trust would furnish a firm letter of intent to a qualified investor, guaranteeing to provide a stipulated amount of money to purchase the property.

4. Armed with the letter of intent, the investor could make a cash offer to the seller, "Subject to obtaining necessary financing."

5. The investor would buy the property, then resell to the trust.

6. There would be a 5 per cent service charge to cover overhead and broker's fees. This could be added to the $500,000 suggested purchase price, making the stipulated advance $525,000.

7. The trust would lease the property back to the investor for twenty years at $52,500 annually. This would double their money in twenty years, netting them 10 per cent interest. Although high interest for the investor to pay, it would be offset by the reduced purchase price obtainable with 100 per cent cash.

The payments of 10 per cent of the $525,000 loan amount annually would be the same as on a regular 6 per cent loan for fifteen and a half years. Thus the first fifteen and a half years might be considered as similar to conventional financing for the in-pocket net after loan payments. The final four and a half years of payment would then constitute the 4 per cent bonus over 6 per cent financing.

8. The lease from the trust would include an option for the investor to buy the property outright at the end of the twenty years for a nominal 2 per cent fee. This would be $10,500 on a $525,000 transaction. The ultimate result would be the same as though a twenty-year loan had been made.

Consummating the Deal

The property was under five-year lease to a national market chain. The lease was "net, net, net," providing that the tenant paid all expenses, including taxes, insurance, maintenance, and repairs. New bona fide offers had already been received in writing for higher rents when the lease expired. All signs pointed to an increasing valuation, making the supermarket an attractive buy.

The investor would have a master lease from the trust, then sublease to the supermarket. His chief problem would be the possibility of having to make payments while the market lay vacant for a period at the termination of the present five-year lease. He therefore could not prudently have entered into such a transaction except with a backlog of income from considerable other holdings to tide him over a possible period without supermarket income. This safety factor, of course, governed the trust's requirement for a ratio of $2 in net worth for each $1 advanced.

An offer of $500,000 was made, with the stipulation that the seller pay the 5 per cent service charge from his proceeds. After negotiation, the deal was consummated by agreeing to his counterproposal to receive $500,000 net, the figure first suggested by the loan broker to the investor.

LOANS NOT SECURED BY REAL ESTATE

Loans unsecured by real estate are all comparatively short-term. Included are the following major divisions:

1. Chattel loans
2. Commercial loans
3. Personal loans
4. Improvement loans

1. CHATTEL LOANS

Loans secured by other than real property are commonly called *chattel mortgages,* providing for loans on personal property, such as automobiles, furniture, and equipment. Chattel mortgages are usually of short term, so that they will terminate well within the life expectancy of the covered chattels.

Interest is figured on a discount basis, approximately doubling conventional interest. Where the interest on an apartment real-estate mortgage might be 7 per cent, the lowest obtainable interest on a refrigerator chattel mortgage would be about 12 per cent, figuring the true cost of 6 per cent discounted. Even this is considered favorable interest for chattels. On auto and other installment chattel mortgages, where the buyer may fail to read the fine print, true interest often runs closer to 30 per cent.

The apartment investor should resort to the chattel mortgage to buy furniture and equipment only when lower-interest and longer-term real-estate financing cannot be obtained. This happens more often with new construction. A builder may be able to finance an apartment structure through a first mortgage but fall short of financing furniture. If he desires to buy furniture he may have to arrange a chattel mortgage.

Most institutional lenders require a chattel mortgage on all furniture and equipment in a building at the time they make a loan, as additional security. This protects them from having such personal property, which may be essential to earning an adequate income, legally salable by an unscrupulous borrower planning default.

Conditional Sales Contract

Like a real-estate mortgage, a chattel mortgage gives legal title to the borrower and is customarily used for loans on chattels already owned. Although popularly referred to as a chattel mortgage, the chattel loan form in almost universal use by sellers is the *conditional sales contract*. This contract serves as a lease, providing that the personal property legally belongs to the seller until paid for in full.

Default

The conditional sales contract strengthens the position of the lender. In case of default, the lender is usually entitled to repossess without legal proceedings of any kind. This power results in much more liberal financing than would otherwise be available.

Repossession provisions may work to the benefit of the borrower if the market value for any reason drops below the outstanding balance. The property may deteriorate faster than expected, or new styles may accelerate obsolescence. An example of the latter is the replacement of 6- and 8-cubic-foot refrigerators by 10- and 12-cubic-footers nationally, as standard apartment-house models. Unless there is a "deficiency clause" or other penalty provision in the fine print, the borrower can be relieved of all further obligation by delivering the chattel to the lender.

A Bargain on the Cynthia Court Refrigerators

The twenty-four Cynthia Court refrigerators were bought, purportedly at wholesale, by the Giacolinis from their countryman on a chattel mortgage contract. The dealer had filled out a simple form bought at a stationery store. Since there is no deficiency clause, we plan to give up these 8-cubic-foot boxes, on which there is a $4,250 balance. In their place we plan to purchase twenty-four new 10-cubic-foot Kelvinators for $3,276, buying the new and larger boxes for $974 less than the outstanding balance on the twenty-four smaller ones.

Kelvinator has promised delivery within twenty-four hours of receiving our order. Before placing the new order, we advise the appliance dealer of our intentions and ask him to pick up the old refrigerators immediately.

Since the appliance dealer padded the cost considerably in the original chattel mortgage, he can repossess and resell the refrigerators at a discount and still not lose money. The retail market value has dropped to about $100 each. If he repossesses he will have cartage, storage, and sales costs. He therefore offers a "bargain":

"If you keep the refrigerators, I will discount $1,000 from the note, cutting it to $3,250."

This opens a new avenue for cutting costs. We mention that we would prefer to get the new, larger boxes but might consider keeping his obsolete 8-cubic-footers if the price is low enough. His discounted note would still include prepaid interest for the remaining term. What is the best he can do for cash?

The dealer says he could use the cash, as business hasn't been so good lately. After further discussion, we wind up with a cash settlement of $90 per refrigerator, or a total of $2,160. This represents a saving of $1,116 over our planned expenditure for twenty-four new Kelvinators.

2. COMMERCIAL LOANS

The most important source of quick cash in sizable amounts to tide over short periods is the *commercial loan*. It is so called because it is usually obtained from commercial banks and is utilized chiefly for short-term business credit. Building up this reservoir of credit will have a major influence on your rapidity of expansion. It will provide ready funds during emergencies, help consummate property and cash-discount equipment purchases, and pay for heavy seasonal expenses like taxes. Having such credit available forms a resilient cushion which enables you to invest with less cash reserves than you would otherwise consider safe. Ready commercial credit is almost the same as ready cash.

The average real-estate owner who concentrates on income property investment will accomplish his commercial-loan borrowing on the strength of his signature, backed up by his financial statement. Commercial loans are also obtained by putting up stock as security, usually earning even more favorable interest rates.

Interest Rates Are Low

Interest usually compares with mortgage rates. If the prevailing mortgage interest is around 7 per cent, a sound commercial loan will cost you, as an apartment owner, about the same. You may discount this from ½ to 1 per cent if you put up stock as security. A large utility may borrow without putting up security, for as low as 6 per cent, a million dollars or so for thirty days to meet a payroll. A utility employee who occasionally puts up stock for security to buy more stock might pay 7½ or 8 per cent on his signature if he wanted to borrow $300 for six months in order to pay his mother-in-law's fare home. Smaller loans like the latter would be made only as personal installment loans except to an established commercial borrower.

Payoff Period Is Short

The commercial loan is normally arranged for a specific period, rather than payable in installments. Some commercial loans are made for only thirty days, others for forty-five, sixty or one hundred and twenty. The usual terms are ninety days or six months, at the end of which time the note is payable in full, including interest.

The note might be renewable for good cause upon its expiration date. At least the interest should be paid. Renewal would be particularly apt to receive favor if some principal payment is made, for example $1,000 on a $5,000 note. Notes may be renewable several times but banks frown on over-all extensions exceeding one year. Some businessmen keep renewing their commercial loans year after year, sometimes reducing, sometimes increasing the amounts, but never paying off. Your credit will be much enhanced and you will be able to obtain increasingly larger loans, if you make a practice of paying off notes in full when due, even though you might have to request a new loan within a month or two.

Fill Purchase and Improvement Money Needs

Besides protecting against emergency or seasonal financial needs, the commercial loan can be utilized to help consummate sales and to handle other purchases and improvements, pending the receipt of long-term funds.

If $5,000 or $10,000 had been needed to consummate the Cynthia Court purchase, the money could have been obtained by the Enterprises through a commercial loan. In the case of the planned improvements at the Cynthia Court, suppose the Monarch Life Insurance

Company had declined to advance any funds till the work was completed. The necessary money could have been borrowed at minimum cost and maximum dispatch through a commercial loan, then paid back from escrow proceeds released after completion of the work.

3. PERSONAL LOANS

The chief distinguishing mark between the commercial and the *personal loan*, besides size, is that the latter is made for personal rather than productive purposes. Normally made to a salary or wage earner with limited resources, it would be repayable in monthly installments fitted to the borrower's earnings, usually for a maximum period of two years. The usual maximum amount is $1,000, so this type of loan would seldom be used by an investor with even modest holdings.

High Interest

Personal loans, like chattel loans, are made on a discount basis, double the interest rate on a corresponding commercial loan. The common interest charged by banks and credit unions is 6 per cent discount, approximating 12 per cent interest. Rates for finance companies specializing in personal loans may run to almost any height conceivable, with 30 per cent being considered low.

In one case with which I became familiar as a telephone supervisor, a wage earner borrowed $5 from a loan shark to cover up from his wife the fact that he had lost this amount shooting dice. He was to pay $1 weekly in interest, which came to 1,040 per cent on an annual basis. He intended to repay the money in a week from dice winnings. Unfortunately he suffered further losses and kept getting deeper and deeper in debt. Within six months he owed $315 in principal, interest, and delinquency charges. The finance company then slapped an attachment on his wages. Only $30 represented principal. I induced the finance company to settle for $50 cash. The employee borrowed this, on my advice, by belatedly turning to his company credit union.

The credit union is a co-operative bank available in over 10,000 companies and in labor unions and other organizations. Total loan funds on hand nationally exceeded one billion dollars by 1960, according to the Credit Union National Association. Members share earnings by depositing savings from which fellow members may borrow at low rates. This should be the first place considered by the wage earner seeking a personal loan.

4. IMPROVEMENT LOANS

The *improvement loan* is a comparatively new type of loan whose use has mushroomed rapidly. It has become a common way of financing additions, repairs, remodeling, and modernization. In dwelling units a certain amount of furniture can be included in the improvement loan. The FHA Title I limit on single-family homes has been increased from $2,500 to $5,000. On multiple dwellings the limit is $15,000, or $2,500 per family unit, whichever is less. Some banks have their own improvement loan programs apart from FHA, in which these limits may be exceeded. FHA improvement loans in 1968 exceeded one-half billion dollars.

Easy to Obtain

Improvement loans are about the easiest to obtain and should be considered when other financing appears exhausted. The entire requirements at the Cynthia Court could readily have been paid for from an improvement loan, a possibility well worth examining if more favorable long-term financing were not available. Improvement loans as a rule are not recorded against the property involved. Thus they are normally available even though there are first and subsidiary mortgages already in effect. If the improvement loan is unusually large, or if the borrower's credit appears extended, the loan may be recorded, making it in effect a subsidiary mortgage. In this regard, most banks are forbidden by law from making second mortgages. Yet they can make a large improvement loan and record it, thus placing themselves in a position similar to that of a second-mortgage holder.

Harder to Pay Back

The improvement loan's chief shortcomings are that it costs more than a conventional loan secured by real estate, is made for a comparatively short term, and consequently requires high monthly payments. Improvement loans are made on a discount rather than a regular-interest basis. The FHA Title I discount rate of 5.5 per cent for loans under $2,500 results in actual interest of 10.69 per cent. The discount interest for loans over $2,500 is 4.5 per cent in 1968. The maximum FHA payoff period has been extended on homes to seven years, and the maximum on apartments to seven years. You are most likely to be held to two years, however, on smaller loans, and three to five years on apartment loans in the $10,000 range.

Here is an example of how this works in practice: An apartment house owner borrowed $10,000 on a non-FHA bank loan in order to buy new furniture and to modernize his building. He signed a note for the $10,000, plus 5 per cent interest of $1,500 for three years, a total of $11,500. Thus the $1,500 interest was "discounted" when he signed the note. He repaid the loan in thirty-six monthly installments, with the thirty-five payments of $319.44 and a final payment of $319.60. This approaches four times the $83.97 proportionate monthly payment to amortize $10,000 of the seventeen-year, 7 per cent first mortgage obtained for the Cynthia Court.

The improvement loan is useful to keep in mind because of easy availability, but its shortcomings should be fully considered before eliminating other loan possibilities. We were able to secure desired funds at the Cynthia Court by refinancing the two existing long-term mortgages. Sometimes it may be necessary to utilize many loans in order to consummate a financing project.

This Is the Church That Loans Built

Following are listed seven loans which I negotiated as board chairman to erect a new church by January 19, 1958, at least a year earlier than would otherwise have been possible.

SAN RAMON VALLEY CONGREGATIONAL CHURCH (UNITED CHURCH OF CHRIST)

Dr. Michael A. Vallon, Pastor

Loans to Pay for Lot, Building, and Furniture
A. First Mortgages
LOAN 1. CONSTRUCTION LOAN FROM BANK OF AMERICA $64,000
Funds advanced as needed to pay construction bills, starting July 1957. Payable $650 monthly, or more, including 6 per cent interest, starting January 15, 1958. To be paid down to $50,000 by January 15, 1959.
LOAN 2. TAKE-OUT LOAN FROM CONGREGATIONAL BUILD-
ING SOCIETY 50,000
Funds available January 15, 1959, to take over previous construction loan. Interest to be reduced to 4½ per cent. Repayable in ten years. (Bank would not have advanced such liberal construction funds except for take-out loan commitment in writing.)

B. Subsidiary Mortgages

LOAN 3. SECOND MORTGAGE FROM BUILDING SOCIETY TO
BUY LOT 10,000

First payment October 1957. Interest 3 per cent. Payable in ten years. This loan was originally made November 8, 1955, as a first mortgage to buy lot. Subordination agreement signed, giving precedence to bank loan.

LOAN 4. THIRD MORTGAGE, GRANT LOAN, FROM BUILD-
ING SOCIETY FOR CONSTRUCTION 5,000

No interest. Due in ten years. Renewable until church funds available to repay into revolving fund for building other churches.

C. Unsecured Loans

LOAN 5. COMMERCIAL LOAN FROM WELLS-FARGO BANK
TO CONFERENCE TO BUY LOT 10,000

This loan was originally made in November 1955, along with Loan 3, in order to buy lot. Interest 4½ per cent. Renewable every six months.

LOAN 6. INSTALLMENT LOAN FROM CONFERENCE TO
BUY LOT 11,416

This pays off Loan 5, including taxes, interest, escrow charges and sanitary-bond payments to take-over date. First payment January 10, 1958. Repayable in five years at 190.27 monthly. Interest 4¾ per cent. (Note: Real-estate taxes apply on lot until church is built and functioning.)

LOAN 7. COMMERCIAL LOAN FROM CONFERENCE TO BUY
FURNITURE 5,000

Funds advanced as needed to pay furniture bills: $1,500 in November 1957; $1,500 in December 1957; $2,000 in January 1958. Repayable January 10, 1959, including 5½ per cent interest.

Except for the close relationship between Conference and church, Loan 6 would normally have been recorded as a fourth mortgage, and Loan 7 would have been secured by a chattel mortgage.

PROGRESS AT THE CYNTHIA COURT APARTMENTS

Within two months after securing finances, all contemplated work at the Cynthia Court is completed. The title company then turns over to us the $9,500 balance held back from their $92,000 escrow. In the next two months the rents of all tenants are raised to the scheduled goal set in appraising the property. The raises take effect one month after delivery of the notices.

Thus, six months after our purchase date, thanks chiefly to favorable financing, we are ready to take another step toward our one-million-dollar goal. A review of our progress, and of the next steps to be considered, will follow in Chapter 30, after we examine aspects of taxes and other operating factors.

To build a fortune, your most important asset will be the maximum use of credit. Ready commercial credit is like ready cash.

Improvement loans are easy to fall back on. Whether seeking funds for improvements or pyramiding, first try long-term mortgages in order to secure the most favorable financing.

PART NINE

HOW TO SAVE
ON YOUR INCOME TAXES

25. HOW TO SAVE TAXES ON
YOUR OPERATING INCOME

U.S. property taxes reached 28 billions in 1968, accounting for 43 per cent of all state and local revenues. The property owner pays many times his proportionate share of taxes for local schools and city and county governments. As a rental owner, he can stay in the black only by passing these tax costs on to his tenants. But the property tax is still the owner's responsibility.

To equalize the tax load, the income property owner can be comparatively exempt from Federal and state income taxes. The latter fall primarily on wages and salaries and on the income from corporate, individual, and partnership business.

TWO MAGIC TAX SAVERS

Substantial income tax savings are available to the income property owner, both in day-to-day operations, to be outlined in this chapter, and in the transfer of property, including buying, selling and trading, to be covered in the next chapter. There are two magic tax savers of major import:

Depreciation
Capital gain

The first offsets operating profits, and the second minimizes turnover profit. Utilization of both is obviously legitimate, within certain bounds, of course. Yet I know of owners of substantial holdings who have taken advantage of neither. Some have paid needless taxes on their operating income because they deducted no allowable depreciation. Others have paid turnover taxes which could have been saved completely.

Although tax savings are available for all, it is amazing how many property owners fail to take advantage of legitimate tax opportunities. Most investors turn over to a C.P.A. or a tax attorney the working out of their tax problems. But it is well to be personally familiar with overall tax factors in order to see that they are utilized to your best advantage. You will seldom find an adviser who will match your keen interest in making the maximum tax-free profit.

In this book I would not attempt a detailed analysis of income taxes, another subject which could fill several volumes. My purpose is to point out guideposts and examples to help you make the most, taxwise, from your property investment. Before consummating a transaction that appears complex from a tax angle, most investors will wish to consult an attorney or accountant expert in tax matters.

TAX GUIDES

Some investors subscribe to weekly tax guides and take comprehensive tax courses. All should prove of value to those willing to give the needed time. The chief shortcoming for other than a specialist like a tax accountant is the mountain of information you may have to cover in order to glean an occasional gem that fits your field of interest. Fortunately you can keep fairly well abreast of general tax trends by studying on a continuing basis the following guides:

Instruction Pamphlet, published annually by the Internal Revenue Service and included with Federal Tax Form 1040. No charge. It is well to review these general instructions each year to obtain a simple, introductory picture of items that may affect your taxes.

Your Federal Income Tax, also published annually by the Internal Revenue Service. Price 60 cents. This is a more comprehensive booklet which should be digested after the above pamphlet. It is intended, according to Russell C. Harrington, Commissioner of Internal Revenue, in the foreword to the 1958 edition, to "give you a well-rounded understanding of the Federal income tax law as it applies to individuals. . . . This booklet was prepared to provide plain-language answers to most of your tax questions."

Included are "many examples which show how the law works in actual situations." Vital information for the property investor is found under a majority of the headings, including the following examples:

Travel and Transportation
Rents and Royalties
Retirement Income Credit
Sales and Exchanges
Condemnations, Involuntary Exchanges
Cost or Basis of Property
Capital Gains and Losses
Sale of Residence
Business and Professions
Accounting Periods and Methods
Bad Debts
Depreciation and Depletion
Installment Sales, etc.
Partnership, Estate and Trust Income
Contributions
Interest Deductions
Taxes
Casualties and Thefts
Other Deductions
If Your Return Is Examined

Tax Guide for Small Business, also published annually by the Internal Revenue Service. Price 60 cents. Although intended for business rather than investment guidance, many useful answers found here are not covered in the previously mentioned publications.

Your Income Tax, by J. K. Lasser, published annually by Simon and Schuster. Price $1.95. After studying the above-mentioned booklets, you will have a foundation on which to build your tax education further. Lasser's tax book (the 1969 edition is its thirty-second annual publication) is the universally recognized authority. As stated on the cover, it is the "original, most widely used tax guide in America."

Mr. Lasser's work is used as a reference bible even by Internal Revenue field agents. I gained special respect for Lasser after reviewing available government publications in connection with a problem involving depreciation. Not finding the answer, I visited the local tax office, expecting the field agent to refer to a government tome. Instead, for his final authority he pulled out Lasser's book.

Bulletin F, published by the Internal Revenue Service. Price 30 cents. To be referred to more fully later. The subtitle explains its scope:

Income Tax
Depreciation and Obsolescence
Estimated Useful Lives and
Depreciation Rates

Depreciation Guidelines and Rules, published by the Internal Revenue Service. Price 25 cents. Intended to replace, but often supplements *Bulletin F.*

TAXES SHOULD BE STUDIED REGULARLY

I scan the first four of these publications from cover to cover each year, in the order listed. Often a helpful item will pop up under a heading which seems at first glance to be unrelated to the field of investment. Although there is considerable duplication, each guide helps to fix ground rules, and each adds a certain amount of valuable information on current regulations.

A little practice will help develop a scanning system whereby you can skim over a page and spot interesting items which you will want to study further. There is no need aspiring to be an over-all tax expert, but it will prove most worthwhile to have a working knowledge of your own specialized field.

KEEP YOUR EYE ON THE BOOKS

You may study taxes with the idea of preparing your own returns, as do many owners who have studied accounting. Or your interest may be only from the standpoint of supervision, as is true of most owners. In any case it is well to keep your fingers in the books in order to spot problems that may require corrective action.

Excessive repair bills on a central refrigeration plant, for example, might guide you to junking the system and installing individual refrigerators. This was done at the Cynthia Court. Excessive furnace repair or fuel bills might point to renovating or replacing the furnace.

An understanding of income taxes may help you make a fortune without a major tax bite to eat into your profits. Personal study and supervision of bookkeeping and taxes may mean the difference between marked and modest success, and even possible failure.

BABES IN TAXLAND

Witness the experience of one working couple with taxable salaries approximating $15,000 a year. The husband was employed as a civil-service engineer. The wife worked as an accounting supervisor for a public utility. She felt this experience sufficient to warrant her taking over, without further study, the books of a 36-unit apartment house which she had inherited.

Some of their investment problems were mentioned to me at a church social. The apartments had not proved the money-maker they had anticipated. The property had been inherited in January of the previous year and they had wound up in the hole because of heavy taxes. They had netted $22,000 in operating income but had paid out about 50 per cent of this in income taxes, leaving $11,000. Loan payments of $8,400 deducted from this left $2,600. In addition they had paid out $7,000 to paint the exterior and the hallways. Thus they were $4,400 out of pocket for the year and were forced to pay this amount from their salaries.

TAX BLINDNESS ALMOST BEYOND BELIEF

I asked how much they had taken as a depreciation deduction. They answered, "Nothing, of course. The property was inherited, so it cost us nothing."

I asked if they had deducted the interest on the loan, and they said no, it had been capitalized. The paint cost, also, was capitalized, rather than deducted from income, because it was such a big expense for one year. Neither of these capitalized items had been depreciated for the year because a full year had not elapsed.

I asked who had prepared their return. The wife said she had turned over all her bookkeeping figures to an insurance salesman friend, who made out income tax returns as a side line. He had previously prepared their returns when salaries constituted their only income. None of his returns had ever been questioned by the Internal Revenue people, so he must be all right.

I pointed out that the government does not question failure to take allowable deductions. Any accountant with rudimentary income-property tax knowledge could have prepared their return so that they would have paid little or no income tax on their apartment income. In fact, this particular tax year they probably could have showed an operating loss which they could deduct from their other income.

Their friend might have had sufficient knowledge to prepare returns for salary and wage earners, whose taxes are practically spelled out in advance. Many a trained accountant might know little about investment property, but at least he should know where to obtain essential information when it is desired. The new apartment owners could be helped most by an accountant who specializes in income property ramifications; he could save them far more than his fees. In addition they would find it worthwhile to familiarize themselves with their tax-free opportunities by studying the tax information described earlier.

THEY COULD HAVE SAVED $12,000 IN TAXES

Examining their possible tax savings revealed that they could have deducted in full in the year of expenditure the $7,000 paint cost and $4,100 paid out in interest. These would be questioned as annual expenses only when a property is bought for quick resale, in which case expenditures incidental to resale are capitalized.

As long as they were capitalized, a partial year's depreciation could still have been taken. Items paid for by July 1, for example, would take a half year's depreciation. A major capital item paid for on December 1 would warrant depreciation for one twelfth of a year. Expenditures spread fairly evenly throughout the year might be grouped, with a half year's depreciation taken for all. For example, if on the first of each month one refrigerator was paid for, all twelve could be grouped in one capital account entitled to a half year's depreciation in the year of purchase.

BASIS FOR DEPRECIATION

On Form 1040 depreciation is taken under the heading of COST OR OTHER BASIS. On inherited property the capital value for depreciation, resale, and other purposes would have no bearing on cost or book value but would be the fair market value, subject to Federal estate tax appraisal. In the case of my church friends, their property was appraised for estate tax purposes at $225,000, which would be the required basis on which to take depreciation. The lot value was assessed at $20,000, the furniture at $25,000, and the building at $180,-000.

Since the building was already thirty years old, figuring a remaining depreciable life of twenty-five years probably would not have been questioned. Thus a depreciation allowance of 4 per cent of the $180,-000 could have been deducted, making $7,200. The furniture could have been allocated in separate accounts for fast- and slow-depreciation items. A composite useful life of ten years would have been acceptable. Depreciating the $25,000 at 10 per cent would have made an additional $2,500, bringing total depreciation to $9,700. Adding this to $4,100 interest and $7,000 for painting would have deducted $20,800 from their taxable net income.

An examination of other clearly deductible management and maintenance expenses which they had overlooked showed that they could have lessened their taxable net by an additional $3,600. This brought to $24,400 the total of obvious deductions which had not been taken. Balancing this against the $22,000 net they had reported would leave a $2,400 loss. This could have been deducted from their salaried income before arriving at their taxable income. In this one year, in their tax bracket, they could have saved $12,000 in income taxes by taking advantage of customary deductions available to them.

WHERE TO LOOK FOR TAX GUIDANCE

As in many other operations, complex tax problems can be readily solved if you know where to look for qualified guidance. The best place to find a capable and reasonable tax attorney or accountant is through your local apartment-house or other owners' association. Other reliable sources include:

Real Estate Board
Chamber of Commerce
Other successful apartment owners
Bank, or building and loan association
Better Business Bureau
Builders Exchange
American Institute of Accountants, or other accounting association

Accountants—public and certified public—from the telephone directory

Bookkeeping service, from the telephone directory

Bar Association, or a lawyer reference service

IT PROFITS TO LEARN THE
RUDIMENTS OF BOOKKEEPING

Even though you have an accountant keep your books, some knowledge of bookkeeping will be most helpful. You will often be able to make suggestions for improving bookkeeping methods to fit your operations, and you will be able to check the financial statements and tax returns prepared for you by others.

Many homeowners save by making out the complete Form 1040, since their taxes and interest along with other deductions normally exceed the fixed allowance. Income taxes and bookkeeping may seem mysterious at first, but they will not prove too complicated if the taxpayer prepares his returns while he is solely a wage earner and, as his estate grows, gradually assimilates the knowledge required to handle more complex problems.

Apartment owners who competently do their own bookkeeping and their own tax returns find that it helps to assure maximum success. If you start handling the books with your first property purchase and keep abreast of tax changes, you can gradually assimilate the required knowledge as holdings increase. I have found that the tax mechanics of a large sale, trade, or purchase are no more complicated than a small one.

WHERE TO LEARN

You can pick up the rudiments of bookkeeping by setting up a household budget and keeping track of income and expenditures. If this is a completely unfamiliar field and you are interested in studying it, consider attending a bookkeeping course at night school a few hours a week. By acting as assistant treasurer of your church, lodge, business association, or other organization you can gain invaluable experience in the fundamentals of bookkeeping and serve at the same time. Or you can volunteer to join a committee that regularly audits books, like the supervisory committee of a credit union.

Volunteers for such service are anxiously welcomed, and you will benefit from the experience and guidance of holdover members. Like casting your bread upon the waters, it may bring you many unsolicited returns. My first experience and interest in finance developed in serving as a trustee, and on the supervisory and educational committees, of a telephone-company credit union.

Tax-Slanted Bookkeeping
Simplifies Preparation of Returns

Keeping books with an eye on the easiest way of transferring ledger entries to an income tax return can transform a possible major headache into a comparatively simple chore. Some bookkeepers enter all expenditures in chronological order in one general account book. At the end of the year they then spend a lot of time and confusion sorting out the various breakdowns needed for income tax purposes. Others content themselves with separating capitalized expenditures from operating expenses, at least saving this one division from year-end separation.

The simplest method is to prepare a separate ledger account, composed of one or more pages, for each entry that will later be made on the income tax statement. Then at the end of the year there will be no sorting at all. To complete your tax return you merely take the following steps:

1. Add each ledger account.
2. List each total as an entry under the appropriate major account on your income tax return.
3. Total the various major accounts.
4. Make the necessary computations to arrive at your taxable income.

I know of salaried couples whose only investment is a home, who spend hours every week fussing with household, employment, and pocket-money entries until income and expenditure are balanced to the last penny. At year end they spend more hours sorting out deductible and nondeductible items. Their entry and sorting hours exceed the time needed for competent accounting on a million dollars' worth of income property.

FOUR MAJOR RENT ACCOUNTS

Many details of tax preparation are spelled out in the publications listed. I therefore will not attempt a complete explanation of every item, but will mention only a few significant areas wherein bookkeeping can be simplified. Tax Form 1040 breaks into four major accounts for apartment house owners under Schedule B, Part II, RENT AND ROYALTY INCOME:

1. Amount of rent
2. Depreciation
3. Repairs
4. Other expenses

Suggested ledger pages for each of these major accounts are indicated on the following pages.

1. AMOUNT OF RENT

The tax return should show the rent from each property. With the Enterprises at the present stage of progress you would show only the Cynthia Court rents. In Chapter 21, "How to Supervise Your Apartment Manager," a monthly report sheet was recommended, headed "Monthly Income." Using this report, signed by the manager, helps to simplify bookkeeping. With the monthly report and duplicate rent receipts on file, it would be necessary to enter on the ledger sheet marked INCOME only the monthly totals for the entire property. This would make only twelve rental entries for the year. Compare this with some bookkeeping practices which include making an entry of each rent received for each apartment. With the Cynthia Court there would be 288 additional bookkeeping entries annually.

At the end of the year the twelve monthly entries would be totaled. Any incidental income, such as that from deposits, coin launderettes, or public telephones, would be added, and the grand income total entered on Form 1040. It is well to indicate other than rent receipts separately, so that there will be no question that all income is reported. For example, you might show total income of $24,060, with an explanatory footnote, "Includes $160 from coin launderette."

2. DEPRECIATION

In 1957, according to an example cited by the Department of Commerce, $18,500,000,000 was charged to depreciation of plant and equipment by U.S. corporations. Over-all figures are not available on income property, the one investment where all the initial cost, excepting land, can be recovered taxwise through depreciation allowances. As trading will be shown to be the major way to cut taxes in pyramiding, so depreciation is the major way to offset operating income.

The more your investment is subject to depreciation allowances, the more you can save on operating taxes. This is the big tax advantage of apartment houses over hotels and commercial property. Investment in the latter includes a comparatively high cost for land, which cannot be depreciated.

The Internal Revenue Service does not dictate depreciation schedules, and it will accept any that are considered reasonable. However, it has indicated what would normally be considered reasonable in *Bulletin F* and in *Depreciation Guidelines,* previously mentioned. *Bulletin F* is considered "outmoded" in some schedules, according to the Internal Revenue Service, but still indicates acceptable lives for items not covered in *Depreciation Guidelines.*

Depreciation on Traded Property

Depreciation allowances on a property taken in trade, as with the Cynthia Court, are figured on the book cost, starting with the first property involved. As an example, here are the steps involved with the Cynthia Court:

1. Take initial cost of A Avenue house.
2. Add cost of house improvements.
3. Deduct depreciation taken on house, including furniture.
4. Add boot given for Belvedere Apartments. This gives book cost of the Belvedere.
5. Add cost of Belvedere improvements.
6. Deduct depreciation taken on Belvedere.
7. Add boot given for Cynthia Court Apartments, arriving at its book cost at time of purchase.
8. Deduct value of nondepreciable lot, leaving depreciable cost.
9. Figure the depreciation (based on comparative values) of furniture and equipment, in a single account.

The balance which would result from deducting the depreciation (step 9) from the book cost at time of purchase (step 7) would represent the current book cost of the Cynthia Court Apartments.

Composite Depreciation Account

It is possible to set up one ledger account for all capital expenditures, including every item except the land value. *Bulletin F* shows a composite useful life of forty years for "good" and "average" constructions, which includes steel, reinforced concrete and brick. This would give an allowable deduction of 2½ per cent annually. For frame or frame-and-stucco construction, like the Cynthia Court, rated "cheap," the suggested composite deduction is 3 per cent, indicating a useful life of thirty-three and a third years.

Depreciation Guidelines does not differentiate construction qualities, listing only one composite life of 40 years for apartments. This is an example of greater useful detail in *Bulletin F*.

Separate Ledger Accounts

A property owner can break down every item of furniture and equipment into a separate depreciation account, but this would be a needlessly time-wasting procedure. *Bulletin F* states that the most generally used segregated accounts for business firms are:

1. Buildings
2. Machinery and equipment
3. Office furniture and fixtures
4. Transportation equipment

While separate ledgers might be arranged for each of these classifications, the average apartment-house owner will find that two of these depreciation accounts are sufficient:

1. Buildings
2. Furniture, fixtures, machinery and equipment

Buildings

Bulletin F indicates that where a building is separated from the equipment for depreciation purposes, a reasonable useful life for standard or sound apartments is fifty years, 25 per cent longer than the composite life of forty. So-called cheap construction like the Cynthia Court is not thus projected in the bulletin. Adding the same 25 per cent factor to the composite figure of thirty-three and a third years would give a separated building life of forty-one and two-thirds years. Rounding this to forty years would be considered reasonable.

The Cynthia Court is already thirty years old. There would be only ten years of life remaining if we started with the day of erection. However, in setting up depreciation on an older building a reasonable adjustment should be made, taking into account the market value and the state of maintenance and rehabilitation. In some cases adjusting to 50 per cent of the full life, or twenty years, would be acceptable. In this case adjusting to 60 per cent, or a twenty-five-year remaining life, would normally not be questioned. This would mean an annual allowable depreciation deduction of 4 per cent of the book cost of the building.

This analysis helps to emphasize the tax advantage from investment in older buildings. Where the Cynthia Court would now merit a 4 per cent depreciation allowance, the same investment and income in new construction of the same quality would normally be offset by a 2½ per cent annual depreciation allowance.

Furniture, Fixtures, Machinery and Equipment

Neither *Bulletin F* nor *Depreciation Guidelines* shows a composite life for apartment furniture, etc. but the former shows approximately twelve years and the latter ten years for hotels. Apartments might experience a similar life expectancy. If the furniture is very old a composite remaining life as low as five years might be acceptable.

At the Cynthia Court most of the fixtures and equipment are as old as the building, but the furniture is only a few years old. The newer and older items could be shown separately if desired. Major added items, like the hall carpets, have an indicated six-year life. The new refrigerators have an indicated life of eleven years. They could also be allocated to separate depreciation accounts. For simplicity all but the building could be included in one depreciation account. A composite life of ten years in this case would seldom be questioned, giving a composite annual depreciation allowance of 10 per cent.

Land Improvements

Where there is appreciable landscaping and paving it pays to set up a separate account for Land Improvements, depreciable in 20 years, as explained in Chapter 27.

3. REPAIRS

For income tax purposes, all noncapitalized expenses are broken into two major accounts, REPAIRS and OTHER EXPENSES. With a rented home, like the A Avenue house, or a duplex, all repairs might run only $100 or so in a given year. A small sum like this would not require further elaboration. On a larger building like the Cynthia Court, where repairs, such as painting, might entail thousands, more detail should be given.

After determining that an expense is a repair item, it should then be listed on an appropriate ledger sheet. The number of separate repair accounts may fluctuate from year to year, varying according to the size of the property and the expense activity. The Internal Revenue Service is not interested in every detail of your expenses, but they would like to see a reasonable breakdown. The more information you can show on a reasonable basis, the more they will be satisfied that you are making a complete and honest return.

Break Down Unusually Heavy Group Expenses

If you have unusually high expenses in a particular account, it is well to split the account further. For example, in most years you might normally include all furnace and hot-water-system repairs under PLUMBING REPAIRS. With apartments like the Cynthia Court your annual bills might run between $100 and $200. In an exceptional year you might have repair expenses of $250 on the furnace and $150 on the hot-water system. Any such peak fluctuation from the normal might be suspect unless explained, so it would be well to list the two mentioned items separately.

With an investment like the Cynthia Court, supplemental pages will obviously need to be added to Form 1040 in order to show desired details. Possible repair headings to consider are listed below. The symbol C indicates suggested regular headings for the Cynthia Court or similar apartments:

> Air Conditioning Repairs
> Brick Repairs
> (C) Carpenter Repairs
> Concrete Repairs
> Elevator Repairs
> (C) Electrical Repairs
> Furnace Repairs

(C) Furniture Repairs
(C) Painting and Decorating, Interior
(C) Painting, Exterior
(C) Plumbing Repairs
    Refrigerator Repairs
    Stove Repairs
    Roof Repairs
(C) Miscellaneous Repairs

Consolidate Unusually Light Expenses

If refrigerators and stoves are comparatively new and trouble-free, their repairs may run only a few dollars. They might then be consolidated under FURNITURE REPAIRS. If all painting, inside and out, amounts to only $200 or $300, it could just as well be grouped under one heading, PAINTING AND DECORATING. If a particular heading like BRICK or CONCRETE REPAIRS amounts to only a few dollars and does not fit another designated account, it should be included under MISCELLANEOUS REPAIRS.

4. OTHER EXPENSES

All annual expenditures not listed under REPAIRS are shown under the major heading of OTHER EXPENSES. Suggestions as to breaking down unusually heavy groups, and consolidating unusually light expenses would also hold true here. Following are headings to consider, with the symbol C for probable Cynthia Court requirements:

(C) Accounting
(C) Advertising and Printing
    Attorney Fees and Court Costs
(C) City License and Fees
    Cleaning and Laundry
(C) Insurance, with subheadings for
    Fidelity
    Fire
    Liability
    Robbery
(C) Interest Paid
    Losses from Bad Checks
(C) Payroll Taxes, Employer, including Social Security and
    Unemployment Insurance

Pest Control
Refunds
Rental Commissions and Fees
Rent Paid Out
(C) Supplies, with possible subheadings for
Garden
Office
Janitor
(C) Salaries and Wages
(C) Taxes, Realty
(C) Transportation Expenses
(C) Utilities, with possible subheadings for
Electricity
Fuel
Gas
Scavenger Service
Telephone
Water
(C) Miscellaneous

Regardless of the number of headings you may devise, there will usually be various small items left for MISCELLANEOUS. Included might be a few dollars each for sometimes-optional apartment expenditures like charging fire extinguishers, and Christmas decorations. Into the same pot should be thrown items from the above headings, like PEST CONTROL, and RENTAL COMMISSIONS, when they total only a few dollars.

FIGURE TAX APPLICATION BEFORE TAKING ACTION

If you buy, sell, trade or make a major operations move, and then figure how taxes would apply, you may discover you have lost an opportunity for a substantial saving. Review each major expenditure or transaction from an income tax standpoint and organize your actions to your greatest tax advantage.

The Internal Revenue Service expects you to pay every penny for which you are liable, and it is their business to quickly let you know if they discover a deficiency. Income tax agents will tell you of incorrect arithmetic, whether in yours or the government's favor. However, they seldom advise you if, like my church friends who inherited their apartments, you fail to utilize all your allowable deductions and exemptions. It therefore behooves you not to overlook the many means for saving money to which the Government agrees you are entitled.

A modest understanding of income taxes will help you make a fortune without a major tax bite to eat into your profits. Some personal study and supervision of bookkeeping and taxes will help assure your maximum success.

Phenomenal tax savings are available to you as an apartment owner, but it is up to you to take advantage of them.

26. HOW TO SAVE TAXES
ON PROPERTY TURNOVER

The United States is the only major country at this writing where a tax is levied on long-term capital gains, according to the New York Stock Exchange. Of forty-nine countries considered "capitalistic," only two others, Israel and the Philippine Republic, tax long-term capital gains. Of course even the maximum long-term capital gains tax of 25 per cent for property held over six months appears small compared with the peak individual tax rate of 91 per cent. With a 25 per cent tax bite on turnover profits, it is still possible to pyramid in property investment faster than in any other way. But why handicap your road to a fortune with even this 25 per cent when you can control your operations to substantially reduce the tax, or avoid it entirely?

"THE MATHEMATICS HAVE ALMOST
UNPARALLELED ATTRACTION"

On this subject the eminent tax and accounting authority J. K. Lasser states in the 1955 edition of his book, *Your Income Tax,* mentioned in the previous chapter: "Tax mechanics have certainly made buying real estate a most profitable occupation. . . . We can keep pyramiding equities, and often without too much tax cost. . . . The mathematics have almost unparalleled attraction."

Many of the tax ramifications of property turnover have been mentioned in previous chapters at each stage of progress. As long as a capital gains tax applies to profit on an outright sale, the importance of trading in order to avoid the tax has been emphasized. Mechanics of trading were introduced in our two property turnovers.

We exchanged the A Avenue house for the 5-unit Belvedere Apartments in a simple, direct trade. We then traded the Belvedere for the twenty-four Cynthia Court apartments in a more complex, three-way trade. With this foundation of understanding, we are now ready to explore in more detail various possibilities which will enable you to save turnover taxes. Our discussion of turnover is broken down into ten subheadings:

1. Trading Up
2. Trading Even
3. Trading Down
4. Selling
5. Changing a Buyer to a Trader
6. Transferring Mortgages
7. Selling Mortgages
8. Kind of Property
9. Investor vs. Dealer or Broker
10. Minimizing Possible Losses

1. TRADING UP

No capital gains tax applies when you trade up, giving your property plus a boot for the property you acquire. Thus in the direct trade of the A Avenue rental house for the Belvedere Apartments no tax was involved, even though the trade established an increased value. If the house had been sold and then the Belvedere purchased later, a capital gains tax would have applied to the net sale profit on the house.

When we were ready to trade the Belvedere for the Cynthia Court Apartments, we were at first unable to obtain acceptance of a direct trade. In this case we negotiated a multiple exchange. We traded the Belvedere to the owner of the Cynthia Court, and he in turn traded the Belvedere for the Dunroamin summer home. From a tax standpoint, it was important that we consummated a direct paper trade to the Cynthia Court owners, actually transferring title of the Belvedere to them. The fact that they immediately made another exchange would not affect our tax-free position.

Essential to guard against would be a short cut of this procedure by transferring title direct from us to the ultimate owner of the Belvedere. This would establish a sale and purchase rather than a trade, and it would produce a taxable capital gain on the Belvedere.

Both of the foregoing trades were simple from an income tax standpoint. In each exchange we paid a bonus, thus establishing that we were trading up. The tax thinking on such transactions is that you are maintaining a continuous investment in productive real estate.

2. TRADING EVEN

An even exchange, where you neither give nor receive boot, gives you the same free-tax treatment as a trade upward. In one example of a profitable even exchange, an enterprising investor traded a duplex, improved like our A Avenue property, for a deteriorated 4-unit apartment house. He had paid $11,500 for the duplex and had spent $1,700 cash plus one year of part-time labor on improvements. His book cost was thus $13,200. The market value of the duplex when exchanged was $18,000, since he had increased the monthly rents to $90 per unit.

The capitalized income value of the 4-unit house was $27,000, with $67.50 monthly rents per unit. Even with a 25 per cent depreciation factor because of the deteriorated appearance, the market value was still $20,250. The owner of the 4-unit house was an elderly widow who was anxious to sell her run-down property, which suffered chiefly from a lack of interior and exterior paint. She was happy to trade for a spick-and-span duplex.

The new owner of the 4-unit building increased its value within two years to $38,000 by nominal improvements, mostly do-it-yourself, including complete painting, which enabled him to increase the rents to $95 per unit. The income value, market value, potential value, and book cost of the traded duplex as compared with the acquired 4-unit property had no bearing on taxable capital gain. The transaction was tax-free as long as a bona fide across-the-board trade was made, with no boot given or taken.

3. TRADING DOWN

You trade down whenever you participate in an exchange in which you take boot in addition to another property. This device may interest you when you are ready to dispose of a piece of property at any stage of progress, especially if you should feel like partially liquidating after your estate exceeds $1,000,000.

Trading down, along with taking back a mortgage, gives you a possible means of selling at a profit and still minimizing your taxes. Any clear book profit would of course be as clearly taxable, at least on a capital gains basis. But there are many tax considerations as to how and when the gain would be payable.

An Example of Tax Savings on Trading Down

A couple in their early sixties had pyramided their net estate to over $2,000,000 in apartment house equities. They decided to gradually sell their apartments and spend most of their time traveling around the world, seeking both tourist havens and off-the-track sights. An example of how they liquidated profitably at tax savings involved trading down an apartment building similar to the Cynthia Court. The market value was $240,000. All actual figures are rounded out to simplify illustration.

They had paid $135,000 ten years previously and had spent $15,000 on improvements, making their cost $150,000. This was depreciated $40,000, however, by the time of exchange, bringing their book cost for tax purposes down to $110,000. If they sold for $240,000 cash, less approximately $10,000 sales expenses, they would have a tax liability on a capital gain of $120,000. Their profit, in their tax bracket, would have been subject to the maximum alternative capital gains tax of 25 per cent, amounting to $30,000.

Instead of selling for cash, they took in trade a lower-valued property and juggled the financing so that they wound up with considerable cash and profit, and with little tax to pay. Here is the way the arrangements were made:

An investor who owned an industrial property with a market value of $40,000 desired to build his estate by trading for a larger property, an apartment house The industrial property was under twenty-year net lease to a national trucking concern at an annual rental of $4,000, with the tenant paying all operating expenses; it was free and clear of loans and was taken in as the entire down payment.

There was a $65,000 loan against the apartment house. The apartment owners arranged to pay this off, and they took back from the buyer a twenty-year first mortgage of $200,000 at 7 per cent, the first payments to be due the following year.

The over-all turnover net profit of $120,000 represented 50 per cent of the $240,000 contract and sale price. Thus the apartment sellers were liable for a 25 per cent capital gains tax in the current year only on 50 per cent of the $40,000 down payment, represented by the market value of the industrial property. This resulted in a capital gains tax for the current year of $5,000 instead of $30,000, saving $25,000 in taxes for the taxable year.

The $100,000 balance of the profit was spread over the twenty-year period of the loan, 50 per cent of the principal payments being shown as profit in each succeeding year.

How the Seller Raised Nontaxable Cash from His Mortgage

To raise cash without affecting tax liability, the apartment sellers borrowed $145,000 at 6½ per cent for twenty years from their bank, hypothecating their first mortgage as security. The $65,000 existing mortgage was paid off. After paying the $10,000 sales commission and setting aside $5,000 for the capital gains tax, the sellers realized $65,000 in-pocket cash.

The bank collected the mortgage payments, credited the lesser payments on the bank loan, and placed the balance in the apartment sellers' account. Their mortgage payments gave them a net income in addition to repaying the bank loan, and they also made a ½ per cent profit on the loan interest.

4. SELLING

A similar financial arrangement can be made on a sale where no exchanges are involved. In the above trade the apartment owners could have taken $40,000 in cash, and the tax liability would have been the same. But they probably could not have sold for as high a profit as on a trade.

Having established the tax on the value of the industrial property, the apartment sellers turned around and sold it within thirty days, cashing it out completely. They received a cash down payment of $15,000 and the $25,000 balance from an insurance company loan, which was transferred to the buyer. No additional tax liability was involved, since they sold at the same price as the trade valuation, and no depreciation had accrued.

Spreading Tax Liability

To spread tax liability over the period of a loan, watch that the down payment, plus the excess of a transferred loan over book cost, plus principal payments during the year of sale, do not exceed 30 per cent of the contract price. The latter is the sale price less any transferred loans. If loan payments, other than interest, are arranged for the year of sale, the down payment must be reduced sufficiently below 30 per cent to safeguard the deferred-tax rules. Some sellers have taken a full 30 per cent down and then found the deferred-tax advantage voided because of subsequent principal payments the same year. A common device is to take 29 per cent down, leaving a 1 per cent safety margin for errors in calculation, then deferring the first principal payment until the next tax year.

100 Per Cent Financing

Besides spreading taxes, taking less than 30 per cent down enables sellers to obtain more favorable prices. Some sellers stretch out their tax payments even longer by taking no down payment at all. They can afford to sell on such a basis only to buyers who have established a reputation for improving rather than bleeding property.

In one case a $165,000 property was sold with 100 per cent financing to an established investor. The seller owned the building free and clear and took back a fifteen-year, 7 per cent first mortgage for the entire sale price. His $55,000 net profit was subject to no tax liability the year of sale except for the proportionate amount he received on the principal payments.

Note Should Be Secured

In another transaction the sellers owned a $150,000 property free and clear. To reduce the lender's risk by speeding the increase of the buyer's equity, they took back three notes:

1. Note secured by first mortgage of $100,000 at 6 per cent, payable in fifteen years
2. Note secured by second mortgage of $25,000 at 7 per cent, payable in ten years

3. Unsecured promissory note for $25,000 at 7 per cent, payable in five years

The sellers preferred the last note unsecured because the buyer was a substantial property owner. Default would have made his entire estate liable, rather than only the single property purchased. After the transaction was consummated and the mortgages and the deed transfer were recorded, the sellers came to preparing their income tax return. They figured all tax liability would be spread over the period of the notes. Similar cases have often not been disapproved.

To their chagrin it was ruled on audit that the unsecured promissory note did not fall under the deferred-tax-payment rules. Taxwise, like Federal reserve notes it constituted full payment of the amount in the year the note was given. They had to pay the same tax on the $25,000 promissory note as if they had received $25,000 in cash. This full liability could have been avoided merely by securing the last note by a mortgage, either a third loan on the property sold or a secured loan on other property. It is not unusual to complete a 100 per cent financing transaction by taking as a down payment a mortgage on real estate unconnected with the purchased property.

5. CHANGING A BUYER TO A TRADER

When we took over the Cynthia Court, we converted the sellers to trading by devising a three-way trade. The reverse procedure should be kept in mind when you are ready to dispose of property and have an eager cash buyer. An investor might be willing to make a fair cash offer for the Cynthia Court, for example, and have no property to trade. You want to trade for other apartments instead of selling for cash. Here is one commonly used method:

You find a half-million-dollar apartment house which you would like to own. You arrange a contract for your buyer to buy this building, then you trade the Cynthia Court for it, thus utilizing the purchasing power of your cash buyer to secure the property you desire. There are two problems to watch here:

From an income tax standpoint your buyer must actually take title to the other property before transferring it to you.

Unless adequately controlled, your buyer may decide to keep the other property, instead of relinquishing it for the Cynthia Court.

A Surer Method of Control

Although the foregoing procedure has often been used to change a buyer to a trader, an alternative method is safer and proves easier to arrange. Many experienced traders would first bind the buyer to a firm purchase contract, to keep him under control. The contract would state: "Subject to intermediate transfer of ownership to be arranged by seller."

Next a direct trade would be consummated for the half-million-dollar property, "subject to the sale of the Cynthia Court." You actually trade for the larger building. The larger owner takes title to the Cynthia Court and then consummates the sale to your cash buyer.

6. TRANSFERRING MORTGAGES

It should be re-emphasized that in all trades or sales the transfer of existing mortgages constitutes payment, taxwise, to the seller. The effect should be weighed carefully in computing tax liabilities. If there is a loan against property being sold at a profit, it is often advantageous from a tax standpoint to pay it off. If the seller prefers not to put up funds, he can usually take back a first mortgage and raise the necessary money by hypothecating.

Examples of such hypothecation have been mentioned in Chapter 24, "More Ways to Borrow Money," and in this chapter under "Trading Down." In the latter example, the apartment sellers hypothecated their $200,000 first mortgage as security for a $145,000 bank loan. If, instead, they had arranged a $145,000 first mortgage and transferred it to the buyer, their tax liability would have radically changed. Their full $120,000 profit would then have become currently taxable. Here is how the tax picture would have altered:

The $35,000 excess of the $145,000 transferred loan over their $110,000 book cost would have been figured as additional down payment. Added to the $40,000 valuation of the industrial building taken in trade, this would have increased their down payment to $75,000.

Their contract price, for tax purposes, instead of being the same as the $240,000 sale price, as when a purchase money mortgage is taken back by the seller, would be slashed in half. First the transferred mortgage would be deducted from the sale price, leaving $95,000. Then any mortgage excess over book cost, in this case $35,000, would be added, making a contract price of $120,000.

The adjusted down payment of $75,000 in relation to the adjusted contract price of $120,000 would be more than double the 30 per cent maximum down payment allowed in order to receive deferred-tax treatment.

The entire $120,000 net profit would have been subject to a $30,000 tax, the same as if the sellers had received all cash.

This illustrates the tax contrast often arising between the customary transferring and the less common hypothecating of mortgages. To summarize, a purchase money mortgage taken back by the seller, then hypothecated to raise money, is not included in the down payment, and is included in the contract price, both computations making it easier to meet the 30 per cent factor. A transferred mortgage, on the other hand, is deducted to arrive at the contract price, thereby adversely affecting the 30 per cent down-payment treatment. Also any transferred mortgage excess over book cost is counted as down payment.

7. SELLING MORTGAGES

Putting up a purchase money mortgage as security to borrow does not affect deferred taxes. However, selling the mortgage outright accelerates the tax application. If a mortgage is sold at a loss below face value, this loss could then be taken into account in figuring taxes. In any case, the amount realized at the time of the mortgage sale would be currently subject to the proportionate taxable gain.

In one case a liquor distributor paid a $25,000 tax because of selling a mortgage, when he could have deferred the tax or could have saved it entirely. He first sold a 24-unit apartment house to a friend for $125,000, taking back a 6 per cent first mortgage for the full amount, due in fifteen years. He had bought the apartments fifteen years previously for $62,500, and depreciation had lowered his book cost to $25,000, making his profit $100,000. Up to this point he was entitled to defer his tax over the fifteen-year period of the mortgage.

In the same year he turned around and traded the mortgage at face value for the warehouse building which he had been leasing. He and his bookkeeper, who was experienced only in preparing business tax returns, figured that his gain could still be spread over fifteen years. Both transactions were consummated and recorded. The bookkeeper subsequently blithely filed the tax return.

Vitriolic were the recriminations when the Internal Revenue Service demanded $25,000 in capital gains taxes for the sale year.

The distributor could have retained his deferred-tax advantage if he had borrowed about $75,000 on his first mortgage by hypothecation to make a down payment on the warehouse. The balance of $50,000 could have been handled easily by a mortgage on the warehouse.

Or he might have left his mortgage unfettered by borrowing $75,000 on the warehouse and giving the seller a $50,000 second mortgage. The payments taken in and paid out could have been arranged to offset each other.

His best solution would have saved him $25,000 by avoiding a taxable gain. He could have traded his apartments for the warehouse, then let the warehouse owner sell the apartments by taking back the $125,000 mortgage. The final results, except for tax liability, would have been the same. Here was a clear-cut case of throwing away $25,000 through tax blindness.

8. KIND OF PROPERTY

Generally speaking, the exchange of any properties held for productive use qualifies under the tax-free rules. The properties do not have to be identical in character, as with the exchange of the A Avenue rental house for the Belvedere Apartments and of the Belvedere for the Cynthia Court. We have cited other types of exchanges, such as an industrial building for apartments. Also permissible would be such trades as a ranch for apartments, or apartments for a hotel.

A problem arises when an investor proposes to trade a property obviously not productive, such as his home, for income property. A home can be traded tax-free for another. However, trading a home at a profit for an apartment house involves a taxable gain.

If the Enterprises had traded their home as the down payment on one of their three purchases, their profit would have been figured by balancing the market value of the purchased property against the allowance for the home. If, for example, the fair allowance on the trade were $5,000 more than the cost, a $5,000 gain would be taxable.

How to Save Taxes on a Home-for-Apartments Trade

As with most property transactions, an investor faced with this type of problem has a perfectly legal way to save taxes. He can rent his home prior to making the trade, thus converting it to income property. Then he can trade up and avoid tax liability. As plainly as this is spelled out by the Internal Revenue Service, it is surprising how many owners of older homes where land values have mushroomed sell at high profits. They pay a healthy tax on their gain and then, as often as not, buy a piece of income property with the remaining proceeds. With a little forethought on tax implications, all the proceeds from the home could have been exchanged tax-free for an equity in income property.

The chief warning here, as with all transactions involving tax matters, is to make sure there will be no question of good faith in converting nonproductive to income property. The home should actually be rented to a bona fide tenant, even though it may be for a short time. Retain bookkeeping entries of rents received, backed by provable duplicate rent receipts, to show that you have collected rents. In cases of such conversion, keep tenants' names on file, so that they can be contacted for verification if needed.

9. INVESTOR VS. DEALER OR BROKER

As an average investor who buys, sells or trades on a sporadic basis, you are entitled to capital gains treatment on profits. You are subject to the maximum 25 per cent alternative capital gains tax in case of a long-term sale, or trading down, and subject to no tax in case of trading up or even. Taking time, effort and money to improve property, in addition to producing more income and turnover profit in the long run, also helps preserve your identity as an investor.

Broker

A real-estate broker handling the same transaction is normally considered to be carrying on property deals as part of his business. He is therefore liable for full income taxes on an ordinary income basis on profits from either sales or trades.

There are various ways in which some brokers circumvent this rule. Some take advantage of an investor's favorable tax position by setting up separate corporations, or by buying and selling through dummy individual title holders, who are owners in name only. There are many legal maneuvers available, and there are also many that are probably questionable. Suffice it to say that an investor who is not also a real-estate agent need not be concerned with the disadvantage of a broker's position from a capital gains standpoint.

Dealer

To retain capital gain advantages, the investor must beware of having his activities construed as those of a dealer or a speculator. The latter is primarily interested in quick sales, rather than improvements and income production. The boundaries between investment and speculation are not exact. Too many sales in one year might tag the seller as a dealer. In one state, for example, more than three sales in a tax year constitutes dealing, taxwise, while three or fewer are considered within the bounds of investment.

10. MINIMIZING POSSIBLE LOSSES

Anyone following the precepts set forth in this book discounts the possibility of taking a loss. However, there is always a chance for misjudgment or misfortune. In such an event continuing success may be governed by ascertaining as soon as possible that a mistake has been made. If it appears that there is little chance for gain and a chance of loss if a property is held, a loss can be minimized, and sometimes avoided, by quick liquidation.

A mistake can be liquidated by cashing out rather than holding out. Many a business bankruptcy could have been avoided if the bankrupt had taken a loss as soon as he realized his financial difficulties. Property owners can sometimes turn a potential loss into a gain by astute trading, or they may take a loss to offset taxable profits, thus minimizing the effect of the loss.

Taking Tax-Allowable Loss on Home

Many a homeowner subject to sudden relocation finds that he has to sell in a hurry and take a loss. It usually takes close to three months to sell a home. His loss is compounded if he has to leave before selling, the idle house deteriorates while uncared for, the lawn turns brown, and the backyard fills with weeds. Unfortunately, in such a case none of his loss can be claimed as a deduction for income tax purposes.

The loss can be alleviated, both in amount and by compensating income tax allowances, if the homeowner first rents his residence and then puts it up for sale. Finding a desirable, responsible tenant who will properly care for the property normally presents no problem, while finding a buyer is comparatively time-consuming.

Sometimes the tenant can be converted later into a buyer. If the house is rented with an extra charge for professional gardening, at least the garden will be kept in presentable condition. In some such cases the price might be held so that the owner turns his potential loss into a small gain, or at least a sale at cost.

If a loss finally results on the sale of a residence which is actually rented, any such loss becomes deductible. One point to watch for here is that the deductible loss may be reduced by the market value at the time of conversion to rental property. The fair market value is figured as the probable resale price if you were not forced to sell, and it might be about the same as your cost. The fair market value may reduce your deductible loss, but it cannot be utilized to increase your loss or reduce a possible taxable gain.

Here are examples of various tax applications:

If cost and fair market value at time of conversion are both $15,-000, and you sell for $13,000, you have a $2,000 deductible loss.

If the cost is $15,000 and the fair market value at time of conversion $14,000, and you sell for $13,000, you have a $1,000 loss for tax purposes.

If the cost is $15,000 and the fair market value $16,000, and you sell for $13,000, you have a $2,000 loss.

If the cost is $15,000 and the fair market value $17,000, and you sell for $16,000, you have a $1,000 gain.

Liquidating Deductible Loss on a Trailer Court

In one case, a widow inherited a ranch, which she sold at a $15,-000 profit over the appraised value at time of inheritance. She used the cash proceeds to buy a trailer court. A real-estate friend who made the sale assured her this was a trouble-free, sound, money-making investment.

Within a few months the widow realized she had made a poor buy. The trailer court was strictly a troublesome business, rather than an investment operation. The income was seasonal and failed to measure up to expectations. Also there were innumerable headaches from constant turnover in tenants, unstable managers, and heckling from local health, police, and building inspection authorities.

The widow decided to dump the trailer court, and she sold for $70,000 net, taking a $15,000 loss. The new buyer had a chance to make money on the court, as he intended to operate it himself. He put up $25,000 cash, and the widow took back a $45,000 first mortgage, payable in ten years at 7 per cent interest.

The widow set her sights on a desirable 40-unit apartment house, with a sale price and market value of $260,000. There was a 5½ per cent FHA loan of $160,000, payable in twenty-five years. Another broker friend said that the owner was anxious to sell out and move to Florida, and that he would accept a substantial discount if he received a minimum of $50,000 in cash.

Retrieved Loss Also Cancels Profits on Ranch

The widow hypothecated her first mortgage to borrow $35,000 at 6 per cent from her bank. She then offered $200,000 for the apartments, including a down payment of $40,000 cash. Negotiations resulted in her buying the forty apartments for $210,000, putting up $50,000 cash, and assuming the $160,000 FHA mortgage. Thus she still had $10,000 in cash from her hypothecated mortgage for an operating and improvement reserve.

The $15,000 loss taken on the trailer court canceled out her profit from the ranch sale. In this case she was better off, taxwise, selling the trailer court and taking a deductible loss, than she would have been if she had worked out a three-way trade for the apartments. A trade upward would have precluded her taking a tax loss.

By raising cash from the liquidation of her $15,000 loss, she had bought a desirable new property at a $50,000 discount. Thus her saving was more than three times her loss, transforming a shaky venture into a sound investment.

Income property offers you unmatchable tax-free opportunities for pyramiding a fortune.

27. MORE WAYS TO PROFIT
BY TAX SAVINGS

(Lecture to National Apartment Association Annual Convention Las Vegas, Nevada, October 16, 1968)

There have been a number of changes in income tax laws since my first book was printed. While there has been no major effect on investment opportunities, some points are especially significant for income property owners.

The new edition of my book incorporates applicable tax changes. I will cover these items, including references to both old and new tax laws and regulations.

How Apartment Owners Can Get Social Security

Little old ladies often grab me at lecture and other appearances to ask questions. As my hair grows thinner it seems that all these girls keep looking younger!

A peppy little lady stopped me in the hotel lobby and said, "I'm 64 and been a widow for many years. I own an 8-unit furnished apartment house free and clear of any loans. It's close to downtown. I get by as it is, but I'd be sitting pretty if I could only draw Social Security in addition to my rents.

"I could have a lot more fun going to Apartment Association Conventions and other meetings. Don't you think the Apartment Associations ought to push getting Social Security for all apartment owners?"

I said, "No. Why make all apartment owners pay Social Security taxes for themselves, when anyone who wants to can qualify?"

She said, "My C.P.A. tells me Social Security is impossible for me to get under present laws. Is he wrong? How do you think I can qualify?"

I said, "Your C.P.A. is correct for normal apartment operations, where you don't provide personal services. But all you have to do is make a change in your operations. Provide hotel service, like maid service and linens, to over half of your units. This means at least five of your eight apartments.

"Then you can file your income tax returns under Business Operations, instead of Investment Rents. That will qualify you for Social Security with self-employment income, rather than investment income."

She asked, "Must I do the maid's work myself?"

I said, "No, it doesn't matter whether you do it yourself or hire the labor as long as you provide the service."

She said, "Bless you. I'll be seeing you at all the National Conventions from now on."

Then she gave me a big kiss—just as my wife came along—so we both had some more questions to answer.

More Retirement Advantages for Owners

The availability of Social Security is an important provision for the smaller property owner approaching retirement. An owner of several apartment buildings has to change only one to hotel-type operations to qualify. It would be reported under Business Operations and the other regular apartment buildings would stay under Investment Income.

A taxpayer of sixty-five has many other advantages, of course, like Retirement Income Credit, taking two exemptions instead of one, and being able to sell a home for cash up to an adjusted net price of $20,-000 without tax on any profit.

TAX ADVANTAGES FOR APARTMENT MANAGERS

An apartment manager's income should be reported for Income Tax, Unemployment, and Social Security purposes. This automatically qualifies the manager for Social Security at retirement age. Many keep their cake and eat it, too, by continuing to work as managers while drawing Social Security. A manager's free apartment should be reported at less than market value for payroll purposes.

The manager's compensation can be arranged to result in higher income to the manager with tax savings for both manager and owner. Some owners pay their managers a full cash salary, then charge regular rent on their apartments. For example, in a 30-unit building with an apartment valued at $150, they would pay the manager $200 cash, then charge $150 for the apartment, resulting in a $50 net cash salary. But the manager with this arrangement has to pay income taxes on a $200 salary, and both owner and manager have to pay payroll taxes on this amount.

With the same basic deal, if you give the manager a free apartment in exchange for services, plus $50 cash, then the manager is not required to pay income taxes on the apartment value. This is because living there is a condition of employment. The tax saving represents extra income to the manager.

Also a manager's free apartment is commonly valued at two-thirds the market value for payroll purposes, with a maximum valuation of $75. This is the law in California, and similar provisions prevail in other states. This adjustment reduces unemployment, disability and Social Security taxes for both employee and employer. It also increases the maximum that an apartment manager can actually earn while drawing Social Security benefit payments.

Take All the Depreciation the Law Allows

The biggest advantage a property owner has to increase net revenues is in decreasing income taxes by taking all the depreciation the law allows. Even though you wind up with substantial in-pocket income, this can usually be offset entirely by depreciation—if you use beneficial accounting practices.

It pays to keep interested in figures to get the most out of life as an apartment investor, and it is perfectly legitimate to figure taxes to your best advantage.

When you first take over a property is the crucial time to set up depreciation accounts for your benefit. That is the time to segregate costs of various items, such as land, buildings, and furnishings.

You can take no depreciation on the basic land, so you should allocate its cost as low as possible, as long as it will appear realistic if you are audited. Then, in contrast, you want to allocate as high a percentage as possible to fast depreciating items. You can include all furniture, fixtures, and equipment in one blanket account, then depreciate, say, at 10 per cent over a 10-year life. Or you can select fast-wearing items like carpets, drapes and upholstered furniture and depreciate them quicker, say for 3- to 6-year lives.

Don't Overlook Land Improvements

After you have built up these fastest depreciating accounts as much as can appear realistic, the next faster depreciating item, often overlooked, is Land Improvements, as suggested in Depreciation Guidelines. This covers paving, sidewalks, landscaping and such items. All can be depreciated when new on the basis of a 20-year life. Of course this can be shortened to between 10 and 15 years on older properties.

40-Year Life for New Apartment Building

Now you have deducted first, the minimum allocated cost of nondepreciable land; second, the maximum cost of fastest depreciating furniture and fixtures; third, the allocated cost of land improvements. These depreciations are normally scheduled faster than your buildings, which are the fourth item that absorbs your remaining cost.

The Internal Revenue Service suggests depreciating a new apartment building over a 40-year life. Naturally, an older building, like the Cynthia Court in my book, can be depreciated faster, depending on age and condition. The rate would normally run between 5 and 3 per cent, spread over 20 to 33⅓ years.

STRAIGHT-LINE VS. ACCELERATED DEPRECIATION

Now that you have allocated your accounts, the next decision is whether to take straight-line or accelerated depreciation. Two hundred per cent declining balance depreciation, double straight line, was started to encourage new construction and the purchasing of new equipment by investors. The idea was that you could double your depreciation the first year to help offset your initial outlay. Then the depreciation would decrease each year until it fell below the amount for straight-line depreciation, thereby offsetting the accelerated depreciation you took in the beginning.

Speculator-builders and investment trusts got hold of this potential bonanza with a bright and perfectly legitimate idea. They made good profits on a tax-free basis by taking the big double depreciation for 2 to 5 years. Then they unloaded their properties long before depreciation dropped below straight line.

The first owner who rents can take 200 per cent of straight-line depreciation, whereas any but the first rental owner can take no more than 150 per cent. Bear in mind you don't have to be the first owner, but the first who rents. You can still take 200 per cent if you buy from a builder who has not rented.

The new laws are intended to penalize the in-and-out speculator without having much effect on the long-term investor. If you take accelerated depreciation and sell within 10 years you have to declare, on a sliding scale, as ordinary income the amount of depreciation that exceeds straight line. What can you do about this?

Basically, if you intend to resell a building within a few years of purchase, it would usually be advisable to take only straight-line depreciation. Then any profits from resale after holding at least one year would be at capital gain rates, 50 per cent of ordinary income, with a maximum rate of 25 per cent. On the other hand, if you expect to hold the property for many years, you could safely take the highest accelerated depreciation allowable.

Keep in mind that after you have allocated the costs of your original purchase, your additions and improvements can usually be depreciated on a varying basis. For example, you might do some remodeling and depreciate it over a 20-year period, even though your main building is depreciated for 30 or 40 years. You might put in new carpets and drapes and depreciate them over 3 years, as another example, and also on a 200 per cent declining balance basis, even though all your other depreciation is longer and straight line. Also, if you use at least a 6-year life, you may deduct 20 per cent of the cost of new furniture and equipment as additional First-Year Depreciation, up to a total bonus deduction of $2,000 on a single return and $4,000 on a joint return.

Many Deductions Are Often Overlooked

Real estate and other taxes and interest on your loans are, of course, deductible operating expenses, along with many other items. Some of them are often overlooked, especially by beginning property owners. A number of legitimate expenses are allowable as soon as you become an investor.

For example, the 1968 law says you can deduct 10 cents a mile for all use of your auto for investment purposes, up to 15,000 miles per year. Then you can deduct 7 cents per mile for all additional mileage. This covers you, your family and your employees. You should include trips to your properties for supervision, and also trips to look over prospective real estate you are thinking of buying. Don't forget shopping trips to buy supplies and equipment. You might visit several equipment dealers before buying stoves or refrigerators. Or you might send Junior to the hardware store to buy a monkey wrench for your apartments. After taking your mileage allowance, you can still deduct for parking fees and tolls.

An apartment owner with more extensive holdings might deduct the entire expenses of one or more autos. An easy way to account for auto expenses is to fill out U.S. Treasury Form 2106, Page 2, covering "Automobile Expenses, Basis, and Depreciation." I have visited several Income Tax offices, but none keep this form in view with the standard forms like 1040. They always keep it hidden under the counter. The information is not offered to you, but you're welcome to copies if you ask for them.

DUES AND ENTERTAINMENT DEDUCTIONS

A member of a professional organization, such as an Apartment Association, can deduct his dues and the cost of attending meetings, seminars and conventions. Both husband and wife can include travel, food, lodging and entertainment expenses. Better keep track of it all —unless you are afraid to show your wife or husband! Guidance on travel and entertainment, and also gift expenses, is covered in I.R.S. Publication No. 463, which is free.

PUBLICATIONS AND OFFICE EXPENSES

You may deduct the cost of professional magazines and books that help improve your operations and add to your investment education. My own books are good examples, along with tax books, like J. K. Lasser's.

If you keep an office in your home you can deduct a proportionate cost of house expenses, including depreciation, utilities, insurance and repairs. For example, if you have a 5-room house, and one room is set aside as your office for investment purposes, then you can deduct one-fifth of your home operating expenses. And you can take depreciation on 20 per cent of the cost of your home.

Besides office space, you can deduct for any portion of your home set aside for storage and repairs for investment purposes. For example, one investor I know converted his garage to a storeroom for storage and repair of apartment furniture, and all of its proportionate cost was deductible.

MORE DEDUCTIONS

Don't forget to keep track of such deductible items as medical expenses, sales and gasoline taxes, and miscellaneous contributions. A recent allowance permits you to deduct a flat 5 cents per mile for use of your auto for charitable purposes, such as attending Red Cross, Scout, or church committee meetings.

Deductions for contributions are limited to 20 per cent of the adjusted gross income except when made to certain church, hospital, government or other listed organizations, where the limit is 30 per cent. If you make more of these contributions in one year than the 30 per cent maximum allowable, you can carry the excess over for five future years.

ADVANTAGES OF PROPERTY CONTRIBUTIONS

The latter choice might be particularly appropriate where you contribute property. You can take credit for the full market value on donated property without paying a capital gains tax. For example, the market value on a piece of property contributed to your church is $10,000 and cost you only $1,000 several years ago. You can take credit for the $10,000 value and pay no capital gain on the book profit of $9,000. You can spread the contribution forward for up to 5 years.

Or you can consider the option of donating a portion of the property at a time. For example, each year you can deed to your church a 10 per cent undivided interest in the property, thus spreading the deduction over ten years.

Some advantages of splitting up portions of property for charitable contributions may also apply to gifts, say, to relatives. For example, you want to give a free-and-clear $24,000 fourplex to your son or daughter without paying a gift tax or disturbing your $30,000 lifetime gift exemption. You are allowed a tax-free gift of $3,000 per year to any person. So you could give a one-eighth portion of the $24,000 property per year for eight years, for example.

You could speed this up to four years by including your child's spouse, deeding one-fourth each year, for example, to your daughter and her husband. Suppose they have six children whom you want to include in your deed? This makes eight persons, with $3,000 tax-free for each, so the whole property could be given tax-free in one year.

Where a husband and wife own property together, each can give $3,000 worth of property, thus doubling to $6,000 the maximum annual amount to any person.

A NEW LOOK AT TURNOVER PROFITS

Now to look at saving money on turnover profits after you have built up the net income and therefore the market value of your apartments. If you trade for a larger property this is considered a continuation of the same investment, and generally not subject to tax. If you sell for cash and have taken no accelerated depreciation since January 1, 1964, you pay half the ordinary tax rate, with a maximum capital gains tax of 25 per cent. If you take back a mortgage of 70 per cent or more, you can spread your profit over the life of the mortgage. This is why many sellers refuse to take all cash, and insist on heavy financing, giving the buyer an opportunity to acquire property with a low down payment.

There is a new gimmick in a recent tax change whereby you can sell for all cash at a big profit and still pay a low tax if you have been coasting along with income offset by depreciation for the past 5 years. This is called Income Averaging. An unusually big income in one year may be taxed according to the average tax paid in the previous 5 years. This could be of special advantage to a broker taxed as a dealer, or to an investor who has taken a lot of accelerated depreciation that is taxable on sale as ordinary income.

LOAN PROCEEDS ARE FREE FROM INCOME TAXES

It usually pays to trade up when you start with smaller properties. Larger holdings are easier to supervise because they can support competent resident managers to handle operating details. Once you have developed a desirable property, it often pays to retain it and refinance to get funds for more pyramiding. One investor paid $100,000 for a piece of property, including improvement costs, and later borrowed $150,000 on it. This gave him $50,000 in extra cash to start new pyramids. The loan has to be repaid, of course, but you don't have to pay a cent in taxes for money you receive from financing, even when loans exceed costs.

HAVE YOU EVER BEEN AUDITED?

I have often been asked, "Have you ever been audited?"

Since my first book came out I have been audited four times, twice by the Federal Government and twice by the State of California. Their second audits concerned the royalties on my books. They wanted me to pay all the taxes in one year, even for money received over several years. I appealed all the way to Tax Court and finally won.

Incidentally, my appeal was settled on the basis of some juggling of income between different tax years, a compromise on paper. But it all came out even, so I didn't have to pay any more Federal taxes. The State of California said they would go along with whatever Uncle Sam decided after I appealed to Tax Court. Because of different sliding rates, the juggling between years resulted in the State's owing me. So they closed the case by mailing me a refund check for $350!

The first auditors from I.R.S. and the State came to delve into my real estate operations. One of the agents said his boss had read in *Time* how I made a million net in real estate on a virtually tax-free basis. The boss said, "Look up Nickerson's returns." Then he said, "Audit him with a fine tooth comb. I don't believe he could be worth that much and pay so little taxes."

CLEAN AS A HOUND'S TOOTH

Normally the statute of limitations runs out after 3 years, unless they can prove fraud or gross underpayment. They audited me from the first realty purchase I ever made, just in case they could uncover something. Luckily, I had been waiting for such an audit all these years and was fully prepared. I had kept all my books and every scrap of paper showing expenses, purchases, trades and sales, where I got the money and where I spent it, down to every individual receipt for even the smallest item.

They asked, for example, "Where did you get the $15,000 you paid down on this apartment house? You don't show it anywhere as income."

Contrary to common law, with the tax people you are guilty until you prove yourself innocent. If they find where you have spent any funds, they take the position it is taxable income unless you can prove otherwise. In this case my documents showed that the money came from refinancing another apartment house after I had improved it. Of course, as mentioned, you don't pay taxes on money you get from financing.

The auditors spent two weeks going over all my files. When they got through one revenue agent said, "Your operations are certainly clean as a hound's tooth. I've audited a lot of books. But until I checked yours I never realized how you could build a million-dollar fortune and pay hardly any income tax. I'm going right out and buy your book myself!"

Be Cooperative

Just in case you are audited, be cooperative in answering questions. But don't volunteer information you are not asked for. You might open up a new subject the agent hasn't even thought of, then waste a lot of time explaining yourself. If an agent claims you owe more tax than you think is right, don't hestitate to fight back. If you feel you are weak on a particular point, it often pays to compromise and save a lot of time by paying a small assessment.

Before making a final agreement, take time to investigate applicable laws and regulations and seek competent advice from an accountant or attorney specializing in real estate. Your local Apartment Association should be able to make a good recommendation. If you still believe you are in the right after investigation, don't compromise. Fight it out with the Agent, then his Supervisor, if necessary, then the I.R.S. Appellate Division. If you don't win there, take your appeal to Tax Court, as I did. You also have the alternative of appealing to the U.S. District Court.

Although you will normally need a qualified tax attorney or C.P.A., I appealed all the way to Tax Court with no such assistance. I wanted to gain firsthand experience, so my advice would be of greater help to other property owners. And it was more of a challenge to take on the government attorneys single-handed!

If you fight for your rights, the odds are heavily in your favor that you have a good chance of winning, either partially or completely. Keep in mind that the Tax Court cannot possibly handle more than 20 per cent of the cases filed. Thus 80 per cent must be settled before they go to Court. This gives you odds of 4 to 1 in your favor that you will gain all or at least some concession if you have the will to fight.

The Chances of Your Return's Being Audited

As an example of I.R.S. scheduling, all of the more than sixty million individual returns filed in 1958 were checked by the government for accurate arithmetic. A cross section were pulled at random and received a thorough audit. The approximately 20 per cent which showed incomes over $5,000 were given a complete study, and all returns over $25,000 were audited in detail. Whether such an audit results in a visit to your office, or in an invitation to bring all your records to the local income tax office, depends on the Internal Revenue Service analysis.

Reasonable income in relation to investments, and reasonable deductions and exemptions according to income, will normally be accepted without further question. But apparently insufficient listing of income, claiming of unallowable exemptions, and unreasonable deductions may bring the tax auditors swooping to check over your every bookkeeping entry. In this event, a receipt or other acceptable evidence may be demanded for every item of expense.

I should mention that audits often result from listing legitimate expenses in the wrong schedule. For example, you would normally list interest on mortgaged apartments under rental expenses. But suppose you get an unsecured improvement loan on the property? Where do you list that interest?

Many owners list all such interest on unsecured loans under Itemized Deductions. To a tax computer this looks like a personal expense and distorts personal deductions beyond a reasonable limit. Just this one item may result in selecting your return for an audit. Make it a point to keep the computer happy, and list all such expenses under the proper business or investment schedules.

The Internal Revenue Service reports that one out of every 28 returns was challenged in the fiscal year ended June 30, 1957. Close to $1,700,000,000 in additional income taxes resulted from the more than two million corrected returns. In the early 1960s the I.R.S. leaned to less quantity and more so-called "quality" audits, making in-depth studies that bordered on harassment. Their intensive "fishing expeditions" antagonized the innocent and proved insufficiently productive to compensate for the additional auditing time. Such nit-picking audits have generally been abandoned. The trend in 1968 is to turn more of the fishing over to computers, and spread more reasonable audits over a greater number of taxpayers. Their goal for 1968–69 is to audit 5 per cent of all returns, but it appears this target will be reduced 1 or 2 per cent by proposed government economizing.

KEEP RECORDS

To sleep well nights, always be prepared for a thorough audit. Take no deductions or exemptions on which there is a question, after checking available guides, until you receive specific approval from the Internal Revenue Service. Make your return as honest and complete as possible.

Maintain complete records. Retain receipts, cancelled checks and other evidence for at least five years as proof of income and expenses. And maintain permanent records regarding all realty purchases, sales, trades and financing.

Render unto Caesar the things that are Caesar's, but don't pay more taxes than you have to. Take advantage of all tax-saving opportunities.

As long as you are prepared, and your returns are accurate and appear reasonable, the chances are you will never be questioned.

PART TEN

DEVELOPING YOUR ESTATE

28. HOW TO OPERATE UNDER GOVERNMENT REGULATIONS

The income property owner operates under many different forms of regulation and control. Wartime-inaugurated Federal "defense area" rent controls, covering five million houses and apartments, were abolished by December 31, 1953. In the preceding two years, controls had already been dropped by local approval in many communities, including Atlanta, Houston, Los Angeles, Oakland, San Francisco, and Seattle. Congressional authority for Federal controls died completely April 30, 1954.

Local controls were adopted in the states of Connecticut, New Jersey, and Massachusetts, and in the cities of Baltimore and Philadelphia, but by December 1957 they had been dropped. Judicial rulings have differed, some approving and some repudiating the continuation of controls except in war. Philadelphia, for example, imposed controls by city ordinance from 1953 to December 1956, when the Pennsylvania Supreme Court ruled that no emergency existed which warranted imposition.

At this writing, in 1968, controls are still in effect, under state local-option provisions, for two-thirds of the 2.1 million privately owned dwelling units in New York City, although dropped in various parts of the state since April 30, 1953. Besides local control in New York City, rent-control regulations are still in effect on a national basis under specified FHA-insured projects, including Sections 207, 213, 220, 608, and 908. In 1958, for example, close to half a million FHA-insured rental units were still subject to rent control.

479

ALWAYS SOME REGULATION AND CONTROL

Although rent ceilings and regulations may subdue progress, our objective of pyramiding equities to a million dollars is still feasible under such controls. Although some present controls may be abolished or modified, others may be retained for some years. According to a 1958 letter addressed to me by John S. Wagner, Director of Public Information for the New York Temporary State Housing Rent Commission:

> New York State took over rent control on May 1, 1950.
> The present law will expire on June 30, 1959. However, the rent law has periodically been renewed for two-year terms. It is anybody's guess whether controls will be extended again for the entire state; *but it is pretty safe to assume that New York City will have rent control indefinitely* [italics mine].

With rent controls on the way out everywhere else in the U.S., why should New York City anticipate indefinite continuation? Mainly because, country-wide, 60 per cent of families own their homes, whereas in New York City 70 per cent are renters living in multiple dwellings of three units or more.

Whether restricted by rent controls or not, apartment operations are generally subject to state housing laws and various municipal and county ordinances. Departments charged with enforcing conformance to their codes include:

Fire
Police
Health
Sanitation
Urban Renewal
Building, including subbureaus, such as
    Electrical
    Plumbing

CHECK PERMIT RESTRICTIONS

As long as you keep a decent building and plan no remodeling, you may seldom hear from any of these departments, except for an occasional or annual inspection. If you request a permit to remodel, representatives of all departments may descend on you, demanding as a condition to issuing a permit that your entire building be brought up to date to meet new codes devised since its erection. Mandatory improvements which might involve considerable cost include complete electrical rewiring and conduiting and complete replumbing for vents and drain lines.

Before letting a contract for extensive alterations, be sure that a permit can be obtained that will not require major changes not contracted for. Added costs may be too great for the planned remodeling to be worth while. Repairs or replacements, like installing new carpet and painting at the Cynthia Court Apartments, normally would not entail extensive changes. Neither would minor conversions of space, like converting the refrigerator room to a launderette. But additions or alterations, such as adding dwelling rooms and changing basements or attics to apartments, might be permitted only by updating a whole building.

Usually such contingencies are subject to modification. For example, I wished to add six new apartments to the front of a 3-story, 6-flat building similar to our Belvedere Apartments. Adding two units to the third story would have invoked the state housing code and would have necessitated rewiring and replumbing the entire building at a cost of $8,000. This was saved by changing plans to include only four additional apartments on two floors. Additions up to two stories came under only the city code, which did not require modifying the rest of the building.

DON'T FIGHT CITY HALL

Observe the time-proved axiom that it seldom pays to "fight City Hall." Code inspectors and rent control authorities have a responsibility to carry out their jobs. Administration of their regulations is usually far from exact, apt to be subject to much interpretation and modification.

Upon visiting regulatory offices, I have heard owners publicly rant of unjust controls and loudly accuse an administrator of being inefficient, biased, and vicious. Naturally the official will be inclined to discount their side of a controversy involving a complaint. And, to guard against circumvention, he may intensify his policing to the point of harassment.

HONEY OUTDRAWS VINEGAR

Your improvement purposes can best be accomplished if you appear co-operative and reasonable. Give full compliance to obvious and unquestionable regulations, and rulings will more often be made in your favor when controversial borderline cases arise. Even if adverse rulings are made, you may still be successful in winning alleviating modifications.

INFLEXIBLE FRENCH CONTROLS
RESULT IN SLUMS

Rent controls generally are designed to hold rents to a level in effect on a given "freeze" date, with little regard as to whether the rent was below market levels at the time. At this writing the most drastic controls appear to be in France, where rents on older housing are still frozen at prewar ceilings. Rents are so unrealistic in the face of present inflation that many owners would prefer that the government confiscate their property for taxes. Strangely enough, I know of cases where the French government refused to take the hapless owner off the hook when so requested, forcing him to continue losing money.

With property operating at a loss, owners carry on no upkeep or maintenance. When strictly inflexible controls allow no profits, deterioration is accelerated and investment properties are inevitably converted to slums before their time.

OWNERS CAN MAKE ENDS MEET
ONLY BY SUBTERFUGE

Tenants who stay put get ridiculously cheap rent. But new tenants pay terrific bonuses. Prospective newlyweds postpone sanctified marriage for years, waiting for a tenant to move or die, while they raise the necessary bonus. In one typical case which I investigated in Paris, the annual rent for a desirable 2-bedroom apartment was $500.

An elderly couple had rented the apartment since 1928. The husband died, and the widow stopped paying even this cheap rent. She eventually fell two years behind, and the owner was still unable to evict her under the tortuous rent control and eviction laws.

The owner had many tenant-applicants waiting in line. One desperate couple, who had postponed their church marriage for two years while waiting for a vacancy, boosted their bonus offer to $10,000. The owner offered the widow half, $5,000, less the $1,000 in arrears, to vacate.

The tenant resisted the offer. It developed that she was averaging $35 weekly subletting the spare bedroom to tourists. She finally settled for $5,000 in-pocket cash, then moved to her sister's home in Rouen.

Bonuses are strictly illegal of course. Owners are supposed to file all vacancies with the government rent registry. Many hopeful tenants have been on the registry preferred list for years, waiting naïvely for a gratuitous vacancy. They may have to wait out their lifetimes unless there is a change in French controls. Rare is the owner who lists a money-losing vacancy, when his only chance to recoup is by extracting a bonus.

NEW-CONSTRUCTION GIMMICKS

In France, as in New York City, new construction is not subject to control. Many beautiful luxury-type apartments are being erected. Even though there are no vacant apartments in all of France, little new privately built housing goes up for the low-income tenant who needs it most. Builders, catering to heavy-bonus payers, have introduced many new gimmicks to extract exorbitant profits and circumvent possible later application of controls.

Outstanding examples are a number of dwellings recently erected on the Riviera as co-operative housing, where each tenant has to buy his apartment. Apartments that might cost $10,000 each to build are sold on a co-operative basis for $25,000. Some of the apartments are actually operated as co-operatives. Several which I checked were only dummy co-ops with control retained by the builder through shares held in the co-op corporation. The tenants prorate regular operating costs, plus a substantial additional amount for management. The latter plum goes to the builder, who thus refutes the saying, "You can't have your cake and eat it." After collecting a 150 per cent profit on his sale, the builder retains the position of a rental owner by continuing to collect a highly profitable return for management.

A COMPARISON OF OTHER COUNTRIES

Before returning to the U. S., let us take a brief look at my on-the-ground observations on the effect of the continuation of controls in other countries.

GREAT BRITAIN'S ECONOMY HAMPERED BY EXCESSIVE CONTROLS

Several government attempts have been made to relax rent controls in England, but always too much opposition has arisen from tenant groups. Wartime restrictions have continued in most phases of economic life. This, along with nineteenth-century union restrictions against mechanization, contributes to a great extent to the lagging of the British economy. Billions in American aid have been poured down their regulatory rathole in a vain attempt to bolster an economy hampered by excessive controls. If these billions had been used for productive purposes, as in Germany, you would see more rapid new building to replace the block after block of structures that have lain gutted and useless for decades.

GERMANY'S FREE ECONOMY IS BOOMING

In marked contrast is the booming economy in Germany, where wartime restrictions against free enterprise were generally abolished early. Germany used her American aid to promote rather than restrict investment opportunities. Germany in defeat was devastated worse than victorious England before the war ended. But Germany has recovered, caught up with, and surpassed England economically, largely because of its greater encouragement of individual enterprise.

ITALY HAS DECIDED TO FOLLOW THE GERMAN EXAMPLE

Italy has taken a realistic look at results in England, France and Germany, and has decided, after considerable hesitation, to follow the German lead toward free, rather than controlled, economy. Effective January 1, 1958, a 20 per cent increase was permitted in the rents that were frozen during World War II. Additional increases were scheduled until decontrolled rent levels were attained.

U.S. CONTROLS ARE MORE FLEXIBLE

Although originally designed to freeze rents, postwar controls in the United States are more flexible, having been modified to allow owners a reasonable profit. Even during the war, when controls were comparatively rigid, there were many legal means of raising rents. Chief among them was the provision for "hardship cases," where rents on the freeze date were unusually low, or where expenses increased to the point of eliminating profits.

Now that the war is long over, the apartment house owner's lot has been alleviated even in the remaining rent-control stronghold of New York City. A comparison of New York's with the former Federal controls shows a great deal of similarity. Most of the changes in pattern by the former tend toward greater flexibility. New York State new construction after February 1947, for example, is exempt. The owner in New York City, or any other rent-control area, should consider implications in relation to his operations and then study appropriate local regulations before taking action.

The discouraged owners of about one-fourth the 1,400,000 rent-controlled apartments in New York City have watched their units drop below the slum line, offsetting $8 billion spent for government-sponsored housing. However, other individual and institutional owners are able to make profits through continuing renovation and modernization and taking advantage of all rent-raising opportunities.

FHA-REGULATED RENTALS

Federal controls on other than FHA-insured housing have been abolished by Congress. But the Federal Housing Administration perpetuates "rent regulations" nationally under the National Housing Act, continuing to control rents under various Sections including 207, 213, 220, 608, and 908. At the present writing there seems to be no program for abolishing these regulations, which are designed basically to restrict the return on investment. Rent raises generally can gain approval to offset increasing expenses, such as higher tax, insurance, and labor costs. Otherwise the chief means of raising rents is by adding a service or facility not included in the FHA-insured mortgage.

One outstanding example of increasing profits under Section 608 regulation concerned forty desirable 2-bedroom apartments in an above-average rental district. The neighborhood had been semi-industrial when the apartments were built, but it was rapidly growing into a choice rating because of new commercial and housing developments. The rents were frozen at the original rental of $75. The original owner took no steps to secure approval for a raise, even though expenses had risen. Finally, discouraged by the difficulty of continuing operation under controls, he sold out to a new investor at the existing rental value, far below both reproduction and potential-income values.

BASE RENT RAISED BECAUSE OF INCREASED EXPENSES

Similar apartments not subject to Section 608 controls were renting for $125 in the area. The new owner studied steps which could raise his rents to comparable levels. Various costs, including school district, city, and county taxes, had risen considerably. In local-control areas like Massachusetts, owners had received blanket authorization to raise rents 30 per cent because of increased costs. In a suburb of Chicago, FHA approved Section 608 increases up to $10.75 per unit.

In this case the new owner presented his cost figures to the local FHA office and received approval to raise all rents 20 per cent to $90. This one move alone increased the gross rental and the net profit $7,200 annually, raising the income valuation by $72,000.

SERVICES DECREASED OR CHANGED TO SAVE EXPENSES

One of the chronic headaches of the previous owner had been the laundry room, where the tenants were furnished free use of old-fashioned, nonautomatic washing machines. These frequently broke down, demanding constant repairs. Not only the owner but the tenants, too, were unhappy, because machines were often out of service, laundry had to be slopped from one broken-down washer to another, and suds and water usually lay on the concrete floor of the drab, unpainted laundry room.

Converting to a coin-operated launderette was an obvious solution. The previous owner had asked permission from the FHA office and had been refused on the ground that the tenants would be charged for service now included in the rents. The new owner polled the tenants with the following questionnaire:

ARE YOU SATISFIED with the PRESENT LAUNDRY FACILITIES?
Would you prefer a new, modern, house launderette, with automatic washers and dryers? The additional cost would be covered by coin operation, with a smaller charge than in commercial launderettes. Please mark preference and return to Manager.

Prefer new launderette——
Prefer no change——

Only one tenant out of the forty voted to retain the old laundry, thirty-nine voting for a change. Many had already been taking their laundry to a commercial launderette, and of course they welcomed a cheaper and more convenient service in the apartment building. After seeing the poll results, the local FHA office sanctioned a coin launderette. The owner had a commercial company install new automatic washers and dryers, equipped with coin collectors. The launderette company paid for the equipment, including installation and maintenance, and paid the owner 25 per cent of the gross income. This eliminated laundry repair and replacement costs for the owner, and it added an average of $30 monthly income.

SERVICES OR FACILITIES ADDED
TO INCREASE INCOME

To make the tenants even happier with the change, the owner brightened the laundry with a sunny yellow ceiling and cheery pink walls. With dryers in the launderette, tenants no longer needed so much outside space for drying. There was an extensive concrete-surfaced drying yard in the rear of the apartments, with long lines on poles. These were removed, and two umbrella-type dryers were installed in a small space, for tenants who occasionally desired outdoor drying. Enough ground was saved to mark off ten parking places, for each of which the owner was able to collect $5 monthly.

The previous owner had allowed outgoing tenants to rerent to friends at the low-ceiling rents. The new owner stopped this cozy arrangement for perpetuating tenancy, taking over the customary authority to choose tenants. All the apartments were unfurnished except for stoves and refrigerators. Many of the tenants were Air Force personnel, subject to transfer. As they vacated, the owner completely equipped each apartment with new furniture. The cost averaged $600 per apartment for furniture retailing at $1,200.

Unfurnished 2-bedroom apartments not subject to control in the area rented for $125, even though they averaged less space. The furniture was an added item not subject to the FHA-insured mortgage. The owner charged enough, with FHA approval, to obtain closer to market value on the entire accommodation. The furnished apartments rented readily for $140, including $90 for the rent-frozen apartments and $50 for the furniture.

Twenty-one months after the apartments were taken over by the new owner a broker brought a cash offer which would have given $100,000 net profit, but the owner refused to sell. There were still other means in mind to increase net income.

This specific example of increasing values under Section 608 regulations has been duplicated under other types of FHA-supervised mortgages, and under area rent controls. I checked two $1,000,000 housing projects in different areas under FHA control other than Section 608. Adding furniture at above-normal profits was the common practice. Furniture charges ran from $25 monthly for 1-bedroom to $50 for 2-bedroom rental units. In both projects, it should be mentioned, wear and tear was excessive because of renting to families with children. This was offset in many instances by collecting a damage deposit, ranging between $50 and $100.

The added income from furniture rentals offered a sound method for increasing net profits under FHA regulations.

Your improvement purposes can best be accomplished if you cooperate with regulatory administrators. Observe the time-proved axiom that it seldom pays to fight City Hall. Remember that honey outdraws vinegar.

Flexible rent controls in the United States have been modified to allow improvement-minded owners a reasonable profit. Although rent regulations may subdue progress, our objective of pyramiding equities to a million dollars is still feasible under controls.

29. HOW TO AVOID PITFALLS

Six months after taking over the Cynthia Court Apartments, our net worth for investment purposes exceeds $100,000, as will be detailed in the next chapter. It is amazing how many friendly salespeople turn up with attractive suggestions as soon as you become established as a successful investor with a six-figure net estate. Their stated purpose is always to make you a lot of easy money, but their actual objective is usually to transfer assets from your pocket to theirs.

Before examining further the investment possibilities ahead, it would be well to consider how to avoid pitfalls which might dissipate rather than develop your estate. The best way to avoid pitfalls is to understand them. Earlier in the book I cited checks to help insure against mistakes in buying income property. The purpose of this chapter is to show money-losing pitfalls which have proved particularly attractive to successful income-property investors.

BEWARE THE UNKNOWN

It is a common but false doctrine that success in one field assures success in another. The key to avoiding mistakes is to stay in your proved field of investment, as most money is lost in trying an unknown business or speculation. If you scrutinize every glittering promise of quick and easy money against this sound precept, you will not go far wrong.

I will not attempt to cover the hundreds of petty and grand bunko schemes, which are more of a business nature and about which the Better Business Bureau can give complete information. My chief purpose is to describe the pseudo investments to which owners of apartment houses and other income property have proved susceptible. There are some ventures so close to the property investment field that many an experienced owner has failed to recognize the chasm of separation. Formerly carefree and prosperous apartment operators have blithely sold proved income property for ventures which doomed them to bankruptcy.

THIRTEEN PITFALLS THAT MAY LEAD TO BANKRUPTCY

All the pitfalls listed have been proposed to me at one time or another, giving me the opportunity to examine their potentialities and drawbacks in detail. They are:

1. Resorts
2. Motels and hotels
3. Unproductive property
4. Distress property
5. Unfamiliar businesses
6. Partnership gimmicks
7. Buy-back contracts
8. Advance-fee financing
9. Overmortgaged properties
10. Lending money
11. Oil and gas leases
12. Gentleman-farming
13. Advice from paper profiteers

1. RESORTS

Certain inducements are called "sucker bait" by knowing realtors. Resorts head the list of bait for property-minded investors. Some, ideally located and operated, pay good returns. A great many operate at a loss. Your first resort may be not only your last resort but also your last investment, if you go broke too late in life to feel like making a fresh start.

An Unfortunate Example

In one unfortunate case, a couple in their fifties jumped at the chance to trade their free-and-clear 18-unit apartment house for a summer resort, where they anticipated retiring. They did not realize that a resort is not an investment like an apartment house, but a seasonal business operation. The apartments were worth $100,000, and the broker told the owners he could get them $150,000 on the trade. The resort was quoted at $200,000 on the basis of the cost of replacement, and by projecting seasonal receipts on a twelve-month basis. However, on the basis of optimistic income possibilities, the maximum value of the resort was about $75,000, as the owner had actually been losing money for the previous three years.

On the basis of comparable values, the couple should have received a boot of $25,000. But they gave a boot of $50,000, in the form of a mortgage on the resort, thus paying double its worth. They failed to make a realistic examination of the property taken over, merely because they thought they were making $50,000 in excess valuation of their own property. After trading in their apartments, the couple slaved for two years, vainly trying to make their resort pay expenses. It was finally foreclosed because they couldn't keep up the loan payments. In the sad aftermath, the husband shot himself and the wife was committed to a state insane asylum.

Quoted below are resort baits which were presented to them, and which are commonly dangled before the unwary.

False Income

"You can make a big income from rooms, meals, bar, pool, picnics, and bathhouse. Each is a juicy money-maker, and you could make a living off of any one of them."

The income from many means of production looks good on paper. One resort bought by another apartment owner earned only 25 per cent of the income listed. The statement showed heavy income for Christmas and Easter vacations, and for six solid months from May 1 to November 1. This appeared reasonable to an apartment owner used to year-round occupancy.

Actually the place was empty except from Memorial Day to Labor Day, a period of slightly more than three months. Even during the season the resort suffered from "weekenditis." Most guests came up only for weekends, leaving accommodations only partly occupied in midweek.

False Tax Savings

"You can save incomes taxes by covering up odd income like picnic fees, and by doing all your personal entertaining and having your own de luxe vacation tax-free."

Even after honestly including all receipts, there will seldom be an income tax, because there will be no net income. Only exceptional operations stay out of the red on a twelve-month basis. You might make money during the season, but this will be more than offset by heavy overhead, including especially high labor and insurance costs.

False Leisure

"You can easily get help to take care of all the headaches, and you can sit back and lead the life of Riley."

Instead of relieving headaches, resort help turns out to be the main headache. You cannot promise security, since you expect to lay off all but stand-by employees at season's end. Employees in turn have no feeling of permanent loyalty. Many fail to stay for the season, some leaving after their first pay check. Others leave when you need them most, when the work gets heavy, like a peak Fourth-of-July weekend. You find yourself enjoying your anticipated leisure by testing your endurance, filling in the gaps left by suddenly decamped cooks, dishwashers, garbage collectors, bartenders, waiters, maids, masseurs, lifeguards, gardeners, *et al.*

Liquidating Loss on Resort

Many resort buyers who, like the first couple, find themselves losing money, compound their mistakes by holding out for an additional season or two, trying to recoup their losses. Seldom does this lead anywhere but to bankruptcy. Our second investor, who found his receipts only 25 per cent of expectations, had traded a 24-unit apartment house for his resort. As the season progressed he borrowed on another apartment house in order to carry his terrific overhead.

At the end of the season he took a comparatively small loss by trading the resort to a large labor union, which planned to use it as a private club. The relieved resort owner took in trade a grocery store leased to a national chain. The market values of both properties were about equal, but the grocery store had a $5,500 larger mortgage, constituting boot to the seller.

The next year the grocery store was coupled with a 12-unit apartment house, and the two properties were traded together for a desirable 40-unit apartment house. Although a mistake had been made trading the 24-unit property for the resort and he had taken a $5,500 loss dumping the resort in exchange for the grocery store, the loss was recouped completely, and a small gain added. The investor wound up as well off as if he had initially made a profitable trade of his 24- and 12-unit buildings for the 40-unit building.

Taxwise he was better off. Taxes would not have been affected on a direct trade, as they were not affected in trading the grocery store for the 40-unit apartment house. But the $5,500 loss represented in trading the resort for the store was fully deductible, since boot had been paid. The loss could have been applied to offset gains, or it could have been spread over the year of loss and the next five years, at a maximum of $1,000 per year.

False Value on Basis of Reproduction

The salesman may say, "You're getting the buildings at half the cost of reproduction, and the land free. You can't go wrong with such a bargain."

Income is always the controlling yardstick on income-property valuations, with other factors, like reproduction costs, being subsidiary. This is most true with resorts, where reproduction may not have the slightest bearing on income value. A de luxe resort castle built on the edge of nowhere at a cost of $1,000,000 is worth only $10,000 if its net income is $1,000 per year. And it may be absolutely worthless if it cannot produce sufficient income to offset expenses.

One Man's Profit May Be Another Man's Loss

Resorts, like all business operations, are heavily responsive to the peculiarities and abilities of their owners. A change in ownership can quickly change money-makers to money-losers, and also the reverse. Whereas a certified profit-and-loss statement on an apartment house usually can be taken as a basis which you can at least match, the same is not true of business, and especially not true of resorts.

Two brothers and their wives, with six children ranging from fourteen to twenty-one, traded the equities in their homes, in the early spring, for a modest resort at a valuation of $20,000. They knew the resort had lost money the previous year, but this failed to discourage them. The depreciated reproduction value of the buildings, according to an insurance appraisal, was $110,000. There were 625 acres of sparsely forested land. The two families figured that they had bought a gold mine.

By the end of Labor Day weekend they had netted approximately $8,000, based on actual out-of-pocket expenses and actual income. None of the ten family members had enjoyed a day's rest all summer, and they were all anxious to sell out. Two of the older children wanted to marry, which would have meant fewer hands for the next season.

Another Man's Loss

By Thanksgiving an enterprising resort broker had managed to trade the family summer venture for a 12-unit apartment house, at a valuation of $75,000. The apartment seller accepted at face value the $8,000 net for six months' operation from April 1 to October 1. He and his wife had always wanted to own a resort, because they loved to entertain, they liked country life, and they anticipated that they could improve considerably the net figures of the previous owners.

The main point overlooked was the value of the labor on the part of the ten family members. Not a cent had been taken out for their wages. The next year's gross income of the new resort owner was about on par with the sellers'. But by the time labor costs and off-season overhead were paid for, expenses exceeded income and the new owners faced the next Thanksgiving completely broke.

2. MOTELS AND HOTELS

As an example of an unsound buy, we cited a hotel operation, the Margie-Joe, in Chapter 9, while seeking a $40,000 apartment house. Many an apartment owner looks at an income statement on motels and hotels based on full house rentals, and he thinks he is getting a terrific buy on the basis of scheduled income. As mentioned before, these operations are subject to seasonal and weekend fluctuations that may drop their actual income to a half or even a tenth of a scheduled full house.

Motels and hotels, like resorts, are business rather than investment operations. Labor costs are excessive compared to apartment houses, and so are replacement and other operational costs. Many pay high gross returns, but they seldom prove successful in paying net income except with experienced and high-priced management.

"Hot Bed" Income

A favorite bait dangled by motel salesmen is "hot bed" income from renting the same room more than once a night. Most motels close to metropolitan areas earn some such extra rentals. But the actual amount is greatly exaggerated and rarely makes up for off-season and midweek vacancies, to result in the equivalent of 100 per cent occupancy.

A suspicious buyer may ask to see a C.P.A.'s tax statement as to actual income and expenses, which is considered a reasonable request on business properties. The broker or seller may wink and say, "You don't think the tax return shows anywhere near the actual income, do you? Why, some of these beds are rented out five or six times a night. Do you think we're crazy enough to show Uncle Sam more than one rental a night? I tell you hot beds are where the real money is, in motels, and if you're smart you won't be paying any income taxes on all this extra money any more than we do."

Uncle Sam sanctions legitimate deductions but hardly condones illicit evasions. He might say that anyone buying on the basis of evading taxes deserves to be fleeced. Any suggestion of making money illegitimately, by tax evasion or otherwise, should be examined with a jaundiced eye and considered as prima-facie evidence that the offered property is not for you. A sound investment, like a sound church, does not need to harp on the wages of sin in order to win your interest.

3. UNPRODUCTIVE PROPERTY

A basic precept we have previously mentioned is that one should buy only property that pays for itself. Sometimes you may be tempted to flout this admonition. Speculation in unproductive property may be considered if you have large holdings. It is extremely dangerous economically for your sole or major investment. There are three major categories of unproductive property of which you should be wary:

Vacant land, including lots
Empty apartments
Unleased stores and warehouses

Vacant Land, Including Lots

Buying unimproved land is purely speculation, rather than an investment. Committing all, or most, assets to such purposes is extremely unsound. You might make a fortunate choice and reap spectacular rewards. On the other hand, your choice might lie comparatively valueless for some time, all the while eating up overhead in taxes and interest. I have known of speculative land purchases which have proved worthless, yet owners have continued throwing good money after bad by keeping up taxes and assessments. This is like buying oats for a dead horse.

Even if you make a sound choice and earn a capital gain, nine times out of ten you could make more by putting your money into productive apartments that pay off loans and operating costs in addition to turnover profits.

Empty Apartments

Two or three vacancies in an otherwise full 24-unit apartment building, like the Cynthia Court, should give no cause for worry, as they should readily be filled. Be especially wary of apartment houses, like the Floradale mentioned in Chapter 9, where most or all of the units are empty. The projected income schedule may be even more than double the actual potential.

A favorite sales lure advertises an empty building as being capable of producing extremely favorable returns, based on promised potential rents. The sucker who bites finds to his disillusionment that he can rent only for less than half the advertised amount. A buyer's chief safeguard is to make sure a property is actually producing income and not merely promises.

Although you may buy with the potential in mind, never pay for the promise of a high potential. Always buy on the basis of present income, and on the basis that the present income will be fairly sustaining. Any potential increases should be considered potential profit after you build up a property and put potential rentals into effect.

Unleased Stores and Warehouses

A vacant single-tenant commercial or industrial property is an obvious red flag for the wary investor. Such vacancies should never be bought except by a holder of substantial properties, who will not be hurt financially while he looks for a tenant. Negotiations to consummate an industrial or commercial lease are sometimes protracted for years. I know of several cases where neophyte investors have put all their savings into one such white elephant and lost everything through failure to keep up loan payments and taxes.

On commercial properties with long leases you can borrow heavily for a term that matches the lease. You can seldom borrow any significant amount on a month-to-month lease, or for a period that extends beyond the term of a lease. These lending stipulations point to the uncertain income from business properties not protected by long-term leases. You should, therefore, be wary of business properties which have tenants on monthly leases or at the end of long leases. Such properties are subject to sudden vacancy.

One investor considered buying a large warehouse, the main storage facilities for a major department store. A twenty-year lease, providing for net payments of $50,000 a year, was to expire in six months. The broker assured his client the department store was eager

to renew the lease even at a higher figure, in view of increased reproduction values. The property was listed for $350,000, making it ap-
parently a good, sound buy. The investor asked my opinion of the
possibilities.

"If the twenty-year lease has only six months to run, the department
store would already be asking to renew, unless they intended to move.
Why don't you call them and ask what their intentions are?"

It developed the department store was already building a new,
larger warehouse in another area. The present building was too small
for their expanded operations. Besides, they considered it obsolete for
modern warehouse methods. The wooden floors and low-capacity elevators were designed for labor-costly hand-operated trucks. Their new
building would have concrete floors, and elevators designed to handle
heavy mechanical trucks. It would also have a sprinkling system,
which would slash insurance costs. The present building could be converted to modern specifications only at prohibitive expense.

This obsolescent building was vacated in six months when the lease
expired. It was still empty at this writing after several years and the
owner was still fruitlessly seeking a new tenant.

4. DISTRESS PROPERTY

An investor bent on improving property may be led into buying
buildings too far gone for rehabilitation to be profitable. Such an example was cited in Chapter 4 under the heading, "Old, Beat Up and
Rough, and No Foundation." In Chapter 9 another example was
given under " 'Unrestricted' Means Slum Property." Another distress
property was the to-be-condemned Faraway Meadows Apartments
covered in Chapter 17.

The rule of thumb to keep in mind on contracted improvements, as
previously emphasized, is that every $1 spent on rehabilitation should
increase the value at least $2. Otherwise improvement money is better
spent elsewhere. A do-it-yourselfer should generally expect to increase value $4 for every $1 spent, else he has wasted both money
and labor.

Do-It-Yourself Dreams That Turned into Nightmares

Many misguided do-it-yourselfers fail to value their personal labor
when planning work projects. I know a master electrician who, whenever he has saved a little money, lays off from his regular work and
spends his time converting an old-fashioned farmhouse into a modern

"ranch style." He has been doing this for the last six years, rebuilding from the ground up. It takes him about four times as long to do the carpenter work, the chief skill required, as it would a master carpenter. All the time he could be earning $6 an hour as an electrician. With the major transformation he has in mind, he would be much better off continuing to work as an electrician, and contracting all other labor to build a new home just the way he wants it.

A worse nightmare involved a fellow telephone engineer who spent fifteen years converting an abandoned 1-story winery into a rambling suburban ranch home. In his case not a dollar was spent for hired labor. With his wife and their two children he devoted nearly every vacation and weekend to the house transformation. Extensive drain lines were dug and a cement septic tank was built, both by hand, taking six months to complete a job that could have been finished by experienced workmen with mechanized equipment in a few hours. Conversion of the dream home by personal hand labor became an obsession. Everything had to be completed and perfect before they moved in. All this time they rented a small house in the city and drove twenty miles to and from the project.

The original winery building and the one-acre lot cost $10,000. Construction materials by the time of completion came to $12,500. Furniture and furnishings cost $5,000. Taxes, interest, utilities, and other direct expenses came to $7,500. This brought the total outlay to $35,000 without counting commuting costs.

The ironic conclusion was that by the time the house was ready for them to move in the two children were married. The engineer and his wife got lonesome in their 4-bedroom ranch house. They decided to sell and move back to a small place in the city. They finally sold for $35,000 net, breaking even for their direct outlay. But their fifteen years of concentrated part-time labor had earned nothing.

Other Causes of Distress

Distress property may fall to such a state not only because of its own deterioration, but also because an entire district has deteriorated into a slum. In addition, relocation of highways and other developments may change a property from choice to distress.

In one case, two luxury motels of more than a hundred units each were built in an unzoned farm area beyond the city limits. Before county-wide zoning was inaugurated several heavy industries moved close by. Included were a smelly fiberboard plant, several large truck terminals, and two slaughterhouses. High-profit night-club business soon deserted the motels in favor of newer ones on the other side of the city. Commercial and tourist travelers followed after.

In another case two traders outfoxed each other. A luxury resort stood on a transcontinental highway which was to be relocated five miles away. Federal funds were responsible for changing the two-lane road to a four-lane freeway. The chief source of steady revenue for the resort was drop-in trade from the highway for drinks, meals, and rooms.

The owner figured that he made a smart exchange by trading even for a motel of comparable value on the outskirts of a city 150 miles from his resort. At no time was it ever divulged to the buyer that contracts had been let to move the highway, so he bought on the basis of the previous full year's receipts.

After the exchange was consummated and all papers recorded, the erstwhile resort operator found his newly acquired motel in the same distress as his abandoned resort. The same highway was to bypass the motel, leaving both highway dependents high and dry.

5. UNFAMILIAR BUSINESSES

Whenever you feel inclined to invest in a business you know nothing about, check the proposition with your local Better Business Bureau. This precaution alone should save you financial headaches.

In Chapter 3 it was mentioned that if you go into a new business your chances of failure are four to one, compared with odds of four hundred to one that you will succeed in property investment. Some businesses are even more prone to failure than the average. All have proved alluring to apartment owners, including:

> Appliance stores
> Bars and restaurants
> Businesses involving new and untried patents and inventions
> Contracting, either general or craft
> Unproved distributorships

An unfortunate combination involved a salaried San Francisco architect who sold his duplex house for $12,000 net cash. He then paid $10,000 to buy an unproved distributorship for an untried invention, a self-righting wheel for trailers. The territory was the Southern states. This appealed to the embryo distributor because his home town was Savannah, where he looked forward to returning as a big-wheel businessman.

The architect had no sales experience and had a shy personality. He was assured, "You don't have to do any selling. The wheel will sell itself. Just show this money-maker to auto dealers and trailer manufacturers, and they will snap it up."

Not only did the wheel not sell. It didn't even hold up. The architect bought a secondhand house trailer for $1,000. He removed its two heavy-duty wheels and installed the "Little Self-Righter," as instructed by the inventor. He packed in wife, son, and all the household equipment the trailer would carry, then started merrily out to challenge the Sierras and Rockies.

The wheel bearings burned out rolling downgrade in Arizona. There was a week's delay waiting for a new wheel. Most of the household equipment, in the interim, was sacrificed to secondhand dealers to lighten the load. The new wheel made it to Memphis, where the distributor decided to start reaping his harvest.

In the next month he failed to make a single sale and was stone broke. He phoned his previous employer collect, asking for his job back and fare home. Happily, he was a good architect, and his employer was glad to provide both.

6. PARTNERSHIP GIMMICKS

A favorite way for shysters to defraud the unwary is to advertise "Partner wanted." They take in an investor, get control of his funds, then decamp. The new partner is left shorn of his money, in exchange for which he is saddled with the responsibility of paying the piled-up outstanding bills.

Many property investments are made on a sound basis by partnerships or syndicates. These might prove worthwhile, especially for those who in the beginning are chary of lone-wolf operations. When partnerships are worthy of consideration, all investors should put in an equal amount and reap an equal benefit, or earnings should be in proportion to investment. Partnerships to be wary of include those which involve a return disproportionate to the risk, on the investment either of time or of money.

Unequal Money

A case of unequal money involved a widow who received $300,000 insurance money when her husband died. A real-estate friend induced her to put all the money into a prosperous hotel which was available for $1,000,000. The friend had no investment funds, and neither he nor the widow had hotel experience. The realtor suggested that they go into the hotel business in partnership. They would retain the present management, and neither would interfere with operations. However, the broker would share the risk by taking over a half ownership. The widow asked how he could do this if he had no funds.

Very simple, he told her. She would put up her $300,000, half for herself and half for him. He would give her a $150,000 second mortgage on his half of the property. That way they would each be investing $150,000. They would share the profits, and out of his half he would give half to her to repay the $150,000 note. He would share 50 per cent of the risk, but she would get 75 per cent of the profits until his note was paid.

The widow actually acquiesced to the suggested agreement. She didn't stop to think that if the venture failed she would lose $300,000, and the broker nothing. He even held out his $25,000 cash commission, paid for by the seller from the proceeds of the widow's cash.

Unequal Time

In a case illustrating disproportionate time, another inexperienced widow put in $100,000 and an experienced investor $100,000, to buy a $750,000 block of apartments. The investor was to take care of all management. The customary fee for this service in the area, which the previous owners had been paying, was 5 per cent of the gross receipts. In discussions preliminary to the purchase, the investor suggested he would discount this to 2 per cent, to which the widow readily agreed. Since they were close friends, nothing about a management fee was put in writing.

After the deal was consummated the widow received advice from many friends who had no experience in property operations. She refused to sanction her partner's drawing the management fee. The partnership turned the friends into bitter enemies. The investor would not manage the property without the agreed compensation for his time. The widow would not approve her partner's earning more than she. Both lost by their failure to compromise. The management was put back into the hands of the realtors who had sold the property, and they were paid their customary 5 per cent fee.

Unequal Return for Risk Involved

Acrimony often develops in a partnership between relatives or friends when one puts up all the money and the other puts up all the experience. They start out with an agreement that an equal return will be fair, as funds and experience are equally necessary to start a successful business. If the business goes broke, the experienced partner has lost a certain amount of time and energy, but the investor may have lost his life savings.

This would be equitable for those choosing to take such a venture, if it proved successful and all profits were shared equally. But if the business is extremely successful, the partner with experience resents the great amount of money made by the investor in proportion to what he has put in, even though the business could never have started without the investor's money. Either there is continual wrangling, or the investor consents to sell out. Henry Ford paid his backers handsome millions for invested thousands. In such a situation the average investor may be forced to sell at far below his equitable share in order to keep peace, particularly if there is a close family relationship.

7. BUY-BACK CONTRACTS

A slicker may induce a somewhat wary investor to buy into an enterprise he would not otherwise consider, by guaranteeing to buy back if the buyer is not satisfied. In one such case, a broker took in a small gift shop as his commission on a large apartment sale. He resold the gift shop to an elderly couple in exchange for a 12-unit apartment building. The couple were intrigued with the tremendous markup, as high as 1,000 per cent on some specialty items. A Mexican charm bracelet, for example, cost 18 cents and was marked up to $1.95.

On paper the net profits looked fabulous. However, the apartment owners were on the fence about closing the deal until the broker gave them a written "buy-back guarantee." He contracted to buy back the gift shop at the stipulated trade value of $75,000 at any time within twelve months if the couple became dissatisfied.

1,000 Per Cent Times Zero Equals Zero

It was not long before the couple found that the gift shop earned insufficient income to pay the overhead, let alone compensate the wife for her full time. The shop was in a poor, back-street location. They arrived at the simple arithmetical conclusion that a 1,000 per cent profit on no sales is nothing.

The couple told the salesman they wanted to exercise the buy-back privilege. The broker advised them that the buy-back contract was made by a corporation he had set up for business purposes. The corporation had gone broke and had no assets with which to buy back. Sure enough, on reading the fine print they found that a washed-out corporation was legally responsible, and not the broker. Meanwhile the latter had sold the apartments, which had been recorded in his name alone.

A buy-back contract is only as sound as the integrity of its contractor. Many shysters sell flimsy businesses, cashing in on a buy-back sale, then skip out. Some cache their assets and go bankrupt. Others, like our 1,000 per cent gift-shop seller, cover up through a corporation, repudiating liability for assets outside the corporation.

8. ADVANCE-FEE FINANCING

A come-on for the unwary seeking financing is the advance-fee racket. If conventional sources, such as banks and insurance companies, fail to meet your requests, you may turn to a loan broker. As covered in Part Eight, loan brokers serve a useful function by getting money seekers and lenders together. Most of them are legitimate operators, who expect to be paid 1 to 5 per cent fees from loans secured. The only advance fee customarily asked for would be an appraisal fee, required to pay for appraising the property. This would run from .1 to .5 per cent. Sometimes a stand-by fee, not exceeding 1 per cent, may be asked by reputable brokers as guarantee that an applied-for loan will be taken if granted. The stand-by fee would otherwise be returned.

Unscrupulous brokers may ask for heavy advance fees, ranging as high as 10 per cent. One such operator demanded a $5,000 advance fee to secure financing to build a $200,000 motel. The total fee was to be 5 per cent, making $10,000. Leaving a balance of $5,000 to be paid from loan proceeds made the project appear more legitimate to the borrower. The loan broker said that the $10,000 would be added to the required $200,000, making a total loan of $210,000.

The $5,000 in advance was to apply in part toward the expenses of making up a brochure. Expensive-looking sample brochures were shown. In addition there would be expenses for taking traffic and population surveys and opinion polls, plus the cost of entertainment "for the right parties who control the money." All this sounded logical to an apartment house owner trying to build a motel and finding financing much more difficult to secure than on apartments.

The would-be motel builder paid the $5,000 advance fee and

waited for completion of surveys, brochure and loan. The broker left word with the secretarial service handling his calls that he had to leave suddenly on a trip across the country. He had "received word of being able to get hold of easy union money" and would be back shortly with loan funds firmly committed.

Sad to say, the broker never returned, nor were his whereabouts ever discovered. It *was* discovered that he had bilked others to the tune of $60,000 in advance fees before his sudden departure.

Except for nominal appraisal or stand-by fees, paying in advance for financing is like paying an attorney a flat fee in advance to sue for damages. If the damage suit has any merit, the attorney will usually prefer a contingency arrangement, as he should make more by taking a percentage. So it is with financing. If your application has any merit, a legitimate broker will take his chances on being paid from prospective loan proceeds.

9. OVERMORTGAGED PROPERTIES

New mortgages from conventional lending agencies are a good guide for appraising property values. But the size of a loan, even from a bank, should never be taken at face value. Always appraise a property on its income, and then on its reproduction cost, irrespective of existing loans. Sometimes loans exceed market values. Many FHA 5 per cent, thirty-five-year loans on large apartment projects exceed present market values, where the improvements or the neighborhood have deteriorated. Buildings under unimaginative or vampire management have depreciated faster than thirty-five-year loan amortization.

Blanket-Mortgaged Assets May Diminish

In some cases the value of assets under blanket mortgage may diminish piecemeal below the outstanding balance on a loan. This might happen, for example, where there is originally a blanket mortgage placed on several properties, some are released to permit sale, and the property remaining under the mortgage is worth less than the amount of the loan.

In one case an owner secured one blanket loan to cover his desirable 48-unit apartment building and two new ventures, a winery and sixty acres of subdivision land. He borrowed enough to pay for all streets, utilities, sidewalks and curbs. After the work was completed, he prepared to repay the loan and reap a rich harvest from selling off lots. Then the roof fell in. First the winery went sour. Due chiefly to lack of experience, his costs so far exceeded income that he closed it down.

Then the adjoining city enlarged its borders, taking in his subdivision. The city forbade his selling a lot until he went to considerable additional expense. His streets, although wide enough to meet the county code, were eight feet too narrow to comply with the city code. The city would not permit a lot to be sold until the streets were widened.

Receiving insufficient payments from the unhappy subdivider, the bank foreclosed on the winery and subdivision. At forced sale $400,-000 was received and credited against the $750,000 blanket mortgage. This left as a balance against the apartment house a mortgage of $350,000. The market value of the apartments at the time was approximately $250,000, which was $100,000 less than the outstanding loan.

The bank would no doubt have foreclosed also on the apartments, except that the borrower owned considerable other property. In exchange for the $400,000 payment on the blanket loan, the bank agreed to leave the apartments in the borrower's hands, giving him an opportunity to pay off his loan.

This chain of events happened while the apartments were under rent controls. Controls were abolished within a year of the foreclosure. As a sequel, the investor decided to forgo ventures with which he had no experience, and concentrate on developing apartments. By installing a small heated swimming pool and other improvements, at a total cost of $5,000, he subsequently raised the income value of the forty-eight apartments to $410,000. The property was sold for $400,-000, with the buyer taking over the outstanding loan.

Judgments May Exceed Values

In another not uncommon case, a lender may get a court judgment when a borrower's liabilities pile up and exceed diminishing assets. An auto dealer borrowed $50,000 from a private lender on the strength of obtaining a new-car franchise. The money was loaned against his business as an individual owner, making all his assets liable. The new auto dealer had been an outstanding sales manager, but he was unfamiliar with other phases of management. He soon went broke, and the lender slapped a judgment on his remaining assets. About all that was left was a 4-unit apartment house with a market value of $40,000, which the dealer had recently inherited free and clear. Rather than take over the apartments, the lender took back a mortgage for his $50,000. The chastened auto dealer agreed to pay this off from his reinstated salary of $1,500 monthly plus bonuses as a sales manager.

A Sight-Unseen Appraisal

An overmortgaged property on a smaller scale involved a modest 5-room house in a country area. Its ready market value was about $6,000, but it had acquired a $10,000 mortgage, which resulted in a $15,000 sale. Here is how the loan and the sale were consummated without lender or buyer ever seeing the property:

A retired couple listed a 30-unit apartment house for sale for $195,000. They received a trade offer of the 5-room house free and clear, plus $25,000 cash, plus a $140,000 first mortgage. The couple asked the broker the value of the house, and he said that after it was fixed up a little it would probably be worth about $15,000. This brought the trade value of the apartments up to $180,000, which happened to be the rock-bottom price at which the couple intimated they would sell.

The apartment sellers did not want to take in any property, but they agreed instead to take a $10,000 mortgage on the house, if the buyer would throw in an additional $5,000 in cash. The buyer was unable to raise more cash. The transaction was consummated by increasing to $145,000 the first mortgage taken back on the apartments. Neither the broker nor the apartment sellers had ever seen the 5-room house, basing their actions solely on a flattering photograph and on a flowery description written by the owner.

The retired couple hypothecated both mortgages to obtain a loan from their bank. The bank accepted the $10,000 mortgage as additional security, although it was not required, and its value therefore was not verified. The bank took over collecting the payments on the mortgages.

Two Realtors Take In the Valueless Country Home Equity at $5,000

Next, the buyer of the 30-unit apartment house was approached by another broker, offering twenty-one apartments which were being sacrificed by an elderly widow for $90,000. A new transaction was concluded with the following arrangements:

The Buyer took over the twenty-one apartments. He traded in two properties with paper equities of $20,000. The 5-room house with the $10,000 mortgage was valued at $15,000, giving an equity of $5,000.

In addition, a $30,000-actual-market-value 4-unit apartment house with a $15,000 mortgage gave an equity of $15,000. The widow carried back the balance of $70,000 as a first mortgage on her apartments.

The Widow accepted on condition that the brokers, two partners, take the country home in payment of their commission due from her, amounting to $4,500. Since the bank now held the $10,000 mortgage, the brokers figured that the bank had made the original loan, which could not have exceeded 60 per cent of its appraised value. From this they estimated the house's value at approximately $17,000, giving them a $2,500 margin in which to cash out their $4,500 commission. They, too, never took the trouble to drive 150 miles to inspect the house, planning to turn it over to a nearby realtor to sell.

The Brokers took back a $1,500, two-year second mortgage at 6 per cent from the apartment buyer for disposing of his $30,000 4-unit property. Their pig-in-a-poke country house they found impossible to sell for any amount in excess of the mortgage. Seeking some solace, they decided to share their acquisition as a summer home. Unfortunately, doubling up caused bitter wrangling between the two previously friendly families. There were arguments over sharing of chores, accommodations, and the costs of food and utilities. Then, when they found they could not live together, controversies arose over whose turn came when, and over house rules about entertaining outside guests. Ultimately the shared summer home broke up what had been a beautiful partnership.

Don't Hesitate to Verify Appraised Valuations

The two brokers could have saved themselves their difficulties if they had made an on-the-spot appraisal and had checked with fellow realtors in the area. Also they could easily have discovered the true status of the loan by a phone call to the bank.

When in the slightest doubt regarding a mortgage, don't hesitate to check with the mortgage holder. Institutional moneylenders seem to have an unwritten law not to divulge exact appraisals, but they will usually give you the desired information if they are properly approached.

You can ask a loan officer point-blank, for example, "What is your appraised value?" He may hesitate and say, "I'm not supposed to give this out." But in most cases he will give you either the exact figures or enough hints for you to draw sound conclusions. It pays to be alert. One officer told me that appraisal information was regarded as confidential. He then contrived to "check with his secretary about his appointments" and left his desk for several minutes. All the while the bank's complete appraisal sheet lay face up directly in front of me, turned for easy reading.

10. LENDING MONEY

Capital is the lifeblood of your progress. To insure success you should keep it continually working for your benefit, until you reach your goal through pyramiding equities. If you are then ready to rest on your laurels, you might well consider switching from property ownership and money borrowing to money lending. You might wish to gradually sell off some holdings, taking back mortgages in order to increase profits and decrease taxes.

Excess funds might then well be invested in other mortgages, as knowledge gained through property ownership will help chart a true course for mortgage lending. You can make realistic appraisals if you lend only on property with which you have become thoroughly familiar. If you gain experience in appraising and borrowing for purposes of buying, selling, and trading apartments, the same experience should give you a sound basis for mortgage lending on apartments.

Be Wary of Unfamiliar Fields

Be wary of lending in a field unfamiliar to you. Loans should be made strictly on the basis of sound risk. When approached for loans, consider the following:

> Four-to-one chances of failure confront any new business.
> This risk is amplified if starting capital is easily borrowed from a friend or relative, rather than restricted by the rules of a conventional lending agency.
> The quickest way to lose a friend or embitter a relative is to lend money which he proves unable to pay back.

11. OIL AND GAS LEASES

Apartment owners accustomed to basing valuations on the yardstick of income are susceptible to the bait of high returns from oil and gas leases. This does not refer to barren and unexplored oil and gas land, the speculative shortcomings of which should be obvious. A trap for the unwary investor covers actually producing oil or gas.

A typical case involved a statement showing a 24 per cent net annual income for the previous years' production, based on the available bargain at which the "money-maker can be stolen from some Indians who inherited the oil land and don't know any better."

In this instance an apartment owner sold his income property, which paid a solid 10 per cent net, and bought $50,000 worth of gas leases. The 24 per cent royalties, he thought, would repay his principal in a little over four years and leave him riding the gravy train thenceforth.

Royalties Soon Fizzed Out

The gas wells were almost depleted, and both gas and royalties soon fizzed out. In the twelve months after purchase, royalty production was $4,200 instead of the expected $12,000. Within another two years the wells were depleted beyond economical handling. Royalties ceased entirely before the get-rich-quicker had gleaned a total close to the $12,000 which he had expected as annual income.

The chief blind spot for the investment-minded is that wells, regardless of babying, do not give forth forever. Such royalties are purely a return of capital rather than income, until the total receipts equal the capital invested.

12. GENTLEMAN-FARMING

Another field toward which income property owners are particularly susceptible are the attractions of so-called gentleman-farming. Probably exceeding the sales appeals for resorts are the blandishments that spring forth to lead inexperienced city-bred investors to the farm. This refers, of course, not to the pure hobbyist but to the investor who buys a farm with expectations of making money.

Farming, with today's mechanization and specialization, is strictly a business operation, requiring experience and training. Farms that pay are tending more and more to be run like factories. There are plenty of farmers who make good money from their investment, labor, and management know-how. To be successful, most of them spend a good deal of time studying to improve their operations, taking courses from the county farm adviser, and sending their sons to the state agricultural college.

Your Own Horse and a Swimming Pool

It is amazing how many city dwellers who have never lived on a farm succumb to the beckoning country life of gentlemanly ease of which they dream. Here are some excerpts from rosy farm brochures appealing to their dewy-eyed expectations:

A few hundred [or thousand] acres, give or take a few.

Something that pays good, producing plenty for luxury living.

Raising all family fruit and vegetables.

At least one horse for each member of the family.

Enough cows, chickens, turkeys, geese, ducks, and pigs to make the family self-sustaining and fill in the picturesque setting.

No income taxes on produce consumed by the owner.

Discounted taxes on profits, especially with a little sideline hobby, like purebred dairy cattle, or thoroughbred horses.

A couple of foals or heifers repays the cost of breeding stock.

Making all kinds of easy government money, from subsidies, soil banks, conservation ponds, and other practices.

Lots of leisure between bountiful harvests, the only real work time.

Swimming pool and sun deck in the back yard, built for practically nothing by the hired hands between chores and harvests.

Mint bed for juleps by the springhouse.

Trout and wild-duck pond on the south forty, installed by the government free, for conservation purposes.

Tax-free housekeepers and gardeners, paid for from farm profits.

These blandishments could go on and on, portraying more of the dreams that nightmares are made of. Fanciful as the foregoing may seem, they are a fair sample of the promises of some farm salesmen. Suffice it to say that experience tends to show there is no such possibility as making money by leisurely and inexperienced gentleman-farming. Many city apartment owners have traded or sold out and bought farms and have been forced into a bankruptcy sale within a year, giving experienced farmers a chance to buy their equipment cheap. Some are lucky enough to cut their losses in time by selling at a sacrifice, before fleeing back to the city.

It is hard to run a farm successfully without working your shirttail off doing the tilling, planting, weeding, pruning, spraying and harvesting, the seasons for which seem to overlap one another in an endless chain; not to mention the handling of stock, which continues throughout the year.

Trained experts continue each year to take over more acreage from unsuccessful small farms. That is why the average acreage per farm and the average production per acre keep growing larger, while the number of farms keeps growing smaller. The number of U.S. professional farmers continues to drop because over half fail to make more than a substandard living. What chance is there then for the amateur?

Absentee Farming

Discount heavily also the promised returns from absentee ownership, especially in land across the country, where fruit, nuts, clover seed, and gladiolus bulbs always grow better even than the greener grass on the neighbor's lawn. You may be regaled with stories of high profits at little cost of money or grief. But absentee farming, on either partnership or co-operative basis, is more risky than on-the-ground operations as a gentleman farmer, where you can at least see what is going on. Unproductive land may be sold at outlandish prices, and promised income may be entirely nonexistent.

13. ADVICE FROM PAPER PROFITEERS

Successful investors have lost out by following the advice of those who have failed in their personal ventures or who have never ventured at all. Many who have never succeeded in personal investments are eager to tell you how to conduct your affairs. Their suggestions are usually prefaced by such phrases as "In your place, I . . ." or "If I were you . . ."

The typical Paper Profiteer predicts horse races and the stock market, and he talks of big killings. He starts out by saying, "Last week if I had followed my hunch, I would have made five thousand dollars in U.S. Steel." These paper profits keep building until he states his coups as though they were actually made: "Last month I made ten thousand in General Motors."

If you ask why these paper profits are not converted into real money by laying dollars on the line, he says, "I haven't enough money for that." The bluff of one such was called by suggesting he mortgage his free-and-clear $30,000 home in order to capitalize on his always-winning hunches. His reply was "I couldn't do that. I've got my little nest egg salted in insurance and a savings account for a rainy day, and I'll never owe a penny on my home."

One might think that following tips that never lose would be a sure road to fabulous wealth. But the Paper Profiteer suffers from a special type of amnesia which causes him to forget the mistakes in his choices. Like the fisherman exaggerating his catch, he also has another disease, called "balloonitis." This causes him to add zeros to an originally planned figure in a successful coup.

Skepticism and investigation are the best defenses against money-losing schemes.

30. HOW TO BUILD MORE PYRAMIDS

It is May 20, 1967, six and a half months after taking over the Cynthia Court Apartments. It is time to review our progress and plan for the future. Apropos, there are three major subjects:

> An Appraisal of Where We Stand
> Profitable Steps to Choose
> How to Build Up Your Credit

An Appraisal of Where We Stand

We have completed all planned improvements and have put into effect our proposed rent schedule, with a slight upward adjustment. Our present schedule, because of charges for extra tenants and a few upgraded rents, shows $2,585 monthly. We had projected $2,538.

To appraise where we stand, we will add our present equity in the Cynthia Court to our present cash balance. Here is a statement of our cash balance:

CASH BALANCE, MAY 20, 1967
Investment cash on hand. November 25 bank
   statement $6,827
Additional savings for 6 months at $50 monthly   300
Net in-pocket rentals from Cynthia Court
   Apartments   4,740
   Gross rentals collected, 6 months $14,112
   Operating expenses (Fixed $3,248; Re-
   pairs, Supplies and Sundries $261)   −3,509

Net operating income before loan payments	10,603	
5 loan payments of $1,172.50, principal and interest	−5,863	
Net income after loan payments	$4,740	
. *Loan proceeds less improvement costs*		15,176
Net first mortgage increase	$20,600	
Net second mortgage increase	3,922	
Total loan increases	24,522	
Loan and escrow charges	−568	
Net loan proceeds	23,954	
Improvement costs, including paint, carpets, landscaping, refrigerators, miscellaneous	−8,778	
Loan proceeds less improvement costs	$15,176	
TOTAL CASH on HAND		$27,043

In figuring our present net estate for investment purposes, we exclude the value of home and personal belongings. These have been omitted throughout the book except when a complete financial statement was made for the bank. All our expansion has been based on pyramiding an original $2,500, plus $50 monthly in savings.

EQUITY IN CYNTHIA COURT

We appraise our present equity in the Cynthia Court by applying the formula explained in preceding chapters:

1. Figure gross annual income ($2,585 monthly schedule times 12)	$31,020
2. Deduct fixed expenses	−6,495
3. Arrive at annual net scheduled income	24,525
4. Multiply by 10	× 10
5. Obtain present market value	245,250
6. Deduct outstanding loan balances First mortgage $91,133; second mortgage $37,195	−128,328
7. PRESENT EQUITY	116,922
Add investment cash on hand	27,043
PRESENT NET WORTH for INVESTMENT PURPOSES	143,965

In the three and a half years since November 1963, when we selected, in Chapter 5, our first rental house from the $10,000 properties in the newspaper ads, we have advanced well over the six-figure plateau. Checking back to our more conservative Step-by-Step Formula to a Million Dollars in Chapter 2, we find ourselves $19,081 over our twelve-year goal of $124,884.

With the estate, experience and knowledge now gained, and with average luck, we can cut our estimated time in half. Allowing six months to search for new investments, we can reach our million-dollar goal in an elapsed time of ten years rather than twenty.

PROFITABLE STEPS TO CHOOSE

With cash on hand of $27,043, and a net worth of $143,965, we could hold back $3,965 for an operating reserve and still have a round $140,000 for reinvestment. What is the next profitable step to take?

Up to this point we have progressed vertically, building on one pyramid. We may continue vertically, trading for a larger building. Or we may build our estate horizontally, starting new pyramids. We have developed a good income producer, large enough to pay for a competent manager. We may well retain the Cynthia Court instead of trading further upward. After obtaining maximum financing, we now have three major alternatives to consider:

1. Trade up for a larger building.
2. Trade for two or more smaller apartment houses and start a new pyramid with each.
3. Keep the Cynthia Court, and start a new pyramid with other assets.

1. TRADE UP FOR A LARGER BUILDING

Any of these alternatives might prove most profitable, depending on the best buys that develop. In each case, before expanding further, it pays to obtain as much cash as possible by refinancing. Often the most favorable loans, approaching or exceeding costs, can be floated after desired improvements are completed and income and value are increased. With the Cynthia Court, acceptable financing has already been secured, predicated on income after partial improvements.

You Will Be Swamped with Sales Calls

In reading ads and talking to realtors, it is well to point out the various possibilities you might consider and to keep an open mind as to your next move. Let realtors know that you are open to suggestions. You will consider trading up for a larger property, or across the board for two or more smaller buildings. Or you might consider buying with up to $22,000 cash down. You will be swamped with calls offering all kinds of lucrative-appearing inducements. It behooves you to keep your head and consider well the pitfalls cited in the previous chapter. Regardless of the decision you make, if you stay in the income property field, specializing in apartments, you are not apt to go far wrong.

A Bargain in the Half-Million-Dollar Range

With our $140,000 in cash and equity available for investment, we could shop for an apartment house in the half-million-dollar price range. To give an idea of the possibilities we might consider, here is an example of a trade consummated at this level:

An owner of two apartment houses, one of 18 units and one of 40 units, bought a rundown additional building with 21 units for $105,000. By improvements and compensating rent increases, he built up the value on the 21-unit building in one and a half years to $205,760. His loan balance was then $63,000. He secured a new seventeen-year, 7 per cent loan in the amount of $95,000, banking $32,000 in cash. This left an equity of $110,760. He advised several brokers that he was interested in trading his approximately $110,000 equity for a larger property in the $400,000 to $750,000 range.

Within three months a 160-unit bargain was presented, an attractive 8-story apartment hotel in one of the most desirable rental districts in Metropole. Two brothers owned the property, inherited from their father. They were anxious to sell out and dissolve partnership. The apartments had actual gross income for the previous year, according to a certified statement, of $158,387. The annual expenses came to $96,024, leaving a net income of $62,363. This made the fair market value $623,630. The asking price was $750,000, showing a net of approximately 8 per cent, instead of the customary 10 per cent. There was a loan balance of $370,000.

Operations Cried for Improvement

The building was in top condition, built of Class A steel construction, with brick veneer. Kitchens and baths had been recently modernized, and little was needed in the way of property improvement. The depreciated replacement value was appraised by insurance appraisers at $1,500,000.

The biggest cost factor was the hotel type of operation. Apartments were rented on a monthly basis, but they received costly hotel service. Included were daily maid service, consisting of cleaning, dusting, bedmaking, and changing towels. Bed linen was changed every other day. Once a week, complete janitor service was rendered, including thorough vacuuming of carpets and rugs, and scrubbing down of baths and kitchens. Labor and supervision alone cost $49,094 a year. Linen replacements came to $2,929, and house laundry cost $5,558.

For reasons obvious to an improvement-conscious investor, the property was not paying anywhere near its net-income potential, which should have been closer to its $1,500,000 replacement value. Whereas the expenses were on a high-cost hotel basis, the rentals were on a monthly basis at about a level which should have been earned without hotel service. Either one of two radical corrections should be made: (a) changing to daily and weekly hotel rates, or to monthly rates at similar levels, increasing income more in line with present costs, or (b) changing to conventional apartment operation, retaining present income, but slashing services and costs.

An experienced hotel operator would have chosen the first step, inaugurating profitable hotel rates. Additional money-makers would include installing a bar, a restaurant and a garden in place of the clotheslines on the roof, and leasing to concessions in place of the large storeroom on the valuable ground floor.

The apartment-minded buyer planned the second step. He estimated savings of $8,487 on linen replacement and laundry. Labor and supervision costs could conservatively be cut by $25,000, approximately in half, making total savings of $33,487 on wages and linen. Adding this to the present net of $62,363 would result in a new net of $95,850, and a new capital valuation of close to $1,000,000.

A trade offer was made, representing a purchase price of $510,000, including the 21-unit building at $210,000 and a boot of $300,000. An exchange was finally consummated with the following arrangements:

The boot was increased to $400,000. Figuring the 21-unit building at its market value of $205,000, this meant a price of $605,000 for the 160-unit property.

This $605,000 valuation, less the outstanding $370,000 first mortgage, gave an equity of $235,000 to the brothers.

The $205,000 valuation, less a $95,000 first mortgage, gave an equity of $110,000 to the up-trader. One of the brothers agreed to take the 21-unit property as sole owner, representing his total net proceeds.

The remaining boot came to $125,000. The second brother took back a second mortgage for $110,000 as his total net proceeds, equaling the value of the first brother's equity in the traded-in property. The second mortgage was to be for seventeen years at 7 per cent, the first payments to start in one year, after the buyer had time to reorganize operations.

The remaining boot came to $15,000. This represented the proportionate sales commission assumed by the up-trader, which was the obligation of the brothers. Two brokers, one representing each party, had agreed to a flat commission of approximately 2½ per cent, because of the size of the transaction. In view of their receiving a $5,000 cash commission from the up-trader, they agreed to take a $15,000 third mortgage on the larger building. This was recorded as a single mortgage, secured by two $7,500 notes, one payable to each broker at $75 monthly, including 7 per cent interest.

After all the foregoing financing, the up-trader still had $27,000 cash in reserve from the loan he had arranged on his 21-unit building.

Immediately after taking possession of the hotel-apartments, the new owner notified all tenants of a change from hotel to conventional apartment operation. All rentals were on month-to-month leases, subject to thirty-day notice. Rents were to remain the same, but maid and janitor service on the owner's account were to be discontinued one month later. Linens, dishes, pots, and pans could be bought by the tenants at a substantial discount, averaging $75 per apartment. Otherwise they were to be sold elsewhere.

Many tenants threatened to move, but most of them stayed after shopping for other accommodations. Vacancies were readily filled at similar rents. Half the tenants started doing their own housework. Of the rest, some contracted direct with former employees to continue full maid and janitor service. Others arranged for this service on a much-curtailed basis.

Close to $11,000 was raised from selling linen and kitchen supplies. Nominal vacancy losses because of the shuffle reduced rental income $3,000 below the previous year, but the incidental $11,000 sales increased the net receipts by $8,000.

One year later, the operating net had exceeded $100,000. Salaries and wages were reduced to $18,100, saving $31,000 as compared with previous operations, instead of the estimated $25,000 possible labor savings. The new rental schedule was nudged slightly higher than on the take-over date. Management was now much simplified after eliminating all the labor and tenant headaches of hotel operation. Merely by this change in operations valuation was raised in twelve months from the $605,000 purchase price to $1,000,000.

More Money-Making Improvements

We should not leave this case history without mentioning additional improvement and financing steps taken. The apartments were in a zoning appropriate for professional offices. A low bid of $18,000 was accepted to convert the large ground-floor storeroom into six doctors' offices. The contract also covered walling-in two small storerooms from basement garage stalls. The latter had been adequate for earlier vintage autos, but were too small for newer models. A realtor specializing in professional leases secured ten-year leases on each doctor's office at $175 monthly, increasing the annual income $12,600. This resulted in a new capital valuation exceeding $1,125,000.

New Financing

On the strength of a new operations statement after the foregoing was put into effect, the owner secured a new first mortgage of $550,-000 payable in twenty-five years at 7 per cent. He paid $18,000 to the contractor and paid off the three mortgages, which amounted respectively to about $260,000, $110,000, and $14,000. These expenditures totaled $402,000, leaving $148,000 in cash proceeds from the new loan. The three previous loan payments were consolidated to a single monthly payment of $3,888. This left approximately $65,000 annual in-pocket income.

2. TRADE FOR TWO OR MORE SMALLER APARTMENT HOUSES AND START A NEW PYRAMID WITH EACH

Favorable opportunities may be presented, enabling you to take over several smaller buildings, each of which may form the base of a new pyramid. You might trade the Cynthia Court, for example, for three or four buildings in the 4- to 12-unit range. Or you might trade for smaller properties and take in a second mortgage, to boot. Then the properties and the mortgage could each be used as down payments on larger buildings.

Using Buildings and Mortgages for Pyramiding

One transaction of this combination nature was recently consummated. An investor had improved his 21-unit building in the previous three years from a purchase value of $80,000 to a resale value of $165,000. There was a $45,000, fifteen-year, 6 per cent loan which he hesitated replacing, without exploring other possibilities, because of low interest and a 5 per cent payoff penalty. The owner advised various brokers that he was interested in trading down for two or more smaller apartment houses in need of improvements. He would also consider taking back a second mortgage, if needed to complete an exchange.

A realtor brought to his attention two 8-unit buildings in separate desirable rental districts. Rentals were considerably below the market. Both buildings were in good condition, except for a sad lack of paint. Their owner, an elderly widower, lived about a hundred miles out of town and owned the properties free and clear. The widower had stipulated that he would sell outright and, for tax reasons, take back mortgages of at least 71 per cent. He would also consider trading up for a larger, choice building, if it had a capable and happily married manager who would not give him any headaches.

The managers of both of his 8-unit apartments were middle-aged widows about twenty years his junior. He had no routine supervisory procedures, such as those recommended in Chapter 21. Both managers ran the owner ragged with picayunish calls, phoning him long distance, collect, at least once a week about minor tenant complaints and exaggerated emergencies. Neither had a husband to handle minor repairs or routine protective maintenance. The owner received an unreasonable number of $5 to $50 repair bills for replacing washers and mending faucets, steps, railings, and plumbing, heating, hot-water and electrical equipment. Each widow, incidentally, had set her cap on promotion from apartment manager to the owner's household manager. Their constant hints of marriage probably added to the widower's reasons for selling.

One 8-unit house, with four efficiency and four 1-bedroom apartments, was listed at $27,500. The other, with eight 1-bedroom apartments, was listed at $42,500. These valuations were based on the existing combined net rentals of $7,000 annually. Investigation revealed sound buildings in need of paint. Many of the rents were half their market value, largely because both buildings were almost filled with pensioners who were friends of the respective managers.

Expenses were pushed out of line because each manager received a $40 monthly salary in addition to a free apartment. A competent manager, with a husband to handle minor repairs, could be secured for a $40-monthly allowance on the regular apartment rent. This meant that one apartment rental in each building was lost because of overpayment of the manager.

A Four-Part Trade-In

The widower liked the spick-and-span condition of the 21-unit building. He was especially attracted by the efficient and comely manager of thirty, who had a husky railroad-yardman husband, and a curly-haired, cuddly three-year-old daughter. For running the 21-unit building, the manager received a free 3-room apartment, plus $25 monthly cash, plus cleaning charges.

Both parties traded properties on the basis of ten times the annual net. The exchange was consummated on the following terms:

The twenty-one units were valued at $165,000, subject to the $45,000 first mortgage. This gave an equity of $120,000.

The two 8-unit properties were valued at $70,000, free and clear. Deducting this from the $120,000 equity left a boot of $50,000.

The widower owned considerable stock of which he sold $30,000 worth. He paid $25,000, half the boot, in cash, and paid his broker a $3,500 cash commission, amounting to 5 per cent of his sale value.

The developer paid a $5,000 flat commission, retaining $20,000 cash. He took back a second mortgage on the 21-unit building for the $25,000 balance of the boot, payable $250 monthly, including 7 per cent interest.

Three Pyramids in Process

Thus the widower's trade-in involved four parts: two 8-unit properties, a $25,000 cash payment, and a $25,000 second mortgage. Each of these gave the developer a potential foundation for a new pyramid. The $20,000 netted in cash, for example, could have been used to buy a property in the $75,000 to $100,000 range. Usually with such holdings, better deals can be made by planning three up-trades, reserving cash for improvements and for sweetening an exchange.

Pyramid 1

Within sixty days the developer traded his $25,000 second mortgage at face value, plus $5,000 cash, as a $30,000 down payment for another property. The purchased building had 32 rental units, including 27 apartments and 5 ground-floor stores. The location was on a main boulevard in a fair neighborhood shopping district. The property was in fair shape except that it was badly in need of exterior painting, and the much-patched roof needed replacement. These detractions brought the purchase price down to $115,000, although the market value on the basis of low rents was $140,000.

Pyramid 2

Within six months, the developer had more than doubled the net income on his two acquired 8-unit properties. A change in managers and compensation rates gave the owner an additional $2,040 income. After painting and decorating, general rent raises were established, bringing the total net to $15,160. The new capital value of approximately $150,000 was earned by improvement expenditures of $10,-000. About $4,000 had been spent on the smaller building, and $6,000 on the larger. These outlays brought the cash netted from the 21-unit trade down to $5,000.

Three months later the owner secured a new $27,000 first mortgage on the smaller building. This was only $500 under his purchase price, $4,500 under his purchase-price-plus-improvement costs. The cash in hand from this series of transactions was now $32,000.

The smaller 8-unit building was traded at a $65,000 valuation, subject to the newly secured first mortgage, giving an equity of $38,000. Twelve thousand dollars cash was added to make a $50,000 down payment on a $175,000 industrial building, leased for ten years to a telephone company. After paying a $3,250 commission to his broker, the improver now had $16,750 remaining cash.

Pyramid 3

A $45,000 first mortgage was obtained on the larger 8-unit house, bringing the available investment cash up to $61,750. A year after the original trade a new exchange was consummated, trading in the remaining 8-unit property, plus $25,000 cash, on a 48-unit building valued at $260,000. The 8-unit building was valued at $95,000, subject to the new $45,000 first mortgage, giving an equity of $50,000. This made a down payment of $75,000. After paying $25,000 cash, plus a commission of $4,750 for disposing of his 8-unit house, the investor still had $32,000 in cash. This could be used to start a new pyramid, or to develop the properties in pyramids 1 and 3.

The example of these three pyramids exemplifies how fast your expansion can be accelerated after you gain experience in buying, improving, financing and exchanging income properties. The more experience you get, the more conservative you will consider our one-million-dollar formula. This particular investor took four years to pyramid from a $5,000 initial investment to the acquisition of his 21-unit property. He then spent three years making improvements, taking at least twice as long for do-it-yourself as would have been necessary for contracted work. Any lost time was recovered speedily when he disposed of his 21 units. By trading down for smaller buildings and a mortgage, and starting three new pyramids, within one year he had acquired three properties, each of which exceeded his 21 units in value.

3. KEEP THE CYNTHIA COURT AND START A NEW PYRAMID WITH OTHER ASSETS

The preceding major possibilities of trading up for a larger property, or down for several properties, have worked out advantageously. The third major choice would be to keep the present apartments and buy additional property with the proceeds of savings and financing.

Keeping the Cynthia Court

Trading up for a larger building was the logical step when we were ready to dispose of the A Avenue house and the 5-unit Belvedere Apartments. With the Cynthia Court's 24 apartments we have arrived at an economical property to operate. It is small enough to be handled by one couple, a manager and her husband, with a full-time job elsewhere, as a handy man. It is large enough to warrant paying enough pocket money to obtain a desirable manager who can be given the responsibility of handling most day-to-day operating decisions. It is a soundly built, attractive building in a good rental location. It is therefore a desirable property to retain on a long-term investment basis.

Starting a New Pyramid

With $22,000 available for further investment, a $4,000 to $5,000-odd cash reserve being adequate at this stage of operations, what would be our probable selection? The easiest to handle, and the most profitable, would normally be the largest single building that could be bought with sound financing. This would point to apartment houses in the $75,000 to $100,000 range. Or two properties, similar to the Belvedere Apartments when they were acquired, might be bought in a range of $35,000 to $50,000 each. The possibilities of starting little pyramids are limitless.

Too Many Peanuts

Another possibility, especially in smaller communities, would be to buy seven or eight duplexes or houses in the range of the A Avenue house when purchased. FHA-insured financing at the 90 per cent level is available for up to a 4-unit building at this writing, in a commendable attempt to encourage the combination of home and rental ownership. With such financing, $22,000 could purchase twenty $12,000 houses and duplexes. This would be a time-consuming investment from an operations standpoint, although buying one or two houses or duplexes as a starter is the usual way to begin pyramiding.

Some investors get started with rental duplexes and single-family homes, and they expand profitably in the same field, especially in rural and suburban communities lacking large apartment houses. Yard and building maintenance and management problems intensify with several 1- and 2-unit rentals under separate roofs, however. Consolidating rental units under one operation, where larger buildings or complexes are available, reduces problems and costs, percentagewise, and increases net. An owner of a 24-unit building like the Cynthia Court, with an efficient manager, may have fewer problems requiring personal attention than the owner of one lone duplex.

Best of All

The best possibility of all, if the Cynthia Court is to be retained, is to start a desirable new pyramid with as little funds as possible, get the new project under way, and then start others on a continuous investment program. With our Cynthia Court stage of experience, growth potentials may develop that might have seemed too amazing to consider possible when we were in our early stages of pyramiding equities.

PYRAMIDING $100 TO $100,000
IN TWO AND A HALF YEARS

In one pyramiding operation recently concluded $100 mushroomed to $100,000 in two and a half years. First a 60-by-200 residential lot was bought with $100 down, in a resort area that had become dormant. The out-of-state sellers had listed the unproductive lot for $1,950. They were anxious to dump at any price, since they had been paying taxes for close to thirty years.

The buyer, an experienced apartment improver, learned that a new hotel and golf course were going in. He offered $1,000, with $100 down, the balance to be carried by the owners on a first mortgage. The sellers accepted. They paid the $100 cash as a sales commission, leaving them with a $900 mortgage for their net proceeds. Buying the lot would normally be considered pure speculation. In this case, with only $100 cash being ventured, the sellers financed nine times the buyer's equity.

TRADED LOT FOR A NEW DUPLEX

The lot was traded free and clear in part payment for a new, completely furnished duplex house with a market value of $17,500. The up-trader borrowed $3,600 on a six-month commercial note. With this he paid off the lot mortgage and gave a cash boot of $2,500 to the duplex seller. A $7,000 first mortgage was obtained on the duplex, excluding the furniture, through a building and loan association, the proceeds going to the seller. Taking over this mortgage made the buyer's total book cost $10,500, including the unencumbered furniture.

At this point the pyramider had pledged his personal credit to the extent of $3,600. From this he now had $200 in-pocket cash, recovering his original $100, plus a $100 bonus.

TRADED DUPLEX FOR A 4-UNIT APARTMENT HOUSE

Next the duplex was traded for a furnished 4-unit house and an adjoining lot, both of which were free and clear. Normally exchanging for a larger building, in the 6- to 10-unit range, would have been more advantageous, except for the opportunity of obtaining cash from financing the mortgage-free 4-unit property. The buyer obtained from his bank a first mortgage of $8,500 on the 4-unit building, excluding the furniture and the adjoining lot. The seller of the latter was well satisfied to receive the following:

> $3,000 cash
> Duplex furniture, unencumbered
> Duplex, subject to first mortgage, now paid down to $6,600
> $7,000 note, payable $75 monthly, including 7 per cent interest. This note was secured by three distinct mortgages:
>> First mortgage on the adjoining lot
>> Second mortgage on the 4-unit house
>> Chattel mortgage on the 4-unit-house furniture

Deducting the $3,000 cash paid to the 4-unit seller from the $8,500 loan left $5,500 cash for the up-trader. From this his $3,600 short-term note was paid off, leaving him with $1,900 additional in-pocket cash. In exchange for his initial investment of $100, he now had $2,100 cash, plus his equity in the furnished 4-unit property and the adjoining lot. With a market value of $22,500, based on low rents, and encumbrances of $15,500, on the take-over date the buyer's equity amounted to $7,000.

The 2-story 4-unit building was basically sound and fairly well maintained, except that the exterior was badly in need of paint. In addition, four rooms on the top floor were due for paint. The furniture was fairly modern and in good condition. The pyramider expected to use most of his $2,100 to slick up the 4-unit house, then trade for 8 to 18 units. He had spent only $180 to trim the shrubbery and paint the front of the building and had raised the rents sufficiently to increase the value to $30,000, when a more fantastic opportunity developed.

TRADED 4-UNIT PROPERTY FOR A 40-UNIT APARTMENT HOUSE

Normally an intermediate trade would have been necessary before a 30- to 40-unit building could be acquired. This stepping-up process was short-cut. The next exchange involved trading the 4-unit building for a 40-unit apartment house in one leap, accomplished by the magic power of credit and financing.

THE 40-UNIT OWNER WAS ANXIOUS TO DEAL

The owner of the 40 units was an experienced motel operator who had previously traded his equity in a small motel for the apartments. He was anxious to sell for two reasons: He needed the proceeds in order to buy a high-income-paying motel, which he intended to operate himself; and the motel was about four hundred miles distant and would tie him down, so he wanted to be free from management of the apartments.

The apartment owner offered to trade his 40 units for the motel, but the owner of the latter would not consider taking in a large property. The two parties agreed on a sale price for the motel. After they had negotiated around the apartment owner's available cash, and the maximum second mortgage the motel owner would take back, $40,-000 additional down payment was needed to conclude the sale.

The buyer was willing to pay the $40,000, but he could raise no more funds except by selling his apartments. The seller refused to take back more financing on the motel, or to take additional notes from the buyer. He said he would consider either a small property or other notes for part of the $40,000.

THE 4-UNIT OWNER ENTERS THE TRANSACTION

At this stage of negotiations, the 4-unit owner entered the picture, having been advised by a broker that the apartment owner was anxious to make a quick deal. The 40-unit building had a first mortgage of $185,000, and a market value of $265,000, based on low rents and high expenses. Its owner thus figured his equity at $80,000.

The 4-unit property was valued at $30,000, subject to mortgages paid down to $15,000, giving an equity of $15,000. Learning that the apartment owner needed $40,000 to make his motel deal, the 4-unit owner offered his $15,000 equity plus a $25,000 second mortgage on the 40 apartments, for a total purchase price of $225,000.

The apartment seller next ascertained that the motel owner would accept the $15,000 4-unit equity plus the $25,000 note from the third investor. With this commitment, after a bit of sparring, he accepted the offered 4-unit trade.

RENT RAISES FOLLOW IMPROVEMENTS

Practically all the furniture and fixtures in the 40 apartments were fairly new. The interiors had been recently painted. The major shortcoming was the dilapidated-looking exterior, as the stucco building had not been painted since it was built 30 years before. The exterior had been let slide because such a large expenditure was involved, compared to piecemeal painting of apartments.

The buyer had spent $1,500 of his remaining $1,920 cash to pay the sales commission on his 4-unit house. He needed $8,000 to pay for completely painting the exterior, modernizing landscaping, and handling other miscellaneous improvements. The property was already mortgaged to the hilt with conventional loans. To increase his reserve and to take care of improvements immediately, the owner borrowed $12,000 on a 4½ per cent discounted, seven-year bank improvement loan.

All improvements were completed within forty-five days of purchase and the rents were immediately raised. The new owner was also able to increase his net income by reducing labor and other operating expenses by $3,000 annually. This, along with increased rent, raised the capital valuation to $335,000.

Loans of $185,000, $25,000, and $12,000 totaled $222,000. This gave the owner, within thirty months of his purchase of the initial lot, an equity of $113,000. His $4,420 cash reserve gave him a net estate of $117,000, bought entirely from the fruits of financing and two and a half years of pyramiding of an initial investment of $100.

HOW TO BUILD UP YOUR CREDIT

Since financing is the key to consummation of nearly every profit-making transaction, it would be well to summarize some of the factors which will help to build up your credit. Your ultimate borrowing power will be controlled not only by your financial statement, the soundness of the project you want to finance, and the way you present your case, but by your borrowing history.

Pay Special Attention to Building Unsecured Credit

In the unsecured-credit field more than any other it is necessary to build a satisfactory borrowing record to be able to obtain quick cash when desired. A solid credit reserve offsets the need for a heavy cash reserve. Good unsecured credit enables you to:

1. Pledge to the maximum your assets in hand, so that you can consummate bigger purchases than would otherwise be possible.
2. Pick up ready cash when needed to enhance a deal, as with the $3,600 borrowed when trading a lot for a duplex.
3. Obtain quick cash to expedite improvements and resulting rent raises, as with the $12,000 improvement loan cited above.

"Honesty Is the Best Policy"

Honesty is more important than assets in building credit. Be as completely honest as possible with your lender. Show not only that you are able to repay, but that you consider it a cardinal sin not to pay as promised. Be conservative in setting a repayment schedule, holding payments as low as possible, but attempt at all costs to meet your due dates, once the schedule is agreed on.

A Cardinal Sinner

I know of a misanthrope, worth a half-million dollars in unencumbered property, who cannot even obtain a small improvement loan because he has earned a reputation for failure to keep his word. In his younger days he used to obtain loans and would not make payments until forced to by the deadline of foreclosure. Just to be cantankerous, he doesn't pay contractor's bills until taken into court. His reputation has been found out and recorded by credit agencies. As a result, now that he would like to build money-making new apartments on some of his lots occupied by decrepit, older buildings, he cannot borrow a cent!

LAY YOUR CARDS ON THE TABLE

If circumstances change from the anticipated, lay your cards on the table as quickly as possible. Don't wait until a note is due to inform your banker that you cannot meet it. Let him know as soon as a reversal is indicated. Give him the up-to-date picture, your plans for recovery and repayment; then ask for a new loan to take the place of the old one.

Although you should plan to repay short-term loans when due, businessmen often renew commercial loans before paying them off. In such a case, if you are businesslike and indicate how you can recover with the help of additional funds, not only can you secure an extension of time, but often you can obtain a larger loan to pay off the old one and give you added cash.

BORROW MORE RATHER THAN LESS THAN YOU NEED

Many wise investors borrow increasing amounts when the money isn't actually needed, so that they can establish a reputation for repaying larger loans as promised. It is a sound precaution to borrow more rather than less than needed. This gives you a reserve cushion, especially to insure having funds on hand for initial repayment. The $12,-000 loan just mentioned, for example, exceeded by $4,000 the improvement money actually needed. The loan was based on normal costs, and the expenditures were based on shrewd contracting.

You might institute a remodeling program that would necessitate emptying out tenants for a temporary period, thus curtailing your income for a time. If you borrow exactly what you estimate needing and run into extra costs, you will be caught short. If your costs run as estimated and you don't refill your apartments as rapidly as anticipated, your rental income may not be sufficient in the interim to make loan payments as expected. But if you borrow an extra thousand or so over needs, this cushion can be used to meet payments when due, thus preserving your credit.

You can impair your credit, and your peace of mind, if you borrow less than you need and, as a result, fall behind on your payments. But you will not be censured for borrowing more than you need. The more you borrow when you don't need the money, the more your credit ceiling will be raised when financing gets tight.

GUARD YOUR CREDIT ZEALOUSLY

Credit, like love, may languish if not continuously nourished. Do not allow your credit to die through neglect. Maintain periodic financial contacts, so that you will keep your credit alive when needed.

You will earn credit ratings higher than the average obtainable if you build a reputation for

Paying your loans and other bills when due, and
Transfusing rather than bleeding property values.

As you pursue a sustained program of buying property subject to improvement and then making the necessary money-making improvements, lenders will welcome you with open arms. You will be considered a prime borrower, entitled to the most favorable financing possible. Top credit will follow you, as your natural due, all the exhilarating days of your creative investment life.

Many are the ways of pyramiding equities to a million or more. All depend on favorable credit, geared to creative investment.

POSTSCRIPT

The opportunity to make a fortune is here every day. Under free enterprise opportunity knocks not just for the favored few but for everyone who aspires to better himself. And opportunity knocks not just once, but many times. All you have to do is open the door.

Jesus said, "You shall know the Truth, and the Truth shall make you free."

If you will embrace these fundamental investment truths of free enterprise I present to you, they will set you free to make a million dollars, or whatever you earnestly aspire to as your share of the Great American Dream.

INDEX